# SOVIET-
# AMERICAN
# RELATIONS
# AFTER THE
# COLD  WAR

# SOVIET-AMERICAN RELATIONS AFTER THE COLD WAR

Edited by ROBERT JERVIS
AND SEWERYN BIALER

Duke University Press  *Durham and London*

© 1991 Duke University Press
All rights reserved
Printed in the United States of America
on acid-free paper ∞
Library of Congress Cataloging-in-Publication Data
appear on the last page of this book.

# CONTENTS

Acknowledgments    vii

Introduction    1
Robert Jervis

1  Will the New World Be Better?    7
Robert Jervis

**Part I   Soviet-American Relations and Domestic Changes**

2  American Reactions to the USSR: Public Opinion    23
Ole R. Holsti

3  American Reactions to Changes in the USSR    48
Robert Dallek

4  Do the Changes within the Soviet Union Provide a Basis for Eased
Soviet-American Relations? A Skeptical View    61
Colin S. Gray

5  Reform, Democratization, and Soviet Foreign Policy    76
William Zimmerman

6  Is Socialism Dead?    98
Seweryn Bialer

**Part II   Soviet-American Security Under Relaxed Tensions**

7  The Soviet-U.S. Relationship and the Third World    109
Harold H. Saunders

8  The Soviet Opening to Nonprovocative Defense    133
George H. Quester

9  East and West in Eastern Europe    148
Charles Gati

10 Soviet Policy in East Asia: The Quest for Constructive
Engagement 164
Donald S. Zagoria

11 Rights, Rituals, and Soviet-American Relations 183
Alexander J. Motyl

12 The UN Rediscovered: Soviet and American Policy
in the United Nations of the 1990s 197
Toby Trister Gati

13 Environmental Protection and Soviet-American Relations 225
Glenn E. Schweitzer

**Part III Some Policy Choices**

14 America's Strategic Immunity: The Basis of a
National Security Strategy 239
Eric A. Nordlinger

15 Taking Peace Seriously: Two Proposals 262
John Mueller

16 Averting Anarchy in the New Europe 276
Jack Snyder

Conclusion 302
Robert Jervis

Notes 315

Index 351

# ▰ ACKNOWLEDGMENTS

This volume was made possible by a grant of the Ford Foundation as part of a project on the political psychology of Soviet-American relations. The staffs of the Research Institute on International Change and the Institute of War and Peace Studies, both at Columbia University, managed the project and the two conferences that shaped this book.

Two anonymous reviewers for Duke University Press provided excellent comments and provided the needed stimulus for final revisions.

When we started drafting these essays in the spring of 1988, we sought to be daring. But as so often is the case, events outran the imaginations of scholars as well as of diplomats. We make no claims for a crystal ball herein. Instead, we have tried to explore the terrain of possible Soviet-American conflict and cooperation in the next decade. In doing so, we have assumed that glasnost and perestroika will not be reversed —although we have not attempted to plot their probable courses of development—and that the USSR will not disintegrate (an assumption that until recently was so obviously sound that it did not need to be stated).

As the chapters in this book show, it has become even more difficult than usual to treat domestic politics and foreign policy as though they were independent—to analyze states as though they were "billiard balls" in Arnold Wolfer's felicitous term.[1] Most obviously, the enormous changes in Soviet politics and policies are the result of both domestic and international forces, and the changes are manifest in both realms as well. We cannot separate the contributions of domestic dissatisfaction and international pressure in producing these changes. Indeed, it is probably less accurate to think of two forces acting independently as it is to think of a complex interaction in which the result cannot be understood by trying to summarize the impact each would have had alone.

The traditional Realist model of international politics glosses over domestic politics, public opinion, and state-society relations in favor of stressing how each state reacts to an international environment composed of other major states. This view is often normative as well as descriptive. It implies if not asserts that public opinion is more subject to passion than to reason and that its influence on foreign policy is likely to be pernicious. As Ole Holsti notes in chapter 2, during much of the Cold War analysts saw American public opinion as flighty and irresponsible.[2] In the late 1940s it was seen as an obstacle to standing up to Soviet aggressiveness; in later years it was often seen as fanatically anticommunist and inhibiting realistic negotiations. But although public opinion is indeed important, it is neither so irresponsible nor so autistic as is often believed. Instead, as the recent change in the American view of the Soviet Union indicates, it is strongly influenced by events in the world. While any of us may find the balance of opinion in the general public misguided at any particular time, the American public does judge what other nations are doing and call for the United States to respond appropriately.[3]

In an analysis that remains both brilliant and controversial, Louis Hartz argues that the unique American social structure and history —particularly the lack of an aristocracy and therefore of a bourgeois revolution against it—have produced not only a strange pattern of domestic political thought and practice, but also have conditioned America's views of the world.[4] Americans saw bloody revolutions as unnecessary and left-wing movements and governments as unnatural and a threat. Writing from the perspective of the early 1950s, Hartz saw these views as enormous handicaps. Yet he also foresaw that America's involvement with the world could alter this perspective, producing not only a more reasonable foreign policy, but greater domestic tolerance as well. This view now seems much more plausible than it did a decade ago.

The American public has been influenced not only by the great changes in Soviet foreign policy, but also by the equally dramatic changes in Soviet domestic politics. Contrary to the expectations generated by most traditional analyses of international politics, both the public and the elites in the West have sharply altered their perceptions of the extent to which the Soviet Union is a menace to Western society because of the growth of pluralism and the decline of communist ideology within the Soviet Union.[5] Robert Dallek notes Reagan's reply to a reporter who reminded him as he walked through Red Square in June 1988 that he had earlier called the Soviet Union an "evil empire": "You are talking about another time, another era."[6] A widespread belief is that countries that do not oppress their own people are not a menace to others and that countries which are less oppressive than they used to be are less threatening than they were before.

This judgment is not—or is not only—a moralistic one. It is implicitly based on an empirical theory of the sources of national behavior. Although rarely fully articulated, the interrelated claims are that when national leaders are responsible to the public and the state apparatus is significantly controlled by the civil society, aggressive impulses are less likely to surface and are more likely to be controlled if they do. So it is not surprising that those who reject this theory and see national rivalries as growing out of geostrategic realities believe, as does Colin Gray, that even far-reaching changes within the Soviet Union will lead the core of the Soviet threat untouched.[7] Furthermore, William Zimmerman's analysis of the opinions of Soviet emigrés reveals that while there are links between the desire for economic reform and opposition to foreign policy adventures, the connection between attitudes toward democratization and foreign policy preferences are much weaker.[8] Indeed, Seweryn Bialer argues that many of the values and concepts of socialism still exercise a strong hold in the Soviet Union and will severely inhibit its transformation to a tolerant, democratic, market-oriented society.[9]

If the traditional view that foreign policy is a product of the external environment is correct, then history cannot have a happy ending. As long as there are independent states, there will be sharp conflicts if not wars. If one focuses primarily on states, not only does the Soviet Union still appear powerful and therefore menacing, but the disintegration of the Soviet sphere of influence in Eastern Europe will also automatically be seen as producing international strife.[10] This is not to say that the belief that foreign policy is closely related to domestic politics and social structure automatically leads one to view recent developments with complacency; there are many ways the Soviet Union and the states of Eastern Europe can develop in nondemocratic and oppressive ways. But if the nature of the state strongly influences its international behavior, then democratization at least holds out the chance for peace. Furthermore, as John Mueller argues, changes in values within modern states can make wars less likely, even if the states remain authoritarian.[11]

The twentieth century has seen a waning of the belief that wars are honorable for any reason other than self-defense. But, absent a large measure of trust which can perhaps be induced by similar domestic political systems and common values, wars can still grow out of insecurity. Thus if Soviet-American relations are to have much less conflict than they have had, it will be necessary for both sides to adopt political and military postures in which the defense can be distinguished from and is stronger than the offense, thus permitting mutual security. As George Quester notes, the Soviet Union has moved sharply in this direction in recent years.[12] Furthermore, this stance has been made much more feasible by the Soviet abandonment of control of Eastern Europe, with the consequent end of the necessity for it to maintain the offensive capability to intervene in that region and the creation of a de facto buffer zone.

But whether the superpowers can move to adopt defense-dominant postures in the absence of domestic changes which reduce their conflict is questionable. As Donald Zagoria notes, there are many potential conflicts of interest between the United States and the USSR in Eastern

Asia, which even the changes in Eastern Europe have left untouched.[13] As long as each side defines its interests competitively and seeks security through advantages over the other, a high degree of tension is to be expected. A changed conception of national interest is made possible by several factors, however. First is the growing sense on both sides that it is difficult if not impossible to attain a meaningful competitive advantage in the strategic nuclear balance. Building a few more weapons will not provide much help; an enormous building program is likely to trigger a matching response from the other side. The United States has particular freedom to redefine its security interests because of its relative immunity from foreign threats.[14] But nuclear weapons and the consequent ability to deter attack by a second strike capability give both sides a large range of choice. Thus the USSR was able to give up its control of Eastern Europe without increasing its vulnerability to external attack, something which would not have been true in the pre-nuclear era. Second, domestic priorities and economic concerns are increasingly important. For the Soviet Union, at least, this requires lower defense budgets and greater cooperation with the other superpower. For the United States, it means that as long as the Soviet Union is not seen as a terrible menace, opportunities for both saving money and turning attention elsewhere are to be welcomed. Third, dealing with problems of the environment permits, if it does not require, joint Soviet-American efforts.[15] Fourth, as foreign policy becomes de-ideologized and the conflict of values between the superpowers decreases, both public and elites on both sides are less inclined to believe that what is good for one side is bad for the other, with the result that worldwide competition can decrease. Thus in September 1989 the Soviet news feature agency Novosti said that the Soviet Union has "abandoned the naive stance [whereby] a country whose ties with the United States were strained was considered a friend of Moscow."[16]

As both a cause and a consequence of relaxed tensions, the United States and the USSR can look at each situation and alternative not in terms of how it puts either of them at an immediate advantage or disadvantage with regard to the other, but in terms of how it affects their long-run relationship, one from which they both can benefit.[17] Furthermore, as Harold Saunders notes, the relationship is likely to evolve in conjunction with increased popular participation. Although few political analysts foresee the demise of sovereignty and state power, many note a noticeable erosion as subversive ideas spread across national boundaries. Thus Alexander Motyl points to the contradiction between national sovereignty and the idea that one state—and the people within it—can have a say in human rights issues within another state.[18] Indeed, even before the rise of Gorbachev, it was astonishing the degree to which the Soviet Union and other states accepted as legitimate the notion that adversaries could meddle in their internal affairs. Although for a decade this acceptance coexisted with a refusal to make substantive modifications in oppressive internal practices, the implicit recognition of international standards of tolerance and free expression eased the way for some of Gorbachev's reforms.

These standards may also have helped undermine the legitimacy of the East European communist regimes, which were overthrown in the fall of 1989 by vastly increased popular participation. Although these changes were made possible by the permission if not pressure of Gorbachev and the Soviet regime, these were popular revolutions which also showed the power of cross-national movements of ideas. The dissidents-protesters-revolutionaries in each country were influenced by the continuing liberalization within the Soviet Union and the stirrings of their colleagues in other Eastern European countries.[19] Furthermore, it seems quite likely that the success of these anticommunist revolutions will in turn influence the political struggle within the Soviet Union. The notion of world politics as dominated by state-to-state relations simply cannot catch what is happening.

In part because states are coming either to choose or to tolerate a wider range of forms of international interactions than they have been accustomed to during most of the Cold War, they may also find a greater role for world organizations. Thus it may not be accidental that some of Gorbachev's most far-reaching proposals have concerned the revitalization of the United Nations.[20] To permit, let alone to encourage, a wider role for international organizations means both subjecting the country's policy to greater public scrutiny and a willingness to compromise and even be outvoted on some issues. It indicates an openness to the idea that the international community might exist on more than the rhetorical level. As Saunders notes, it is also consistent with placing a higher priority on constructing viable relationships with other countries than on seeking short-run competitive advantage.[21] In a parallel manner, greater Soviet involvement in international economic institutions will require it to accommodate to prevailing norms and values and to adjust its domestic arrangements accordingly.

None of this means that traditional diplomatic arrangements and institutions will be disregarded. Indeed, it is hard to imagine intensive cooperation without them. Perhaps the most important issue facing the superpowers—and not only them—is the unification of Germany. It is interesting that three of the instruments that are now being deployed were established for very different purposes: NATO, designed primarily to reassure the West Europeans and secondarily to deter the USSR; the European Community, established to encourage Western European economic growth and to provide a counterweight to American power; and the Conference on Security and Cooperation in Europe, continued after the Helsinki agreements in order to make limited gains within the Cold War framework that had just been put in place.[22]

Changes are coming so rapidly that our thinking—let alone a book that needs to be set in type—cannot keep up with them. It is still hard to believe that at the end of 1989 the president of the Soviet Union would have to declare "I am Communist, a convinced Communist. For some that may be a fantasy. But for me it is my main goal."[23] Furthermore, by early 1990 it was apparent that this description was questionable if not invalid. Likewise, even weeks before it happened, it would have been hard to believe not only that there would be a revolution in Romania, but also that in the middle of it the French and Americans would have considered urging the USSR to intervene, that the Soviets would reject the suggestions, and that if they had intervened, they would have done so on behalf of forces that would have been considered counterrevolutionary a short time before.[24] These avowals and events make clear, if preceding ones did not, that we are in a new era. It is easy to exaggerate the clarity and simplicity of superpower politics in the Cold War years, but the new era—whatever it may be—is likely to be much more complex. The number of significant actors will increase and the connections among them will multiply. As citizens, many of us are hopeful that these changes will realize more of our values; as scholars, we are both intrigued and daunted by the difficulty in understanding unfolding developments. Here, we cannot claim to have covered all aspects of the emerging situation, let alone to have arrived at a set of firm conclusions. But we hope that the chapters that follow will at least stimulate further thought on how the United States and the USSR are likely to contend and cooperate in a world that is hard to understand within the framework of our standard ideas and concepts.

We are seeing the most dramatic changes in world politics that have occurred since the end of World War II. Events are moving so fast that the boldest speculations of a few years ago now are tame. But it is clear that the Cold War is over—and in a real sense the West has won it.[1] We have avoided a world war or turning ourselves into a garrison state, and the values of democracy and liberalism have spread throughout the world. Containment has had many of the effects George Kennan predicted.[2] It is interesting to recall the words of the group he headed in Project Solarium, Eisenhower's general policy review of 1953:

> [To bring] about an alteration in basic Soviet aims . . . , the U.S. should seek to convince the men in the Kremlin of the fallacy of the fundamental concepts upon which their policies are based, and without which these policies are neither intelligent nor intelligible. We should try to persuade them, by our words and our deeds, that their delusions regarding world economic and political affairs have already led them into absurd follies and will lead them into personal and national disaster. In particular, we must seek . . . to disprove their beliefs concerning us and to demonstrate that the world situation in general, and Western civilization in particular, have not conformed and will not conform to Communist prophecies. We must try to make them realize that in seeking to undermine and destroy the Free World, they are in fact steadily incurring burdens and risks which sooner or later will undermine and destroy Soviet Communism. We must try to stimulate within their minds a growing and gnawing awareness that the theories which have enslaved them are not only morally evil, but are historically outmoded, scientifically unsound, and practically unworkable.[3]

## A Better World? How Bad Was the Cold War?

If we are entering a new era, it is appropriate to ask again the question Carl Becker posed in 1944: "How better will the new world be?"[4] This cautionary note—which proved all too warranted forty-five years ago—may at first glance seem misplaced. Who could mourn the passing of the Cold War? But we should note the positive features of the era. First, and most important, peace has been maintained between the superpowers. Of course, the causes can be disputed and, in particular, it may have been maintained in spite of rather than because of a high level of Soviet-American rivalry. But we should not ignore the basic fact that we are living through the longest period of peace between the major powers that has ever existed in recorded history. Many attribute this to the inescapable fact that a Soviet-American war would be enormously destructive, in significant measure because of large nuclear stockpiles.[5] Others, even more optimistic, argue that modern states have found that war is not a cost-effective way to reach their goals.[6] These characteristics presumably would not change even under dramatically relaxed Soviet-American tensions, but the question of how safe the new era will be should not be quickly dismissed; I will return to it later.

A second feature of the Cold War that was welcome—at least to the superpowers—was its relative stability. Of course, there have been many important changes in world politics since 1945—decolonization and the economic rise of Germany and Japan, to take only the most obvious ones. But on issues of greatest importance to the superpowers, the world in 1988 looked remarkably like it did in 1948. Although we often talk about living in an era of rapid change, Great Power politics have changed much less since World War II than was true for any long period in previous history.

That both sides maintained their vital interests unimpaired is related to the third beneficial characteristic of the Cold War—crises have been rare. Each superpower was cautious because it expected the other to defend what was of most concern to it. Putting aside the confrontations in the first five years of the Cold War attendant on the working out of their spheres of influence, the belligerence of the superpower rhetoric has not been matched by the proximity to armed conflict. The dangerous crises of the 1950s were Sino-American clashes, with the Soviet Union only being involved indirectly. Berlin and Cuba have been the only sites of severe Soviet-American crisis after the initial period; we have gone without such a confrontation for a longer period than that which usually intervened between Great Power wars in the past. Indeed, as both a cause and effect of the patterns previously mentioned, the superpowers developed "rules of prudence" to see that the frictions between them did not become unmanageable.[7] Of course none of this could guarantee that if the Cold War continued, it would have remained under control. Good luck perhaps played a major role in the past. Nevertheless, the new world can be better only if it maintains this record of accomplishment.

This is not to deny that there are good reasons to be glad to see the Cold War pass. First, and most obviously, it was characterized by some danger and significant levels of fear of nuclear war, especially in mass as opposed to elite opinion.[8] Of course, the danger of superpower nuclear war can be totally extirpated only by abolishing nuclear weapons. While most hardheaded academics have argued that this is simply unrealistic, in part for technical reasons but largely because no superpower leader would in fact be willing to give them up, it is interesting that Reagan and Gorbachev seemed to be quite serious about doing so. Nevertheless, skepticism seems warranted, if only because the superpowers are not the only ones with nuclear weapons. While nuclear weapons and the Cold War arrived together, the passing of the latter does not mean the abolition of the former. Indeed, among the greatest challenges of the new world will be dealing with nuclear dangers without the simplifying framework that superpower dominance imposed.

A second undesired aspect of the Cold War was the high level of defense spending. Although its effects on the economy can be debated, at this point the burden seems high and the desire to reduce it in part explains the changes in Soviet and American domestic politics that we are witnessing. But if both sides restructure their forces to stress the defense, as befits the goals of stability and nonprovocation, their new postures may not come cheap. Furthermore, not all superpower arms are procured out of fear of the other; a world in which the other superpower is not much of a menace is not one without call on Soviet or American militaries. Indeed, if the new world is more unruly than the old one, savings might be surprisingly small.

A third undesired characteristic of the Cold War was the compulsion for each side to check any perceived advances by the other. This meant that conflicts anywhere in the globe could affect, and be affected by, Soviet-American relations. It is a commonplace to note that the era of Great Power peace has coexisted with an extremely large number of wars in the Third World, some of them extremely bloody. There probably is no simple answer to the question of whether there would have been more or fewer wars absent the Cold War. Likewise, Third World conflicts probably have had a differentiated impact on Soviet-American relations. On some occasions, such conflicts have become occasions for Soviet-American conversations or even cooperation because of the fear that, without such efforts, the superpowers could be drawn in. In other cases the results were to increase Soviet-American tensions. "SALT lies buried in the sands of the Ogaden," argues Brzezinski.[9] Even if this is an exaggeration, the assumptions of the Cold War meant that any conflict in the Third World could worsen superpower relations even if the issues were intrinsically trivial.

A new world of relaxed Soviet-American tensions will surely decrease if not end the propensity to impose superpower conflict upon local conflicts all over the globe. Indeed, if the Cold War is not to be resurrected, Third World conflicts will either have to end or to be disconnected from superpower relations. Because the former is unlikely— on the contrary, they could easily increase as the superpowers withdraw —the latter will be necessary. The history of the seventies and eighties shows what an irritant "regional issues," as Reagan called them, can be.

The superpowers have been deeply involved throughout the world for three reasons. First, some areas are crucial because they are sources of needed raw materials—the Persian Gulf is the best if not the only example. The end of the Cold War will not end these conflicts, although it should attenuate them by reducing each side's fear that the other may try to isolate it economically. In any event, they constitute a small minority of the cases. More fall into a second category—areas where either or both sides want to spread their values. Here the changes in the superpowers and their relations matter even more. If both become less ideological, they will care less about having third countries develop in their image. If they come to see the other as not representing their polar opposite and complete evil, they will be less concerned if Third World states take on some of the other's values. The deideologization of Soviet policy (both domestic and foreign) is particularly important here as it removes a potent reason for them to support radical regimes.

During the Cold War, probably the most important reason for the superpowers to be concerned with conflicts in the Third World was the worry that victories—especially military victories—by the other side or its clients would undermine the state's reputation and credibility. Belief in "domino dynamics" were very powerful, at least in the United States.[10] As Soviet-American relations greatly improve, these beliefs will be badly undercut, just as the diminished fear of falling dominoes has paved the way for better relations. Each side will have less reason to expect the other to take advantage of momentary weaknesses; the other side will not be seen as primarily responsible for events in the Third World; the importance of Third World dominoes themselves will be less. But the kind and extent of the connections between Third World events and superpower relations will depend in part on the sorts of understandings the United States and the USSR evolve and the perspectives they bring to bear.

## Causes of the Cold War

Having examined the welcome and unwelcome features of the Cold War and how they might be transformed, it is useful to examine briefly the factors that caused the Cold War and inquire how many of them are likely to continue to operate in the future. Whole libraries have been written on the sources of the Soviet-American conflict, and I will not attempt to resolve the numerous and important disputes. Instead, I will discuss five factors which I think most analysts would agree were important.

First, the Soviets are clearly correct to argue that the conflict was not only between two powerful states, but also was between two different social systems. Contrary to the claims of Realism, one reason why each side perceived the other as a threat was the nature of the other's domestic political system. Marxism-Leninism—at least in the variant that reigned in the Soviet Union throughout most of the Cold War —held that capitalism is ineradicably hostile to socialism and will crush it if it can. As Lenin put it: "As long as capitalism and socialism exist, we cannot live in peace; in the end, either one or the other will triumph."[11] International politics is, to a significant extent, a reflection of class politics. Thus the 1988 disagreement between Foreign Minister Eduard Shevardnadze and Yegor Ligachev is significant. "The struggle between two opposing systems is no longer a determining tendency of the present era," argued the foreign minister. "We proceed from the class character of international relations," replied Ligachev.[12] The former view has prevailed; as the participants in the Soviet debate realized, the consequences are great and far-reaching.

The American worldview similarly stresses the domestic sources of foreign policy. The Wilsonian heritage (which predates Wilson) is strong; democracies are seen as peace-loving, dictatorships as aggressive.[13] Communist regimes are especially to be feared because of their revolutionary impulses. This view has deep roots in the American social structure. As Louis Hartz so brilliantly showed, America was founded as a "bourgeois fraction"; never having been a feudal society it never experienced a middle-class antifeudal revolution and never saw strong domestic radicalism. As a result, it has great difficulty understanding revolutions and left-wing regimes, almost always seeing the former as unnecessary and instigated from abroad and the latter as violent and unnatural.[14] This view was reinforced by twentieth-century history: the disturber of the peace in 1914 was authoritarian; those in the 1930s were totalitarian. During the war, plans for the reconstruction of Germany and Japan prominently featured their democratization: not only was this good in itself, but it also was deemed necessary for ensuring that these countries would not resume their aggressive ways.

Following the same reasoning, officials in the Pentagon assumed that the greatest threats would arise from states that were totalitarian rather than from ones that had specific conflicts of interest with the United States.[15] In 1946 an admiral told Secretary of the Navy James Forrestal: "If we fought Germany because of our belief that a police state and a democratic state could not exist in the same world, it must necessarily follow that we could not afford to lie down before Russia." Arthur Hays Sulzberger summed up this position well: "Only people who have a Bill of Rights are not the potential enemies of other people."[16] Thus Thomas Patterson and John Gaddis argue that the Soviet domestic system was one of the main reasons why the United States perceived Russia as a threat in the immediate postwar period. As the latter puts it, "the Soviet Union combined—as no other country in the world at that time did—two characteristics that Americans found particularly objectionable: arbitrary rule and ideological militancy."[17]

Having deep roots in the American perspective, this kind of view continued throughout the Cold War. In 1952 a National Intelligence Estimate argued: "The USSR is a totalitarian state and experience suggests that totalitarian states are subject to internal pressures and compulsions which may result, without warning, in . . . war."[18] Thirty years later, President Reagan stated the other side of the coin: "Governments which rest upon the consent of the governed do not wage war on their neighbors."[19] As the Soviet Union has changed, so has the American perception of threat. The changes in Soviet politics and society mean that many of the old Wilsonian reasons why the Soviet Union would be expansionist no longer hold. Gorbachev understands this. He ended his interview with *Time* in September 1985 with these words: "In conclusion I would like to express an idea which can be regarded as cardinal to our entire conversation. It was said justly that foreign policy is an extension of domestic policy. Since this is so, I would ask you to give some thought to the following: since we are undertaking such challenging domestic plans, what external conditions can we be interested in? I leave it to you to provide the answer."[20]

Thus, contrary to what Realism prescribes and predicts, American liberals and conservatives alike believe that a more liberalized, open Soviet Union will follow a very different foreign policy. Although some conservatives may remain skeptical about whether the changes will prove lasting, their views on the linkage between domestic and foreign policies are more consistent that those of the liberals. Conservatives have usually argued that the foreign policy of the Soviet Union is linked inextricably to its repressive, if not totalitarian, domestic system. Many liberals have denied this, instead seeing the Soviet Union as reacting more to its international environment. For liberals, then, the current changes, although fascinating and central for Soviet domestic politics, should be less important. But the deeply felt Wilsonian impulses of liberals have proved stronger than their need to be consistent.

If in 1945 each side was ready to perceive the other as a threat because of the nature of its domestic system, a concrete issue was at hand to crystalize the conflict: the future of Europe and, more particularly, Germany. In the early 1970s the Quadripartite Agreements on Germany and Berlin and the Helsinki structure ratified the postwar division and made possible a degree of security and stability which the Soviet adventures of the late 1970s and the Reagan rhetoric of the 1980s could not disturb. More than anything else, it was Gorbachev's decision to liberate Eastern Europe which both transformed détente into the end of the Cold War, and opened the door to possibilities and dangers that are likely to be central to Soviet and American concerns for some years to come.

A third issue that while not causing the Cold War, fueled it was competition in the Third World. Indeed, as conflict in Europe and Sino-American strife abated, the Third World became the main arena and stake for Soviet-American competition. So it is not surprising that the decline of détente in the 1970s largely can be explained by unregulated competition in the Third World. The nature of these situations precluded solutions along the European lines: there were no clear lines of status quo to be mutually recognized, and the local actors were—and still are—both unstable and have sharply conflicting ambitions. But forces have been at work to draw much of the venom from Third World conflicts. Most obviously, both superpowers are disillusioned with what is to be gained by apparent victories there. Neither side sees its clients as highly reliable; neither expects Third World countries to develop rapidly in ways that gratify the superpower's values and self-image; neither thinks that military adventures in the Third World are likely to be cheap.[21] Particularly important are the changes in the ruling Soviet coalition; Gorbachev's support no longer depends, as Brezhnev's did, on making gains in the Third World.[22]

The fourth source of the Cold War is more obvious and more general —the expansionistic drives on the part of one or the other superpower. This, of course, raises the central issue of the origins of the Cold War, but for our purposes all that is required is to ask whether there is a plausible case to be made for either country now being strongly aggressive. It is hard to answer in the affirmative. Even if the revisionists are correct that after World War II the United States sought to keep the world open for American capitalist expansion, little remains of this impulse that would conflict with the Soviet Union. Clearly, the greatest problems for American capitalists are posed by their European and Japanese counterparts: the Soviet Union is more a potential market than an economic threat. At least to an American observer, the case of Soviet goals has been more ambiguous in the past, but now it is hard to believe that the Soviets would try to increase the areas of the world they control. After having given up Eastern Europe, why would they risk war or even serious conflict to try making gains elsewhere?

The fifth source of the Cold War is the security dilemma. An elemental fact of international politics is that the way in which a state tries to make itself more secure often has the unintended and undesired consequence of making others less secure.[23] Conflict and wars can occur even if neither side is dissatisfied with the status quo; states can be expansionistic not because they are strongly driven to increase their values, but because they believe that greater power and influence is needed in order to ensure that others do not menace them. In the most extreme cases, a state may believe that, in the words of a Russian czar, "That which stops growing begins to rot."[24] There is then no way, the state believes, to protect itself without encroaching on others. Mutual security is simply impossible. Both sides seemed to believe this in the years immediately following World War II, in part because each believed that the other's domestic system meant that it was extremely difficult to live with. The United States doubted whether it could be secure as long as the Soviet Union was powerful; Soviet leaders probably doubted whether they could be safe as long as the capitalist world existed. These fears have almost disappeared; with good reason, both sides now see that they can live with each other and that trying to undermine the other's security may not be in their interest.

Technologies as well as beliefs are now more compatible with mutual security. Thanks to nuclear weapons, each side now maintains its safety, not by the ability to defeat the other militarily, but by the fact that any major war would be enormously destructive for all concerned.[25] Each side can gain a large measure of security by maintaining a robust second-strike capability; doing this is not incompatible with the adversary doing the same thing.[26] Mutual security is not automatic, however, and I will discuss the subject more in the concluding section.

## Moving to a New World

Although most Cold War dangers have passed, moving to a world of greatly reduced Soviet-American tensions may not be easy or even safe. Transitions are notoriously difficult; developing new patterns is usually much more difficult than maintaining established ones. As many scholars have noted, the "rules" of the Cold War have allowed each side to make fairly accurate predictions of what the other side was likely to do. Each side learned how to behave in order to keep the other's response within reasonable bounds. Gross miscalculations, like those leading up to the Cuban missile crisis, were rare—although, of course, complacency should be tempered by the fact that any one such incident could lead to world war. Developing new understandings will not flow automatically from reduced tensions.

This is especially true because the coming era will have few historical precedents. In the past the leading states have been rivals if not enemies.[27] By the same dynamic, one source of previous rapprochement between Great Powers was the need to work together against other rising powers. Thus the Anglo-French entente of 1904 was brought about in part because each side realized that it needed to settle its colonial disputes with the other in order to husband its resources against increasingly powerful challengers. This is not quite what is happening now. Certainly Europe, Japan, and even China are increasing their economic and military might, and the latter has been seen as a serious threat by both superpowers. In the early 1960s the United States explored the possibility of cooperating with the Soviet Union to prevent China from developing nuclear weapons, but the Soviet Union was not interested; in the late 1960s and early 1970s the Russians made even stronger overtures, but it was the Americans' turn to rebuff them.[28] But although some analysts argue that the United States and the USSR need to cooperate to restrain China,[29] the dominant belief is that the danger is limited and can best be met by measured conciliation. The grounds and support for uniting against either Japan or Europe are even less.

But if there is no single rising party that represents a clear menace to both sides, I do not think it is an accident that better relations are coming about at a time when both realize that they are in relative decline when compared with much of the rest of the world.[30] The pattern of the rise and decline of great powers is relevant, but should not be mechanistically projected into the future.[31] The rising powers may be America's economic rivals, but they are not its political enemies. Furthermore, none of them is likely to displace the Soviet Union in terms of military power, let alone replace America in its world role.[32] Nor does the Soviet Union fit the old pattern. It never was dominant; its economy, we now know, has been a disaster for years; its challenge was not so much new rising powers as older foes.

Nevertheless, the erosion of both superpowers' strength has encouraged them to cooperate. First, they now place a higher priority on encouraging economic growth. Of course, in previous periods as well, concern with economic growth loomed large. Thus one source of dissatisfaction with the last years of the Eisenhower presidency was the belief that unless American productivity increased, its economy soon would be surpassed by that of the Soviet Union. But the current preoccupations are likely to last much longer and to contribute to better relations with the Soviet Union. Furthermore, to the extent that new American economic policies will increase frictions with allies, better relations with former adversaries will be strongly desired.

A second consequence of relative decline is that both powers feel they have fallen prey to "imperial overstretch," to use Paul Kennedy's term.[33] Foreign adventures require resources that are now increasingly scarce. Thus although the United States and the Soviet Union may not have strong common interests in the Third World—with the important exception of limiting proliferation—they do have converging interests in limiting their expenditures and commitments there. But to do this, each needs the other's tacit assistance: even in an era of greatly reduced tensions, it will be difficult for one superpower to pull back if the other does not.

The recession of superpower influence can create as well as mitigate conflicts. And even if the superpowers have previously declared their lack of interest in an area, their attitude may change as when disputes actually occur. This is less likely to be the case in the Third World—although this possibility cannot be dismissed—than in Eastern Europe. The problem is twofold. First, political disputes within and between these countries, long submerged by Soviet dominance, will break the surface, in all likelihood with major violence. Second, it will be hard for the superpowers or Western Europeans to remain indifferent to the bloodshed even if they do not find the issues of intrinsic importance. Assuming they can resist the Cold War temptation to believe that they must support the faction opposing an element supported by the other superpower, the local dispute need not produce animosity among outsiders. But although outsiders prefer Eastern Europe to be stable and peaceful, they have only limited ability to produce that result and will find their political vision and skills put to severe tests when conflicts break out. I will turn to this problem in the concluding chapter.

## Conclusions

For the newer world to be a better one, it will have to maintain the benevolent characteristics of the Cold War. Most important, it will have to keep the peace between the superpowers. At first glance, this would not seem to be a problem; if the United States and the USSR could avoid a war while their relations were hostile, they should surely be able to do so when their relations are much better. But because the interaction between states forms a system in which outcomes are often different from intentions, the problem is not so quickly dismissed. For example, good relations could lead either side to press the other hard in the belief that the adversary would make a major concession rather than endanger the valued atmosphere and pattern of concord.[34] Such behavior contributed to the decline of détente in the 1970s. As the United States and the USSR increase their cooperation, they move away from the older arrangements in which what each side could not tolerate was relatively clear. It will then be important for both sides to maintain a sense of limits—not only an appreciation of the limits on the extent to which cooperation is possible, but also an understanding of the limits to the other's activities that each state is willing to accept. Of course, there will be both conflict and uncertainty here. The superpowers may not be sure of their own interests as the configuration of world politics changes. Furthermore, even greatly improved relations will not do away with all competition, and therefore will not do away with bargaining and bluffs. Although pressures to deny the other side any gains will decrease as the level of conflict falls, it will still be in each's interest to keep the other out of disputed areas. Dangerous games of chicken can still occur with lowered stakes.

Even with greatly improved relations, nuclear deterrence will still remain. Indeed, it may be a necessary foundation for greater cooperation. Although security without nuclear weapons is possible, the non-nuclear past was punctuated by frequent wars among the great powers. Furthermore, now that the superpowers have become accustomed to equating security with the ability to destroy the adversary, returning to older forms would probably prove unsettling, especially without some way to overcome the familiar obstacles to complete nuclear disarmament. Nuclear weapons can facilitate cooperation because they permit their owners to be indifferent to many events and outcomes which in earlier eras had to preoccupy them, often causing significant conflict. In a nuclear world the state's security only minimally depends on others. Isolationism becomes possible, indeed often attractive if security is the state's main goals. Thus while nuclear weapons were not sufficient for the Soviet Union to decouple its fate from Eastern Europe, they were necessary for that policy. Second-strike capability enabled the Soviet Union to physically protect itself without controlling its neighbors, which was not true in the past.[35]

The challenge is to see that military policy serves, rather than undermines, the improved relationship. Here unilateral measures may be as important as joint ones.[36] Both sides need to be able to protect themselves while limiting the extent to which they threaten the other.[37] In the area of nuclear strategy, mutual security is possible if the superpowers forego the notion that in order to deter the other side, they must be able to fight a war in a way that leaves them better off than the adversary. In other words, they must move away from policies based on the idea that deterrence requires the capability to gain a relative advantage over the other side. The reason is obvious: such a stance rules out mutual security. This goal is within reach—at least on the general strategic level—when each side believes that the other is deterred by the realization that war would be mutually disastrous no matter who came out somewhat "ahead."

In a parallel way the prospects for mutual security are strongly influenced by the bargaining tactics that states imply. For either side to stress its overall military superiority, its right to dictate the settlement of a wide range of disputes, or its general resolve is to create a strong security dilemma because the adversary cannot easily retreat without endangering many of its values. In the same way, a state that employs the tactic of "the rationality of irrationality"[38]—for example, pretending not to understand how serious the crisis is or feigning a lack of self-control—may prevail, but the long-run consequences will be unfortunate if the other side concludes that it cannot deal with the state on reasonable terms.

By contrast, the use of claims, threats, and military forces linked more closely to the particular issue and to the state's well-established interests in protecting its position can succeed without simultaneously menacing the other's ability to maintain its core interests. Thus commitment, especially when linked to important intrinsic interests, can be used to safeguard one side's concerns without threatening those of the other: each side can be committed to defending the principles and areas of the world that matter most to it when these are less important to the other side. But as the Soviet Union abandons its sphere of influence it will take greater intellectual imagination and political skill to devise mechanisms to keep the peace within the previously stable regions and develop new patterns of superpower relations. Indeed, the recent Soviet pattern of being so reasonable as to conform to almost every Western position may prove troublesome if and when the USSR reverts to more common bargaining practices. The West may then find it hard to predict where the Soviets will take a firm stand, what issues it considers vital, and where it sees Western demands as intolerable.

There are great opportunities to make the new world a better one, but this will not occur automatically. The easing of Soviet-American hostility removes many dangers, but new ones may arise. Skill, statesmanship, and sensitivity to the interrelations between foreign policy and domestic politics will be required on both sides. While the changes within the Soviet Union probably were a necessary condition for creating a safer and more peaceful world, they are not sufficient to reach that end. The dangers of the Cold War are familiar but this does not mean that they are the only troublesome possibilities. Politics has a way of surprising us, often unpleasantly. Future historians will judge our generation harshly if we fail to do our best to anticipate important problems and devote ourselves to dealing with them.

# PART I
# SOVIET-
# AMERICAN
# RELATIONS
# AND
# DOMESTIC
# CHANGE

On February 27, 1946, Senator Arthur Vandenberg asked his colleagues in the Senate, "What is Russia up to now?" He was not the first to ask that question, and he certainly would not be the last. George Bush is only the most recent president to take part in what has been an almost perpetual debate on the issue. During recent years American interest in the question of Russia has been enhanced by both external and internal developments. Since 1985 Mikhail Gorbachev has provided the Soviet Union with a style of leadership that seems light years removed from that of his immediate predecessors; even those most skeptical about the significance or permanence of glasnost or perestroika agree that Gorbachev possesses political and public relations skills unmatched in recent Soviet history. At the same time, the American president who excoriated the Soviet Union as an "evil empire" in 1983 was, within five years, meeting regularly with Gorbachev and describing him as "my friend." The first year of George Bush's presidency witnessed a dramatic acceleration of improving relations between the superpowers, highlighted by Soviet acceptance of regime changes in precisely those countries where the Cold War began with the imposition of one-party Stalinist governments after World War II.

**Public Opinion and Foreign Policy**

At least three classes of "theories" have been used to explain how the American public reacts to foreign affairs in general and, more specifically, to the Soviet Union. The first viewpoint depicts the public as a dangerous constraint on effective policy making. Its intellectual roots include Walter Lippmann's iconoclastic post-World War I—but pre-polling era —works (1922, 1925) that emphasized the wide gap between the democratic ideal of the concerned and informed citizen on the one hand, and, on the other, the great mass of people whose busy lives leave them little time, opportunity, or even inclination to ponder and develop informed opinions on public issues. Thirty years later, Lippmann had become more alarmed, regarding the public as not merely uninformed, but almost invariably wrong:

> The unhappy truth is that the prevailing public opinion has been destructively wrong at the critical junctures. The people have impressed a veto upon the judgments of informed and responsible officials. They have compelled the government, which usually know what would have been wiser, or was necessary, or what more expedient, to be too late with too little, or too long with too much, too pacifist in peace and too bellicose in war, too neutralist or appeasing in negotiation or too intransigent. Mass opinion has acquired mounting power in this country. It has shown itself to be a dangerous master of decision when the stakes are life and death. (Lippmann, 1955:20)

A similar theme was developed by Gabriel Almond after World War II. Drawing on a growing body of polling data and fearing that the American public might lapse into a mindless isolationism, he depicted public opinion as a volatile and mood-driven constraint upon foreign policy: "Perhaps the gravest general problem confronting policy-makers is that of the instability of mass moods, the cyclical fluctuations which stand in the way of policy stability" (1950:239). Six years later, Almond restated his thesis, focusing not only on the instability of moods, but also on their generally inappropriate character. He told the National War College, "For persons responsible for the making of security policy these mood impacts of the public have a highly irrational effect. Often public opinion is apathetic when it should be concerned, and panicky when it should be calm" (1956:372, 376). The Lippmann-Almond thesis was given further support in a classic discussion by Converse (1964) which found that foreign policy attitudes among the mass public had relatively little structure. Jean-François Revel's critical observations about American reactions to the Soviet Union are a more recent reiteration of the theory that the public is always out of synch with reality, especially on foreign affairs (1978:15).

A second theory depicts the American public quite differently, although not necessarily in a more flattering light. Rather than focusing on volatility and mood cycles that generally have a strong negative correlation with events in the real world, this theory emphasizes certain continuities in public opinion, with special attention to a Manichean world view. For the public the appropriate metaphor for world affairs is the cowboy movie, with its "white hats" and "black hats," simplistic plots, violent shoot-outs as the characteristic mode of conflict resolution, and the inevitable triumph of the good guys. According to this viewpoint, Americans regard communism as the great evil and the Soviets as its agents. To the extent that public opinion has been a factor in American foreign policy, it has buttressed, sustained, and perhaps even cast into concrete the one constant in Washington's post-World War II diplomacy: a reflexive anticommunism that serves neither the national interest nor prospects for peace and stability.

There are at least two broad variants of this theory. According to the first, public opinion is the victim, for it has been manipulated into a hard-line anti-Soviet position by the ruling class and its faithful handmaidens in the media and other key institutions. Because public opinion has no autonomous life of its own, it is also of limited relevance in any effort to understand American policies. This viewpoint may be found in several "revisionist" histories of the postwar era. A second version locates an irrational anti-Sovietism in certain elements of American culture. For example, Robert Dallek has written of an "unthinking anticommunism" that serves several nonrational needs, including as "a convenient excuse for not facing up to troubling domestic concerns" (1983:xvii, xviii).

Until recently, something like the Lippmann-Almond view of public opinion and foreign policy has been widely accepted. In part this acceptance can be traced to the dominance of the realist perspective on international politics. The several schools of realism share a skepticism of the Wilsonian faith in public opinion as the bedrock and ultimate guarantor of sound diplomacy and peace; indeed, according to many realists, one needs to bring public opinion into the analysis only to explain deviations from rational foreign policy, for the public has neither the knowledge nor the patience to pursue the national interest intelligently.[1] The Lippmann-Almond thesis has also been sustained by opinion polls which have yielded ample evidence of the public's limited factual knowledge. Innumerable surveys reveal such stunning gaps in information as X percent of the public are unaware that there is a communist government in China, Y percent believe that the Soviet Union is a member of NATO, or Z percent do not know whether the United States is supporting the government or the rebels in El Salvador, Nicaragua, or Angola.

Nevertheless, the Lippman-Almond thesis which posits an uninformed, volatile, and structureless public opinion has been subject to considerable critical scrutiny during recent years. Several studies have revealed that public opinion is in fact characterized by more structure and stability than predicted by the mood theory (Caspary, 1970; Russett, 1990; Wittkopf, 1986; Page and Shapiro, 1984; Ladd, 1983; Oldendick and Bardes, 1981; Bennett, 1972; Hurwitz and Peffley, 1987; 1988). More importantly, when attitude changes take place, they seem to be neither random nor 180 degrees removed from the true state of world affairs. Rather, the changes appear to be "reasonable, event driven" reactions to the real world (Page and Shapiro 1984), even if the information base from which they are drawn is marginally adequate at best. Thus, the revisionist thesis is not based on surveys that most Americans can name all members of NATO or the key actors in the various Central America conflicts.

Revisionist studies have thus given rise to a third view emphasizing the rational rather than the irrational to explain how the public changes or retains its foreign policy opinions. Page and Shapiro contend that "virtually all the rapid shifts [in public opinion] we found were related to political and economic circumstances or to significant events which sensible citizens would take into account. In particular, most abrupt foreign policy changes took place in connection with wars, confrontations, or crises in which major changes in the actions of the United States or other nations quite naturally affect preferences about what policies to pursue" (1984:34). Similar conclusions have emerged from other studies (Bennett, 1972:742; Free and Watts, 1980:50; Wittkopf, 1988:5). An interesting variant of the "rational public" thesis stipulates that the public attempts to moderate American behavior toward the USSR by expressing preferences for a conciliatory stance from hawkish administrations while supporting more assertive policies from dovish ones (Nincic, 1988). To the extent that one can generalize from this study to other periods or other aspects of foreign policy, it further questions the Lippmann-Almond thesis, for it identifies the public as a source of moderation and continuity rather than of instability and unpredictability.

Before turning to the data, two important limitations must be noted. First, the standard constraints on the uses of survey data—including discontinuities in topics, frequent changes in question wording, biases in questions, and the like—certainly exist here. The fact that Soviet-American relations have been the central concern of American foreign policy since World War II has not ensured the existence of standard data sets that lend themselves readily to longitudinal analyses. Second, this chapter is not a definitive test of the alternative theories of public opinion and foreign policy.[2]

### Images of the Soviet Union and Soviet Leaders

During two periods since World War II polling organizations have frequently asked the public about Soviet foreign policy goals. The first period, 1946 to 1953, witnessed a steady erosion of wartime cooperation between Moscow and Washington, the start of the Cold War, and the death of Joseph Stalin. The second, since 1976, has been marked by the end of détente, a rapid turnover of Kremlin leadership, and the apparent end of the Cold War.

The proportion of Americans who believed that the Soviet Union was merely acting defensively by "building up protection against being attacked in another war" declined steadily between 1946 and 1949. The invasion of South Korea, widely assumed to have at least tacit Soviet support, further reduced to a minority of one in ten those who believed that the USSR was acting out of defensive concerns. After a lapse of more than a quarter century a similar question was again posed regularly but with more diverse set of response options. As was the case earlier, the results appear to be at least moderately sensitive to international events. Whereas in 1978 only 18 percent of the respondents believed that the Soviet Union was willing to risk war in a quest for global domination, that figure more than doubled within four months— an interval highlighted by the Soviet invasion of Afghanistan. Conversely, the later 1980s have seen a steady if unspectacular decline in the proportion of the public which believes that the USSR will use any means, not excluding war, to achieve essentially unlimited ends. Indeed, three "Americans Talk Security" surveys in 1988 revealed that increasing numbers of respondents attributed defensive motives to the Kremlin. By the end of 1988 those who believed "protecting its own national security" to be the driving force behind Soviet policy outnumbered those who described it as "world domination" by a margin of 65 percent to 28 percent (ATS-2, ATS-7, ATS-12).

Until recently, polling organizations rarely asked the American public to evaluate individual Soviet leaders. Even the death of Stalin in 1953 did not elicit a Gallup national survey on the implications for Soviet-American relations of his demise or for assessments of his successors.[3] The lack of interest in specific Soviet leaders changed dramatically with Mikhail Gorbachev's rise to power. Indeed, the frequency with which pollsters have asked the public to assess Gorbachev may be a good indicator of his manifest public relations skills.

Although the results reveal a considerable range of responses, in part arising from inconsistency in the wording or context of questions, one rather remarkable constant runs through the results: not a single survey found that as many as 40 percent of the public expressed a negative opinion of Gorbachev. By 1988, those with a favorable view typically outnumbered his detractors by margins 2–1 or more. A May 1989 CBS/*New York Times* poll found that two-thirds of the respondents believed that both Gorbachev and Bush were willing to make real concessions to improve relations between the superpowers. However, although two-thirds of voters trust him more than previous Soviet leaders, only 14 percent trust him "a great deal" (ATS-7:116–17). For many Americans, apparently including Presidents Reagan and Bush, a close link exists between favorable assessments of Gorbachev and improvements in relations between the superpowers. Such a linkage can also have its limits. Gorbachev's relative youth, apparent good health, and evident political skills suggest that he would normally enjoy a long tenure, but the détente of the early 1970s also points to some of the hazards of personalizing international relationships.

## Soviet-American Relations

Almost as soon as the United States entered World War II, polling organizations started asking the public to appraise the prospects for postwar Soviet-American relations, focusing on the probability that the Russians could be trusted to continue wartime cooperation with the United States. None of the many wartime surveys found a plurality that answered the question in the negative. In the wake of the Yalta Conference, which President Roosevelt reported had resolved a number of outstanding issues between the "Big Three," affirmative responses outnumbered the negative ones by 2–1. Another Gallup poll yielded similar results immediately after Russia joined the war against Japan, as Stalin had promised to do at Yalta. From those high points there was a steady but irregular erosion of public trust in the Soviet Union that coincided with a confrontation over Iran as well as the failure of various foreign ministers' conferences to resolve such issues as peace treaties for Germany and Austria. As late as December 1946 a plurality of the public remained confident about cooperation between Moscow and Washington, but by 1949 the optimists had shrunk to a small minority.

Two decades later Harris surveys began asking Americans to assess the prospects for Soviet-American agreements "to help keep the peace." The results summarized in table 2.1 trace a pattern that looks quite consistent with international developments. Those who felt that agreements were possible outnumbered the nay-sayers by 12 percent in July 1968, but following the Soviet invasion of Czechoslovakia in August, the number of optimists fell from 49 percent to 34 percent. The developing détente between the superpowers was also reflected in public opinion. In 1973, strong majorities, reaching a peak of 69 percent, answered that it was possible to reach such agreements. By the time Harris had stopped asking the question in 1975, that figure had dropped to 45 percent.

Although strictly comparable data are not available for the Gorbachev period, there are many indications of increasing optimism about cooperation between the superpowers. A 1988 survey found that only

Table 2.1  "Do You Think It Is Possible for the United States
and Russia to Reach Agreements to Help Keep the Peace?"

| Date | Poll | Can Reach Agreements (%) | Not Possible (%) | Not Sure (%) |
|---|---|---|---|---|
| March 1951 | Gallup* | 44 | 46 | 10 |
| July 1968 | Harris | 49 | 37 | 14 |
| August 1968 | Harris | 34 | 50 | 16 |
| December 1968 | Harris | 40 | 48 | 12 |
| August 1970 | Harris | 52 | 32 | 16 |
| June 1971 | Harris | 54 | 33 | 13 |
| February 1972 | Harris | 56 | 34 | 11 |
| May 1972 | Harris | 52 | 38 | 10 |
| June 1973 | Harris | 59 | 22 | 19 |
| November 1973 | Harris | 69 | 20 | 11 |
| December 1974 | Harris | 59 | 26 | 15 |
| December 1975 | Harris | 45 | 39 | 16 |

*Wording: "Do you, yourself, think it is possible or impossible for the United States to reach a peaceful agreement with Russia?"

19 percent of the respondents felt that improving relations between the two nations "will *not* lead to any lasting, fundamental changes." In contrast, 57 percent felt that the changes will be fundamental and lasting, "though the two countries will never be allies," and a surprisingly high 23 percent predicted that "one day" they would indeed be allies [ATS-6:64]. By the end of 1989, when asked to look ahead to the end of the millenium, two-thirds of the respondents stated that "The Soviet Union and the West will be living peacefully together" (De Stefano, 1990).

Pollsters have periodically asked Americans to assess the probability of American involvement in a nuclear war.[4] In 1954, a year after the Soviets successfully tested a hydrogen bomb, almost two-thirds of the respondents in a Gallup survey expected such a war. That proportion declined sharply during the détente period, but concern about nuclear war has not completely vanished. In response to frequent questions on the issue during the 1980s, between one-third and one-half of the public expected the United States to be involved in a nuclear war within a decade; however, at the end of 1989 that figure had dropped to 8 percent (De Stefano, 1990).

Although the "nuclear freeze" movement peaked with successful referenda on the issue during the first Reagan administration, concerns about the consequences of nuclear war persisted. A 1987 *Newsweek* survey revealed overwhelming (84 percent) agreement with the proposition "There would be no winner in an all-out nuclear war, both the U.S.

and Soviet Union would be completely destroyed." Indeed, fear of nuclear war appears to be a driving force behind several important changes in public opinion on foreign affairs, including increasing support for arms control and greater acceptance of military parity between the superpowers (Yankelovich and Doble, 1983; Public Agenda Foundation, 1984, 1988). Whereas during the early 1980s a clear majority favored American military superiority, more recently approximately half the participants in several surveys have accepted parity (*Newsweek*, 1987; ATS-1; CBS/*New York Times*, 1988).

A data series on trends in Soviet-American relations covers a twenty-year period, beginning just before détente and continuing to the present. The results are generally consistent with trends in relations between Washington and Moscow. Harris and Potomac polls during the early 1970s found that significant proportions of the public felt that those relations were getting better. Likewise, five 1988 ATS surveys revealed that at least 60 percent of registered voters felt the trend to be toward better relations. These results are buttressed by polls asking respondents to describe more specifically the relationship between the two superpowers. Not surprisingly, very few respondents have depicted the Soviet Union as a "close ally" in any of the surveys, but there has been a marked increase in those who believe that the Russians are "friendly, but not close allies." Between 1984 and 1988 those selecting the term "unfriendly and an enemy" to characterize the USSR declined from more than 50 percent to fewer than one in three, and the percentage of public depicting the Soviet Union as "unfriendly" fell from 90 percent to 63 percent.

The period since Mikhail Gorbachev's accession to leadership has also seen a flurry of survey questions concerning the level of Soviet threat to the United States. The past few years have witnessed a declining sense of threat from Russia. One must be cautious about attributing too much significance to figures from any single survey; nevertheless, the finding of a 1988 ABC/*Washington Post* poll—respondents who believed the Soviet Union is "not at all" a threat to the United States (12 percent) outnumber those who regarded the USSR as a "very serious threat" (11 percent)—appears to symbolize a sea change in opinion. An ATS survey at the end of 1988 revealed comparable results, with only 9 percent describing the USSR as a "very serious threat," and 54 percent stating that it is either a "minor" or "not at all" a threat (ATS-12:58).

Support for nuclear arms control, either general proposals or specific agreements, has been one of the constants in public opinion since the 1950s. One could almost say that most Americans have rarely seen an arms control proposal that they did not like; the SALT II agreement, which eventually lost the widespread support it originally enjoyed, is the only exception to this generalization. More recently the Inter-mediate-range Nuclear Forces (INF) Treaty received overwhelming approval. Should START negotiations involving 50 percent reductions in nuclear weapons be completed successfully in 1990, the treaty would appear to have an equally strong base of support. No doubt both INF and START gain a measure of acceptance because they were endorsed by a popular president whose harsh anti-arms control rhetoric during the 1980 presidential campaign endowed him with the image of a leader who would not rush into unfavorable agreements. But that support does not appear to explain fully public enthusiasm for arms control; in some cases it may not even be a necessary condition. Numerous polls and referenda revealed widespread approval for a nuclear freeze during the early and middle 1980s even though President Reagan repeatedly denounced the proposal.

Indeed, public support for arms control is so strong that it appears to transcend at least two potentially important barriers. First, many among the public continue to believe that the United States trails the Soviet Union in military capabilities. However, at least some respon-dents may also regard arms control as a way of ensuring that the gap between the two nations does not widen, especially in an era of less abundant funding for the Pentagon. The data also reveal widespread skepticism about the Soviet trustworthiness. Americans have a favor-able view of Soviet leader Gorbachev, but his popularity has only par-tially eroded the opinion, held by a vast majority during the pre-Gorbachev era, that the Soviets cannot be trusted to honor agreements. It thus appears that some Americans prefer the risks of Soviet cheating on an arms treaty to those of an uncontrolled arms race. However, the limited scope of the INF treaty probably contributes to this preference among risks, and it should not be assumed that a more general agree-ment, especially one that would be more difficult to monitor, would elicit similar enthusiasm.

The generalization that Americans support both arms control and at least military parity with the Soviet Union is supported by responses to a question concerning the risks of continued arms acquisitions ver-sus falling behind the Soviets in nuclear weaponry. We do not have com-parable data from the period before the Carter-Reagan defense buildup, but figures since 1982 reveal a public almost evenly divided on the issue. Although support for defense spending peaked during the early 1980s, at least in part because of some fear that arms races are at best futile and at worst they add to the risk of nuclear war, concern persists about falling behind.

## American Policies Toward the Soviet Union

Should the United States be tougher or more accommodating in its dealings with the Soviets? This question has been posed several times during the past decade, and a somewhat comparable question was included in a Free-Cantril survey in 1964. Although the latter poll took place in the aftermath of the Cuban missile crisis—a period that included the Test-Ban Treaty, the "Hot Line" agreement, and generally less confrontational relations between Moscow and Washington than had been the case during the turbulent years between the Berlin "deadline crisis" and the missile confrontation—a substantial 61 percent of the respondents agreed that the United States should "take a firmer stand" in its dealings with the Kremlin. However, there were definite limits on what a "firmer stand" should entail; the same survey found only 20 percent who favored "rolling back the iron curtain." Sixteen years later, in the wake of the Soviet invasion of Afghanistan, two-thirds of those responding to a CBS/*New York Times* poll also felt that the United States should "get tougher." During the Reagan years, however, every survey save one (taken immediately after the destruction of Korean Air Lines flight 007) has revealed that Americans prefer trying "harder to reduce tensions with the Russians" to a more confrontational policy. By 1988 the tension-reduction option was favored by a margin of almost 3–1 (ATS-10), even though there continues to be some support for a policy of "rollback" (ATS-8:141). A year later, respondents who felt that President Bush should do more to help the Soviet Union "deal with social and political change taking place there" outnumbered by more than 4–1 those who stated that he was doing too much.

Just before gaining the Republican presidential nomination in 1980, Ronald Reagan asserted in an interview for a friendly newspaper that the Soviets were the sole source of international problems (House, 1980). Although he was elected in a landslide that fall, survey data suggest that most Americans reject such a Manichean diagnosis of world problems. The proposition that "the U.S. has to accept some of the blame for the tension that has plagued U.S.-Soviet relations in recent years" elicited agreement from three-quarters of the public. That three polls, undertaken by different organizations over a span of more than five years (1982–88), yielded almost identical results lends greater credence to the data. Respondents to a 1988 survey also agreed by a margin of 2–1 that "The U.S. often blames the Soviet Union for troubles in other countries that are really caused by poverty, hunger, political corruption and repression" (ATS-7:57). These figures would seem to cast some doubt on the thesis that a moralistic and hypocritical American public is incapable of transcending a "black-white" assessment of world affairs.

A comparison of President Reagan's general job approval rating with that for his handling of relations with the USSR reveals the following pattern.[5] During Reagan's first two years the two scores were remarkably similar. His general rating then rose from a nadir of 35 percent in January 1983 to a peak of 65 percent at the time of his 1984 reelection, but his Soviet scores lagged substantially behind. Both ratings improved in 1985, but at the end of the following year the Iran-Contra fiasco led to a precipitous decline in approval for Reagan's overall job performance —from 63 percent in October to 47 percent two months later—from which it recovered only at the end of presidency. In the meanwhile, his ratings for handling relations with the Soviet Union increased, reaching a peak that coincided with the Washington and Moscow summit meetings.

More generally, the data indicate that after the honeymoon of 1981, Reagan's strongest approval ratings on Soviet policy tended to come during the second term, a period marked by regular meetings with Gorbachev, progress on arms control, and a general easing of tensions between the two superpowers. By June 1988 a Harris survey found that the president's high approval rating on Soviet policy (67 percent and on his performance at the Moscow Summit meeting far outstripped his overall job rating (54 percent). This suggests at least two interpretations linking public opinion to foreign policy that are not mutually exclusive: (1) Reagan was driven to seek a rapprochement with the Soviets in order to bolster his domestic ratings and, perhaps, his standing in history; and (2) whether or not bearbaiting was good domestic politics in 1980, by 1985, the year Gorbachev assumed Soviet leadership, the domestic climate of opinion had changed sufficiently to make dancing with the bear a more attractive option.[6] Comparable figures for President Bush indicate that his performance rating increased sharply after he announced that he would meet with Gorbachev at Malta.

Since 1974 the Chicago Council on Foreign Relations (CCFR) has conducted surveys at four-year intervals which include some questions on the importance of various foreign policy goals. "Containing communism" has been among the goals in each of the polls, and the 1982 and 1986 polls also asked respondents to rate the importance of "matching Soviet military power." Substantial proportions of Americans rated both of these as "very important" foreign policy goals, and very few considered them to be "not important." However, neither of these ranked within the top four goals. More specifically, "matching Soviet military power" ranked only eighth among fourteen possible goals in both 1982 and 1986, and in *each* of the four CCFR surveys, three goals received more "very important" ratings than either of the items relating directly to the USSR: "worldwide arms control," "protecting the jobs of American workers," and "securing adequate supplies of energy."

## Opinion Leaders

The Lippmann-Almond thesis not only took a very skeptical view of public opinion, but it also emphasized that the "irrational tendencies" of the public were "counteracted by the attentive public" and opinion leaders (Almond, 1956:377). Important elements of the Lippmann-Almond thesis are no longer accepted as axiomatic, but the concept of a stratified public has survived more or less intact; debates focus less on the existence of strata than on their size and the boundaries between them

The post-Vietnam period has witnessed growing interest in the foreign policy views of opinion leaders. In addition to several one-time surveys of various leadership groups (Barton, 1974–75; Russett and Hanson, 1975; Sussman, 1976; Chittick, 1986, 1987; Koopman, Snyder, and Jervis, 1989, 1990; Peterson, forthcoming), two projects have each surveyed opinion leaders four times since the mid-1970s. The Chicago Council on Foreign Relations has conducted surveys of both the general public and small samples of leaders in 1974, 1978, 1982, and 1986 (Reilly, 1975, 1979, 1983, 1987). Their data have also been widely used for a number of impressive secondary analyses by Mandelbaum and Schneider (1979), Schneider (1983), Wittkopf (1986, 1987, 1988), Wittkopf and Maggiotto (1983a, 1983b), Maggiotto and Wittkopf (1981), Herrmann (1986), Chittick, Billingsley, and Travis (1990), and others. The Foreign Policy Leadership Project (FPLP) has also conducted leadership surveys at four-year intervals since 1976, with responses from well over two thousand leaders in each of the four studies.

The 1984 and 1988 FPLP questionnaires include an item that asks respondents to assess the source and motives of Soviet foreign policy by expressing agreement or disagreement with several propositions that have been central to the debate about "what is Russia up to?" For example, does the Soviet Union behave much like a typical great power? To what extent does its foreign policy reflect the imperatives of Marxist-Leninist ideology? The fundamental nature of the Soviet political system? Is its foreign policy driven by fear or by inherently expansionist propensities? Do Russian leaders have a high or low propensity for risk?

The results suggest a tendency to avoid both extremely soft/optimistic and hard/pessimistic interpretations. An overwhelming majority (82 percent) agreed in 1984 that "The Soviet Union and the U.S. share a number of foreign policy interests such as prevention of war, arms control, and stabilizing relations between them," and by 1988 that figure had increased to 89 percent. Almost equally large proportions also expressed agreement with the propositions that the Soviets have a low propensity for risk and that their external actions "often stem from genuine fears for Russian security." (Responses to another question, however, indicated that in 1980 and 1984 fewer than a third of the leaders regarded the invasion of Afghanistan as a manifestation of genuine security fears.) More than 60 percent of the leaders believed that Soviet foreign policy goals are "inherently expansionist," and a majority stated that the goals are guided by Marxist-Leninist ideology. However, whereas in 1984 about a third of the respondents agreed that the Kremlin's foreign policy goals are similar to those of a typical Great Power, 47 percent did so in 1988.

Several items in the 1984 and 1988 FPLP questionnaires deal more or less directly with aspects of Soviet foreign policy. The results leave little doubt that most American leaders continue to regard the Soviet Union as an expansionist power, both in general (78 percent in 1984, 73 percent in 1988) and with respect to such specific undertakings as its invasion of Afghanistan. However, the data also reveal a rather consistent trend toward a somewhat less malign view of Soviet foreign policy. This pattern emerges not only with respect to the items cited previously — in 1980, for example, 85 percent of the respondents ascribed expansionist motives to the USSR — but also on several others. Whereas in 1980 three leaders in five agreed that, "Détente permits the Soviet Union to pursue policies that promote rather than restrain conflict," four years later only 45 percent did so, and by 1988 the comparable figure was 39 percent. Moreover, there was a tendency to regard the USSR as less menacing within the global context. Although fewer than 40 percent of the leaders taking part in the 1984 and 1988 surveys believed that the communist bloc is irreparably fragmented, more than two-thirds of them were inclined to regard revolutionary forces in the Third World as nationalistic rather than as Soviet or Chinese pawns.

A question first introduced in the 1980 FPLP questionnaire asked respondents to identify the two most potent threats to American security during the remainder of the millenium. The 1980 respondents gave strong emphasis to threats emanating from the Soviet Union in the form of its military buildup and its activities in Third World areas. They also accorded considerable importance to dangers arising from a variety of unresolved domestic issues, whereas the rich nation-poor nation gap, the population explosion, and unwarranted American interventions abroad gave rise to less concern.

Responses in 1984 and 1988 revealed dramatic changes. In 1984 many still viewed Soviet activities as a major threat, but by 1988 far fewer leaders regarded a military gap between the United States (21 percent) or Soviet actions in the Third World (25 percent) as one of the top dangers. No doubt the large American military buildup of the previous decade assuaged some fears. Whereas in 1980 "a growing gap between rich nations and poor nations" was checked off by only about a quarter of the leaders, in 1984 it emerged as the most widely cited threat, and in 1988 it ranked second only to concern for such domestic issues as crime, decay of cities, unemployment, inflation, and racial conflict. Between 1980 and 1988 there was also a substantial increase in the percentages of those who cited "uncontrolled growth of the world's population" (from 13 percent to 24 percent) and "American intervention in conflicts that are none of our business" (from 8 percent to 17 percent).

The Chicago Council question on the importance of various American foreign policy goals was also posed to both CCFR and FPLP leadership samples, providing an opportunity to place their concerns with the Soviet Union within the context of a broader agenda of foreign policy issues (table 2.2). Items relating to containment, matching the Soviet military buildup, arms control, and defending allies bear directly on Soviet-American relations, whereas several others are almost wholly devoid of any East-West connotations.

Although between one-third and one-half of the leaders surveyed by the CCFR and FPLP rated "containing communism" as a "very important" goal, a pattern of responses that has remained relatively stable, it never emerged as the dominant or superordinate goal. Arms control has consistently been accorded a higher priority than containment. Even when the "defense consensus" was nearing its peak in 1980, well over half of the leaders rated arms control as a "very important" goal. Moreover, by 1988 responses to the item on "matching Soviet military power" indicate far less concern for that goal than for bringing the arms race under control. Another strategic goal—defending allies—elicited rather different responses in the two surveys, but the trend in both surveys is the same. Polls in the immediate post-Vietnam period revealed a somewhat skeptical stance, but in subsequent years American leaders have accorded increased importance to extended deterrence.

For many leaders the highest priority items on the nation's foreign policy agenda encompass a number of nonstrategic issues, including but not limited to energy availability, international economic cooperation, the standard of living in the Third World, hunger, the global environment, and Third World debts. Each of these goals was accorded greater importance than either containment or matching Soviet military power in one or more surveys, and in some cases the data also reveal a trend of growing rather than diminishing concern for these issues.

The data in table 2.2 also permit comparison of leaders and the general public on foreign policy goals relating to the USSR. Arms control has consistently been rated as a "very important" goal. Leaders have tended to place it at or near the top in every survey, whereas for the public it has generally ranked just below energy and job security in importance. Somewhat smaller percentages in the public and leadership samples have also regarded "matching Soviet military power" as important. Compared to leaders, the general public has accorded greater importance to containment of communism, but leaders attributed greater importance to a closely related goal—"defending our allies' security." One possible explanation is that leaders are more inclined to accept concrete commitments to allies, and to be somewhat less enthusiastic about the more open-ended and somewhat vaguer goal of "containing communism."

These data do not offer much sustenance for the theory that American leaders, as a whole, are wedded to a chiaroscuro image of world affairs in general or, more specifically, of the Soviet Union. Although President Reagan was quite successful in obtaining support for several aspects of his program, notably with respect to tax cuts and defense spending, and his personal popularity remained high, the evidence suggests that he was less successful in persuading opinion leaders to accept some central elements of his diagnosis of world affairs or of Soviet foreign policy. On balance, American leadership assessments of the Soviet Union appear "moderate," a judgment that those who believe the Soviet Union to be a uniquely aggressive and expansionist power that would attack its adversaries at the first sign of Western weakness will surely not accept. Nor will those who believe that the USSR is just another major power which has only acted defensively in the face of a hostile environment dominated by those determined to undo the results of the 1917 revolution. "Moderate" means that many opinion leaders tend to accept the following propositions. Soviet foreign policy derives from multiple motives rather than undimensional ones; relations between the United States and the Soviet Union are often better described as non-zero-sum rather than zero-sum; and however troublesome those relations might be, the Kremlin is not the sole source of American foreign policy problems.

### Demographic Factors and Opinions About the Soviet Union

If past is prologue, the evidence suggests that public opinion will continue to reflect events in American-Soviet relations, but a prognosis may also be illuminated by examining the demographic factors associated with opinions and whether the data reveal sharp cleavages based on ideology and party, as was true in 1984 among opinion leaders (Holsti, 1988). Are there significant generational or gender gaps in opinions on

Table 2.2 The Importance of Various Foreign Policy Goals for American Leaders and the General Public, Chicago Council and Foreign Policy Leadership Surveys, 1974–88 (% "very important")

| Importance Attached to Each Goal | The Public | | | |
|---|---|---|---|---|
| | CCFR 1974 | CCFR 1978 | CCFR 1982 | CCFR 1986 |
| Containing communism | 54 | 60 | 59 | 57 |
| Matching Soviet military power | — | — | 49 | 53 |
| Helping to improve the standard of living in less developed countries | 39 | 35 | 35 | 37 |
| Keeping peace in the world | 85 | — | — | — |
| Worldwide arms control | 64 | 64 | 64 | 69 |
| Defending our allies' security | 33 | 50 | 50 | 56 |
| Promoting and defending our own security | 83 | — | — | — |
| Promoting the development of capitalism abroad | 16 | — | — | — |
| Securing adequate supplies of energy | 75 | 78 | 70 | 69 |
| Helping to bring a democratic form of government to other nations | 28 | 26 | 29 | 30 |
| Protecting the interests of American business abroad | 39 | 45 | 44 | 43 |
| Protecting the jobs of American workers | 74 | 78 | 77 | 78 |
| Protecting weaker nations against foreign aggression | 28 | 34 | 34 | 32 |
| Maintaining a balance of power among nations | 48 | — | — | — |
| Combatting world hunger | 61 | 59 | 58 | 63 |
| Helping solve world inflation | 64 | — | — | — |
| Strengthening the United Nations | 46 | 47 | 48 | 46 |
| Strengthening countries who are friendly toward us | 37 | — | — | — |
| Fostering international cooperation to solve common problems, such as food, inflation, and energy | 67 | — | — | — |
| Keeping up the value of the dollar | — | 86 | 71 | — |
| Worldwide population control | — | — | — | — |
| Promoting and defending human rights in other countries | — | 39 | 43 | 42 |
| Protecting the global environment | — | — | — | — |
| Averting financial crises arising from Third World debts | — | — | — | — |
| Reducing the U.S. trade deficit with other countries | — | — | — | 62 |

the USSR and relations between the superpowers? A number of the 1987 to 1988 ATS survey items provide some basis for exploring the impact of ideology, party, age, and gender on opinions.

Since the end of the Vietnam War sharp ideological cleavages among both the general public and opinion leaders have dominated many foreign and defense policy issues (Holsti and Rosenau, 1984; Holsti, 1987). Responses to forty-six ATS survey items yield some evidence of both

| Leaders | | | | | | | |
|---|---|---|---|---|---|---|---|
| CCFR 1974 | FPLP 1976 | CCFR 1978 | FPLP 1980 | CCFR 1982 | FPLP 1984 | CCFR 1986 | FPLP 1988 |
| 34 | 39 | 45 | 41 | 44 | 38 | 43 | 36 |
| — | — | — | — | 52 | 40 | 59 | 32 |
| 62 | 38 | 64 | 44 | 55 | 59 | 46 | 51 |
| 95 | 71 | — | 76 | — | — | — | — |
| 86 | 66 | 81 | 55 | 86 | 70 | 83 | 68 |
| 47 | 37 | 77 | 44 | 82 | 47 | 78 | 51 |
| 91 | 85 | — | 90 | — | 83 | — | — |
| — | 6 | — | 10 | — | — | — | — |
| 77 | 72 | 88 | 78 | 72 | 84 | 72 | 75 |
| — | 7 | 15 | 10 | 23 | 18 | 29 | 24 |
| — | 14 | 27 | 19 | 25 | 22 | 32 | — |
| 34 | 31 | 34 | 30 | 43 | — | — | 36 |
| — | 18 | 30 | 23 | 43 | — | 29 | — |
| 56 | 44 | — | 55 | — | 43 | — | — |
| 76 | 51 | 66 | 51 | 64 | 56 | 60 | 57 |
| 81 | 50 | — | — | — | — | — | — |
| 31 | 25 | 25 | 32 | 25 | 27 | 22 | 27 |
| 28 | 23 | — | 37 | — | — | — | — |
| 86 | 70 | — | 73 | — | 66 | — | 70 |
| — | — | 73 | 63 | 38 | — | — | — |
| — | — | — | 45 | — | 53 | — | 53 |
| — | — | 36 | 27 | 41 | 33 | 44 | 39 |
| — | — | — | 47 | — | 53 | — | 68 |
| — | — | — | — | — | 44 | — | 45 |
| — | — | — | — | — | — | — | 63 |

agreement and dissensus across ideological lines (table 2.3). By an arbitrary criterion—differences of at least 10 percent between conservatives and liberals—an ideology gap exists on seventeen of the forty-six items, but only five of them find a majority of conservatives on one side of an issue and a majority of liberals on the other. Even conservatives support the INF treaty, the 50 percent reduction of long-range nuclear forces that forms the basis of START negotiations, and a nuclear freeze;

Table 2.3   Differences Between Liberals and Conservatives
on Selected Questions Concerning the Soviet Union,
"Americans Talk Security" Surveys, 1987–88

| Topic | Total | Differences Between Liberals and Conservatives | | Liberal and Conservative Majorities Disagree |
| | | < 10% | 10% + | |
|---|---|---|---|---|
| Image of Soviet Union | 4 | 1 | 3 | 0 |
| Soviet motives and goals | 4 | 2 | 2 | 1 |
| Soviet threat | 3 | 1 | 2 | 2 |
| Soviet policies and actions | 5 | 5 | 0 | 0 |
| Assessments of Gorbachev | 8 | 4 | 4 | 1 |
| U.S. policies | 4 | 3 | 1 | 0 |
| U.S.-USSR relations | 8 | 7 | 1 | 0 |
| Arms and arms control | 10 | 6 | 4 | 1 |
| Total | 46 | 29 | 17 | 5 |
| | (100%) | (63%) | (37%) | (11%) |

*Number of Questionnaire Items* (column group header)

have favorable impressions of Mikhail Gorbachev and trust him at least
"somewhat"; and agree that relations between Moscow and Washington are improving. The sharpest differences between conservatives and
liberals appear on such questions as the impact of defense spending,
the trustworthiness of the USSR, and the extent of the threat from the
Kremlin.

Although President Reagan did not escape scathing criticism from
such prominent conservatives as George Will, Norman Podhoretz, Howard Phillips, and others for his more accommodating stance toward the
Soviet Union, he received high marks from conservatives in the ATS
surveys for his efforts on arms control and for "standing up to the Soviets." This may explain the surprisingly strong support among conservatives for several facets of "détente II." In assessing the Soviet Union
under Gorbachev and in supporting arms control many of them are
probably taking their cue from the most conservative president of the
postwar era.

Although differences between Republicans and Democrats of 10
percent or more may be found on eleven of the forty-six items, only two
issues find a majority of members of the major parties on opposite sides.
Moreover, on some issues Republicans tend to take on a slightly softer
stand than Democrats—for example, in assessments of Mikhail Gorbachev. Again, the probable explanation is that the most visible steps
in improving relations with the USSR, including summit meetings, the
INF treaty, and START negotiations are associated with President Reagan.

While the terms *generation gap* and *gender gap* have become a common part of our vocabulary, solid evidence that they constitute prominent landmarks on the American political landscape is elusive at best, especially on foreign policy issues. The ATS data provide some evidence of both gaps, although not necessarily in the form often suggested. Both men and women under the age of forty tended to express more optimistic opinions about the Soviet Union and more dovish opinions about American policies. More specifically, the most optimistic/dovish responses were recorded by younger men on twenty-nine of forty-six questions. Conversely, the least optimistic/dovish groups were older women (twenty-one items), followed by younger women. Perhaps the most surprising finding is the consistency with which women expressed more skeptical opinions about the USSR than did men, irrespective of age. Although women were more inclined than men to describe themselves as doves (ATS-9:119), men offered more support on all five arms control items by an average margin of 6 percent; expressed more trust in the USSR on six of seven items (6 percent); assessed Gorbachev more favorably on eight items (9 percent); had a more benign view of Soviet motives on six of nine items (3 percent); assessed relations between the two superpowers more favorably on ten of thirteen items (5 percent); and expressed a more optimistic view on the likelihood of nuclear war (10 percent). In the only exception to this pattern, women were more critical on three items relating to the impact of defense spending (6 percent).

This brief analysis suggests that the sharp ideological and partisan cleavages that have characterized public opinion on many foreign policy issues have been somewhat muted on several questions concerning the USSR. This may well be one of the more significant achievements of the Reagan administration.

### Conclusion: Prospects for the 1990s

Opinions about the Soviet Union are important not only because they center on relations between the superpowers, but also because they play a central role in one's entire outlook on international affairs (Herrmann, 1986; Holsti, 1988; Hurwitz and Peffley, 1988). It would clearly be overstating these results to conclude that the public or opinion leaders are generally correct in their views of the Soviet Union, if only because it is usually impossible to identify the "correct" answers with respect to such critical questions as Stalin's intentions or, indeed, those of his successors. Nevertheless, the data suggest that aggregate opinions tend to reflect events and trends in international affairs.

The findings also appear to offer very little support to theories that the American public is deeply steeped in reflexive and unyielding hostility toward the Soviet Union. To the contrary, substantial numbers of Americans appear to yearn for good relations between the superpowers and, when given a reasonable pretext for doing so, they will express opinions to that effect. This is evident in data from the World War II period when the war against Nazi Germany provided a clear mutuality of interests, as well as in evidence from the détente of the early 1970s and the current period of dramatically improving relations.[7] Many Americans believe that future Soviet-American relations will be radically different from those in the past. When asked by a 1987 ABC/ *Washington Post* survey whether relations between the two superpowers are entering into a new era, 76 percent replied in the affirmative. Mikhail Gorbachev was regarded as seriously interested in arms control by 73 percent of the respondents, and 85 percent of them stated that, compared to previous Soviet leaders, he was more interested in improving relations with the United States. These judgments, which are generally supported by other surveys, would appear to indicate a public eager to accept at face value the events that have marked warming relations between Washington and Moscow. Moreover, when asked to identify the reasons for improvements in American-Soviet relations, many respondents leaned toward a benign explanation. For example, when registered voters were asked to identify the two most important reasons for greater Soviet interest in arms control, the most popular answer (50 percent) was "Soviet changes under Gorbachev," whereas only 34 percent cited "Ronald Reagan's buildup of America's military defense" (ATS-1:25). Another survey (ATS 2:36) asked more specifically about the major reasons for the INF treaty. The two most widely cited answers were that Gorbachev and the Soviets are sincerely interested in avoiding nuclear war (65 percent), and that the treaty is a "good deal" for both sides (62 percent).

More generally, American definitions of "national security" appear to reject the view that the Soviet Union is the sole source of threats to it; indeed, those who regard it as the major threat are a diminishing minority. In response to a 1988 question on the most important goals of national security policy other than protecting our own borders, combating drug trafficking was most frequently (22 percent) cited, following by correcting the trade imbalance (18 percent) and reducing nuclear forces (15 percent). Only the next two items, getting communists out of Central America (13 percent) and containing Soviet aggression (12 percent), dealt with Cold War threats (ATS-4:92–93). Another survey revealed that 76 percent of respondents rated "the spread of nuclear weapons to the Third World" as an "extremely serious" or "very serious" threat to national security. Terrorists' activities, the trade imbalance, the Soviet-American arms race, and world economic problems were cited as extremely or very serious threats by more respondents than the 52 percent who gave such a rating to "Soviet aggression around the world" (ATS-1:9). A survey undertaken a year later yielded almost identical results. "Soviet aggression" was again cited as an "extremely" or "very" serious threat by 52 percent of the respondents, but they expressed even greater concern about other threats: international drug trafficking (88 percent), domestic problems such as crime and homelessness (78 percent), nuclear proliferation (76 percent), terrorism (72 percent), world economic competition (57 percent), and the greenhouse effect (53 percent) (ATS 9:51−54). In short, even though few Americans believe that Moscow's challenges are a thing of the past—only 29 percent think that the Russians "will begin to pull back from their attempts to expand their influence in various parts of the Third World" (ATS-1:24) and a majority believes that if we are weak the Soviet Union "will attack us or our allies in Europe and Japan" (ATS-7:57; ATS-12:61)—most of them perceive a world in which challenges to national security emanate from many sources and encompass a wide range of issues.

These opinions no doubt reflect in substantial part the events from 1986 to 1989, especially the frequent meetings between Gorbachev and Reagan, as well as the dramatic turnabout in the latter's rhetoric about the USSR. Although he did not wholly escape criticism, Reagan's own impeccable conservative credentials permitted him to pursue policies that others could have attempted only at considerable political risk. As Richard Nixon told Mao Tse-tung on his historic visit to China, "Those on the right can do what those on the left can only talk about" (quoted in Gaddis, 1982:284−85.) Had Walter Mondale been elected in 1984 and walked precisely the same path in his policies toward the USSR, could he have escaped a firestorm of criticism from many of those who later praised Reagan? Whether President Bush, who is openly distrusted as a "moderate" by many staunch conservatives, can count on similar forebearance remains to be seen. Mikhail Gorbachev's remarkable acquiescence in 1989 to events in Poland, Hungary, East Germany, Czechoslovakia, and Romania made it more difficult for domestic critics to attack Bush as being soft on the Soviet Union, but as William Safire, George Will, Richard Pipes, and A. M. Rosenthal have demonstrated, it is not impossible to do so.

Public opinion would appear to offer substantial support for further development of "détente II," especially on arms control. To be sure, the public remains skeptical and wary of the Soviet Union in many respects; for example, despite Gorbachev's obvious popularity, there is not much inclination to give the Soviets a great deal of credit for withdrawing its armed forces from Afghanistan (ATS-8:73), and trust that the Soviets will live up to agreements, while rising, is still limited to a minority

(ATS-12). Nevertheless, the combination of clearly changing views about the USSR, public support for arms control, and opposition to large increases in defense spending appears to have created a domestic "window of opportunity" for progress on arms reductions.

There are, however, at least two potential dangers to be avoided. First, because such windows do not stay open permanently, as the history of SALT II demonstrates, one cannot assume that the glacial pace of most negotiations will result in timely agreements that take advantage of opportunities to strengthen an arms control regime. More broadly, an overly cautious approach runs the risk of missing a historic opportunity for better superpower relations. As Robert Legvold summarized the challenge: "Do we have the imagination, creativity and courage to respond to the very revolution in Soviet policy for which we have waited half a century?" (1988–89:98).

There is also another pitfall to be avoided: overselling the public on the improving state of the American-Soviet relations for domestic political gains. When rosy predictions of future cooperation between Moscow and Washington turn out to be premature, exaggerated, or both, a sense of betrayal is likely to be reflected in opinion polls. Official efforts during World War II to portray the USSR in idealistic rather than realistic terms, no doubt dictated by the exigencies of the war effort, may also have rather poorly prepared the public to face the possibility that there could be serious divergences of interest concerning settlement of some important issues arising from the war. Pronouncements by Richard Nixon and Henry Kissinger in 1972 and 1973 to the effect that "the Cold War is over" probably contributed to a backlash against détente when it turned out that, among other things, the scope and specific obligations in some of the superpower agreements of that period were loosely spelled out. President Reagan engaged in similar rhetorical excesses about escaping from the awful dilemmas of Soviet-American relations by negotiating away all nuclear weapons or rendering them impotent and obsolete through the Strategic Defense Initiative. On this score President Bush gets higher marks to date. He has also avoided another trap. American leaders have sometimes succumbed to the temptation of making irresponsible comments about Eastern Europe in the hopes of reaping domestic political advantage; recall for example, the promises of "liberation" and "rollback" during the 1952 election campaign. Bush has been notably restrained in this respect, even though it has earned him some criticism for timidity.

## References

Almond, Gabriel A. *The American People and Foreign Policy*. New York: Harcourt, Brace, 1950.

―――. "Public Opinion and National Security," *Public Opinion Quarterly* 20 (Summer 1956):371–78.

"Americans Talk Security" (ATS). Twelve National Surveys on National Security Issues. Winchester, Massachusetts. October 1987 to December 1988.

Barton, Allen H. "Consensus and Conflict Among American Leaders." *Public Opinion Quarterly* 38 (Winter 1974–75):507–30.

Bennett, Stephen Earl. "Attitude Structures and Foreign Policy Opinions." *Social Science Quarterly* 55 (December 1972):732–42.

Caspary, William R. "The Mood Theory: A Study of Public Opinion and Foreign Policy." *American Political Science Review* 64 (June 1970):536–47.

Chittick, William. "On Restoring Foreign Policy Consensus or "'Putting Humpty Dumpty Together Again.'" Athens: University of Georgia: mimeo, 1987.

―――. "Three Headed Eagle Reconsidered." Paper presented at the Annual Meeting of the International Studies Association, 1986.

―――, Keith Billingsley, and Rick Travis. "Persistence and Change in Elite and Mass Public Attitudes Toward U.S. Foreign Policy." *Political Psychology* 11 (June 1990):385–401.

Converse, Philip E. "The Nature of Belief Systems in Mass Publics." In *Ideology and Discontent*. Edited by David E. Apter. New York: Free Press, 1964.

Dallek, Robert. *The American Style of Foreign Policy*. New York: Knopf, 1983.

De Stefano, Linda. "Looking Ahead to the Year 2000." Gallup Organization, 1990.

Free, Lloyd and William Watts. "Internationalism Comes of Age . . . Again." *Public Opinion* (April–May 1980):46–50.

Gaddis, John Lewis. *Strategies of Containment*. New York: Oxford University Press, 1982.

Herrmann, Richard. "The Power of Perceptions in Foreign Policy Decision Making." *American Journal of Political Science* 30 (November, 1986):841–75.

Holsti, Ole R. "Public Opinion and Containment." In *Containing the Soviet Union*. Edited by Terry L. Deibel and John Lewis Gaddis. Washington, D.C.: Pergamon-Brassey's, 1987.

―――. "What Are the Russians Up to Now: The Beliefs of American Leaders About the Soviet Union and Soviet-American Relations, 1976–1984." In *East-West Conflict: Elite Perceptions and Political Options*. Edited by Michael D. Intriligator and Hans-Adolf Jacobsen. Boulder, Colo.: Westview, 1988.

―――, and James N. Rosenau. *American Leadership in World Affairs*. London: Allen and Unwin, 1984.

House, Karen Elliott. "Reagan's World: Republican's Policies Stress Arms Buildup, a Firm Line to Soviet." *Wall Street Journal*, June 3, 1980, p. 1.

Hurwitz, Jon, and Mark Peffley. "How Are Foreign Policy Attitudes Structured? A Hierarchical Model." *American Political Science Review* 81 (December 1987):1099–120.

―――. "Public Images of the Soviet Union and Its Leaders: The Impact on Foreign Policy Attitudes." Paper presented at the annual meeting of the American Political Science Association, 1988.

Kennan, George F. *American Diplomacy, 1900–1950*. New York: Mentor, 1951.

Koopman, Cheryl, with Jack Snyder and Robert Jervis. "Theory-Driven vs. Data-Driven Assessments in a Crisis." *Journal of Conflict Resolution* 34 (Dec. 1990):694–722.

————. "American Elite Views of Relations with the Soviet Union." *The Journal of Social Issues* 45, no. 1 (1989):119–38.

Ladd, Carl Everett. "Public Opinion: Questions at the Quinquennial." *Public Opinion* (April–May 1983):20, 41.

Legvold, Robert. "The Revolution in Soviet Foreign Policy, *Foreign Affairs* 68 (Winter 1988–89):82–98.

Lippmann, Walter. *Essays in the Public Philosophy*. Boston: Little, Brown, 1955.

————. *The Phantom Public*. New York: Harcourt Brace, 1925.

————. *Public Opinion*. New York: Macmillan, 1922.

Maggiotto, Michael A., and Eugene R. Wittkopf. "American Attitudes Toward Foreign Policy." *International Studies Quarterly* 25 (December 1981):601–31.

Mandelbaum, Michael, and William Schneider. "The New Internationalisms: Public Opinion and Foreign Policy." In *Eagle Entangled: U.S. Foreign Policy in a Complex World*. Edited by Kenneth A. Oye, Robert J. Lieber, and Donald Rothchild. New York: Longman, 1979.

Morgenthau, Hans J. *Politics Among Nations*. 5th ed., rev. New York: Knopf, 1978.

Mueller, John E. "Public Expectations of War During the Cold War." *American Journal of Political Science* 23 (May 1979):301–29.

Nincic, Miroslav. "The United States, the Soviet Union, and the Politics of Opposites." *World Politics* 40 (July, 1988):452–75.

Oldendick, Robert, and Barbara Ann Bardes. "Multiple Dimensions in the Structure of Foreign Policy Attitudes." *Social Science Quarterly* 62 (March 1981):124–27.

Page, Benjamin I., and Robert Y. Shapiro. "Changes in Americans' Policy Preferences." *Public Opinion Quarterly* (Spring 1984):24–42.

————, and Glenn R. Dempsey. "What Moves Public Opinion?" *American Political Science Review* 81 (1987):23–43.

Peterson, Sophia. *A Survey of Rhodes Scholars*. Forthcoming. Public Agenda Foundation. *The Public, The Soviets, and Nuclear Arms*. New York: Public Agenda Foundation, 1988.

————. *Voter Options on Nuclear Arms Policy*. New York: Public Agenda Foundation, 1984.

Reilly, John E., ed. *American Public Opinion and Foreign Policy*. Chicago: Chicago Council on Foreign Relations, 1975. Also in 1979, 1983, and 1987.

Revel, Jean-François. "Reflections on Foreign Policy and Public Opinion." *Public Opinion* (July–August 1978):15–17.

Russett, Bruce M. "Democracy, Public Opinion, and Nuclear Weapons." In *Behavior Society and Nuclear War*, vol. 1. Edited by Philip E. Tetlock et al. New York: Oxford, 1989.

————, and Elizabeth C. Hanson. *Interest and Ideology: The Foreign Policy Beliefs of American Businessmen*. San Francisco: Freeman, 1975.

Schneider, William. "Conservatism, Not Interventionism: Trends in Foreign Policy Opinion, 1974–1982." In *Eagle Defiant: United States Foreign Policy in the 1980s*. Edited by Kenneth A. Oye, Robert J. Lieber, and Donald Rothchild. Boston: Little, Brown, 1983.

Sussman, Barry. *Elites in America*. Washington, D.C.: Washington Post, 1976.

Wittkopf, Eugene. "Elites and Masses: Another Look at Attitudes Toward America's World Role." *International Studies Quarterly* 31 (June 1987):131–60.

————. "Foreign Policy Beliefs, Preferences, and Performance Evaluations." Paper presented to the Annual Meeting of the International Society of Political Psychology, 1988.

―――. "On the Foreign Policy Beliefs of American Leaders: A Critique and Some Evidence." *International Studies Quarterly* 30 (December 1986):425–46.

Wittkopf, Eugene, and Michael A. Maggiotto. "Elites and Masses: A Comparative Analysis of Attitudes Toward America's World Role." *Journal of Politics* 45 (May 1983a):303–34.

―――. "The Two Faces of Internationalism: Public Attitudes Toward American Foreign Policy." *Social Science Quarterly* 64 (March 1983b):288–304.

Yankelovich, Daniel, and John Doble. "The Public Mood: Nuclear Weapons and the U.S.S.R." *Foreign Affairs* 63 (Fall 1983):33–46.

# CHAPTER 3 ■■
# AMERICAN REACTIONS
# TO CHANGES IN THE USSR
**Robert Dallek**

The rise of Mikhail Gorbachev to power in the Soviet Union and the advent of glasnost and perestroika have evoked strong reactions in the United States. Seventy years of highly charged feelings about Soviet communism made it inevitable that Gorbachev's proposals for far-reaching change would produce uncertainty among Americans about the meaning of events in the USSR. Although a variety of discrete responses are evident in the United States, it is not enough simply to reduce the American reaction to a few categories of clearly held ideas. Although there are separate, easily identifiable views that need describing, the American reaction seems most notable for its ambivalence, the extent to which contradictory views grip the imagination of many of the same people at the same time. The American reaction to Gorbachev is a blend of fear, hope, illusion, and realism—the same feelings that in one degree or another have characterized the American response to the Soviets from the start of their regime.

In broadest terms, Americans responding to recent developments in the Soviet Union may be divided into skeptics and optimists. Skeptics warn that despite outward appearances of change,[Soviet devotion to communism and worldwide control is as strong as ever. The Cold War will continue, some of these skeptics believe, in muted form for a while, but ultimately these two very different American and Soviet systems will either fall into an apocalyptic struggle or reach some accommodation based on realistic assessments of differences and needs. More pessimistic skeptics see no real hope for fundamental agreement between two such irreconcilable systems and hold to the belief that the long-term survival of America as we know it depends on the eclipse of Soviet communist power. The internal changes occurring in the USSR are hardly a demonstration that Moscow will abandon its drive for global control. Quite the contrary, a stronger Soviet Union at home will be a greater menace abroad.]

By contrast, optimists argue that Gorbachev represents a new day in Soviet history and that much of what is happening in Russia and Eastern Europe is the result of American pressure and example. Soviet inability to keep up with America's military buildup has forced Moscow into the INF treaty on U.S. terms and compelled a turn toward capitalism at home that may signal the triumph of free enterprise in the seventy-year struggle with communism. Indeed, the shift toward political freedom and elementary democracy in Russia and the Warsaw Pact countries, Bulgaria, East Germany, Hungary, Poland, and Romania, may hail the ultimate Soviet acceptance of the United States as the model by which all sensible nations really wish to live.[2]

These reactions to Gorbachev's four-year rule are, on the one hand, notable for their similarity to those that have dominated American thinking about Moscow for the past seventy years, and, on the other, for their simultaneous appeal, however contradictory, to many of the same people. Since 1918 a majority of Americans justifiably have seen their country as locked in a power struggle with the USSR. This concern, however, has repeatedly given rise to exaggerated fears about the capacity of the Soviets to imperil democracy at home and abroad. The Red Scare in 1918 and 1919 and the refusal to recognize the Soviet government until 1933 reflected in part these convictions. Hopes of economic cooperation and the alliance against Nazism in World War II temporarily muted these concerns. But the outbreak of the Cold War in 1946 and 1947, the Alger Hiss and Rosenberg cases, Soviet acquisition of nuclear weapons, communist victory in the Chinese civil war, and the Korean fighting reawakened the fears. The receptivity in the United States to Joseph McCarthy's charges about communist subversion in Washington and to Eisenhower-Dulles campaign rhetoric in 1952 depicting Soviet-American relations as "an irreconcilable conflict" and a contest between "good and evil" were fresh expressions of these old beliefs. They continued in part to shape American foreign policy in the thirty years after 1953: the interventions in Iran and Guatemala in the fifties; the decisions to topple Castro, send American marines into the Dominican Republic, and escalate in Vietnam in the sixties; the contribution to Allende's demise in the seventies; and the support of Nicaragua's contras in the eighties are some examples.

In 1987, when Brown University's Center for Foreign Policy Development and the Public Agenda Foundation described an American victory over Soviet power by 2010 as one possible outcome to Soviet-American relations in the next quarter century, it was the product of the long-standing assumption that this was the only realistic way to deal with an unrelenting foe intent upon the destruction of the American way of life.[3]

At the same time that Americans saw Soviet-American relations as an unresolvable conflict in which one side or the other had to triumph, they also subscribed to the containment doctrine, the idea that American economic, political, and military strength could inhibit Soviet expansion without an apocalyptic showdown. George Kennan gave voice to this policy in 1947 and, as John L. Gaddis has demonstrated in his book, *Strategies of Containment*, it has been continued in one form or another ever since. One alternative future described in the 1987 Brown University-Public Agenda publication is largely an extension of this containment idea. By 2010, the authors of *Four Futures* suggest, the United States and the Soviet Union could "have eliminated the danger of a nuclear war destroying the whole world" and could "have taken major steps to ensure that no regional crisis could erupt into a super-power war." Yet in spite of these achievements, this alternative portrait of Soviet-American relations assumes that the two sides will continue their political competition, and the United States will still have to hold Soviet expansionist impulses in check.[4]

A third general American approach to the Soviets over the years is perhaps best described as Wilsonian universalism—the hope that nations everywhere will accept America's democratic values and by so doing abandon international aggression for a policy of collective security. In this scheme of things, however profound the differences between the United States and the USSR, it is thought possible and even likely that the Soviets will eventually see the light and convert to traditional American economic and political ideas. This hope found fullest expression during World War II when Americans across the political spectrum described the Soviet Union as already converted or rapidly turning into a country resembling the United States. In perhaps the most famous wartime expression of this view, *Life* magazine declared in March 1943 that the Russians were "one hell of a people . . . [who] to a remarkable degree . . . look like Americans, dress like Americans and think like Americans." The NKVD was "a national police similar to the FBI."[5]

This sort of wishful thinking had outlived the war. In the late 1940s Henry Wallace's Progressive party was convinced that Soviet receptivity to collective security and respect for national self-determination were victims of Truman's anticommunism. In this scheme of things, had FDR lived, Washington and Moscow would have continued a cooperative relationship for the foreseeable future. This rosy picture of a friendly, progressive Soviet Union found renewed expression in revisionist writings on the origins of the Cold War in the 1960s and 1970s.

As during World War II, however, this hopeful picture of Soviet Russia as a potential convert to American ideas held considerable appeal to conservatives as well. In 1972, for example, President Richard Nixon told Henry Kissinger: "We constantly misjudge the Russians because we judge them by their manners, etc., and we do not look beyond to see what kind of character and strength they really have. Anybody who gets to the top of the Communist hierarchy and stays at the top has to have a great deal of political ability and a great deal of toughness. All three of the Soviet leaders have this in spades, and [Leonid] Brezhnev in particular. . . . Like an American labor leader, he has what it takes. . . ." He also reminded Nixon of "a big Irish labor boss, or perhaps an analogy to mayor [Richard] Daley [of Chicago] would be more in order." But whomever he called to mind, he was the consummate self-made man with "a great deal of animal magnetism and drive which comes through whenever you meet him."[6]

Even Ronald Reagan, the most conservative, anti-Soviet president since 1945, found the idea of converting the Soviets to American traditions appealing. In October 1985, on the eve of Reagan's first summit meeting with Gorbachev, columnist George Will wrote: "Several years ago I heard President Reagan say approximately this: 'I would like to take the Soviet leaders up in a helicopter over Los Angeles.' (Here I thought: Good, he is going to push them out. But, no.) 'I would point to all the small houses with swimming pools and I would say, Those are the workers' houses!' Surely Ronald Reagan does not think that the hard men of the Kremlin are misguided Lane Kirklands, labor leaders mistaken about how best to raise living standards." Will worried that Reagan viewed Soviet leaders as "susceptible to the taming example of American freedom and affluence. I mention this now," Will added, "because the Washington Post reports that recently the President was flying over New Hampshire and said to the Governor how much he would like to take Gorbachev to 'any house down there' to meet 'the working people.' What does the President think such a visit would accomplish? Perhaps the Gorbachev palm slapped to the Gorbachev forehead, and a thunderstruck exclamation, 'Marx goofed! I have seen the future and lots of kitchen appliances, and it and they work. So dismantle the *gulag*!'"[7]

An impressionistic survey of American reaction to Gorbachev's rule provides some demonstration of how varied and ambivalent it has been. On at least one point, however, almost all Americans who pay some attention to Soviet affairs, or have heard about Gorbachev's reforms, seem to agree: there is some kind of struggle over change going on in the Soviet Union. In May 1988, for example, columnist Anthony Lewis of the *New York Times*, discussed the effort to transform Soviet society and the reality of change in Soviet-American relations. "Virtually every day brings another development that we would have greeted with utter disbelief a few years ago." Offering "random samples" of change, Lewis acknowledges that they are "extremely disturbing to the entrenched bureaucratic class . . . in a highly conservative society." Columnist Flora Lewis of the *New York Times* shared her colleague's view that Gorbachev faced serious resistance to his reforms that could make him "stumble and fall." In Moscow, "orderly change is extremely difficult and risky for those in power." A front-page story in the *Los Angeles Times* on May 31, 1988, confirmed the picture of a divided Soviet Union in which "conservative opponents" of Gorbachev were squeezing "liberal supporters . . . out of a special Communist Party conference called to push forward his sweeping program of political, economic and social reforms." According to Michael Parks, the *New York Times*'s Moscow correspondent, Gorbachev's reform "proposals have split the party, the government and much of the country into those wanting . . . to widen and accelerate the reforms, and those who fear that they will throw the country into chaos and favor more limited and gradual changes."[8]

Both the *New York Times* and the *Los Angeles Times* reported that debate in the Soviet Union extends to matters of language and history. In August 1988 a *New York Times* correspondent described an invasion of American idioms into the Russian language that some Russians feared would dilute their mother tongue and open their society to other corrupting influences. "The onslaught," Bill Keller writes, "is on many fronts, from rock music to politics. But the heaviest infiltration is the terminology of business and economics, where the Russian language, like the state-run economy, is poorly equipped to deal on its own with such concepts as computerization, financing, and marketing. . . . The invasion has brought indignant cries from purists, who fear the mother tongue is being corrupted or, worse, that foreign words are the harbingers of decadent foreign concepts, such as capitalism and break-dancing —known here as 'kapitalizm' and 'breikdensing.'"[9]

In the summer of 1988 the *Los Angeles Times* described an argument in the Soviet Union over Soviet diplomatic history in general and the origins of the Cold War in particular. The article pointed out that a number of Soviet foreign policy specialists had abandoned the picture of foreign policy as an extension of a worldwide class struggle against capitalism and instead had begun to see "the Cold war, the arms race, the division of Europe, [and] regional conflicts from Latin America to Africa to Asia" as equally the responsibility of Soviet and Western actions. Conservative opponents of this "revisionism" objected to the "departure from long-held principles," and warned against sowing "confusion among Soviet people and among our friends abroad."[10]

Not all American observers are convinced that such debates are real. Conservative *New York Times* columnist William Safire asserted during the fourth Reagan-Gorbachev summit in June 1988 that "you really have to be here in Moscow to feel the urge to conform to the new

Soviet nonconformity. Criticism of the old regime is not merely permitted on a scale unprecedented in Soviet life, but it is organized and orchestrated with such gusto that it appears democracy is busting out all over. It's not. . . . The tables in the summit press center groan with booklets in every language peddling the new anti-party party line." Yet for all Safire's skepticism, even he is ready to acknowledge that "not all of glasnost is manipulation."

Safire's is just one voice among what he describes as "a dwindling band" of those who doubt the reality of Soviet change and continue to view Moscow as "the center of tyranny, terrorism and aggression in the world." Safire believes that by helping Gorbachev we may be saving "a system that offers pluralism when in trouble and Stalinism when back on its feet." Yet even as tough-minded an anti-Soviet as Safire is ready to concede his uncertainty: "It may be that the Soviet Union is on the capitalist road and the cold war is ending; but it also may be that Mr. Gorbachev is a Khrushchevian flash in the pan, or is a leader shrewd enough to take advantage of our hopes, as Lenin did with his New Economic Plan. Nobody knows."[11]

Skepticism about Soviet capacity to change is one element in the overall response to Gorbachev's "reforms." "Whether the Communist system is capable of the kind of reform that can bring the kind of success Mr. Gorbachev seeks is another question," Flora Lewis wrote in May 1988. "My own view is probably not. . . ." However much Ronald Reagan has been in the forefront of those ready to believe that glasnost and perestroika are real and hail profound changes in Soviet communism, he also has enduring doubts about the willingness of Soviet authorities to be anything but "profoundly evil" and cunning liars who above all aim to do in the United States. In April 1988, for example, only six weeks before he held his fourth summit with Gorbachev, he made what the *New York Times* called "a thundering attack on the Soviet Union, saying, 'If there is change, it's because the costs of aggression and the real moral difference between our systems were brought home.'" When Secretary of State George Shultz saw Gorbachev in Moscow the next day, "the Soviet leader denounced the President's tone as 'confrontational.'"[12]

During his visit to Moscow in June, Reagan gave symbolic expression to his long-standing conviction that Soviet repression of traditional Western freedoms remains an unresolved problem. In a meeting with Soviet dissidents at the American ambassador's residence and by a visit to a seven-hundred-year-old Russian Orthodox monastery, the president criticized the Soviets for denying their citizens freedom of religion, speech, and travel. The message was not lost on Gorbachev, who declared that support of human rights "should be done without interfering in domestic affairs, without sermonizing or imposing one's views and ways, without turning family or personal problems into a pretext for confrontation between states." By the end of the four-day summit Gorbachev, according to the *New York Times*, was exasperated with "Mr. Reagan's concentration on human rights issues and the President's refusal to endorse the general guidelines for Soviet-American relations proposed by the Soviet leader." In part an endorsement of "peaceful coexistence," a phrase that originated with Lenin and is anathema to American conservatives, the Soviet version of the guidelines was unacceptable to the president and his advisers. Although there was much more symbol than substance to this dispute, it was evidence of continuing American skepticism about Soviet commitments to change.[13]

Doubts about Soviet readiness for fundamental reform is particularly strong when it comes to military doctrine and plans. While most American commentators on Gorbachev's foreign policy see him as eager for a period of calm in Soviet-American relations, they also doubt his ability or desire to reduce substantially military competition with the United States and bring an end to Soviet expansionism. As U.S. Ambassador to the Soviet Union Jack Matlock said at a spring 1988 symposium on "Gorbachev and the Second Soviet Revolution," despite the Intermediate-range Nuclear Forces treaty and a decision to leave Afghanistan, the Soviets "still ship arms to many places around the world and they are not cutting off with the rapidity one would hope for." The Soviets "haven't opened up a new front of military confrontation in the eighties," Matlock added. But "they're still hanging on to some of the more important military penetrations they made in the seventies. . . . It would be premature to conclude that the practices of the past are excluded by current ideological changes." Robert Legvold, professor of political science and director of the Harriman Institute for Advanced Study of the Soviet Union at Columbia University, agreed: "Gorbachev is not about to roll up the Soviet tent and retreat from the global role to which he aspires."[14]

When Secretary of Defense Frank C. Carlucci visited the Soviet Union in August 1988, he bluntly told the Soviets the same thing, saying that he saw little concrete evidence of a Soviet shift to a more defensive military strategy. "No one begrudges you the need for a strong and capable army," Carlucci told a gathering of Soviet military chiefs. "What troubles us is when the Soviet Union continues to develop forces far in excess of defense—and especially when that newly added strength focuses on forces designed for massive offensive operations to seize and hold territory." A report at the end of August 1988 that the Soviets were expanding a Syrian naval base as a prelude to an increased naval presence in the Mediterranean confirmed the feeling in the Defense Department that Gorbachev's rule had done little to alter Soviet expansionist impulses. In a report released in September 1988 by the defense policy subcommittee of the House Armed Services Committee, Democrats and Republicans alike agreed that there had been changes in the rhetorical description of Soviet military goals, but substantive reforms had not been made. Promised changes in the structure of Soviet military forces to make them less menacing to the West might occur in the future, the subcommittee concluded, but they had not occurred yet.[15]

Despite growing evidence in 1989 that Gorbachev was committed to domestic economic and political change, reduced defense spending, and nonintervention toward Eastern Europe where popularly supported governments were replacing communist regimes, some Americans remained doubtful that the Soviets were capable of sustaining real change. In the spring of 1989 Richard F. Cheney, the secretary of defense, predicted that Gorbachev would fail in his reform efforts and would be replaced by someone "far more hostile" to the West. "The task that he [Gorbachev] set for himself of trying fundamentally to reform the Soviet system is incapable of occurring." In November 1989 Zbigniew Brzezinski, President Jimmy Carter's national security adviser, told Soviet officials in Moscow that "No successful precedent exists of transition from a Communist, dictatorial system to a pluralistic, democratic system. . . . It is especially difficult to restructure a statist centralized economy into a functioning market system." Although Brzezinski did not foresee "a return to some kind of Stalinism in the Soviet Union," he also doubted that the near future would bring "truly profound transformations of political and economic institutions and of political culture." Likewise, the economist Robert J. Samuelson observed that the communist "societies are discarding familiar political and economic institutions without any assurance that they can develop adequate substitutes." *New York Times* correspondent R. W. Apple, Jr., echoed the point: the political changes sweeping across Eastern Europe and the Soviet Union made 1989 worthy of comparison with 1848. But a severe testing lay ahead. "It is far easier to topple tired and rotten political and economic structures . . . than it is to build shiny, efficient, lasting new ones."[16]

At the same time that Americans are skeptical about Soviet commitments and their ability to make fundamental reforms at home and abroad, they also have strong hopes that Gorbachev's government will produce far-reaching changes. These hopes rest on the belief that a stagnant Soviet economy, the pressure of U.S. policies, and the irresistible example of a free and prosperous United States are compelling Gorbachev to abandon failed communist means for more practical ones imported from the West.

Ronald Reagan was a leading exponent of these ideas. In response to Gorbachev's reforms, Reagan declared that he no longer viewed the Soviet Union as an "evil empire." "You are talking about another time, another era," the president told a group of reporters during a walk through Red Square in June 1988. Some six months before he had also said that Gorbachev's rule signaled the suspension of the Soviet drive for "a one-world, Communist state." In December 1987, on the eve of Gorbachev's visit to Washington to sign the INF treaty, Reagan declared: "We now have a leader that is apparently willing to say—or has never made that claim, but is willing to say that he's prepared to live with other philosophies in other countries." "The notion that the Soviet Union does not want to take over the world," *New York Times* journalist David K. Shipler wrote, "is certainly a new one for Ronald Reagan and one that many of his conservative supporters deplore as naive." In answer to this charge, Reagan's aides asserted that the president has remained steadfast, and it was the Soviets, not Reagan, who had changed.[17]

And the source of this transformation, Reagan and administration leaders claimed, was American pressure and example. Soviet willingness to eliminate intermediate-range nuclear weapons, discuss major cuts in strategic systems, and withdraw from Afghanistan was less the result of Moscow's severe internal economic problems than of fear generated by America's military buildup and commitment to pursue the Strategic Defense Initiative. "The contribution of the Reagan Administration's defense buildup, its 'evil empire' rhetoric, its Star Wars and 'freedom fighter' programs to the evolution in Moscow cannot be reasonably weighed," Flora Lewis believes. "There's just no way to know whether they pushed Mr. Gorbachev or whether he'd be doing the same things anyway." But whatever the reality, the Reagan administration was convinced that its policies deserved the lion's share of the credit. Furthermore, it viewed the turn toward greater openness in Russia as growing out of the realization that American-style free enterprise and individual liberty are the only means by which Moscow will be able to work decisive improvements in the Soviet economy. Having predicted for a long time that the Soviets might one day realize how shortsighted they are, Reagan believed that the Soviets saw the fallacy of their ways and were giving up the unrealizable goal of imposing "their incompetent and ridiculous system on the world."[18]

It is currently an article of faith in the United States that at the same time the Soviets remain a dangerous adversary they are beginning to accept American habits of mind and are trying to imitate the American way of life. During a meeting with students at Moscow State University, Reagan urged the transformation of Soviet society through American-style freedoms, and celebrated current events in the USSR, "a time when the first breath of freedom stirs the air, . . . one of the most exciting, hopeful times in Soviet history." He described a shared Soviet-American aversion to bureaucracies, and told the students that "I could be looking out at an American student body as well as I'm looking out here and would not be able to tell the difference between you."[19]

Anticipating the tone of the president's trip to Moscow, Shipler wrote on May 29, 1988, that in making his journey, "Ronald Reagan carries the burden of ambivalence toward the Soviet Union that most Americans bear—the suspicions that the Soviet authorities are profoundly evil, the hopes that Russians are just like us, the fear that they are cunning and duplicitous, the belief that they can be reasoned with. As the President goes through the pageantry of the summit conference, he acts out these inner conflicts of perception for all his countrymen."[20]

Evidence of American ambivalence toward Gorbachev's Russia abounds. In the same meeting with Soviet military chiefs at which he objected to their "massive offensive" military power, Secretary Carlucci declared: "This is a unique event. As I look out at your faces, I can't help but think how similar you look to faces I look at time and again in the United States, members of our own military establishment. We have so many similarities. Every step in our dialogue which can improve communications is in our interest and in the interest of world peace."[21]

On May 31, at the start of the fourth Reagan-Gorbachev summit, a human-interest writer for the *Los Angeles Times* described "the increasing and probably inevitable Americanization of Moscow. To say that Marx Street already has turned into Main Street—or ever will—would be a gross exaggeration, even though Pepsi, Coke and Fanta Orange stands are sidewalk fixtures; Astro Pizza has been selling genuine U.S.-style pies to the comrades for the last month, and Baskin-Robbins will sign a deal today to open its first Soviet store in July. McDonald's and Pizza Hut have already announced similar plans." The account goes on to describe Soviet fascination with a television series about America that was "so riveting that Soviets are following a trend that's already afflicted Americans; they're becoming couch potatoes." Interviews with a mining engineer dressed in "Levi corduroys and a button-down Wall Street-style power shirt" and teenagers who drank Pepsi, admired Michael Jackson, and looked "like teens in any U.S. shopping mall" underscored the extent of American influence on Russia.

Even U.S. Information Agency Director Charles Z. Wick expressed amazement at the transformation of Moscow. "I was out walking this morning at 7 a.m. when I noticed some boys fishing off the Moscow River embankment," he said. "At first I just assumed they were American kids. They both had on blue jeans. Then I was startled to realize I had just taken it for granted." Wick did not "think we can Americanize this country completely," because that would be "putting on an American superficial appearance. I think we have much more responsibility to have the Soviets understand our values and our concept of democracy."[22]

At the end of the Moscow summit the *Los Angeles Times Magazine* carried a story by George Stein about "Soviet Chic": "Suddenly All Things Russian Are Red Hot." The article described Gorbachev as number eight on the Gallup list of the ten men most admired by Americans and as the man who "could launch a thousand Soviet missiles or smile over an arms control agreement." Stein cited opinion polls showing "that the suspicion and hatred with which many viewed the Soviet Union has diminished, at least for now": "62 percent of Republicans and 66 percent of Democrats now say the United States can trust the Soviet Union at least somewhat, and 71 percent of Republicans and 74 percent of Democrats say they think the United States can trust Gorbachev in particular." U.S. tourism to the Soviet Union had doubled, and "Surf Russia" T-shirts, with a face of Lenin next to palm trees, were selling so fast in California that boutiques could not keep them in stock. Soviet visitors to the United States are greeted warmly. One participant in a Soviet-American mountain-climbing outing in the Rockies recalled Soviet and American climbers sitting around a campfire singing "Amazing Grace" and "Moscow Nights." A visit by high-ranking Soviet officials to conservative Orange County, California, where they briefed residents on Gorbachev's reforms, evoked expressions of support: "I am a conservative," one man said, "But I want you to know I sympathize with what you are trying to do, and I wish you the best."[23]

Stein suggests that the outpouring of interest and sympathy had a faddish quality to it and might not last very long—an important point in trying to assess American attitudes toward Soviet-American relations in the 1990s. Much of past and current reaction to the Soviet Union rests upon contradictory impulses that can shift almost overnight. "The astonishing thing to me," Allen Kassof, executive director of the International Research and Exchanges Board in Princeton, New Jersey, says, "is how quickly the mentality of conservative America has changed. The hard core aside, you find people who think it very fashionable to engage in relations with the Soviets. . . . How quickly the turnaround. It is as though nothing had ever been wrong and the Evil Empire was 100 years ago, instead of two or three years ago." In a poll done in Orange County in January 1989 a plurality of residents thought the Cold War was coming to an end and listed the Soviet Union as less of a future threat to the United States than the Third World and Japan.[24]

In our dealings with the Soviets we suffer from what political scientist Seweryn Bialer has called a "quick fix" attitude. This attitude "has its sources in the admirable native American optimism and in the 'can do' approach which lead both to impatience with problems which have no visible rapid solutions and to an exaggeration of American ability to influence rapidly both its own allies and a difficult and dangerous adversary." When this quick fix approach combines with "the vagaries of the American political system, the sensationalism of the media, and the impatience of the American public," it leads to swings in attitudes toward Soviet-American relations from "unwarranted optimistic illusions to overly pessimistic exaggerations." The dramatic destruction of communist control in Eastern Europe by spontaneous uprisings in the last months of 1989 exhilirated most Americans. But as the drama of a revolution gives way to the tedium of everyday events and the difficulties involved in bringing long-term change to these countries string themselves out over months and years, American interest in and support for such reforms will likely diminish and perhaps disappear.[25]

Soviet expert Marshall D. Shulman of Columbia's Harriman Institute worries that American opinion toward the Soviets is too unstable to permit significant advances in arms control negotiations in the coming decade. The cautious approach to arms negotiations by George Bush during the first year of his term is one demonstration of Shulman's concern. In 1988 he wrote:

> During the past two years, President Reagan has given his support to the principal of arms-control negotiations with the Soviet Union. But within the government bureaucracy and in our domestic politics, there is not the sufficient support to translate this principal into concrete measures. Although the right wing in American politics has been somewhat isolated by the President, it still has the capability to block further progress. Prospects for the near-term future, beyond the present Administration, are not encouraging, considering that politicians in both parties appear to have concluded that the political center of gravity in the United States is still conservative. The fact is that there is not a politically effective constituency in the United States in support of security through arms control.[26]

The dangers to improved Soviet-American relations from unstable or nonrational thinking in the United States are substantial. This is not to suggest that American attitudes toward the Soviets are wholly unreasonable. In fact, there has been a lot of good sense behind American dealings with the Soviets since 1945. The Marshall Plan, the strategy of deterrence, the Kennedy Test Ban treaty, and Reagan's INF agreement with Gorbachev are just a few examples. Yet the case for a rational foreign policy should not crowd out the less palatable shortcomings in our approach to the USSR. On the one side is what George Kennan describes as "the continuing existence of a substantial, politically influential, and aggressive body of American opinion for which the specter of a great and fearful external enemy, to be exorcised only by vast military preparations and much belligerent posturing, has become a political and psychological necessity." At the opposite extreme is the illusion, similar to that appearing during World War II, that the Soviets are becoming just like Americans.[27]

These views may have more to do with shifts in feeling about conditions in the United States than with Soviet realities. When we feel badly about the state of the nation, as we did at the start of the Reagan term, we tend to see external dangers capable of destroying our internal institutions. When we feel good about ourselves, we tend to think that the whole world wants to become just like the United States.[28] At the beginning of Reagan's presidency, when only 17 percent of Americans thought things were going well in the country, we found considerable appeal in Reagan's view of Moscow as an "evil empire" effectively working to destroy the American way of life. At the end of this term, when 56 percent expressed satisfaction with conditions in the United States, we were ready to accept the picture of a benign Soviet Union transforming itself into a political and economic democracy. "Once you begin a great movement," Reagan said in his Farewell Address, "there's no telling where it'll end. We meant to change a nation, and instead, we changed a world. Countries across the globe are turning to free markets and free speech—and turning away from the ideologies of the past. For them, the Great Rediscovery of the 1980's has been that, lo and behold, the moral way of government is the practical way of government. Democracy, the profoundly good, is also the profoundly productive."[29]

Improved Soviet-American relations at the end of the eighties were mostly the result of Gorbachev's reforms and a sensible American desire for a more relaxed world in which we spend less on costly defense programs. If this improvement is to continue and prosper, however, we will need to be more attentive to realities abroad and less inclined to make foreign affairs an extension of shifting conditions in the United States; parochialism and irrationality ill-serve the national well-being in our dealings with the Soviet Union, or with any other nation.

## ■ CHAPTER 4
## DO THE CHANGES WITHIN THE
## SOVIET UNION PROVIDE A BASIS FOR
## EASED SOVIET-AMERICAN
## RELATIONS? A SKEPTICAL VIEW
### Colin S. Gray

Contrary to the evident tide of official and public opinion at present, it is the central contention of this chapter that there is as much peril as promise in the contemporary course of Soviet-American relations. Mikhail Gorbachev is but the latest in a long succession of reforming czars. It is inconceivable that he could direct and oversee the transformation of the brutal, continental, multinational empire that is the USSR into something so much kinder and gentler that a truly objective basis for a structural improvement in political-security relations would be the consequence. This is not to say that the United States and the Soviet Union are locked into a permanent enmity. Imperial Russia and the United States were functional allies with regard to possible dangers from Britain through most of the nineteenth century;[1] generically similar policy calculation could reproduce that objectively based friendliness some time in the future. But, there is little about Gorbachev's perestroika that carries a plausible promise for the drastic rewriting of the terms and conditions of Soviet-American relations.

Lest there be any misunderstanding, the skepticism which pervades this chapter does not extend to many of Gorbachev's motives. It is entirely probable that Gorbachev sincerely desires to modernize the USSR and no less sincerely desires a period of international political relaxation while perestroika struggles to secure some lasting domestic grip. However, there is no reason to believe that Gorbachev is any more, or less, sincere about his variant of peaceful coexistence and "new thinking for our country *and the world*,"[2] than was his forebear, Lenin. Gorbachev's novel reference to "humankind interest" with respect to the obvious perils of nuclear war is very likely as sincere as it is compatible with the preferences of the general staff.

It is probable that Gorbachev's policy motives are both wholly traditional and close to irrelevant. His leadership role is uniquely important, but changes under way in the Soviet empire are by no means solely the result of one man's commitment to change. Even if Gorbachev personally would like to transform the USSR from ugly continental predator to global good neighbor (by reasonable definition of the neighbors), it seems highly unlikely that Russian/Soviet political-strategic culture, the great institutions of the Soviet state, or plain objective conditions (bearing upon domestic political stability, for the leading consideration), would permit him to succeed—even though the CPSU nominally (to date) has been deprived of its "vanguard" role in favor of a rather authoritarian presidential system of government.

### What Drives Soviet-American Relations?

Soviet-American relations should not be liable to radical restructuring in the face of the words of the latest reforming czar. The decades of variable hostility were not the product of words, of personalities, or of the ever-shifting fashions in beliefs that so alter the tone of domestic politics in the West. Superpower relations in the miscalled Cold War, or "long peace," are nearly totally explicable with reference to the universal logic of the balance of power.[3]

The United States truly arrived as an essential player in the global balance of power in the winter of 1916–17, when her terms and conditions for the allies' purchase of war materials became critical for the continued conduct of the war. However, it was not until 1943 (in the context of policy planning for postwar Europe), and perhaps not even then, that the United States recognized that its statecraft would be a critical factor for the quality of postwar international security. Unfortunately, American appearance as a self-aware superpower—certainly as a power noticeably greater relative to potential peers than great powers usually had been—coincided with both the emergence of the USSR as the latest hegemonic menace to the balance of power in Europe and Asia and the availability of few atomic weapons. The novel mix of peacetime activism in balance-of-power statecraft, perception of Soviet menace, and nuclear peril has encouraged people to view the Soviet-American security relationship as something extraordinary—which it is, *for Americans*—rather than merely as the latest episode in antihegemonic conflict. Failure to appreciate the geostrategic rather ordinary character of their antagonism toward the USSR can spur Americans to the kind of thinking which looks to the rapid and benign transformation of Soviet-American relations.

This is not to deny the unique, or at least unusual, features in the post-1945 history of Soviet-American relations. But a good part of the optimism currently being projected for superpower relations flows from American inexperience in statecraft and from the absence of a mature tradition of prudent behavior in the maintenance of a balance of power.

The baseline for normalcy in the American worldview is the baseline for a country that did not play an essential active role in the balance of power. The Cold War of such ill-renown is magnified in its alleged historical distinctiveness because, in the U.S. experience, it is contrasted not with international politics as typically conducted from the chancelleries of Europe, but rather with the international politics of an age remembered imperfectly as one of American innocence.

Soviet-American antagonism certainly has some ideological content, but that content is more of an overlay than an essential fuel. The Cold War was a balance-of-power conflict, as were the two world wars of this century, the Crimean War, the great wars against Revolutionary and Napoleonic France, and—a century earlier—against the France of Louis XIV. Ideology is a weapon in contemporary international relations, certainly by contrast with the international relations of the 1850s, but it has little to do with what drives the strategic relations of mixed conflict and cooperation among states.[4]

For reasons of ideology, the leaders of the USSR have been rather less respectful of the ideas that other polities have legitimate interests, and that the contemporary international order has value in and of itself, than were the statesmen of Imperial Russia. However, little of significance in Soviet statecraft can be attributed uniquely to the ideology of the regime.[5] The Cold War has been about the balance of power in Eurasia. Rightly or wrongly, successive generations of American statesmen have come to believe that a single power or coalition should not be permitted to dominate Eurasia. With clear reference to the geopolitical theory of the British geographer Halford Mackinder, the U.S. government has stated that "the first historical dimension of our strategy . . . is the conviction that the United States' most basic national security interests would be endangered if a hostile state or group of states were to dominate the Eurasian landmass—that area of the globe often referred to as the world's heartland."[6]

The Soviet polity is heir to the continentalist legacy bequeathed by the Russia of the Romanovs. The unique quality of Soviet threat discerned by Americans has not pointed to anything very extraordinary in Soviet statecraft, but rather to the absence of adequate balancing elements within Europe and Asia and to the novel range and destructiveness of modern weapons. Personalities, policies, and ideological emphases will alter over time. But the USSR—or a Russian successor state—as an inherently insecure multinational empire,[7] can cease to pose a plausible threat to the balance of power only if other states rise to a new preeminence—as did Imperial Germany after 1871—or if the country is paralyzed in its ability to act externally for reason of domestic fragilities, as was the case, for example, for several years after the 1905 revolution.

By virtue of location, size, and political-strategic culture, the Soviet Union/Russia can hardly help posing a threat to the security of its neighbors. Whether or not Gorbachev succeeds with perestroika, whatever success would mean, Russia is going to remain a very large military power which, on grounds of capability alone, must breed anxiety abroad. The military professionals on the Soviet General Staff can go along with "new thinking" or "reasonable sufficiency," and even with paying renewed attention to defense.[8] Those ideas are entirely compatible with, indeed are helpful for, the needs of the Soviet armed forces for qualitative improvement and for an improved ability to protect against new Western strike assets. But the idea of a truly inoffensive defensive defense, as contrasted with a synergistic defense-offense, is an affront to common sense, to likely strategic conditions for the Soviet empire, and to Soviet military science.[9] Soviet military leaders do not need to be told that a thoroughly defensive mode of warfare is an invitation to defeat. "Defensive defense" would concede the initiative to an enemy who, in this case, enjoys a global agility bequeathed by maritime supremacy and a great superiority in defense mobilization potential.

It is close to ludicrous to postulate a Soviet military establishment capable only of functioning defensively at the operational level of war. The objective basis in actual Soviet military power for Western net assessment of threat is unlikely to alter dramatically. The idea of a USSR-scale Switzerland, literally incapable of persuing an "active defense" to the Channel coast, is the realm of dreams.

## Pressures for Change

It may not much matter for international peace and security whether Gorbachev succeeds or fails. On the one hand, a Soviet Union revitalized by a healthy shot of perestroika, and with its tacit social contract between rulers and ruled in good order, would be a more formidable competitor in those security stakes that still have zero-sum features. One may believe that the Soviet Union/Russia and its role in the world would be transformed radically for the better as a consequence of Gorbachev institutionalizing his apparent—and certainly novel—recognition of the classic security dilemma.[10] On the other hand, a Russia whose domestic troubles do not yield to Gorbachev's medicine, although less formidable to other states as a long-term competitor, could probably function as a dangerous, destabilizing factor in world politics. Hypothetically, Russian leaders witnessing the evident failure of perestroika to modernize the USSR might well conclude that the domestic path to the restructuring of the Soviet condition—and particularly the long-term security condition—was proven to be unavailable or politically intolerable; that tacit acquiescence in the slow relative decline of the Soviet Union was unacceptable; and that intimidation and the limited use of armed force offer the superior route for Soviet national security policy as it enters the twenty-first century. These points are not predictions; they are not offered in blithe disregard of the distinctive dangers of the nuclear age, nor are they dismissive of the grand strategic difficulties of translating military pressure into political and economic benefit.

It is obviously true that the USSR is in crisis, is perceived by Soviet leaders to be in crisis, and that that perception of crisis is being exploited to advance reforms as well as careers. However, it is well to remember that, as the old saying goes, "there is a great deal of ruin in a nation (or empire)." Despite allegations to the contrary, the USSR is not on the brink of collapse; the Soviet system, in the most important respects, works well enough for life to totter on, and in some respects, in areas designated as highest priority, the Soviet system works much better than does the U.S. system (e.g., in lead times for designing, developing, testing, and procuring most military equipment). Imperial Russia, and even the USSR, has a history of periodic flurries of drastic reform activity. The Gorbachev era is new primarily in that it is new to most of the people in the West who think about Soviet matters and who have never laid much store by what they might learn from history books.

The pressures for modernization in the USSR, including the possible abandonment of the USSR in favor of a move "back to the future" with some imperial Russian polity, would seem to be nearly identical to the pressures which moved Peter the Great, Catherine the Great, Alexander II (in his reforming period), Lenin, and Stalin, among others, in their turns to direct radical change from above. Russia/the USSR could not compete for sufficient security with a modernizing and intrinsically menacing outside world unless it reshaped its domestic house. Gorbachev recognizes that the Soviet economy is in the process of losing technological touch with the leading economies of the West and the East.[11] Gorbachev's answer to the impending military, and actual civilian, technological backwardness of his country is necessarily twin-headed. Internally, and without success to date, he is endeavoring to find a path toward a more efficient economy. Externally, through the manipulation of greedy and ignorant foreigners, as well as through personal appeal, he seeks to persuade putative enemies that there is little need to compete with the USSR militarily, and that his country is a reliable partner for joint economic ventures of all kinds. Lenin would have smiled on all of this (save for the sidelining of the CPSU)—after all, imitation is the sincerest form of flattery.

Gorbachev is not wholly insincere and cynical in using words and phrases which evoke a positive resonance when translated for Western ears. There can be little doubt that he is genuinely appalled by the prospects of nuclear war (as is his general staff and, indeed, as are all sensible people). Undoubtedly he is massively uninterested in undertaking military operations against NATO; he is sincere in wishing for improvement in the living standards of the Soviet peoples—and not only for considerations of political stability. He would also welcome a lengthy period of international relations sufficiently relaxed to allow reallocation of scarce economic assets away from near-term military production and toward medium-term civilian economic capital improvement and growth (and hence for the potential long-term benefit of the military establishment).

Amid all that is unknown, and notwithstanding his flamboyant personal style of leadership, there are some very important fixed features on the landscape of Soviet policy choice.

1. Gorbachev will not preside purposefully over a process of change deemed likely to imperil the political stability of the USSR unless he has no practicable alternatives, a situation that appears to be approaching rapidly.

2. The Soviet Union is and will remain a super-centralized empire. The Great Russian empire to which Gorbachev is the current legatee was not forged by the voluntary accession of peoples. No Soviet leader has proved willing to experiment with any serious devolution of Moscow's authority upon regional bodies, let alone to risk appearing weak in face of local demands for a much greater measure of self-rule, or, worst of all, independence.

3. Marxist-Leninist ideological baggage is irrelevant to the details and the course of governance, but—and this is a very large *but*—it is still the totemic bulwark proclaiming what remains of the legitimacy of the Soviet political system. Marxism-Leninism is not a manual for statecraft, but it does shape concepts and terms of reference. Autocratic, at least authoritarian, rule is as Russian as borscht. The reasons why the Soviet Union is unlikely to evolve into the condition of a stable and popular pluralistic democracy are at least as much Russian as they are contemporary-ideological.[12] It remains to be seen just how democratic Gorbachev's post-CPSU Russia will be, and how stable.

It would be unwise to attempt crystal-ball gazing concerning the ultimate purposes behind the highest level in Moscow's current commitment to change. There is no way to know what policy ambitions may lurk in the deepest recesses of Gorbachev's mind, how long his tenure of office may prove to be, and how policy choice could alter with evolving opportunities. Most words and actions undertaken thus far under the umbrella of perestroika lend themselves to interpretation either as examples of exactly what they profess to be, or as cases of intelligent grand-strategic management of the interstate competition as usual.

Soviet frontal opposition to NATO's Intermediate-range Nuclear Forces (INF) deployment and to President Reagan's Strategic Defense Initiative (SDI) proved counterproductive. Democracies have a way of finding tolerable coherence and sense of purpose when perceiving themselves to be under threat. However, a peace offensive is potentially devastating to the will to sustain a defense effort. An enduring weakness of a democracy is its inability to discern apparently distant danger through the fog, or smoke screen, of pacific sentiments and friendly gestures. It is always possible that the next several years could witness a gradual, but cumulatively dramatic, change in Soviet political and strategic culture.[13] It is conceivable that whatever Gorbachev's policy motives, he is riding the tiger of a societal and political transformation that truly will produce a Soviet Union vastly different from the bureaucratic autocracy, not to mention the "evil empire," of recent decades. While being properly attentive to the deeply rooted cultural characteristics of a society and polity, one must beware of being captured by rigid "essentialisms."[14] It is always easy to show that "what is" "had to be." By way of contrast, some scholars believe that czarist Russia, without the fatal strains of World War I, might have evolved into a constitutional monarchy. Likewise, some people believe that the development of the USSR was critically and idiosyncratically diverted into the most brutal and brutalizing path imaginable as a consequence of the distinctly noninevitable seizure of Lenin's inheritance by Stalin.[15] The implication of these speculations is that the future of the Soviet Union/Russia could include a course surprising to those disinclined to view history as an ever-dynamic set of possibilities.

By making a virtue of necessity—the political meltdown in East-Central Europe—Gorbachev is closer than any postwar Soviet leader has been to achieving the neutralization of Germany, the withdrawal of the United States from peninsular Europe, and the effective dissolution of NATO. The price of the "peace" that is breaking out is proving expensive for Western security—and it may yet bankrupt us.

### The Military Dimension

NATO, the Delian League of modern history, was founded and developed to provide the political architecture necessary for the organization of Western security in the face of perceived military danger from the East. Unlike the Delian League, NATO has not become an instrument for empire. But NATO is fairly strictly an instrument for the deterrence of

Soviet military attack upon Western Europe. The guardianship of the United States does not weigh as heavily upon its foreign dependencies as did the Athenian hegemony-turned-empire, but it can still be irritating to local pride, as well as potentially dangerous to vital local interests. Alliance with a very great power has always been a distinctly mixed blessing.[16] It seems improbable that continental Western Europe would choose to exchange even the somewhat ragged architecture and practices of NATO—which amount still to a security wardship under the United States—for Soviet (or, almost as likely, German) goodwill. But, the Western Alliance as extant cannot function in its traditional mode in the absence of a perceived military threat from the East.

A central problem for NATO, as noted previously, is that its political cohesion is under both purposeful and incidental assault from Gorbachev's "new thinking," while the likelihood of Gorbachev succeeding in his domestic reform endeavors becomes ever more problematic. The Soviet Union is the beneficiary of a Western goodwill which may undermine the foundations of Western defense, even though the future course and outcome of perestroika is profoundly uncertain. Although there remains considerable inertia behind the NATO alliance, budgetary pressures in the United States, generational changes on both sides of the Atlantic, changes in the ethnic composition of the U.S. public, and trade competition—to cite the more obvious factors making for alterations in policy—already make NATO appear distinctly entropic and old-fashioned (and this is to ignore the structural problem posed by a reunified Germany). If Moscow psychologically can continue to disarm key segments of Western European opinion, then NATO's days truly are numbered, although some residual political framework from the containment era would remain.[17] But NATO as developed in principle, in organization, and in terms of critical obligations between 1949 and 1954, the NATO still familiar in formal purpose, in structure, and in strategy (with the U.S.-extended nuclear deterrent as the instrument of the security guarantee), would vanish rapidly.[18] One should not reflexively lament the passing of old political forms and yesterday's strategic arrangements. However, the issue is whether the gold of good relations, which appears to be very much on offer from Gorbachev's ailing Soviet empire, is of the twenty-four carat or the fool's variety.

Two points merit particular notice. First, the issue really is not Gorbachev's personal sincerity. So, the subject for investigation herein is not framed in terms of a debate over whether the promised changes in Soviet military doctrine and posture are or are not intended as a snare and a delusion. Second, with some good reason it came to be fashionable in the 1980s to consider the USSR a "one-dimensional superpower."[19] That one dimension is, of course, the military. Bearing in mind the enormous uncertainty over the prospects for perestroika's success in restructuring the Soviet economy, nontrivial, if not whole- sale, reduction in the offensive fighting power of the Soviet armed forces —however helpful for domestic resource reallocation—would deprive Moscow of much of its leverage in world affairs. Smiles will accomplish more than threats with regard to Western Europe, but latent threats have their utility and certainly are critical for that quality of political respect or prestige which binds the ever-fissionable materials of empire. Furthermore, a Soviet Union/Russia shaken in the prestige it enjoys and damaged in its self-confidence by the unprecedented retreat from empire in Afghanistan, by the collapse of the structure of communist party rule throughout East-Central Europe, and by the crisis of legiti- macy proclaimed via the formal demotion of the CPSU is unlikely to be willing to devalue the heavily military currency of its international standing.[20] The undiminished Soviet commitment to the moderniza- tion of its strategic forces attests to Moscow's sensitivity to the prestige value of particular kinds of military power.

Before citing the grounds for skepticism over the medium-term significance of the proclaimed changes in Soviet military thinking and posture, it is essential to identify what appears to be occurring in Soviet thought and policy.

1. The Gorbachev reforms and future, rather traditional, Soviet mil- itary goals are by and large compatible. The emphasis upon replacing quantity with quality has been promoted by the Soviet military leader- ship since the late 1970s.

2. The Soviet Union is serious about all aspects of denuclearization —consistent with maintenance of an all-level nuclear counterdeterrence to possible Western nuclear initiatives.

3. Gorbachev does favor arms reduction agreements. They dimin- ish Western will and limit Western license to compete while they pro- vide excuses and reasons for near-term domestic reallocation of scarce resources away from defense research, development, and production.

4. The Soviet General Staff is serious about a more defensive mili- tary posture, although only in the traditional context of defensive- counteroffensive (an offensive defense) military planning. A truly —indeed, strictly—defensive defense would be an affront to strategic common sense, military science, and the lessons of history.[21] A rising level of Soviet interest in defense predated Gorbachev's accession in 1985, and can be attributed in good part to the notably more offensive cast to U.S. and NATO ideas, plans, and capabilities (AirLand Battle, Follow-On Forces Attack, the U.S. Navy's Maritime Strategy, Samuel P. Huntington's influential espousal of the notion of "conventional retali- ation," and so on)[22] in the 1980s. Soviet defense professionals argue that

new generations of advanced conventional munitions (ACMS) are all but removing traditional distinctions between defensive and offensive weaponry.

5. The elusive concept of reasonable sufficiency (for what?) has been embraced and promulgated at the highest level. Its precise meaning is open to debate. The deputy chief of the Soviet General Staff advises that "*all countries* should adopt and consistently implement the 'principle of defence sufficiency' at the minimum necessary level *and should completely renounce the strategy of nuclear deterrence* (emphasis added)."[23]

6. Although the USSR long has denied the thesis that war between East and West is fatally inevitable, the current emphasis being laid upon the importance of the prevention of war suggests that war is deemed to be possible. The Soviet military establishment may be somewhat confused over what is meant by "defensive sufficiency," but it is unlikely to be confused over its inalienable duty to attempt to win any war that cannot be prevented.

Soviet leaders and spokespersons have been talking unusually systemically about national security, acknowledging unambiguously that one country cannot, or should not, seek security at the expense of the security of others. In short, ample grounds exist for optimism. Moscow is talking peace, is undertaking unilateral force reductions, and is endorsing the idea of arms reduction regimes intended to express inoffensive purposes on the part of the High Contracting Parties (including highly unfavorably asymmetrical force reductions). Can it be that George Kennan's original containment hypothesis has been proven correct—as have the arguments of the Reagan conservatives of the early and mid-1980s who argued no compromise with an unrestructured evil empire? What Kennan wrote in 1947 should be recalled: "But the United States has it in its power to increase enormously the strains under which Soviet policy must operate, to force upon the Kremlin a far greater degree of moderation and circumspection than it has had to observe in recent years, and in this way to promote tendencies which must eventually find their outlet in either the break-up or the gradual mellowing of Soviet power."[24]

It is not at all clear that Gorbachev's USSR is "mellowing" in systemic ways of structural significance for the organization of international security. The arms reduction treaty already signed, on INF, works militarily in the favor of the Soviet Union. Indeed, any arms control agreement which forwards the cause of denuclearization, which diminishes available steps for nuclear escalation, and which reinforces the "nuclear taboo," cannot help but harm uniquely the security of the coalition which persists in pretending that nuclear threats comprise the heart of its defense concept (i.e., NATO). The pending START regime, although dramatic in the scale of its *promised* (not actual) reductions (to approximately 50 percent of START-*accountable* central nuclear warheads), is as bereft of a solid strategic rationale for the West as was the INF treaty. Unless one adheres to the witless proposition that the best strategic forces' posture is the least strategic forces' posture, the START possibility promises—as one should expect from the long, disappointing history of negotiated measures of arms control—to have modestly negative implications for a reasonable Western view of the stability of the central balance.

More interesting than either INF or START are the talks on Conventional Armed Forces in Europe (CFE). These talks address the relative capabilities of *the* Soviet military instrument of excellence—its land power. CFE has to be approached in the context both of Soviet claims for a claimed shift to a defensive orientation in both the social-political and the military-scientific wings of their military doctrine—although since they have always asserted the defensiveness of their doctrine, some skepticism is in order—and of recognition of the fact of lively debate in the dimension of military science.[25] Optimists in the West may need to rediscover what their forebears in the 1930s learned through exhausting diplomatic experience: there are offensive policies and strategies, but there are no inherently offensive weapons.[26] At the very least, and granting that offensive operational intentions should provide telltale logistic and deployment signatures, the distinction between offensive and defensive capability often is blurred.

It is possible that Soviet military intentions in Europe are as advertised. Perhaps it is the Soviet purpose to transform their forward deployments—or such forward deployments as residual Pact "allies" fail to see ejected—into garrisons objectively innocent of the ability to threaten to take ground in the West. One must remain agnostic on that important point at present. Furthermore, Christopher Donnelly notes that "the Soviet Army is so uniquely tailored for the offensive (believing it to be the only sensible means of defence in event of war) that to change this in any meaningful way would be the work of years. We cannot expect to see significant results in the short term."[27]

However, as Donnelly also observes, "the Soviet Army faces the need for imminent reform and reorganization."[28] Some of those announced withdrawals of forces that the USSR is claiming as evidence of its novel rejection of offensive ideas and plans, and indeed Soviet proposals for mutual, if asymmetrical, force thinning through CFE, could be held to serve rather traditional Soviet military ideas. By diminishing force to space ratios—not to mention the cumulative impact upon NATO's political cohesion of the aura of détente—the Soviet Union may well be hoping to provide itself with real running room for an armored non-nuclear *blitzkrieg*.[29] It is by no means self-evident that this is the case, but the evidence to date could lend itself to this interpretation among others. Of course, the unexpectedly rapid political collapse of real Soviet authority in East-Central Europe in 1989 has to figure as an important, although not necessarily fatal, potential handicap to rather traditional Soviet campaign designs. The future terms of military engagement in Europe will be different from those of the past because the Soviet army lacks allied contributions of forces and territory for forward deployment. However, the political clout and possible military prowess of Soviet arms are not absolute matters. The key question is what kind—and how much—political-military resistance will face Russia in the new Europe of the 1990s and beyond.

## Conclusions: Reasons for Skepticism

It is the broad conclusion of this chapter that there is probably a lot less to the apparent, announced, or discussed as possibly pending changes in the USSR/Russia than meets the eye. Further, it is concluded that the changes that have happened to date in the structure and behavior of the Soviet empire do not *yet* warrant any radical recasting on the Western part of established international security agreements. I am agnostic, although admittedly leaning toward skeptical, over the prospects for the thoroughgoing benign transformation of Lenin's legacy into a gentler and kinder polity. Indeed, if there is a somewhat different Soviet Union/Russia waiting in the wings of history for its turn on stage, it is likely a more overtly nationalistic and authoritarian Greater Russian/ Soviet empire, rather than a democratic socialist union of Soviet peoples. In addition to those Russians who recall with a strange nostalgia —if only second-hand—the Golden Age of truly firm government under Joseph Stalin, there are many ethnic Great Russians who discern in glasnost, perestroika, and "new thinking" a flabby liberalism that affronts their political culture. Great Russian chauvinism is alive and well in the Soviet empire and may yet recapture its ethnic patrimony if Gorbachev stumbles too badly. Behind the CPSU is a living tradition of Mother Russia that is ethnically intolerant, spiritually arrogant, and deeply respectful of autocratic rule. The *Pamyat'* (memory) movement is an expression of this patriotic Russian tradition.[30]

The broad conclusions just registered rest upon eight principal threads of argument. First, it is likely to be the case that the Soviet empire will be a source of menace to its neighbors (and to those distant lands whose balance-of-power policies support the Soviet empire's neighbors) whether or not Gorbachev's perestroika succeeds in modernizing the Soviet economy. A successfully modernized Soviet economy must mean a Soviet Union/Russia better able to bear the costs of military competition and even of distant empire.[31] A Soviet economy that could not be modernized by politically acceptable methods and policies might present Soviet leaders with the grim alternatives either of acquiescence in long-term decline from super-state standing, or of an attempt to change the terms of the international security condition through near-term exploitation of favorable military balances. I admit to being uncomfortable either with a much more powerful Russia, or with a Russia deeply pessimistic about its future security.

Second, Gorbachev is attempting the strategically impossible, in that he does not seem willing or able properly to align means with ends. There is little room for doubt that the motivating factor behind perestroika, glasnost, and the "new thinking" on foreign policy is the need to revitalize the Soviet economy. Gorbachev requires a relaxed Western world that will extend credits and technological assistance and will slow down the pace of its high-technology military challenge. However, the Soviet problem is not in the system, rather is it *with* the system. Thoroughgoing economic reform almost certainly requires thoroughgoing, systemic, political reform. The dropping of Article 6 of the Soviet constitution on the leading role of the CPSU *could* lead to such reform, but in and of itself it is no panacea for the ailments of today. Then-deputy director of the CIA, Robert M. Gates, characterized the Soviet economic reform problem in the following terms: "Trying to reshape the entire Stalinst economic structure gradually while leaving key problems of price reform and the government monopoly over goods until last is like a phased change from driving on the right hand side of the road to the left. The results are likely to be similar."[32]

Third, Russian culture, geography, and the dynamics of imperial rule all militate against the radical transformation of the Soviet Union as a player in world politics. Of course, states have changed their roles quite dramatically in response to altered circumstances: for example, Portugal, Sweden, Spain, the Ottoman Empire, and more recently the erstwhile great powers of Western and Central Europe (France, Germany, and Britain). But it is virtually inconceivable that a Soviet empire at the peak of its relative military prowess would choose quite voluntarily to attempt to settle permanently for a comfortably semiretired status from the rough and tumble of world politics. Even though severe economic problems may well invite and require severe solutions, the Russian culture, which is the product of a half-millennium of national experience, is not going to be cast off and replaced at the policy convenience of a . reforming czar.

Fourth, if the past is any guide, Gorbachev's reform campaign is likely to be yet another of history's potential turning points where history actually fails to turn.[33] The study of history should not breed cynicism, but a healthy skepticism over the significance of Mikhail Gorbachev's perestroika must be encouraged by the realization that the past three hundred years have witnessed many past instances of perestroika (e.g., in 1763, 1801, 1861, 1907, and 1922, plus the no-less short-lived Khrushchev and Kosygin reforms of the early and mid-1960s). Admittedly, *this time* it might be different. However, the historical record suggests that cycles of reform and repression are entirely Russian/Soviet.

Fifth, even if the most optimistic interpretation of Gorbachev and his evolving program is appropriate, he personally might be run over by the locomotive of history in the form of entrenched vested interests responding to clear and present danger. Whether or not perestroika and "new thinking" on security policy would survive the political demise of Gorbachev is sufficient enough an open question to encourage caution in the West.

Sixth, popular democracies are so prone to fits of enthusiasm for quite different assessments of foreign danger or opportunity that Western policymakers should risk erring on the side of being tardy in their reaction to Soviet policy changes. The Soviet Union could alter its main policy line in the course of an afternoon. The West, however, would require months or years to repair the damage it could impose upon its collective security structures in a burst of enthusiasm for the apparent evidence that peace was breaking out. Moreover, if the Western alliance were to unravel itself in a more or less unplanned reaction to the apparent disappearance of the Soviet threat, one wonders how Soviet policymakers would define their responsibility to their country in such a new situation. European security should not repose upon Soviet goodwill.

Seventh, both optimistic and pessimistic judgments are compatible with current trends in Soviet foreign, military, and arms control policy. It is prudent for the West to assume that the Soviet Union is pursuing its traditional purposes, although with a rather different mix of—and weighting among—means. U.S. influence could not be expelled from Western Europe by threats, but the offering of olive branches bears the promise of yielding that geostrategic effect. One can always hope that the announced changes in Soviet military doctrine in favor of "defensive sufficiency" are as benign as Soviet spokespeople affirm. However, the close fit between Soviet strategic interests, the terms of the INF treaty, their proffered terms for START, and the ground-forces slim-down all lend themselves to a less charitable interpretation. Furthermore, even if Gorbachev means exactly what he has said and written about military matters, he may not fully appreciate the ambivalence of military capability between offense and defense.

Eighth, even at some risk of appearing to argue that he is miraculously right, and even if he is wrong, I believe that the West can best serve the Soviet peoples, as well as its own security, if it declines to ease Gorbachev's policy path—beyond the utterance of encouragement, that is. It is not in the interest of the West for Gorbachev to succeed in economic revival, either of the bloated Leninist polity that is still the Soviet Union, or of an authoritarian Great Russian successor state. This is not to deny that there are dangers for the West associated with policy failure in Moscow. Policymakers in the West probably cannot exercise much influence over Moscow for good or harm. But, whatever influence they can wield should be in favor of obliging Gorbachev to proceed with thoroughgoing political reform.

# CHAPTER 5 ▄▄▄
# REFORM, DEMOCRATIZATION,
# AND SOVIET FOREIGN POLICY
William Zimmerman

A new "great debate" is taking place in Western public policy dialogue concerning whether, and if so how, the United States should assist the Soviet Union in implementing reform.[1] Although currently consensus exists that "something" should be done, the range of views is immense. It extends from⎡those who assert that the United States has an obligation to encourage Soviet reform and who imply that nothing less than the peace of the world is at stake to those who are fearful that reform will weaken Western resolve and vigilance and result in a Soviet Union that is more powerful but no less threatening.⎦

The current dialogue is in many respects a continuation of a larger discussion about the sources of Soviet foreign policy that has preoccupied scholars and politicians in the United States and elsewhere in the West at least since the end of World War II, and arguably since the Bolshevik seizure of power. That discussion in turn should be viewed in the context of the long-standing debate over whether a connection exists between the political system of a state and its foreign policy. At the root of the current discussion, as in so much of the prior dialogue, is whether fundamental political and economic transformations in the Soviet system would result in Soviet foreign policy behavior more conducive to relatively benign East-West relations. In the past, many have argued that *only* the democratization of the Soviet political system would result in more benign international behavior, just as persons have long argued that dictatorships result in war, and democracies in peace. Such a view has a long pedigree in political philosophy and makes most sense if one assumes that behaviors within states are extrapolated to relations between states.[2] Others—George Kennan's "X" article in 1947 remains the most relevant example—have envisaged more than one scenario in which Soviet foreign policy behavior moderates. They, however, would include major domestic political and economic transformations as one circumstance producing such change in Soviet external behavior. In both cases, it has been thought that the aggressive elements in Soviet foreign policy have derived largely from the nature of the Soviet political system and that changes in the political system would result in changes in foreign policy behavior.

Until recently, the issue of whether hypotheses linking major internal reforms and Soviet foreign policy behavior are correct has been an exclusively academic matter and of no relevance to the real world or any imaginable real world in the policy relevant future. Indeed, Western theorists, empirical research, and even powerful voices in the Soviet Union[3] in the early and mid-1980s were much more inclined to emphasize the prevalence of traditional or "neotraditional" patterns of rule in the Soviet Union than to speculate about the prospects that fundamental changes were in the offing in the direction of a more modern polity. By the early 1990s, by contrast, hypotheses about the linkages between internal economic or political reform and Soviet foreign policy had clear relevance. After 1985, when Mikhail Gorbachev became general secretary of the CPSU, the issue of whether links exist between Soviet domestic reform and foreign policy suddenly became highly topical—*aktual'nyi* in the Soviet sense.

At one level, the links are obvious, if only because we have multiple statements by Gorbachev that Soviet foreign policy is directly linked to Soviet domestic policy. Likewise, there are theoretical reasons why we should expect some attenuation in Soviet expansionist proclivities if fundamental democratization and economic decentralization were to occur. One of the more durable generalizations in the literature on comparative foreign policy is that the broadened authentic participation of groups in a polity increases the pressures for domestic resource allocations, and consequently in the long term diminishes the disposable surplus for foreign policy. Moreover, an empirical case can be made that Western-style democracies never fight each other. Likewise, the consequences for Soviet relations with the United States and the West more generally might be immense were the Soviet Union to become a trading state in Richard Rosecrance's terms.[4]

At another, more concrete, level, however, the nature of the links between domestic attitudes and foreign policy positions is neither well documented nor well substantiated. The assumptions that scholars, publicists, and leaders in the Western policy debate adopt about such links seem largely to derive from first principles and their policy positions rather than from any empirical base. The purpose of this chapter is to provide a data-based assessment of the links between attitudes toward reform and Soviet foreign policy. Specifically, I address two questions. Are persons who favor democratization or economic decentralization less likely than others in the Soviet Union to endorse the expenditure of funds for the military? Are they prone to associate themselves with positions indicative of an activist Soviet foreign policy?

## The Approach

My approach is to examine mass and attentive public attitudes, rather than the attitudes of the elite in the Soviet polity. My primary source is the Soviet Interview Project (SIP), a massive, omnibus Russian-language survey conducted in 1983 of 2,793 former Soviet citizens, the majority of whom migrated to the United States in 1979 or 1980. These people are primarily from urban parts of the European Soviet Union, relatively highly educated, overwhelmingly Jewish, and they migrated. The chief difficulty with this survey is that these respondents left the Soviet Union.

In addition, I analyze the results of a survey done in May 1988 for the *New York Times*/CBS by the Institute of Sociological Research of the Soviet Academy of Sciences and present findings from a survey done in the summer of 1989 by the same institute. Both are telephone surveys, the first of 940 Moscow residents, the second of between 250 and 300 respondents each in the cities of Moscow, Leningrad, Kiev, Alma-Ata, Tbilisi, and Tallinn.

Surveys of Soviet citizens also have their problems: They have so far almost invariably been done in cities and usually in Moscow alone, as was the case of the *New York Times*/CBS May 1988 survey. (It is important to note that in the SIP survey and very likely in the real world as well, there is a "Moscow effect"—some responses are systematically different on the part of former residents of Moscow.) They are not part of a national sample, and the responses are colored by Soviet citizens' well-founded suspicions about the questions of strangers. If the primary problem of the SIP data is that the respondents are *outside* the Soviet Union, the primary problem of surveys done in the Soviet Union is that the respondents are *in* the Soviet Union.

Nevertheless, surveys from both sources can, with care, be used as a source for the attitudes of some relevant groups in the Soviet population. Perhaps the most important caveat to enter about both the survey conducted by the Institute of Sociological Research for *New York Times*/CBS and the SIP survey is to urge readers to treat percentage responses (the marginals) with great caution. In both instances, however, the *patterns* detected should be given credence. Intergenerational differences among Moscow respondents for example almost certainly find their counterpart in other European Soviet cities. Likewise, intergenerational differences in attitudes which exist regardless of the respondents' reasons for migration or role in decision to migrate are likely to have been reflective of the state of thinking in the European, urban parts of the Soviet Union at the time of their last normal period in the Soviet Union, the late 1970s.

I share with Timothy Colton the view that mass publics—what he terms "the population"—have some bearing on Soviet foreign policy behavior and that the weight of mass publics in the foreign policy process is increasing as authentic political participation increases. I also regard the role of mass publics in foreign policy as being limited and almost certain to remain that way, the progress of democratization notwithstanding.[5] Consequently, I have also attempted to ascertain the views of those who would constitute a more attentive public, a cohort I have defined as those with some or complete university education. My data sources do not permit parallel analysis of more rarefied notions of attentiveness. Persons with some or complete university education also have attributes associated with an attentive public: they pay greater attention to both Soviet and non-Soviet media than do other Soviet citizens, they often have a nomenklatura position in the Soviet Union, and they have greater access to privileges than do other Soviet citizens.

I am concerned with two foreign policy dimensions which are crucial in assessing the attitudinal implications of domestic transformations for U.S.-Soviet interactions. One pertains to the attitude toward military spending, the other to the proclivity to use military force, especially outside Eastern Europe.

The Soviet Interview Project survey explicitly addressed the respondent's attitude toward military spending by asking whether he or she thought the Soviet Union was "spending too much, too little or about the right amount on the military, armaments, and defense." As in the previous instance, the question was framed with reference to the respondent's attitudes while he or she was in the Soviet Union and before the respondent had made the decision to migrate. Not surprisingly, these respondents overwhelmingly told American interviewers that too much was spent on defense. There was, however, sufficient variance in the responses so that *patterns* of relevance to the attitudes of mass publics in the Soviet Union could be discerned. Moreover, the summer 1989 Institute of Sociological Research survey asked Soviet citizens whether they thought the "14 percent reduction of the military spending suggested by Mikhail Gorbachev at the Congress [was] enough" or not, thus providing a basis for comparison.

With regard to the use of force, the most relevant question in the SIP survey was one that asked whether, during the respondent's last normal time in the Soviet Union (before his or her life was affected by the decision to migrate), the respondent thought the Soviet Union was right or wrong in providing "military aid to North Vietnam after the United States bombed" the latter.[6]

The Moscow survey conducted for the *New York Times*/cbs asked respondents whether they thought the Soviet Union "had accomplished its goals in Afghanistan" (not quite the same as asking whether respondents favored the Soviet action). In addition, two questions in the Moscow survey related to Soviet proclivity to use force. One asked whether the Soviet Union should "interfere in the internal affairs" of another state, the other whether it "should send military aid when asked." Not surprisingly, question construction fundamentally affected response patterns. Only about a fifth of the Soviet respondents said the USSR should interfere in the internal affairs of another country, whereas about three-fifths were prepared to support the Soviet Union's sending military aid when asked. To account for the lability of opinion reflected in such responses, I combined the answers to the two questions. This allowed me to treat as *hawks* those who favored intervention regardless of question construction, to identify a large intermediate group with labile responses that varied with question phrasing (*turkeys*), and to term *doves* those who opposed intervention regardless of the manner the question was phrased.

Two questions in the sip survey indicated attitudes toward economic reform and traditional Soviet economic institutions. These concerned the respondents' posture with respect to collectivization of agriculture and to state ownership of heavy industry. Respondents were asked to place themselves on a seven-point scale,[7] indicating at one extreme that in agriculture they thought the "state should control production and distribution of all agricultural products" and at the other that "all agricultural production and distribution should be private." With regard to heavy industry, they were asked to place themselves along a continuum indicating whether, in their view, the "state should own all heavy industry," or rather that "heavy industry should be owned privately."

Four questions in the sip survey were particularly appropriate to assessing attitudes toward democratization. Attitudes favoring liberalism and opposing traditional Soviet authoritarianism were derived by analyzing two questions. One spoke nicely to the core democratic notion of the market place of ideas by asking respondents' reactions to the proposition "In any society it will always be necessary to keep dangerous ideas from being expressed in public." A second concerned respondents' beliefs in individual rights and the rights of society. They were asked to locate themselves along a continuum the extremes of which were the "rights of accused must be protected even if guilty may go free" and the "rights of society must be protected even if the innocent may go to prison."

The SIP survey also permitted an examination of attitudes relating to participatory notions of democracy. Two questions were relevant: one dealt directly with political participation, the other with strikes. Respondents were asked whether they agreed or disagreed with the notion that "people should be able to participate in any organization even if the organization opposes some government laws" and to place themselves on a seven-point scale ranging from fully endorsing the proposition that "workers should not be able to strike because strikes are costly" to "all workers should have a right to strike even if certain services are disrupted."

The Institute of Sociological Research survey of Moscovites conducted for the *New York Times*/CBS also bore directly on the links between attitudes toward participatory democracy and foreign policy. Respondents were asked whether they agreed or disagreed with the proposition that "demonstrations were appropriate in our society," and whether (in spring 1988) a one party system "promotes democracy" in the Soviet Union.

Finally, both the 1988 Moscow survey and the SIP survey contained data relevant to Soviet attitudes toward Stalin. The Moscow survey asked whether respondents had favorable or unfavorable feelings about Stalin, and the SIP survey contained three questions: Did the respondents, during their last normal period in the Soviet Union, agree or disagree that (1) "Stalin brought rapid economic development to the Soviet Union"; (2) "Stalin was the kind of strong leader the Soviet Union needed in times of crisis"; and (3) "Stalin is blamed for some things he actually did not do."[8] Each of the three propositions picks up on a key element in Stalinism: whether respondents were so anti-Stalinist that they dismissed his role in transforming Soviet society in the first Five Year plan, whether respondents were apologists for Stalin and felt criticisms of Stalin had gone too far, and whether the respondents were sufficiently authoritarian in their basic outlook to believe that a very strong leader is necessary in crisis situations.

## Results of Surveys

Important differences exist in the extent of support for reform across age cohorts in the Soviet Union, both in the sense of economic decentralization and with regard to a more politically open society in which the rights of individuals are not subordinated to the *kollektiv*. The Harvard Russian Refugee Project of the early 1950s found that support for traditional Soviet institutions increased, the younger the respondents and the more the respondents had been socialized to Soviet power. By contrast, a central finding of the Soviet Interview Project data is that

Table 5.1   Changes in Support for Traditional Soviet Institutions
(Year Born by Decades)

| | Entire SIP Survey | | | | | |
| Proportion saying: | 1905–19 | 1920–29 | 1930–39 | 1940–49 | 1950–59 | Total |
| --- | --- | --- | --- | --- | --- | --- |
| "State should own all heavy industry." (%) | 52 (188) $Tau_b = -13, p < .0001$ | 52 (196) | 50 (289) | 35 (233) | 30 (147) | 42 = 1,053 100 = 2,488 |
| "Rights of society must be protected even if an innocent person may go to prison."* (%) | 38 (129) $Tau_b = -11, p < .0001$ | 27 (99) | 24 (124) | 17 (115) | 14 (70) | 22 = 537 100 = 2,435 |
| "In any society it will always be necessary to keep dangerous ideas from being expressed in public." (%) | 59 (63) $Tau_b = -17, p < .0001$ | 62 (78) | 45 (88) | 36 (85) | 37 (58) | 45 = 372 100 = 821‡ |

*Agreeing here are those who answered "6" or "7" to 7-point scale item ranging from "rights of accused must be protected even if guilty may go free" to "rights of society must be protected."

where there are differences in attitudes across generations, younger respondents are more likely to support economic or political reform in directions more akin to Western systems and less likely to endorse traditional Soviet economic and political institutions. (Note, moreover, that these persons had both left the Soviet Union and were interviewed in the United States before Gorbachev's rise to power in 1985). This finding holds controlling for time in the United States and reason of migration. Younger cohorts were more likely than older cohorts to support private ownership in industry, to disagree with the proposition that "it will always be necessary to keep dangerous ideas from being expressed in public," and to assert that "rights of accused must be protected even if guilty may go free." Dissatisfaction with the collectivization of agriculture was high across all age cohorts among those interviewed in 1983 by the Soviet Interview Project interviewers. Notions of reform, consequently, struck a responsive chord in the Soviet Union in the 1980s that resonated better with younger Soviet audiences (table 5.1). Moreover, Soviet surveys such as the 1988 Moscow survey by the Institute for Sociological Research done for the *New York Times*/CBS bear out this overall finding: when Soviet respondents are asked specific questions that reflect attitudes relevant to authentic political participation

Some or Complete University

| 1905–19 | 1920–29 | 1930–39 | 1940–49 | 1950–59 | Total |
|---|---|---|---|---|---|
| 46 | 49 | 45 | 27 | 27 | 36 = 395 |
| (35) | (60) | (142) | (96) | (62) | 100 = 1,099 |

$Tau_b = .15, p < .0001$

| 38 | 19 | 14 | 16 | 10 | 16 = 174 |
|---|---|---|---|---|---|
| (29) | (23) | (45) | (54) | (23) | 100 = 1,097 |

$Tau_b = .08, p = .001$

| 65 | 41 | 41 | 24 | 35 | 36 = 129 |
|---|---|---|---|---|---|
| (15) | (15) | (44) | (30) | (25) | 100 = 363 |

$Tau_b = .13, p < .005$

‡In this and several other cases, only one-third of the 2,793 respondents were asked the question.

—whether demonstrations are acceptable or not in the Soviet context, for instance—younger cohorts are considerably more receptive to views at variance with traditional Soviet institutions and behaviors and more congruent with glasnost and democratization.[9]

These differences do not, however, allow clear-cut propositions linking age cohort and attitudes favoring a more benign Soviet foreign policy. As in the case of the responses pertaining to agriculture, the distribution of responses pertaining to military expenditures in the SIP survey is consistent across age cohorts. Everyone is opposed to the level of military spending. Like the responses pertaining to agriculture, the overwhelming response (92 percent) is that too much is spent on the military. Evidently, moreover, this finding is not substantially contaminated by the respondents having told American interviewers what the latter wanted to hear. A 1989 poll conducted by the Institute of Sociological Research in Moscow, Leningrad, Kiev, Tbilisi, Tallinn, and Alma-Ata revealed that very few were opposed to reducing military expenditures. Of the six cities surveyed, only in Moscow (9 percent) did more than 5 percent of the respondents state they were opposed to the reduction. Indeed, between a quarter and a third of the respondents in Moscow, Leningrad, Kiev, and Alma-Ata said the 14 percent reduction was not enough, a view shared by almost two-thirds of the respondents in Tbilisi and Tallinn.[10]

Data drawn from experiences in the late 1970s suggested that there might be a hawkish tendency among younger Soviet cohorts. Deborah Yarsike and I have shown that, with the important exception of the cohort born in the 1920s (the persons occupying virtually all the current leadership positions in the Soviet Union, even though Gorbachev himself was born in 1931), the younger the former SIP respondents were, the more likely they were to say, during their last normal period in the Soviet Union (which for most of the respondents was in the late 1970s), that the Soviet Union was right to aid North Vietnam militarily. They were also more likely to say that the USSR would win a war if one were to break out and that the USSR was more powerful than the United States.[11]

Persons interviewed in Moscow in the summer 1988 about Afghanistan revealed an opposite trend. The younger the respondent, the more likely he or she was to assert that the Soviet Union had not achieved its goals in Afghanistan [$tau_b$ .12, $p < .0001$]. The intervention measure, by contrast, constructed from responses from the same questionnaire does not correlate with age. In this instance no pattern is discerned.

One can reasonably construct a story about how younger cohorts are more attuned to shifts over time in the global distribution of power and more cognizant of Soviet achievements and failures and in such a way reconcile these findings. For our purposes, however, what bears emphasis is that the 1988 Moscow survey does not lend support to the proposition that by the end of the 1980s it was true that the younger the Soviet respondent, the more likely that person would affirm the appropriateness of Soviet use of force. Rather, the responses to the more general questions about intervention seem to suggest the absence of a trend in either direction.

Ambiguity in this regard should be a caution about the ready acceptance of empirically unsubstantiated generalizations linking Soviet attitudes toward reform and attitudes toward foreign policy. Indeed, as it turns out, when relationships are examined directly, a differentiated and nuanced picture emerges. Attitudes favoring economic decentralization and anti-Stalinist positions correlate significantly with foreign policy attitudes congruent with a less activist foreign policy. By contrast, attitudes consistent with political democratization yield mixed results.

These findings are summarized in tables 5.2–5.5. As table 5.2 reveals, among the respondents as a whole, those favoring state ownership of agriculture are more likely[12] to say that the USSR was right to aid Vietnam militarily (61 percent) than those who favor a mixed agricultural economy (46 percent) or, especially, those who believe that agricultural production should be entirely in private hands (34 percent). Remember, no claim is being made that these percentages are to be found in the Soviet Union, only that the *pattern* had its counterpart in the European parts of the Soviet Union in the late 1970s. Those accepting the traditional Soviet institutional pattern in agriculture are also much more likely (29 percent among the entire group interviewed) than those favoring mixed ownership (10 percent) or exclusively private ownership (4 percent) to assert that the amount spent on military, armaments, and defense was "about right" rather than "too much."[13]

A similar pattern can be observed among the more educated respondents in the SIP survey—those more nearly approximating a Soviet attentive public. Of the more educated among the SIP respondents, those who favor state ownership of agriculture were more likely to characterize Soviet military expenditures as being "about right" than were other respondents and much more likely to endorse the proposition that the USSR was right to provide military aid to North Vietnam after the U.S. bombing.

The same generalization relating attitude to public and private ownership to foreign policy activism occurs in the case of attitudes toward state ownership of heavy industry and our two dependent foreign policy variables (table 5.2). Overall, of those who associated themselves with the assertion that the state should own all heavy industry, 13 percent said that about the right amount was being spent on the military, armaments, and defense compared with 5 percent and 3 percent of those favoring a mixed solution or the private ownership of heavy industry. Likewise, 47 percent of those endorsing state ownership of industry said that Moscow was right to aid Vietnam militarily, whereas 38 percent endorsing a mixed economy and 31 percent favoring completely private ownership took that stance.

Among the more educated respondents in the SIP survey, those saying heavy industry should be state-owned were likewise somewhat more inclined to associate themselves with the proposition that military spending was about right and considerably more likely to respond that the Soviet Union was right to aid Vietnam militarily. In short, the overall pattern seems clear: in mass publics, and generally among attentive publics as well, attitudes are linked that favor economic decentralization and a more benign Soviet foreign policy.

This finding is paralleled in both the 1988 Moscow survey and the SIP survey in regard to Stalin. Those in the entire pool of SIP respondents who agreed that the USSR needed someone like Stalin in a crisis, that Stalin contributed to Soviet economic growth, or that Stalin was often blamed for things he actually did not do were much more inclined

Table 5.2   Economic Decentralization and Foreign Policy Attitudes

| Proportion Saying Soviet Military Expenditures "About Right": * | Entire SIP Survey | | | |
| | State-Owned† | Mixed | Privately Owned | Total |
| --- | --- | --- | --- | --- |
| % of those saying agriculture should be | 29 | 10 | 4 | 8 = 183 |
| | (61) | (50) | (72) | 100 = 2,365‡ |
| | $Tau_b = .22, p < .0001$ | | | |
| % of those saying heavy industry should be | 13 | 5 | 3 | 8 = 176 |
| | (117) | (40) | (19) | 100 = 2,257 |
| | $Tau_b = .15, p < .0001$ | | | |

| Proportion Saying USSR Right to Provide Military Aid to North Vietnam after U.S. Bombed North Vietnam. | | | | |
| --- | --- | --- | --- | --- |
| % of those saying agriculture should be | 61 | 46 | 34 | 39 = 241 |
| | (39) | (60) | (152) | 100 = 641 |
| | $Tau_b = .15, p < .0001$ | | | |
| % of those saying heavy industry should be | 47 | 38 | 31 | 40 = 245 |
| | (117) | (78) | (50) | 100 = 616 |
| | $Tau_b = 13, p < .0005$ | | | |

*Except where noted, all others responded "too much."
†In this and all subsequent tables, responses that are more traditionally Soviet are given first.

to agree with the proposition that the Soviet Union was right to aid North Vietnam militarily and somewhat more likely to respond that military spending was "about right," rather than "too much" (table 5.3). Table 5.3 also reveals that virtually the same observation holds for those with university education in the SIP survey. With one exception, the responses by the more attentive publics in the survey bear out the link between anti-Stalin attitudes and support for a relatively benign Soviet foreign policy.

Table 5.3 reveals the same story concerning views about Stalin and foreign policy postures on the part of Muscovites in 1988. About two-thirds overall of those who gave pro-Stalin responses also said that the USSR had achieved its goals in Afghanistan, and about twice as many anti-Stalinists as pro-Stalinists were disposed to dovish responses regardless how the question of the appropriateness of intervention was posed. The same pattern is detected among those in the Moscow sample with some or complete university education. The conventional wisdom is correct: Stalinists are more disposed to spend money for the military and more inclined to intervene militarily than are non-Stalinists.

Some or Complete University

| State-Owned | Mixed | Privately Owned | Total |
|---|---|---|---|
| 16 | 6 | 4 | 5 = 53 |
| (10) | (10) | (27) | 100 = 1,091§ |
| $Tau_b = .11, p < .0005$ | | | |
| 8 | 4 | 3 | 6 = 52 |
| (29) | (16) | (7) | 100 = 1,056§ |
| $Tau_b = .10, p < .0005$ | | | |
| | | | |
| 73 | 45 | 29 | 36 = 104 |
| (16) | (29) | (59) | 100 = 289 |
| $Tau_b = .23, p < .0001$ | | | |
| 48 | 36 | 23 | 40 = 102 |
| (45) | (39) | (18) | 100 = 280 |
| $Tau_b = 19, p < .0005$ | | | |

‡Of the remainder, nine responded "too little."
§Of the remainder, one said "too little."

The story is more complicated when the links are examined between attitudes toward democratization and foreign policy (tables 5.4 and 5.5). The SIP survey data do not support the view that there is an association between attitudes toward liberal notions of democracy —specifically, the marketplace for ideas, and the priority of individual over social rights. Both for the survey as a whole and for the more educated subset, no relationship exists at all between stance pertaining to the proposition that it is necessary to keep dangerous ideas from society and whether the USSR was right to provide military aid to North Vietnam (table 5.4). Likewise, responses about societal versus individual rights and Soviet support for Vietnam are not correlated.

The story is only slightly different in the case of attitudes toward military resource allocation. Here there is a weak correlation between support for a more traditionally Soviet attitude favoring the priority of societal over individual rights and a greater propensity to assert that military expenditures are about right among the entire cohort of those surveyed in the SIP project. Those with university training who favor societal rights over individual rights are likewise marginally more dis-

Table 5.3   Stalinism and Foreign Policy

| Proportion Saying Military Spending "About Right" by Responses to Stalin Questions* | Entire SIP Survey | | |
| --- | --- | --- | --- |
| | Agreed | Disagreed | Total |
| "Stalin brought economic development to his Soviet Union." (%) | 11 | 5 | 8 = 56 |
| | (36) | (20) | 100 = 740† |
| | $Tau_b = .10, p < .005$ | | |
| "Stalin was the kind of strong leader the Soviet Union needed in times of crisis." (%) | 12 | 4 | 7 = 56 |
| | (41) | (15) | 100 = 754† |
| | $Tau_b = .15, p < .0001$ | | |
| "Stalin is blamed for some things he actually did not do." (%) | 11 | 6 | 7 = 47 |
| | (18) | (29) | 100 = 682† |
| | $Tau_b = .12, p < .001$ | | |

| Proportion Saying USSR Right to Aid North Vietnam Militarily: | | | |
| --- | --- | --- | --- |
| "Stalin brought economic development to the Soviet Union." (%) | 50 | 28 | 38 = 226 |
| | (131) | (95) | 100 = 603 |
| | $Tau_b = .20, p < .0001$ | | |
| "Stalin was the kind of strong leader the Soviet Union needed in times of crisis." (%) | 50 | 30 | 39 = 237 |
| | (134) | (103) | 100 = 611 |
| | $Tau_b = .20, p < .0001$ | | |
| "Stalin is blamed for some things he actually did not do." (%) | 57 | 34 | 39 = 221 |
| | (72) | (49) | 100 = 567 |
| | $Tau_b = .20, p < .0001$ | | |

| Proportion Saying USSR Achieved Goals in Afghanistan: | Entire NYT/CBS Moscow Survey | | |
| --- | --- | --- | --- |
| | Pro-Stalin | Anti-Stalin | Total |
| | 66 | 48 | 56 = 362 |
| | (183) | (179) | 100 = 646 |
| | $Tau_b = .18, p < .0001$ | | |
| Proportion giving pro- and anti-interventionist responses regardless of question formation:   Hawks | 16 | 14 | 15 = 84 |
| | (36) | (48) | |
| Doves | 17 | 30 | 24 = 142 |
| | (39) | (143) | 100 = 581 |
| | $Tau_b = .11, p < .005$ | | |

*Except where noted, all others responded "too much."
†In each instance, four said "too little," the remainder reponded "too much."

Some or Complete University

| Agreed | Disagreed | Total |
|---|---|---|
| 9 | 4 | 7 = 19 |
| (11) | (8) | 100 = 344‡ |

$Tau_b = .09, p < .001$

| 9 | 4 | 6 = 19 |
|---|---|---|
| (11) | (8) | 100 = 344‡ |

$Tau_b = .09, p < .05$

| 7 | 5 | 5 = 17 |
|---|---|---|
| (4) | (13) | 100 = 30 |

$Tau_b = .02, p$ n.s.

| 50 | 27 | 35 = 99 |
|---|---|---|
| (50) | (44) | 100 = 281 |

$Tau_b = .22, p < .0001$

| 49 | 30 | 37 = 103 |
|---|---|---|
| (49) | (54) | 100 = 282 |

$Tau_b = .19, p < .001$

| 59 | 31 | 36 = 96 |
|---|---|---|
| (27) | (69) | 100 = 265 |

$Tau_b = .21, p < .0005$

Some or Complete University

| Pro-Stalin | Anti-Stalin | Total |
|---|---|---|
| 50 | 40 | 43 = 112 |
| (38) | (74) | 100 = 263 |

$Tau_b = .10, p < .10$

| 13 | 8 | 10 = 23 |
|---|---|---|
| (9) | (14) | |
| 22 | 39 | 34 = 83 |
| (15) | (68) | 100 = 243 |

$Tau_b = .16, p < .005$

‡In each instance one said "too little."

Table 5.4  Attitudes Toward Liberalism and Foreign Policy Attitudes

| Proportion Saying Military Spending "About Right" by Response to:* | Entire SIP Survey | | |
|---|---|---|---|
| | Agreed | Disagreed | Total |
| "It will always be necessary to keep dangerous ideas from being expressed in public." | 10<br>(34)<br>$Tau_b = .07, p < .05$ | 6<br>(27) | 8 = 61<br>100 = 760† |
| | Societal<br>Rights | Equal<br>Rights | Individual<br>Rights | Total |
| Should individual or societal rights prevail?‡ | 10<br>(45)<br>$Tau_b = -.04, p < .05$ | 8<br>(76) | 6<br>(45) | 7 = 166<br>100 = 2,235§ |

| Proportion Saying USSR Right to Aid North Vietnam Militarily by Response to: | | | |
|---|---|---|---|
| "It will always be necessary to keep dangerous ideas from being expressed in public." | 39<br>(109)<br>$Tau_b = .00, p$ n.s. | 39<br>(130) | 39 = 239<br>100 = 618 |
| | Societal<br>Rights | Equal<br>Rights | Individual<br>Rights | Total |
| Should individual or societal rights prevail? | 42<br>(51)<br>$Tau_b = -.04, p$ n.s. | 42<br>(113) | 36<br>(78) | 40 = 242<br>100 = 600 |

*Except where noted, all others responded "too much."
†Four said "too little."
‡In each case one said "too little."
§Nine said "too little."

posed to support higher military spending, although among the university educated, tolerance for the market place for ideas and military spending are not all related. In short, it would be impossible to claim that there is a strong relationship between attitudes toward liberal notions of democracy and foreign policy attitudes. Rather, links between attitudes toward liberal notions of democracy and foreign policy are somewhere between nonexistent and trivial.

When we turn from liberal to participatory notions of democracy, the evidence is considerably more mixed. In the case of mass publics in the SIP survey, no relationship exists between attitudes pertaining to political participation and position on Soviet use of force with respect to Vietnam and only a weak relationship exists between attitudes toward participation and military spending (table 5.5). The links between the

| | Some or Complete University | | |
| --- | --- | --- | --- |
| | Agreed | Disagreed | Total |
| | 6 | 5 | 5 = 8 |
| | (3) | (5) | 100 = 350‡ |
| | $Tau_b = .07, p < .05$ | | |

| Societal Rights | Equal Rights | Individual Rights | Total |
| --- | --- | --- | --- |
| 7 | 5 | 3 | 5 = 49 |
| (11) | (25) | (13) | 100 = 105‡ |
| | $Tau_b = -.05, p < .05$ | | |

| | | | |
| --- | --- | --- | --- |
| | 38 | 35 | 36 = 102 |
| | (40) | (62) | 100 = 285 |
| | $Tau_b = .03, p$ n.s. | | |

| Societal Rights | Equal Rights | Individual Rights | Total |
| --- | --- | --- | --- |
| 39 | 38 | 32 | 36 = 108 |
| (14) | (50) | (36) | 100 = 281 |
| | $Tau_b = -.06, p$ n.s. | | |

#Respondents were asked where they would place themselves on a 7-point scale ranging from "rights of accused must be protected even if guilty may go free" to "rights of society must be protected even if an innocent may go to prison."

attitudes toward strikes and foreign policy are slightly clearer but nevertheless not robust. Respondents' position on strikes correlates relatively well with attitude toward military spending but weakly with Soviet use of force in Vietnam. Among the more educated there is no relationship at all between participation question and military spending or between attitude toward participation or strikes and use of force in Vietnam, but a modest and statistically significant relation between attitude toward strikes and military spending. The SIP survey questions suggest that there may be some relationship at the mass level between attitudes toward democratic participation and attitudes toward foreign policy, but not among the more educated respondents.

A different picture emerges when we examine the results of the 1988 Moscow survey. Both overall and among those who have some or

Table 5.5  Attitudes Toward Authentic Political Participation
and Foreign Policy

| Proportion Saying Military Spending "About Right" by Response to:* | Entire SIP Survey | | |
|---|---|---|---|
| | Disagreed** | Agreed | Total |
| "People should be able to participate in any organization even if the organization opposes some government laws." | 12 (21) $Tau_b = -.08, p < .05$ | 7 (42) | 8 = 63 100 = 780† |

| | No Strikes | Sometimes | Right to Strike | Total |
|---|---|---|---|---|
| Should workers have a right to strike? | 18 (51) | 8 (58) $Tau_b = .13, p < .0001$ | 5 (60) | 7 = 169 100 = 2,281† |

| Proportion Saying USSR Right to Aid North Vietnam Militarily in Response to: | | | |
|---|---|---|---|
| "People should be able to participate in any organization even if the organization opposes some government laws." | 36 (46) $Tau_b = .03, p$ n.s. | 39 (192) | 38 = 258 100 = 624 |

| | No Strikes | Sometimes | Right to Strike | Total |
|---|---|---|---|---|
| Should workers have a right to strike? | 50 (40) | 37 (73) $Tau_b = .06, p < 10$ | 37 (128) | 39 = 241 100 = 621 |

complete university education, those who state that demonstrations are not appropriate in Soviet society are considerably more likely to say that the USSR achieved its goals in Afghanistan. In a similar fashion, those who accepted the traditional Soviet notion—embraced for instance by Gorbachev as late as 1989—that a one-party system promotes democracy in the USSR are much more likely to endorse the proposition that the Soviet Union had achieved its goals in Afghanistan.

Even more to the point, those likely to associate with the proposition that demonstrations are all right in the Soviet context and who *disagree* with the statement that a one-party system contributes to democracy (by implication these respondents support multiparty democracy) are also more dovish. Both in the survey as a whole and among the more educated subset, respondents who support Western-style attitudes

|  | Some or Complete University | | |
| --- | --- | --- | --- |
|  | Disagreed | Agreed | Total |
|  | 5 | 6 | 5 = 19 |
|  | (14) | (5) | 100 = 356‡ |

$Tau_b = -.00, p$ n.s.

| No Strikes | Sometimes | Right to Strike | Total |
| --- | --- | --- | --- |
| 9 | 6 | 3 | 5 = 50 |
| (10) | (24) | (16) | 100 = 1,078‡ |

$Tau_b = .09, p < .001$

|  | 37 | 29 | 32 = 103 |
| --- | --- | --- | --- |
|  | (85) | (44) | 100 = 289 |

$Tau_b = .07, p$ n.s.

| No Strikes | Sometimes | Right to Strike | Total |
| --- | --- | --- | --- |
| 43 | 36 | 34 | 36 = 103 |
| (12) | (39) | (52) | 100 = 288 |

$Tau_b = .05, p$ n.s.

toward participation are much more likely to state that the Soviet Union did not achieve its goals in Afghanistan and much more likely to oppose Soviet intervention regardless how the question is framed. Several explanations are possible for the differences. One partial answer is that there is some systematic distortion on the part of those, especially the elderly, in the Moscow survey who are prone to say—to be safe—that everything is right in the Soviet Union. These are people who also say that Russians treat their children better than do Americans. Those who say that Russians treat their children better than do Americans are distinctively more disposed to say that a one-party system facilitates democracy in the Soviet Union and to say that Soviet use of force is appropriate. That, however, is not the whole story. Even among those who state that Russians love their children more than do Americans, those who

Table 5.5 Continued

| Proportion saying USSR completely or basically achieved goals in Afghanistan: | Entire NYT/CBS Moscow Survey | | |
|---|---|---|---|
| | Disagreed | Agreed | Total |
| Controlling for whether agreed or disagreed that "demonstrations are appropriate for our society" | 66 (287) | 45 (121) | 58 = 408 100 = 703 |
| | $Tau_b = -.21, p < .0001$ | | |
| | Agreed | Disagreed | Total |
| Controlling for whether agreed or disagreed that a one party system promotes democracy" in the USSR | 70 (294) | 34 (68) | 58 = 362 100 = 623 |
| | $Tau_b = .35, p < .0001$ | | |

| Proportion Favoring and Opposing Intervention: | | Disagreed | Agreed | Total |
|---|---|---|---|---|
| Controlling for response whether demonstrations acceptable: | Hawks | 18 (69) | 12 (30) | 16 = 99 |
| | Doves | 19 (73) | 30 (75) | 24 = 148 100 = 629 |
| | $Tau_b = .13, p < .001$ | | | |
| | | Agreed | Disagreed | Total |
| Controlling for whether agreed or disagreed that a one party system contributed to democracy: | Hawks | 19 (68) | 10 (19) | 6 = 87 |
| | Doves | 15 (53) | 41 (77) | 24 = 130 100 = 553 |
| | $Tau_b = .26, p < .0001$ | | | |

*Except as noted, all others said "too much."     †Of the remainder, four said "too little."
**The traditional Soviet position is given first.     ‡Of the remainder, one said "too little."

think a one-party system contributes to democracy in the USSR are more disposed to hawkish views concerning Soviet use of force, and those who do not are more dovish.

An additional explanation for the discrepancy in the findings is that Moskovites have more ideologically constrained views than do other Soviet citizens. When the response patterns of Moscow residents in the SIP survey is compared, we find that among them, as in the case of the respondents to the 1988 Institute of Sociological Research survey, views endorsing authentic political participation and right to strike correlate substantially with attitudes toward Soviet support for Vietnam. Of those who endorse authentic political participation, only slightly more than a quarter (28 percent) say that the Soviet Union was right to use force in

Some or Complete University

| Disagreed | Agreed | Total |
|---|---|---|
| 57 | 33 | 44 = 124 |
| (76) | (48) | 100 = 279 |

$Tau_b = -.24, p < .0001$

| Agreed | Disagreed | Total |
|---|---|---|
| 62 | 22 | 45 = 114 |
| (90) | (24) | 100 = 253 |

$Tau_b = .39, p < .0001$

| Disagreed | Agreed | Total |
|---|---|---|
| 15 | 7 | 11 = 28 |
| (18) | (10) | |
| 25 | 37 | 32 = 81 |
| (30) | (51) | 100 = 257 |

$Tau_b = .15, p < .01$

| Agreed | Disagreed | Total |
|---|---|---|
| 17 | 4 | 11 = 25 |
| (21) | (4) | |
| 18 | 47 | 31 = 71 |
| (22) | (49) | 100 = 231 |

$Tau_b = .33, p < .0001$

Vietnam, whereas exactly one-half who disagree approved of Soviet use of force in Vietnam ($tau_b = .17, p < .05, n = 133$). An analogous relationship exists in the sip data for Muscovites when responses about strikes and those concerning Vietnam are cross-tabulated.

It is also possible that in general attitudes even among mass, and especially among relatively attentive publics, have become more constrained during the 1980s. The sip survey is a reasonable reflection of the views of citizens in the Soviet Union at the end of the 1970s. A plausible hypothesis is that the 1988 Moscow survey is capturing in part the development of real thinking about policy preferences, at least in places like Moscow, so, in general, correlations have increased among responses to politically relevant questions. In a highly politically charged and politically engaged atmosphere it may well be that what we are identifying in the 1988 Moscow survey is partly the development of more or less coherent political positions with respect to domestic and foreign policy among mass and attentive publics.

I have argued that substantial linkages between the attitudes of Soviet mass and attentive publics toward economic reform and foreign policy activism. How a Soviet stands on Stalin is likely to provide a useful indication of how that person thinks about Soviet foreign policy. Whether a link exists between attitude toward democratization and foreign policy posture depends substantially on one's definition of democracy. The case is weak for connecting attitudes toward liberal notions of democracy and foreign policy posture. It is possible that by the onset of the 1990s we might find that a linkage had emerged in people's minds between views on the one hand about individual rights and the marketplace for ideas, and views about foreign policy on the other—but that remains to be seen. Certainly, no such link existed at the end of the 1970s for the SIP respondents. Rather, data from the SIP survey indicate that the link between attitudes toward liberal notions of democracy and foreign policy in the Soviet Union are somewhere between nonexistent and trivial. There is a case to be made, though, as the 1990s begin that among mass and attentive publics there is a link between attitudes congruent with support for authentic political participation and those supporting a relatively benign Soviet foreign policy. These findings have important implications for the assessment of the likely evolution of Soviet foreign policy in the 1990s as well as for understanding the sources of Soviet foreign policy behavior.

The evidence mustered herein is that a highly significant and relatively robust link exists between attitudes toward economic reform and foreign policy. This link provides an important reason why Soviet policies should be encouraged in the direction of greater global economic interdependence. For the Soviet Union to increase its trade to levels comparable to other communist states such as Yugoslavia, Hungary, and, more recently, the People's Republic of China, or to that of the other state with an enormous internal market, the United States, would require fundamental decentralization of decision making to enterprises and ministries. Rosecrance and others have made compelling arguments why the foreign policy of a Soviet Union that had become a trading state would differ from its traditional behavior. The attitudinal link between postures favoring the kind of economic decentralization that such global economic participation would entail and a less activist foreign policy suggests an added benefit. Not only would the Soviet Union become entangled in what Harold K. Jacobson terms "networks of interdepedence,"[14] but domestic constituencies favoring a less activist foreign policy would also be strengthened.

The implications of the democratization of the Soviet Union for foreign policy attitudes, however, are less clear-cut and turn in part on one's definition of democracy. Independent of the links between attitudes toward the political system and attitudes toward foreign policy, in an increasingly participant Soviet polity the effectiveness of domestic claimants on resources will almost certainly increase. Thus, the data mustered in this chapter indicate that, however much we may on other grounds welcome the emergence of persons committed to the market place of ideas and to the priority of individual over societal rights, their increased weight in the political process will not increase the likelihood of a more benign Soviet foreign policy. At the same time an intensification of the role of those publics endorsing participatory democratic postures may in fact increase the weight of attitudes favoring a substantially less activist foreign policy, especially in a Soviet Union, which is becoming increasingly politically aware and where attitudes toward domestic and foreign policy are becoming more constrained and coherent. This increase gives the West an additional stake in the democratization of Soviet society.

# CHAPTER 6 ■■
# IS SOCIALISM DEAD?
Seweryn Bialer

In Eastern Europe the first phase of victorious anticommunist revolutions has run its course. In the Soviet Union the guided reform has been overtaken by a spontaneous anti-totalitarian revolution. These qualitative changes constitute the greatest historical reversal of the idea of socialism, which for over a century was in ascendancy on a worldwide scale. Socialism is collapsing not only as a ruling ideology of states, but also as an international political movement and intellectual creed. This collapse is effected not by outside forces, but by the implosion of the socialist-communist regimes, by the popular and intellectual revulsion against "real socialism" and socialist revolutions, and by the rejection of the theory that gave birth to a monster.

By now it is quite certain that Marxian socialism in its most politically meaningful twentieth-century variant, radical Leninism, is dead as a state ideology. Its rejection in Eastern Europe is total; its erosion in the Soviet Union is proceeding at an accelerating and astonishing speed and is by now irreversible. In the remaining communist states it may still survive for a prolonged time in China, but its days in Cuba or Ethiopia are numbered. Socialism in the countries of Eastern Europe and the Soviet Union brought their nations to the brink of social, economic, cultural, and moral disaster and lost any vestiges of legitimacy among the mass public. In the Communist Party of the Soviet Union, not only is the mass membership profoundly and irreversibly disillusioned in its former faith, but, as was shown to be the case in Eastern Europe in 1989, the party elites lack the self-righteous conviction that formerly provided them with the determination and fanaticism necessary for the will and means to rule at any price.

The Communist parties out of power, most of which became in the last decades increasingly irrelevant to the political processes in their countries, have been dealt a mortal blow by the disintegration of ruling communism in Europe. If they persist in orthodoxy, they will continue their slide to the status of small sects of semireligious eccentrics. If they attempt to adjust radically to the new circumstances, they will be open to continuous splits and will become indistinguishable from the moderate social-democratic reformers whom they fought viciously for so long and whom they labeled traitors to the cause of the working class. Furthermore, the "old" social democrats will have an insurmountable advantage over the former Leninists because their credibility is high and they are not tainted by past servility to the masters of the Kremlin. The Communist parties were not of the "left," they were of the "East," and the "East" has crumbled. They have to pay the price of a disastrous past.

Despite the defeat of the Sandinistas in Nicaragua (and almost certain decline and defeat of their brethren in El Salvador), in the underdeveloped regions radicalism and revolutionism are far from dead. Yet with very few exceptions the influence of Marxism-Leninism on these movements is eroding rapidly. The socialist model of governance as practiced in Eastern Europe (or in Ethiopia, or Mozambique, or Cuba) can hardly provide an emulative standard in the light of its disclosed utter mismanagement in all spheres of life. In addition, the radicals and revolutionaries in the underdeveloped countries can no longer count on major help from Russia, and so have no material incentive to follow its old Leninist creed. Increasingly today, and in the foreseeable future, these movements will be shaped by native, local traditions and by what can be called the "politics of rage": by populism, a creed that aims for social justice and equality and can be fiercely nationalistic but has no comprehensive vision of a new order; by individual or mass terrorism that is an expression of frustration and desperation growing from its inability to build mass support; by ethnic, racial, and religious hatred that leads to destructive mass violence.

Marxian socialism, consequently, is dead or dying as an ideology of state rule and management of the economy, as a faith of a once cohesive international political movement, and as a dominant creed of revolutionaries and radicals everywhere. But, contrary to what is often assumed, this is not the end of the story. Marxian socialism still has a future as a "moral creed," as an academic discipline, and, most importantly, as an internalized predilection of working people and even the intelligentsia in countries of disintegrating communist rule.

While the "real socialism" of oppressive rule and disastrous social experimentation is universally recognized as morally abhorrent, the many ideas of the original Marxian socialism are not. Considered not as a theory, not as "socialism of the great vision," but rather as a set of moral injunctions about the elimination of poverty, about the redress of great inequalities of wealth and power, about guaranteeing that democratically elected governments will insure the priority of human needs in the economic system, they provide a skeptical corrective to the practices of modern and modernizing societies. Indeed, sometimes for better, sometimes for worse (when good intentions lead to bad, unintended consequences), these injunctions have been in part incorporated into the ethos of modern capitalism. Although they are not the core operational creed of any major organized group (of course, they are most prominent within the social-democratic parties), they are diffused in sources of origin and points of receptivity to their influence. Dreams and delusions of millennial "scientific socialism" have been rejected, but many of the impulses remain and are fed by concerns of real or imagined inequities of the everyday political and economic processes in capitalist countries. Unless and until capitalism can adequately address problems of equity and community, the ideals of socialism will continue to influence liberals and remain a matter of concern for conservatives.

Because of its vision, it is not surprising that Marxian socialism remains alive on the campuses of the great universities of the United States, Great Britain, France, Italy, Japan, let alone Mexico or Brazil. The difference in outlook between leftists in the West and intellectuals in the East is brought out by the conflicting meanings of the prefix "real" attached to "socialism." For the latter, "real socialism" means the one that has been incorporated into practice, and anything else is an untested or disproved idea. For the former, the socialism in practice is basically "unreal" because in their view it did not follow or was not derived from the authentic ideas of the founders. Further, the only "real socialism" is the original, uncontaminated system of ideas that was misapplied and misunderstood, but which, of course, needs to be brought up to date, revised, etc. Marx said, "An idea, once it gets hold of the masses, becomes a material force." Yet even he would be amazed by the tenacity with which segments of academia stick to his tarnished heritage. Were such tenacity displayed in chemistry departments, the phlogiston theory of fire would still dominate. This persistence of Marxian influence confirms once again that unfulfilled prophecies have, and will retain, a life of their own.

The attitudes of the peoples of Eastern Europe and the Soviet Union have some resemblance to those of many Western intellectuals. That is, while Eastern Europe has rejected the practice of communism and the nations of the Soviet Union are moving in the same direction, yet, among the working peoples of those countries, who suffered most from the consequences of an utopian idea that ran amok in practice, the actual influence of the idea is paradoxically not dead. As a result of many decades of communist rule, people internalized many beliefs and derivative habits that grew out of the original socialist idea or its communist interpretation and practice. One of the leaders of Hungarian liberals (Alliance of Free Democrats), Gaspar Tamas, declares: "We have to fight not only against the communist state and economic system but also against the communism inside each of us." The monopolistic position of "official" socialist ideology, and the communist practice, created conditions under which the peoples under communist rule, most of all in Russia, were infected by a philosophy of dependency instead of self-reliance, of an all-embracing collectivism and conformism over individualism, of commitment to the equalization not only of opportunities but also of outcomes, of rigidity and extremism of beliefs, and of intolerance.

This philosophy can be expressed in truisms that are rooted deeply in folk consciousness, of which the following are only a few:

The state should be mistrusted or even hated, it personifies the "they" against "us"; yet at the same time all well-being derives not from one's own activity, but from the state, which should take care of one's needs and aspirations.

The "collective" always knows better, and, even if it does not, it has the moral authority and right to impose its views; individualism is not only antisocial but also anti-individual, that is to say, it goes against one's own self-interest—happiness, security, prosperity lie in one's submergence into the small group as well as the all-embracing "collective."

Initiative is an attempt to play up to the "bosses"; venturousness is an expression of an unhealthy ambition and of arrogance toward one's peers.

"My neighbors should not be better off than I am," rather than "I should be as well off as my neighbor."

One should be "principled" and rigidly confront beliefs and interests that differ from one's own. Compromise is always "rotten." "Opportunism" does not mean grasping "opportunities," but betraying one's principles.

The deep, popular internalization of the attitudes and habits expressed in communist ideology and practice is supported by ample evidence from public opinion and attitude research conducted in the Soviet Union.[1] Perhaps most alarming is the underlying acceptance of authoritarian solutions and intolerance as exemplified in the endorsement of the death penalty to preserve social order and harmony:

(a) Two-thirds of those polled expressed a desire not only to preserve the death penalty in the Soviet Union (which is applied broadly) but to extend it on a mandatory basis even further.

(b) Over 70 percent selected the option "to liquidate them" in reference to those convicted of murder regardless of mitigating circumstances.

(c) Some 33 percent advocated death sentences for prostitutes, drug addicts, and homosexuals.

(d) About 22 percent demanded killing AIDS victims as well as those born with disabling birth defects.

(e) Nine percent would like to see beggars and alcoholics physically eradicated.

Of those polled, over 25 percent still see the main reason for the terrible conditions in the USSR in a conspiracy of domestic and foreign enemies, and 40 percent still adhere to the view that major concentration of power in the hands of a *national* leader ("our people need a strong hand") is needed all the time or very frequently.

On a more personal level, in their own day-to-day activities 54 percent of those polled said that they prefer a "strogii nachal'nik"—a strict, authoritarian boss. "People's expectation of justice," commented the director of the study, Iurii Levada, "are connected with hopes for the solicitude of the state, and therefore, for authoritarian social policy."[2] Only 19 percent of the people surveyed said they see the main task of the country as the creation of a free, democratic society.

If the Soviet public rejected the basic ideas of socialism, it would endorse economic concepts like the market, the importance of entrepreneurship and individual initiative, and resulting inequalities in the distribution of rewards. Survey data reveal that this is not the case.

While 47 percent of those surveyed believe that what is most needed to turn the economy around is honest, daily labor from everybody, some 55 percent are ready to settle for low wages and salaries in exchange for either easy work or for a guarantee of the stability of the job.

Only 7 percent believe that the existing restrictions on entrepreneurship should be abolished and that the "ceilings" (the upper limits established on wages and salaries) should be eliminated. Only 10 percent express a willingness to engage in their own private economic activities with the attendant responsibilities and risks. Almost 50 percent hold the belief that the state should not permit the existence of millionaires either because to own a million rubles is an evil in itself or because they believe that it is not possible to acquire a million rubles honestly or without exploiting someone else. Thirty percent of respondents consider the main task of the country to be to attain genuine social justice, but "social justice" is interpreted primarily as the denial of high wages and salaries and even more so of entrepreneurial income. In the existing situation of widespread poverty 20 percent of blue-collar respondents nevertheless answered the question, "What are you most dissatisfied with in the current system of labor compensation?" by saying: "The differences in earnings between the various categories of workers are too great."

The absorption of the attitudes and habits derived from communist ideas and practice by the peoples of the Soviet Union, and most significantly by the Russians, will immensely increase the difficulty of building democratic institutions and a working market economy. The peoples of the Soviet Union are increasingly, and it seems irreversibly, rejecting the totalitarian communist system. But in shaping an emerging new system they are guided to a large extent by many principles of the system that they reject. Aside from the physical, cultural, and moral devastation, this is the final legacy left by communism to the nations which it has ruled.

The disintegration of traditional Soviet political and economic institutions, of federal ties between the republics, of regional ties within the republics themselves, and also of the social system of relations and values, are necessary prerequisites to the transformation of bureaucratic totalitarianism in the direction of a politically democratic, socially pluralistic, and economically market-oriented Russia and other nations of the Soviet Union. Of course, the incredible speed and the complexity of the disintegrative processes make it unlikely that the Soviet Union can avoid major convulsions and mass confrontations along the class, ethnic, and political divides. What makes these prospects especially daunting, however, is the extent to which the working people and the intelligentsia, let alone the existing administrative and managerial elites in all walks of life, have internalized the attitudes and beliefs of the rejected communist creed and practice.

The mass susceptibility to traditional Soviet core attitudes makes highly unlikely even a less than rapid and smooth acceptance of the political-economic and social institutions that are being borrowed from Western experience. Those institutions, values, and ways or thinking have no roots in past Soviet (and Russian) reality, collective memory, or even solid organized support. The manifest attraction to the formal paraphernalia of democratic order and market economy is accompanied by ignorance of the essence of those institutions and the way of life that they engender. As in the "original" Russian Revolution, mass perception, and even that of the "Democratic Opposition," is permeated by utopian expectations that carry the seeds of mass disappointment and rejection before the new values are able to take institutional roots.

The anomie left in the wake of the disintegration of bureaucratic totalitarianism in conjunction with the continued strength of political, economic, and social attitudes from the past reinforces the probability of two mass reactions to the predicaments of an extremely difficult and frustrating transition. The first, cutting across all social groups, would be a violent reaction of people who are learning to despise their past, have no hope for the future, and are disoriented by what is happening.

They feel the urge to strike out not simply against the abstract "evil system" but also against the actual "mass persona" of the evil-doers on all levels of social endeavor. Such days of collective revenge-taking may be approaching and may be quite violent; instead of having a cleansing effect on the society, such actions will rather magnify the instincts and patterns of behavior that are inimical to the evolution toward a civil society.

The second reaction that will set in within the national collectivities is already starting to emerge but will have especially significant consequences when it occurs within the Russian nation. Unceasing self-flagellation and a critical onslaught against the feeling of national self-esteem and the sense of historical greatness will bring a backlash well-known from the history of other nations. Such a reaction, aimed at restoring "national pride," can be partly xenophobic and directed against the emulation of foreign models of social organization. It will most certainly be aimed against the "tormentors," i.e., the intellectuals. It will most likely be expressed, even in its more benign or nonviolent form, in the idealization of the Russian past and a preference for archaic and authoritarian forms of social, political, and economic organization. It will be the antithesis of tolerance and will be inimical to all that is necessary for both economic development and democracy. Experimentation, the growth of individual differences, personal initiatives in either the political or the economic realm, will be attacked as "antisocial." Political competition will be seen as a destructive import from abroad.

The progress made by authentic liberal democratic forces in the Soviet Union since 1989 is truly remarkable. But we must see clearly the target of most of their efforts and the arena of most of their successes: the mobilization and guiding of widespread dissatisfaction into a rejection of the existing political and economic system in the face of massive opposition from bureaucratic conservatism and the reactionary Leninist fanatics of the Party apparatus. Their success in providing fundamental organizational forms for new political and economic institutions remains very limited, however. The mass acceptance of those new "institutions" is rather rudimentary and primarily symbolic. Indeed, support for and belief in new social organizations and the parliament have actually declined after an initial period of high expectations. Much more probable in the medium run than a turn onto the road of democratization (even something far short of a stable democratic order in the Western sense) in Russia and the nations of the Soviet Union is the emergence of authoritarian order(s) most likely of an "inclusionary," populist type. In comparison to the "bureaucratic totalitarian" system the emerging orders will almost certainly be of a relatively benign nature—they will come as a blessing for the peoples of the Soviet Union and for the foreign nations who for so long were locked into conflict with the Soviet threat. The forces of liberal democracy in the Soviet Union should be unconditionally supported by the West. But the realistic expectations on which the West should base its plans and actions, at least as long as evidence to the contrary is not forthcoming, should consider as most likely the emergence in the foreseeable future of a Russia that will be neither totalitarian nor democratic.

If this evaluation of the plausible alternatives in Soviet development is realistic, some implications emerging from the implosion of Soviet communism for the international situation and Soviet-American relations suggest themselves:

(1) A unified, totalitarian Soviet Union is a thing of the past—its rebirth is of a very low order of plausibility. To the extent that either Soviet expansionism or Western—and especially American—fear of the USSR was generated by the latter's totalitarianism, an important source of international conflict has been removed.

(2) A fully democratic Soviet Union—or successor states—is also unlikely. To the extent that American support for Gorbachev and extensive cooperation with the USSR rests on the belief that the former adversary is rapidly evolving into a country like itself, current good relations rest on insecure foundations. When the American leaders and public come to realize that the Russian and other peoples of the Soviet Union do not accept American beliefs and values about the free market, individualism, political tolerance, and political and economic competition, there will be a period of shock and readjustment, the final outcome of which cannot be easily predicted.

(3) The military strength of the Soviet Union (or of a separate Russian state) will be sufficient in the foreseeable future to contest regional goals only when they do not enter directly into sharp conflict with the advanced industrialized democracies. The most obvious concrete cause of the Cold War was the perceived Soviet threat to Western Europe; this has disappeared.

(4) The expectations that the Soviet Union, or the nation-states that will emerge from its disintegration, will rapidly become integrated into the "Common European House" in meaningful economic and political terms is unrealistic. This is the goal to which Soviet leaders aspire and which many Western analysts consider to be attainable by the end of the century. Most likely, Russia will be closer to Europe, yet it is highly improbable that it can be a part of Europe. Its economic and political order will preclude this for a long time to come. The hope for creating a truly harmonious international system based on making the

Soviet Union European in values, outlook, and institutions is not likely to be realized. Less extreme and less complete ways of international cooperation will have to be developed. Unrealistic expectations in this area, in tandem with exaggerated hopes for domestic democracy, are likely to produce disappointment and disillusion in the West with consequent damage to the ability to realize the full potential for good relations.

(5) The process of national revival and the rebirth of national spirit may lead Russia into conflicts with its neighbors to the south and with China as well as to attempt to gain influence, although not domination, in Eastern Europe. Both the revival of nationalism and its foreign policy manifestations will cause dismay and conflict with the West. Much will depend on how extreme the developments in the Soviet Union are and how much the West can both moderate them and deploy a careful and modulated response.

(6) The effort of the Western powers will probably be directed toward a measured increase in economic and political intercourse with Russia, thereby keeping alive Russia's hope of becoming a part of the West. The core of Western strategy, however, should be to contain within Soviet borders the turmoil of the new Russian Revolution. The deepening of economic and political relations with Russia, and its hope of becoming part of the West, will constitute the main area of Western leverage in inducing a nonthreatening direction of Russian development. But an adequate American policy requires a realistic understanding that in the foreseeable future the Soviet Union is not likely to develop in the Western image. Aspects of socialism that most Americans find disturbing if not repugnant are very much alive in the USSR; although communist totalitarianism is dead, the good relations that most leaders and members of the public seek will still require cooperation among states of quite different social systems.

**PART II
SOVIET-
AMERICAN
SECURITY
UNDER
RELAXED
TENSIONS**

This chapter is written from the premise that the overall Soviet-U.S. relationship itself—in addition to the issues that concern both nations—is worthy of study. Its focus is how Soviet-U.S. interactions in the Third World intersect, affect, and reveal that relationship.

The threat of nuclear war is justification enough for an extraordinary effort to understand the total pattern of interactions between these two powers, but opportunities reach well beyond. Knowing what enhances or blocks cooperation is critical to the politics of preventing war. Beyond that, new challenges and dangers in a changing world could bring nations—even former adversaries—together in productive new modes of cooperation.

That premise imposes on this chapter and on the Soviet-U.S. dialogue a demanding focus—the point at which two agendas intersect. One could write or have a discussion on the changes in Soviet and U.S. policy thinking about the Third World. Much could be said. Or one can discuss, as this chapter does, how those changing policies are revealed concretely through our interactions in the Third World, and then how they in turn intersect, affect, and reveal the changing overall Soviet-U.S. relationship.

To put the point into two practical questions that policymakers on both sides will ask about the actions of the other: What are they doing and why? Can we cooperate—why or why not? Another way of asking the second question: Do actions increase suspicion and mistrust and weaken the relationship necessary for cooperation? Or do they provide evidence that we are acting openly, not threatening the other, and opening the door to cooperation that might strengthen the relationship?

Looking from that last question to the future, the policymaker comes to a far-reaching question: Is strengthening the relationship itself a legitimate objective? If we cooperated, would we enlarge our capacity to pursue interests that neither of us can pursue effectively alone?

This chapter is written against the backdrop of American and Soviet rethinking of our respective roles in the world and ways of pursuing our interests—what we can and cannot achieve acting alone on the global stage. We both want to avoid nuclear war, and rethinking has brought new concepts of security into focus. But neither of us is clear about what we want in the Third World—individually or in relation to each other. Yet our fears, anxieties, and anger toward each other have often been most sharply expressed there. The Third World will pose some of the most pressing challenges to our common future. What we have learned there about our strength and its limits and about our relationship has already refined our sense of how today's world works.

A corollary premise is that we may know our relationship better —and strengthen it when that serves both nations' interests—if we do some rethinking together. The mechanisms are in place. Official talks about regional conflicts became regular in the mid-1980s. Nonofficial dialogue had already broadened and deepened as citizens became frightened at the absence of a serious relationship between governments.

This is not a treatise on what Americans and Soviets are saying about their Third World policies as this book goes to print. Instead, it offers a perspective and a framework for study and dialogue—a framework to be used, tested, refined, and developed as a context for acting and enriching insight into the relationship. It is not a chapter about the past or present; it is a chapter about walking into the future. The approach is intended to grow and change with experience.

## A Changing World and the
## Soviet-U.S. Relationship

Thoughtful Americans and Soviets are learning both in their bilateral dealings and through experience in the Third World that familiar concepts of international relations often do not accurately picture how nations relate. Traditional tools of statecraft do not reliably produce results expected of them. Other instruments of change are not used as creatively as they could be. Principles of law and ethics do not reach deeply enough into the interaction among nations to guide policy and conduct.

In the past, Soviet-U.S. discussions have often become sterile because each side has used the traditional vocabulary of international relations with its own definitions or resorted to principles not always realistic in today's world. By the early 1990s thinkers on both sides were moving toward concepts and vocabulary that reflected the world, but the experience has just begun. We must be precise and work out ambiguities together.

Five observations about contemporary international relationships broaden perspective on Soviet-U.S. interaction. Although I write as an American, my talks with Soviet colleagues suggest that many would agree generally, or at least find these a reasonable starting point for discussion.

First, more and more problems confront nations that no one nation can deal with alone—partly because these problems cut across national borders and partly because more centers of influence affect the course of events. This observation causes both Americans and Soviets to reflect on the nature and limits of national power used unilaterally outside relationships with other nations concerned with the same problems.

Even protecting a nation's security and identity—the state's ultimate responsibility—may not be possible without cooperation between adversaries who share a common security problem such as possessing nuclear weapons. The concept of "common security" assumes that no state can achieve absolute security and that the threat of destruction from preemptive attack cannot be reduced if an adversary feels insecure. No power can reduce the threat of nuclear destruction by itself; such powers can only do so together.

The interactive nature of security is even more apparent in Third World situations. Some conflicts there could draw the superpowers into nuclear confrontation, yet neither can impose solutions on Arabs and Israelis, Afghan factions, or Indians and Pakistanis. Sporadically the superpowers think about the advantages of acting in complementary ways or jointly. Within those conflicts, one nation can only achieve long-term security in relationship with adversaries. Neither Arabs nor Israelis, for instance, can end their conflict alone; they can only do it together. Beyond conflicts of power, no one nation can deal with many of the cross-border issues that threaten humankind. The Soviet Union and the United States increasingly see common interests in dealing with some of these as causes of instability that could threaten security: proliferation of nuclear, chemical, and biological weapons as well as conventional arms, especially missiles; environmental changes; and hunger, disease, and poverty.

Second, underlying the proliferating state centers of influence is a broader popular participation both within and between nations. Focusing on the political energies and interaction of communities of people —not just on state institutions—leads to different use of familiar concepts.

The increasing involvement of people in domestic and world politics demands new awareness of the human roots of state policy, interests, and conflict in international relationships. Change seems to swell more from the bottom up than from the top. More people interact more quickly. What one leader says or does is heard, seen, and assessed in hours by another's constituents. Beyond leaders, people in many nations are more aware of each other as human beings, not just as institutional abstractions. Fear, suspicion, rejection, mistrust, hatred, and misperception are often greater obstacles to peace than inability to resolve technical problems.

Both the USSR and the United States have encountered the consequences of this increased popular role and discovered that their own interaction can become intertwined with those consequences. Each saw aims thwarted by popular movements in Vietnam and Afghanistan. Each experienced a unique role in the lives of those Jewish people who founded the State of Israel and sees a need to deal with the fears and aspirations of Israelis and Palestinians as well as with their political institutions. The popularly based Khomeini revolution in Iran shifted the strategic balance between superpowers, and each had trouble relating to the governing authority that emerged. Soviets worry about potential interaction between Islamic movements in Iran and Afghanistan and the Moslems of Soviet Central Asia, and Americans worry about a potential flood of refugees from south of their border if economic, social, or political conditions become intolerable for large numbers there. Both recognize the consequences for the Soviet-U.S. relationship of a bloody climax in South Africa that puts them on opposing sides. Both are struggling with the impact of popular movements in Europe in 1989 on their individual security and on their relationship.

Third, traditional instruments of statecraft often do not reliably accomplish what is expected of them. As we watch the widening involvement of publics and civil societies, we focus more and more on political instruments used in the political arena for changing political environments so that publics will encourage and sustain new approaches.

Nuclear weapons cannot be used, and even non-nuclear weapons make war prohibitively costly as a way of bringing about change, pursuing interests, or resolving disputes. Negotiation—normally considered the peaceful alternative to force—does not initiate change. Change is initiated and shaped in the political arena. Negotiation may define, crystallize, and consolidate change already begun. But until politicians transform the political environment, negotiators are unlikely to succeed. Or if they do reach a technically sound agreement, it may not be fully implemented or have the intended consequences.

These three observations about our changing world lead to two further thoughts about how nations relate. These thoughts do not supplant traditional concepts. They do transform those concepts by placing them in larger contexts. Practitioners and scholars across disciplines are already redefining familiar concepts and enlarging the range of tools for shaping change. My aim here is a conceptual framework that could integrate these insights for fuller understanding of the Soviet-U.S. relationship.

I do not think it is adequate today to focus primarily on states amassing military and economic power to pursue rationally defined interests in competition with other states. Relations between nations today are increasingly a continuous political process of complex inter-action among policymaking and policy-influencing communities on both sides of a relationship. As more people participate, change often takes place through that interaction on many levels at once rather than mainly through a linear series of government actions and responses. Beyond the power and policymaking of individual states acting on each other, we see a total pattern of interaction—the overall relationship—between two nations.

People have lived by the dictum that one state should not be involved in another's politics. That is not realistic today. Relationships among constituencies across borders are facts of life. Interaction—direct or empathetic—between Soviet dissidents and Americans affected gov-ernments' ability to ratify arms reduction agreements. Soviet and U.S. leaders act in each other's political arenas day by day whether they choose to or not. An element of Israel's power is its ability through U.S. friends to manipulate the U.S. Congress. Israelis and Palestinians by merely existing are part of each other's politics and policymaking. Americans' and Soviets' perceptions made each nation seem a threat in the other's eyes.

In Soviet-U.S. competition in the Third World, cross-border influ-ence has been seen with reason as one side trying for exclusive posi-tions at the other's expense. A sensible approach is not to condemn such interaction, but to build relationships in which mutual respect keeps that interaction within limits that define the identity and integ-rity of each party. Such interaction may even suggest imaginative approaches to common problems.

Shifting focus to that political process incorporates two important dimensions of experience into our thinking. First, we pay more atten-tion to the large political environment in which people reach funda-mental judgments about peace, war, negotiation, and economic change. Second, when we turn to that political environment, we introduce ways of influencing those judgments and therefore the course of change by political action rather than only by contests of force. If power is ability to influence the course of events, power today may emerge as much from the political ability to conduct that interactive process creatively as it does from wielding military or economic power or being an unyield-ing negotiator.

To add this political dimension to thinking about national power is to open the door to a range of political instruments that are not coercive but persuasive and sometimes even cooperative. The root of the word *political* leads to the citizen—the human being. Political instruments form ideas and perspectives that have organizing and directing power—organizing power as they become widely accepted ways of understanding events and directing power because of the actions that flow from them.[1]

My main point flows from this picture of relations among nations as a political process of continuous interaction: we need a concept to describe how nations relate large enough to encompass that process itself. Such a concept must include but go beyond the power, structures, decisionmaking, and formal positions of individual states and the instruments of state they use to get what they want from each other. It must go beyond describing the international system in the metaphor of a chess game.

To capture the totality of this dynamic interaction, I am suggesting the concept of *relationship*. In some languages the concept is better conveyed by the phrase "the total pattern of relations or interactions."

At first hearing, relationship is such a commonplace word that we hardly notice it, but when we stop to think about relationships that sustain us as human beings, we begin to feel the concept's power and depth. We also recognize that focusing on relationships causes us to change the ways in which we know, think, and act. Moving from "us and them" or "I" and "you" to "we" produces a palpable shift in mental gears.

Commonplace words often acquire new meanings only when we imbue them with new ideas. The problem in accepting any word to capture how nations relate today may be that we still think of states and power politics.

Three finer points are also important: (1) There are different levels, kinds, or qualities of relationship—conflictual or cooperative, immature or mature, destructive or constructive. (2) Relationships are dynamic. They reflect kaleidoscopic shifts among factors that affect them, and they may change in character over time. They regress or mature and contract or enlarge their capacity to do what needs to be done. Good relationships may sour, and bad relationships may improve. (3) An overall relationship will involve many different interactions—or relationships—among subsets of people. That different use of the word may cause some confusion, but normally as with many rich words, context will make the meaning clear.

I have been asked whether I see relationship as a condition or a creation. I believe it is a condition more often than we recognize. I also believe that developing mature relationships that generate peaceful and mutually satisfying solutions to problems that no one nation can deal with alone is both a goal and a creative human experience. Given the problems humankind faces, a concept such as developing and sustaining problem-solving relationships among nations may have to subsume concepts of power politics if humankind is to survive.

Experience suggests that relationships combine four characteristics. The quality of a relationship will result from the degree of development within each area and the overall combination of these factors in specific periods of time and in given situations. (1) There is a recognized coincidence or mutuality of interests and needs—both practical and psychological—in a situation. (2) Cumulative interaction generates perceptions about motives and behavior patterns. Interaction on many levels creates new opportunities for changing the pattern of interaction. (3) As communication deepens and real interests and needs are increasingly understood, more sensitive limits are introduced to let each party know when it is respecting or transgressing the other's interests. (4) At some point a constructive relationship may evolve with a political foundation and character of its own based on the need to act together. Both partners may come to value the relationship as an extension of themselves in pursuing complementary or common interests. In time, the interaction can generate cooperative problem-solving behavior as a norm.[2]

To apply the concept of relationship to nations is not simply to transfer personal qualities, values, and experience to them. Nations do have institutional characteristics beyond the sum of their citizens.

To use relationship this way is to focus on what happens between nations when they interact. The process of interaction itself—the relationship—becomes worthy of attention by scholar and policymaker.

Changing relationships becomes a political aim rather than simply forcing concessions or beginning negotiation. Curbing confrontation, resolving conflict, or cooperating requires seeing what grows in the space between leaders and people if they define problems together as affecting common interests and work together over time on solutions. As they probe underlying needs, a relationship grows. As the relationship grows, the political environment changes. Nations can do more than they first thought possible. They need not surrender individual identities; to the contrary, the relationship may enlarge the potential of each. As time passes, the relationship itself acts as a brake against purely self-centered acts. Focusing on relationship causes leaders to think and act differently from the way they would act if they were playing chess and tending balances of power. They concentrate less on sending signals, threatening, or negotiating and more on discussing, analyzing, and solving problems.

Writing about the Soviet-U.S. relationship requires a strong word of caution. It does not imply that the USSR and the United States have become trusting friends—even with the changes of the Gorbachev era. That would be incorrect. The two nations are locked into a relationship by common possession of nuclear weapons and now by recognition of other common interests. The issue is to understand their interaction and how to conduct the relationship to produce security and other results that serve common interests. Relationship seems more useful in capturing that interaction than the idea of two nation states as rational actors dealing with each other in some kind of strategic game. It adds peaceful instruments for conducting the interaction with less danger.[3]

Focusing on the Soviet-U.S. relationship requires reflecting on our experience in each area of relationship and on how our understandings of relationship differ and converge. The remainder of this chapter discusses Soviet-U.S. interaction in the Third World in that context.

### Interests as a Function of the Soviet-U.S. Relationship

Understanding a relationship starts from probing the real interests of each nation—what each wants to achieve and avoid and, above all, why. The changing world described previously requires a richer concept of national interest and consequently a broader picture of how interests are defined as realistic guides to policymaking. The quality of relationship changes as mutual understanding of interests deepens—and perhaps above all, as people begin to understand interests partly as a function of their relationship.

If one pictures states pursuing objectively defined interests with regard to other states, a concept of interests as defined analytically by officials of the state will suffice. My experience from twenty years in U.S. government policymaking, working with five presidents, suggests that a purely analytical statement of interests is not an adequate touchstone for a president in setting the nation's direction.

In dialogue with Soviet colleagues, I have put the point this way: A president will start from an analytical statement of interests provided by the experts in the National Security Council system. Sometimes they will disagree about exactly how to describe the U.S. interest in a situation, and at best they may give the president different points of view. After considering those expert views of the national interest, the president will then go into the political arena to sense the exact emphasis concerned Americans place as they define that interest or to test the politics of building support for pursuing one interest over others.

Soviet colleagues at first insisted that objectively defined interests exist and guide Soviet policy; it was only the particular character of the

U.S. political system that caused Americans to see interests differently. In more recent discussions, one Soviet colleague reflected: "There are group interests, there are state interests, there are personal interests, but there are also objective national interests. . . . We must determine the system of interests on both sides as they apply to each situation."[4]

It remains appropriate to speak of interests as they may be defined in state institutions, but an interest of the nation must also reflect what the people of the nation are "interested" in. Recognizing that nations have different governing systems, I include "policymaking and policy-influencing communities" in the interaction between nations. I also see them as involved in defining interests as interests guide policy. The identity of those communities will vary widely from nation to nation.

If one uses the concept of national interest this way to understand another nation's behavior, one must identify what may be involved beyond an analytical statement of interests. I suggest probing in three areas.

The first area involves probing deep-rooted human fears, hopes, wounds, perceptions, and cultural values that form human beings' sense of what is vital in protecting their identity. To the surprise of some who use the concept of interests in a routine way, real interests are not easy to define or talk about. Saying exactly what we fear or want and how much can raise complex questions. Recognizing why we really define interests as we do may reveal premises more visceral than analytically defensible — and perhaps even more important for that reason. We each need to know who the other is in the full sense of knowing a person's or a people's identity. Each of us needs to understand where the other is "coming from." What does each really want to achieve and avoid generally and at this moment and why? Probing those questions does not just produce the familiar analytical definition of state interests. It also explores those dimensions of interests with roots in the historical and cultural experience, human feelings, and political processes of nations.

Soviets try, for instance, to understand the U.S. interest in Israel. Objectively, the United States seems to have more at stake in Arab oil. Americans recall their human commitment to survivors of the unique horror of the Nazi Holocaust, feelings of guilt among U.S. Jews and non-Jews after the Holocaust, respect for Israeli achievement and the unique cohesion of the Jewish people, the pervasive civic energy of Jewish Americans, the deadly serious commitment and organization of the Jewish community, and the Old Testament biblical education of American Christians. These feelings rest in the American experience of providing a haven for the persecuted, resisting excessive exercise of government power, and protecting individual rights through its constitution and courts. The U.S. commitment to Israel defies objective definition as a strategic commitment, but no president of the United States could sit idly by and see Israel seriously harmed.

The second area involves understanding priorities. Defining interests as they actually guide policy requires deciding how much we want something in relation to other interests that may compete for the same political and material resources. Knowing the personal and political processes by which competition among interests and advocates is resolved and priorities are set is also a key element in understanding a nation's working interests.

At the end of the 1980s, for instance, Soviets who once defined as a paramount interest global support for class struggle and liberation movements explain that their main interest now is developing their own socialist society. To understand that as a statement of real interest and not as a tactical shift to lull us requires understanding why Soviets changed their minds. A shift for human reasons may have great credibility.

Third, defining interests is further complicated when—as with two nations such as the USSR and the United States—interests are defined partly as a function of a relationship. Each defines interests not only as what it wants for itself, but also often in relation to the other's presumed interests.

As the USSR and the United States interact in the Third World, the interests of one are often defined partly as a function of interests perceived to lie behind the other's actions. At a minimum, whatever our own interests, we often also define interests in terms of our global competition—what we want to deny the other. Or if we both want to change a situation as in Afghanistan or Angola, we can work out arrangements that meet the minimum interests of each. Further, as we work together on common problems, we reflect on the overall relationship and ask: If conducting the relationship to deal with one common problem enhances ability to deal with another, does that create interests of the relationship itself? Might the relationship itself have interests worth identifying, pursuing, and protecting?

Détente foundered in the 1970s partly because we did not mutually understand how actions would affect interests broadly defined. Unless the concept of interest is enlarged, it is hard to illuminate how Third World situations intersect the overall Soviet-U.S. relationship. The 1979 Soviet invasion of Afghanistan did not threaten territory vital to U.S. national security. The act of invading confirmed for Americans their deep-seated fear that Moscow was still bent on spreading its system of centralized political control—a system Americans saw as the epitome of all they had opposed in winning their own freedoms. Henry

Kissinger in cutting the Soviets out of his Arab-Israeli shuttles might have served a Soviet interest in settling a dangerous regional conflict. But Soviets read his action as saying he did not see détente as a relationship between cooperating equals.

As one Soviet colleague put the point, we do not always distinguish accurately between internal and external causes of regional conflict. At worst, each will see the "hand of imperialism" or "the subversive actions of the Soviet Union" behind conflicts that have essentially indigenous origins. To put the point in its worst sense, each of us has a tendency to wrap a local conflict into the Soviet-U.S. contest.

Ideology introduces a particularly complex element into the definition of interests in the Soviet-U.S. relationship because American and Soviet ideologies are historically intertwined. Since Marxism was born as a critique of Western capitalism from within, Soviet and Western philosophies as they affect policies have been locked together, partly as functions of each other. Each side's approach to the world is seen in part as the product of the way ideological and policy differences are resolved within each political system. The nature of the internal political systems is part of the threat each sees in the other.

In a July 1987 *Pravda* article, "New Philosophy of Foreign Policy," Academician Evgeni Primakov wrote: "Interstate relations in general cannot be the sphere in which the outcome of the confrontation between world socialism and world capitalism is settled."[5] He went on to underscore the importance of political measures in ensuring the security of states but left unanswered the question that came immediately to an American mind: If not in interstate relations, how will the "confrontation between world socialism and capitalism" be played out? Will states compete by proxy instead of directly, or will a new relationship evolve? The answer remains open. But Soviet statements have become steadily clearer.

Some Americans still say that competition or conflict between Soviet and U.S. interests will remain inevitable out of normal geopolitical reality. Others believe we will often have different interests and aims but also suggest the interaction might gradually become less ideological and more a normal competition—or even cooperation—between states.

In a September 1987 article in *Pravda*, Gorbachev, along with others, opened the possibility that the Soviet approach to nations in the Third World had begun to change:

Unconditional observance of the UN Charter and the right of peoples sovereignly to choose the roads and forms of their development, revolutionary or evolutionary, is an imperative condition of universal security. This applies also to the right to social status quo. This, too, is exclusively an internal matter. Any attempts, direct or indirect, to influence the development of 'not one of our own' countries, to interfere in this development should be ruled out. Just as impermissible are attempts to destabilize existing governments from outside.[6]

The notion that, in some states, change at a given moment might not be historically inevitable and that governments are entitled to maintain the status quo seemed to differ sharply from the traditional view that change is an objective reality with which the Soviet government has an interest in aligning itself through whatever means it chooses.

Subsequently, Foreign Minister Eduard Shevardnadze in a report to the Foreign Ministry in July 1988 took an additional step in stating that Soviet interests do not lie in promoting class struggle: "Generally speaking, it is difficult to reconcile the equating of international relations to a class struggle with a recognition of the real possibility and inevitability of peaceful coexistence, as a higher universal principle, and mutually advantageous cooperation between states with different sociopolitical systems." He went on to develop the point further:

If mankind is moving toward a unity of diversities and toward a community of equals who freely choose their own path—and it undoubtedly is moving toward this—then our interests consist in strengthening in every possible way our unique socialist individuality and essence and heightening their attractiveness to the rest of the world.

If mankind is able to survive presently only under conditions of peaceful coexistence—and it is undoubtedly incapable of ensuring its future under conditions of permanent confrontation—then does not the conclusion arise that the conflict of the two systems can no longer be viewed as a leading trend in the modern world?

The socialist states in the competitive struggle must . . . show that socialism can provide man with more than any other sociopolitical system.

That is our main national interest.[7]

Gorbachev seemed to affirm the trend in his December 1988 speech to the UN General Assembly:

Freedom of Choice is a universal principle that should allow for no exceptions.

It is not simply out of good intentions that we came to the conclusion that this principle is absolute. We were driven to it by an unbiased analysis of the objective trends of today. . . .

This objective fact calls for respect for the views and positions of others. . . .[8]

On the U.S. side, President Jimmy Carter's administration redoubled the American emphasis on respect for basic human rights and declared this commitment to be a U.S. interest in shaping relationships with other nations. During the 1980s the United States established federally funded institutions and programs to strengthen democratic organizations in the developing world. Some of the rhetoric behind this movement has stated as its explicit purpose rolling back the spread of Marxist-Leninist regimes. Other statements simply underscored a U.S. commitment to universal values, many of them incorporated in UN documents.

On the threshold of another opportunity for a sounder Soviet-U.S. relationship, we each need to accept that a key to changing a relationship is changing how each side defines its interests in relation to the other. It is now common in Soviet-U.S. dialogue to hear, "We must move from a zero-sum view of our relationship to a positive-sum view." If both are serious about strengthening the relationship, each must be honest—with itself and hopefully with the other—and precise about its real interest in promoting its social, political, and economic system in particular places. Or if each is willing to live with the system that citizens of a country choose, they must reach a common understanding of what defines a genuine act of self-determination that neither the Soviet Union nor the United States will see as threatening to itself. They must be able to distinguish a presence sought for ideological interests or for achieving exclusive influence from normal relations between great powers and countries in the developing world.

### A Continuous Political Process of Complex Interaction

The frequency and intensity of interactions between states affect the character of their interaction, and as nations interact over time, each may modify its actions in light of what it learns of the other's reactions. Beyond these basic points, three others are essential to understanding how nations relate in today's world.

*Complexity of interaction.* Even the interaction of state institutions is difficult to explain fully without describing both the intertwining of issues and the breadth of interaction among significant elements of whole bodies politic. As the interaction becomes more complex, each body politic influences the other's behavior in more ways.

One difference of view that plagued détente throughout the 1970s was the slow recognition of how specific issues affected the overall relationship and the ability to cooperate. Soviets tended to think of individual issues as dealt with by state institutions on the analytical merits of each issue, whereas Americans stressed the connections among issues as policymaking and policy-influencing communities interacted.

U.S. leaders explained how issues become intertwined in American politics, and sometimes they explicitly linked issues to demonstrate what, in their view, a cooperative interaction required. All issues the USSR and the United States deal with together are interrelated because each partner's actions affect the other's perception of readiness to cooperate. Americans saw the invasion of Afghanistan—against a backdrop of Soviet moves in Angola and Ethiopia and missile deployments in Europe—as the final blow to ratification of the SALT II agreement. The American perception was not so much formed by analysis as by fear and distrust of Soviet intent affirmed, in their view, by that Soviet action. In the mid-1980s the Soviets came eventually to acknowledge such a connection. Until then, they had argued that the administration could have shaped public opinion to avoid the connection if it had wanted to.

This difference in view reflects differences that have characterized the two political systems. If changes in the Soviet political and social system progress, Soviet leaders may pay more attention to how U.S. actions affect their political constituencies and ability to act. Some Soviet citizens, for instance, warned that U.S. backing for the Afghan resistance in acts that humiliate the Soviet Union after its forces withdrew could give Gorbachev's enemies ammunition for attacking his domestic reform program.[9]

*Interaction as political process.* A corollary to the complexity of interaction is recognizing the process of interaction itself as the context for changing its character. One important difference in approach that hindered Soviet-U.S. cooperation in the 1970s was the degree of emphasis placed on political processes for changing a situation in contrast to focusing primarily on the goal itself and mechanistic diplomatic steps for achieving it. The United States increasingly focused on changing political environments to make progress toward solutions possible. The Soviets emphasized outcomes with less thought about how to get from here to there.

The United States in the 1970s, for instance, described the Arab-Israeli peace process that produced five interim steps toward peace as negotiations embedded in a political process. Each step changed the political climate to enable another step not previously possible. Soviet colleagues even in the early 1980s saw the U.S. emphasis on an open-ended political process as a U.S. effort to avoid the issues of a just settlement so as to allow superior Israeli military power to work its way.

They urged a conference to define a settlement, initially with less emphasis on how the political environment for substantive solutions might be developed. By the late 1980s, the Soviet approach under the Gorbachev-Shevardnadze leadership reflected far greater appreciation for political process.

Again, the difference in the 1970s and early 1980s may have reflected the different character of the two systems. Americans emphasize political process because they know the difficulty of taking steps that a divided body politic cannot absorb all at once. U.S. leaders have had to deal with Americans' reactions to Soviet actions in the Third World and elsewhere. Soviet colleagues were accustomed to a government that could make decisions within a small group—such as those around Brezhnev who decided to invade Afghanistan. They had less vivid need to think about the political environment in which policy is carried out. While they may seem to have paid careful attention to political processes in trying to bring pro-Soviet organizations to power through the international communist movement, the emphasis was on controlling the levers of power rather than on changing the political environment from the ground up. Under Gorbachev they seem to be moving away from this approach—as are some Americans in recognizing the frailty of reliance on unpopular right-wing governments. If that Soviet position proves to guide Soviet policy and the United States focuses more on human rights and less on blocking the USSR, both may begin to work from more comparable views of political process. If so, the quality of their interaction will change.

*Intimacy of communication.* Perceptions that grow out of action and reaction with limited communication and understanding may be correct or inaccurate, but they begin to determine how two parties deal with each other. They affect credibility and mistrust and the choice between resort to force or reason. As two nations recognize the interdependence of their interests through interaction, the quality of their interaction may change. Much of that can happen through state-to-state communication in formal diplomatic exchanges.

Beyond simply stating governmental positions is a depth of communication that normally takes place outside formal channels but is often most revealing of real interests and needs, political dynamics, priorities, identity, and purpose. Some say that such communication is not possible between governments—only between individual human beings. Others say that officials are human beings who ought to have the capacity to explain what is important to them. Whatever the capacity of governments, the proliferation of dialogue among American and Soviet citizens across the spectrum of common interests—including the full range of issues in the Third World—evinces concern that government communication is not deep or broad enough to provide a sound basis for the complex interaction that characterizes the relationship.

## Regulation and Limits in Relationship

As interaction becomes more complex and growing communication deepens understanding of the real interests and needs of each side, increasing attention is given to regulation of that interaction with more sensitivity to limits so each party can know when it is respecting or transgressing the interests and needs of the other. These limits define what each sees as threatening. Communication may deepen further, and a shared interest in maintaining the limits may appear. The reflections that follow use Soviet-U.S. interaction in the Arab-Israeli arena to explore the evolution of limits in their relationship.[10]

*Minimal regulation.* Since the early 1950s, the two powers competed for influence in the Middle East. Using military, economic, and diplomatic support for regional states as instruments in their competition, they saw that competition as a zero-sum game. The Soviet offer to fund the Aswan Dam in Egypt after the United States backed away was seen as a coup for Moscow. The United States succeeded Britain in providing military aid to Jordan to block Soviet influence there. In the context of this highly competitive, often hostile relationship, the imperative of avoiding nuclear confrontation emerged as the one fundamental shared interest regulating their competition, especially in the mid-1960s after the Cuban missile crisis.

*Tacit regulation.* As the two nations interacted over time, one began to discern implicit "rules of the game" which seemed to develop in practice. These led toward tacit regulation of competition. Such practices have sometimes been called "regimes."

For instance, Soviet and U.S. behavior during the 1967 War and after seemed increasingly to reflect a tacit rule of the competition that both powers would state their specific interests clearly when those interests were threatened. On the hotline in June 1967, for instance, both were explicit about their commitment to stay out of the fighting to avoid being drawn into confrontation. On the last day of the war as Israeli forces fought closer to Damascus, the Soviets used the hotline to state their sharp discomfort.

As experience accumulated, some precision emerged in defining and recognizing limits. In 1967, 1969 and 1970, and 1973 those limits on the Soviet side seemed to be drawn at threats to the heartlands of Egypt and Syria. On the U.S. side, the limits were defined as preventing any transgression of Israeli territory. Each also seemed to understand that trying to establish an exclusive position in any of the major countries would cross a dangerous line.

Each power also seemed to want to move each Arab-Israeli crisis quickly back into a diplomatic framework—normally under UN auspices—for dealing with basic issues in the conflict. While the two have gone remarkably far on occasion in using the Arab-Israeli conflict as a vehicle in their own competition, they found common interest in moving the conflict to a diplomatic track after three military showdowns (1967, 1969, and 1970, 1973) showed that a settlement could not be imposed by force. This tacit assumption has led in some cases to explicit cooperation. Paradoxically, they also saw that diplomatic instruments used to lay foundations for a settlement provided yet another source of influence—the demonstrated capacity to influence the course of events. For seven years in the 1970s the United States cut Moscow out of those efforts partly to gain advantage in their competition.

The Soviet Union and the United States seem to have been most cautious when their overall relationship was most uncertain. This was true during the 1967 War and in 1983 when U.S. Marines were in Lebanon, Sixth Fleet aircraft were over Lebanon, and Soviets were manning Syrian air defense missiles. The two were most daring in their own competitive military involvement during the War of Attrition along the Suez Canal in 1970, when they had developed enough of a relationship to be more confident of their ability to avoid confrontation but were still testing each other in the process of building that relationship. During those military actions, they also seemed to be working from a tacit principle of avoiding direct exchanges of fire between Americans and Soviets.

*Explicitly regulated competition.* Soviet colleagues have often pressed for going beyond tacit practices in regulating competition to write a "code of conduct" or "principles" to govern our competition in the Third World. Americans have felt that universal rules are so vague and subject to reinterpretation in each situation that they are not precise guides to behavior. They can lead—as did the Basic Principles agreement of 1972—to more misunderstanding than stability in the relationship. But continuing discussion about applying operational principles in specific situations or making tacit practices more explicit can focus probing discussion of objectives and possibilities for cooperation.

Some of the principles being discussed at the beginning of the 1990s that would make up a code of conduct are familiar. They are central to the UN Charter, and they appear in bilateral documents. Others are less familiar and are emerging from experience in Afghanistan, the Middle East, southern Africa, Central America, and Kampuchea. The Soviet government in its new emphasis on the United Nations has given fresh attention to them.

A first is "non-intervention." In the Soviet-U.S. context, that means neither superpower should introduce its military forces into regional situations. While the principle is generally understood, specific cases have revealed different interpretations. Soviets say their troops in Afghanistan did not violate the principle because they were "invited," leaving aside that the inviting leader had emerged from a Moscow-backed coup. Some Americans found that the invasion of Grenada did not violate the principle because the "safety of Americans" was at stake and also the evidence of communist stockpiling jeopardized the "security of the hemisphere." Similarly, the introduction of U.S. troops into Panama in 1989 was justified on grounds of protecting Americans and enforcing respect for international principle. Soviets questioned the presence of American units in the multilateral force placed in the Sinai under the Egyptian-Israeli peace treaty when Soviets blocked a UN force there. Americans and Soviets have even discussed whether one could define legitimate and illegitimate intervention.

A second principle, written by the Americans into the Basic Principles agreement of 1972, is that neither side should seek unilateral advantage in third-world conflicts. Within the decade when the agreement was written, Soviet-supported military forces intervened in Angola and Ethiopia to back one side over another in civil wars, and the United States cut the Soviet Union out of the Arab-Israeli peace process, in part to consolidate Egypt's and hopefully Syria's move away from the Soviet Union. The principle may be valid, but its utility involves much more precise common understanding of how each side defines the other's advantage.

Third, with intensified efforts in 1988 toward reducing conflict in Afghanistan, Kampuchea, and Southern Africa, "national reconciliation" was advanced as a principle for finding compromise settlements. The principle is again generally commendable but is more or less useful depending on its application. For instance, the United States has argued in Afghanistan that it would not be a valid political process if the government established during Soviet military occupation simply drew some opponents into its governing structure. The Soviet position has been that the government of the past ten years has made fundamental changes, has won a position of authority in the Afghan body politic, and cannot be ignored in a settlement. The U.S. view of true national reconciliation is that the symbols of both government and opposition in the ten-year civil war should step aside and a government should be formed reflecting the balance of forces in the country—not the balance of forces under an Afghan government supported first by Soviet military force and then by military, economic, and security assistance. In the U.S. view, the requirements of true reconciliation are (1) a political process in which Afghan parties can come to terms with each other without outside interference and (2) superpower willingness to accept the outcome of any reasonable process. A similar argument surrounds the end of civil war in Angola.

Another principle which is philosophically accepted but not agreed in application is "self-determination." Americans defined a political process they would regard as a legitimate process of self-determination in Nicaragua. Initially, it seemed that Soviets would have difficulty accepting self-determination if it seemed to lead to the alteration or fall of the Sandinista government. Of course, elections in early 1990—on top of late 1989 events in Eastern Europe—demonstrated an evolution in Soviet thinking. Soviets have described an international conference to which the Palestine Liberation Organization might come to negotiate steps for exercising their right of self-determination, and the United States has expressed reservations because it has opposed an independent Palestinian state, even when it knew that would be the outcome of an exercise of free Palestinian choice.

These are but four examples of the problem of finding principles that each superpower will accept without qualification as a guide to action. At the very least, each requires some discussion—and possibly disagreement—about exactly what it would mean in application.

*Psychological limits.* Underlying the tacit or explicit practices and principles that may regulate competition are limits reflecting sensitivity to the human dimensions of interaction between two nations. A refrain that runs through most discussions of the Soviet-U.S. relationship in regional conflicts is the repetition of Soviet insistence that the United States treat the Soviet Union as an equal. "We are your nuclear equals; you must treat us as your political equals." Protecting identity and self-esteem can be as important as avoiding threats to analytically defined interests.

Rarely is this feeling more sharply expressed than in the Arab-Israeli arena. Remembering Soviet bitterness at Kissinger's exclusion of Moscow from the Arab-Israeli peace process in 1974 and 1975, Americans in February 1988 heard Soviets say that the peace initiative Secretary of State George Shultz was bringing to Moscow on his way to the Middle East would be judged partly on whether Shultz intended genuine cooperation. After they understood the approach, Soviets judged that "it was another solo U.S. performance." The thought that Secretary Shultz in 1988 or Secretary James Baker in 1989 might not have political permission from the U.S. body politic to engage fully with Moscow on this issue touched raw Soviet nerves.[11]

The related American feeling has been deep suspicion that Soviets are trying to achieve equal participation without equal investment. In the early 1980s, Americans repeatedly said Moscow could not expect to be an equal participant in the peace process until it had restored the same kind of working relationship with Israel it had with Arab governments. (The Soviets as well as the Arabs rightly insisted that the United States meet the same standard by establishing a normal relationship with the Palestinians.)

More broadly, a subtle Soviet feeling comes through in dialogue that Americans treat Soviet society as inferior. In some dialogue, politeness causes participants to avoid the subject. But some Americans say bluntly that facts such as the executions and concentration camps of the Stalin era, the Berlin wall, and continued denial of emigration well into the 1980s affected American attitudes negatively. Beyond that, Soviet policies toward Soviet Jews and Israel played into the U.S. body politic and affected the Soviet-U.S. relationship. The important point is not to trade charges about human rights violations but to understand how one nation's domestic experience affects the larger relationship—in this case why Americans feel that appropriate limits include concern for human rights.

### The Evolution of a Problem-solving Relationship

As the interdependence of interests increases, as interaction leads to greater knowledge and communication, and as limits become more sensitive to real interests and needs, a sense of relationship may grow. Then cooperation results from explicit understandings or from acting within an understood context. The capacity to cooperate takes on value in its own right. Self-conscious problem-solving behavior comes to characterize the interaction, and it acquires qualities of its own that both partners value as an extension of themselves in pursuing shared interests. Partners diagnose situations together; envision alternatives, analyze obstacles, and define operational problems together; and design courses of action together. The relationship almost acquires interests of its own.

Gorbachev seemed to capture the spirit of this point in his 1988 UN address: "We are speaking of cooperation which could be more accurately termed co-creation or co-development. . . . one comes to the conclusion that if we are to take into account the lessons of the past and the realities of the present, if we are to reckon with the objective logic of world development, we must look for ways to improve the international situation and build a new world—and we must do it together."[12]

Such a relationship between nations does not develop quickly, probably can never develop completely, and is unlikely to be irreversible. We can nevertheless try to recognize such a relationship in its growth and focus on strengthening it when that seems to serve interests.

*Experimenting with cooperation.* As the Soviet Union and the United States have moved from tacit practices regulating competition toward more explicit regulation and more sensitive limits, they have consulted, coordinated, communicated deeper concerns, and even cooperated. Those experiences in cooperation and complementary action have begun to provide insight into the nature of the constraints on their cooperation.

In the Arab-Israeli arena since 1967, with the notable exception of the first Reagan administration, the two powers have talked seriously up to a point on occasion about an Arab-Israeli settlement. After the 1967 War, both supported UN Security Council Resolution 242 and the secretary general's appointment of a mediator to try to resolve the conflict. In 1969 they discussed elements of a settlement to determine whether they could present a common proposal and, with their combined weight, persuade regional parties to accept it. In the last days of the 1973 War, U.S. Secretary of State Henry Kissinger flew to Moscow, drafted Resolution 338 with Soviet Foreign Minister Andrei Gromyko and agreed to co-chair the Middle East peace conference that eventually met in Geneva in December 1973. After the three interim agreements of 1974 and 1975 mediated solely by the United States, the efforts of President Jimmy Carter and Secretary of State Cyrus Vance in 1977 to resume the Geneva conference led to a joint Soviet-U.S. statement of October 1, 1977.

Those experiences in studying together approaches to the conflict's root causes demonstrated the constraints on cooperation. Both powers have felt limited in the distance they could take from the positions of their Middle Eastern friends for two reasons. First, each has become quite open since the early 1970s in acknowledging that it cannot force or persuade its friends to accept a settlement they felt did not fulfill their objectives. More basically, the underlying issue was how achieving a settlement would change Soviet and U.S. influence with regard to the other. Neither has been ready to cooperate if cooperation seemed to enhance the the other's overall position. The two came closest to genuine cooperation in late 1973 and in 1977, when their cooperation on bilateral issues was at its most mature, although in neither case could cooperation be sustained. The ultimate obstacle lay not in absence of a common view of a sensible approach to that problem but in the Soviet-U.S. relationship itself.

*Cooperation in relationship.* If both nations could envision an Arab-Israeli settlement they could live with that neither could achieve alone, then Moscow and Washington would face two choices in conducting their relationship in the Arab-Israeli arena. On the one hand, they could define precisely their respective interests there to avoid threatening moves that could trigger a nuclear confrontation. In other words, they could go on trying to regulate their competition by tacit or explicit practices or principles. That would be a significant start. Or, in addition, they could talk together directly about how to resolve the conflict in a way that would not concede an undue advantage to either. That is the real issue, but discussing it would require a more mature relationship than has existed.

As long as the Soviet Union and the United States do not discuss directly their separate definitions of the problems they face in the Arab-Israeli arena, they will find it difficult willingly to share influence in the area. For the Soviet Union, the problem since 1945 has been to push back Western encirclement based in this area. The United States, on the other hand, has defined the problem as winning eventual Arab acceptance of Israel while also building its own relationship with key Arab states to keep oil flowing and curb Soviet influence. Probing these fundamental views would be a start in figuring out whether each could reduce the other's sense of threat.

More basic, each seems to feel that sharing the appearance of ability to shape events would somehow diminish its global stature. Some of this feeling results from problems in the Middle East, but underlying those is the chemistry of the Soviet-U.S. competition. Israel as the U.S. friend, for example, retains predominant military strength, and the United States has not wanted to undermine that advantage without a clear-cut Soviet-supported Arab commitment to final acceptance of Israel within negotiated borders. The United States has felt—right or wrong —that Soviet interest lies more in enhancing influence in Arab states than in assuring Israel's security. But U.S. leaders have also sometimes wanted to demonstrate regionally and globally that Soviet military and diplomatic support could not help Arab friends achieve their goals—that only the United States could. These feelings explain why cooperation is guarded. Reluctance stems as much from the suspicion and fear on each side about the other's basic intentions in the contest for world power as from issues in the Middle East.

Although the two powers have talked extensively about the substance of these issues in their diplomatic exchanges, they seem to have engaged in remarkably little sustained conversation—with the possible exception of Kissinger's more private conversations with Soviet Ambassadors Anatoly Dobrynin and Gromyko—about the conduct of the relationship itself. The Baker-Shevardnazde conversations may also have a political dimension. Such communication has been most productive at the political level (often in a back-channel setting) rather than at the diplomatic level because politicians seem freer in discussing real interests and constraints. When such communication does not take place, the two powers still tend to rely on indirect signals—military alerts, visible increases in defense spending, and hostile rhetoric—rather than in talking directly about the conduct of the relationship. Official conversations still do not seem to be marked on either side by much self-revelation about real interests in relation to each other.

*Thinking in relationship.* As Americans and Soviets reflect on our interaction in the Third World, we need to explore what differences it might make to think from the perspective of our overall relationship. The questions that follow are one framework. They do not take the place of shared analysis of regional roots of conflict and approaches to resolution. They may provide a second and simultaneous level of analysis relevant both for resolving regional conflict and for shaping the Soviet-U.S. relationship.

1. What is the situation as each sees it? To what extent do we define it as a function of the Soviet-U.S. relationship? What do our differences in interpreting the "facts" reveal about our separate interests and aims? How does each see the other's involvement as threatening?

In Nicaragua, for instance, Americans in the 1980s needed to define exactly how they saw developments there as threatening the United States. We needed to explain to Soviet colleagues why some—rightly or wrongly—saw Moscow using instruments from the international communist movement or associated revolutionary movements to assert influence beyond normal relations among states—influence that would give excessive advantage to the Soviet Union.

Conversely, in Afghanistan, Soviet colleagues still need to define precisely what degree of Soviet influence Soviet interests require. They express historic Soviet concern that Afghanistan at the Soviet back door not be used as a staging base for hostile forces. In addition, as they argue the need for a compromise solution which does not reflect absolute victory or defeat for either side, is it possible to talk partly in terms of what Moscow and Washington—setting aside for purposes of analysis the Afghan factions—would regard as the elements of a compromise settlement they would not regard as giving excessive advantage to the other.

2. As we study alternative political processes for changing a situation, can we identify both steps that might help resolve the regional problem and steps that might, at the same time, enhance capacity for future Soviet-U.S. cooperation? What blocks cooperation, and what slows removing obstacles?

As events in Afghanistan and Angola-Namibia unfolded, some Americans at the end of the 1980s voiced concern that negotiated arrangements had ratified outcomes that would consolidate Soviet positions that the Soviets could not win militarily. Those Americans believed the outcome of negotiations on southern Africa would leave the present Soviet-supported government in control in Angola and open the door to future control in Namibia by the Southwest African People's Organization (SWAPO), which they also saw as susceptible to Soviet influence. In Afghanistan, they believe enough elements of the communist government will remain in place to sustain Soviet influence even without military presence.

In each case, changing the political situation on the ground is complicated enough. Underlying the problem of finding approaches to the local problem is finding approaches that would not seem to produce a settlement excessively advantageous to either the Soviet Union or the United States. Unless those situations evolve so as to leave each side with a different perception of the other's intent, the relationship will not grow.

3. What would be evidence that the Soviet Union and the United States are treating each other with mutual respect—that we are treating each other as equals?

We use the phrase "mutual respect" routinely in diplomatic parlance. We need to discuss openly exactly what that means to each of us in each situation. We have already spoken of what would it mean for Americans and Soviets to treat each other as equals in the Arab-Israeli arena and of the impact of human rights issues on attitudes toward each other. Discussing the principle in a wide range of situations could deepen sensitivity to underlying interests and concerns in a wide variety of situations.

4. What practices or principles are we using to regulate our competition? What level of relationship does our behavior in each situation exhibit?

As we look to the future, for example, in the Persian Gulf area or in South Africa, Americans and Soviets have a chance to develop scenarios of how situations there might unfold. Our aim would be to identify situations that might bring our interests into conflict and to talk through in advance practices, rules of behavior, or principles for preventing confrontation and steps that could even lead to cooperation.

Richer formulations of these questions may arise if the relationship deepens, and new situations will pose new fears and new challenges in cooperation. The purpose here is only to establish a different framework for study, dialogue, and policymaking that will illuminate more fully how Soviet-U.S. interaction in the Third World intersects, reveals, and affects the Soviet-U.S. relationship. Insights gained could enlarge the capacity of nations to prevent war, resolve conflict, and enhance the quality of life as humankind looks toward the third millenium of the common era.[13]

# CHAPTER 8

# THE SOVIET OPENING
# TO NONPROVOCATIVE DEFENSE
### George H. Quester

As on so many other fronts, a remarkable development has emerged in the Soviet Union's discussion of military strategic issues. Where the Soviets for years had stressed the priority of nuclear disarmament, basically arguing that their conventional forces were posing no threat to Western Europe, the advent to power of Mikhail Gorbachev produced a series of much more forthcoming Soviet statements.[1] These statements have admitted that there is a conventional armaments problem which is indeed "asymmetrical" and which has roots in "geopolitical" factors. That is, they admit that the deployments of U.S. and other NATO nuclear weapons may indeed have come in response to some *real* Soviet conventional military threats over all the years since World War II, rather than being simply the product of the malicious imaginations of the capitalist world.

With their emphasis on defensive weapons in place of offensive weapons, on "nonprovocative defense" or "defensive defense" (so that capabilities should be stabilizing on their own, regardless of what either side thinks about the other side's intentions), such Soviet statements are tied in logically with a new endorsement of "sufficiency." As the Soviets, who have led the world in their commitment to investments in tanks and other vehicles of mobile warfare, admit that the tank is a cause of tension, we have been experiencing a frankness and honesty which the most wildly optimistic analyst would not have predicted.

Skeptics could note, to be sure, that words by themselves could not produce any kind of relaxation in the West until the words were matched by deeds, by the kinds of reconfiguration of Soviet forces needed to eliminate their potential for offensive thrusts westward. If most of the more forthcoming statements emerged from senior civilians, or from junior analysts outside the military, with less echo of this by professional military officers, were the statements tangible and valuable?

Yet, if the Soviet admission of responsibility for the lack of crisis stability in the Central European confrontation of conventional forces was not by itself a sufficient condition for the relaxation of tensions, it nonetheless might have been a necessary precondition, and it did offer a promising opening. To repeat, however pessimistic anyone wanted to be about how much all of this yet amounted to, none of the more hawkish and suspicious analysts of Moscow's policies and intentions would have expected such Soviet pronouncements as have occurred since the mid-1980s.

Why would the Soviets be in a mood to admit that they had been posing a conventional military threat to the European members of NATO, to concede that their tank forces had held these countries in a sort of potential grip, perhaps ever since 1945? Why would Gorbachev and his colleagues become so ready to talk and negotiate seriously about giving up this grip, about reconfiguring the Warsaw Pact (and NATO also—the Soviets were not saying that *all* the offensive potential of conventional forces sits on their side) so that neither alliance can effectively attack the other—after decades of telling Western Europe that the communist world had no *intention* of ever launching aggressive warfare, and that the West should accept and have faith in such statements of intention? A number of contending theories remain plausible for this remarkable change of Soviet public posture, because the Soviet Union, even with glasnost, has not yet become such an open society that we can instantly know which reasoning is at work.

## Alternative Interpretations of the Soviet Shift

One line of logic would simply assume that the Soviets had been sincere for decades in expressing worries about whether the *nuclear* weapons deployed to Western Europe would be fired by neo-Nazi West Germans or by Americans, or by anyone else, knowing that such weapons would directly or indirectly produce a devastation of the USSR. If Moscow had at length seen that this wiring-in of nuclear escalation risks was the direct result of the inherent possibility of a Soviet conventional invasion of Western Europe, then the quid pro quo for eliminating the Western nuclear threat may finally have been realized to be a relaxation of the Eastern conventional threat.

As a second explanation for the Soviets' willingness to become engrossed in conventional disarmament, it is also possible that Gorbachev and his associates are driven by financial considerations.[3] Maintaining sizable conventional forces is an expensive proposition. Gorbachev's economic reforms in perestroika may achieve economic gains in the long run, but for the short and medium term, they would even set back the Soviet economy, because the average Soviet citizen has become so unused to market mechanisms and incentives. A hefty reduction in the defense budget, avoiding extensive competition with the United States in new strategic nuclear systems and avoiding the drains of manpower and resources imposed by conventional weaponry, might thus be the only way of giving Gorbachev the economic elbow room that he so desperately needs.

The third explanation for the new Soviet willingness to discuss their own conventional threat to Western Europe might, rather than an accessory to the economic reforms of perestroika, simply turn out to be another natural illustration and instance of glasnost. The Soviets are freer now to tell the truth, to discuss things honestly and openly, rather than sticking by official pronouncements and the party line, and hence they may just be describing what they see—which is what other people have been seeing for a long time. Any reference to the strategic complications produced by geography is a reminder, after all, of what Mackinder outlined at the beginning of the twentieth century,[4] a geopolitical fear that any power at the center of the Eurasian continent will have a military advantage over the continent's peninsulas. The British worries about "the great game" against Imperial Russia in the nineteenth century had been that Russian forces could as easily move against China as against India, or against Turkey or Scandinavia or Japan or the center of Europe, especially once channels of transportation such as the Trans-Siberian railroad were completed. If it was a taboo for Soviet commentators ever to face up to such geopolitical considerations, the taboos are now generally being lifted, and realities can be discussed.

Yet there is more to be addressed in open discussion than simple geopolitics, for the weapons one procures also affect the threat others feel. Burdened by something over which they have had no control in the configurations of geography, the Soviets have nonetheless exacerbated this, ever since World War II, by investing heavily in tanks and other mobile-warfare platforms, platforms far more effective than even the railroad for amplifying the threat of Russia's position on the continent. And if this kind of policy choice was previously kept from open discussion in the USSR (while it produced a great deal of open, and worrisome, discussion in the West), it is taboo no longer.

## Soviet Trickery?

Yet another interpretation has been introduced, that Gorbachev's discussions of conventional weaponry were yet another trick in the never-ending Soviet campaign to weaken the NATO alliance and dominate Western Europe.[5] Given that the Soviet statements amount to admissions of criticisms that have been directed at Moscow for three or four decades, this kind of trickery would indeed have to be fairly subtle and indirect but it might still be effective if the West were to be lulled into a false sense of security, and then woke one day to discover that Soviet tanks could roll into Frankfurt and Brussels more easily than ever (or even into Paris, if the French were somehow lulled into giving up their *force de frappé*).

As has been our situation ever since 1945, moreover, the issue has never been only whether the Soviets would actually launch such a war. A most important accessory has been the mere prospect that such a war would always be possible, with the subtle intimidation of Western political processes that could go along with this.

The worry has thus at times been that seemingly new and reasonable Soviet discussions of conventional arms control will be used to accelerate the nuclear disarmament of Europe, without at the same time being translated into really meaningful reduction of the Soviet ground forces' potential for advancing into the West European peninsula. The publics of Western Europe and the United States, always of two minds about the nuclear escalation threat (liking the way it deters Soviet aggressions at lower cost, dreading the possibility that the bluff would be called, to cause an escalation to the destruction of all the cities of the Northern Hemisphere), would race to complete the process initiated in the INF agreement, that is, race into a de facto acceptance of the old Rapacki Plan "making Europe safe for conventional war."

Skeptics about the significance of any Soviet verbal discussion of "defensive defense" thus contended that only a major drop in Soviet force totals and Soviet military spending could be meaningful. More important than a drop, of course, would be a reconfiguration of such forces so that they were less disposed toward the offensive and forward motion. There is some interesting evidence that Warsaw Pact maneuvers have shifted to being more often tests of the Soviet ability to stand and hold a line, rather than "defending the Soviet motherland" by rolling into Frankfurt and Brussels. The more offensive type of maneuver has not yet been eliminated, however, having only fallen to a smaller portion of the total.

Perhaps it is too early to rule out totally the possibility that this is all a Soviet trick and bargaining ploy; there are probably at least some Soviet officers who have been ready to go along with it simply on this interpretation. Yet, to repeat, the concessions that the Soviets have made in their verbal pronouncements are indeed remarkable.

Most important, such pronouncements have helped the West to slow nuclear disarmament in Europe for the immediate future, rather than putting pressure on the NATO governments to speed it. "Even the Soviets" have been saying that the next appropriate round of disarmament arrangements should be in the conventional sector, coupled with admissions that Soviet tank totals are a big portion of the problem. If this was Soviet trickery, it was of a very complicated sort. More probably, it is more than trickery, drawing in the wider array of Soviet interests noted previously.

### Fears of Western Conventional Military Power?

A possible explanation is yet more complicated. Gorbachev has had reason to fear Western conventional military capabilities as the side-effect of all that he was initiating in glasnost and perestroika, and more generally as the result of the so dramatically demonstrated fragility of the Warsaw Pact. Western calculations by which the Soviets had such a tremendous conventional force advantage always tended, on a "worse-case" basis, to assume that the Poles and Czechs and Hungarians would be fighting on the Soviet side. If these nationalities had been assumed to be more lukewarm about the aggressions Moscow had launched, the NATO defense task would have looked somewhat easier. And if some or all of these countries had rebelled against communist rule, with their armed forces perhaps joining with their people in a resistance to the Soviets, a worst-case analysis for Moscow could then have expected U.S. and West German tanks to be moving eastward, rather than Soviet tanks moving westward.[6] However well-meaning and genuinely desirable Gorbachev's moves to glasnost and perestroika might be, they have been opening bottles sealed for decades.

If the ultimate goal of a serious conventional arms control negotiation (avoiding the sterile arguments about parity and numbers which have characterized the long-running MFR or MBFR negotiations) was thus to reduce the totals of tanks, armored personnel carriers, mobile artillery, and bridging equipment, the reduction would have to apply to both sides, and would lessen any potential of NATO forces for moving to the aid of Poles, Czechs, or Hungarians.

The worst of all strategic situations is not where one side can attack the other profitably, but where *either* can see gains in such an attack and fears that the other must be contemplating such an attack (or where each has to fear that the other is fearing such an attack and contemplating preemptive action). The dangers of offensive capabilities (in the counterforce sense) and first-strike incentives are well understood for the interactions of strategic nuclear forces, but they are just as relevant for the face-offs of conventional forces. "A war nobody wanted" is what may have happened in 1914, when offensively inclined forces faced each other.

It may thus simply have been Soviet propaganda when U.S. fighter-bombers or the Follow-on-Forces-Attack (FOFA) strategy were portrayed as favoring the attack—but it may not.[7] Although NATO has far fewer tanks than the Warsaw Pact, its tanks are sometimes argued to be quali-tatively superior.[8] There was always less chance that a Belgian tank would ever turn against the forces of the United States compared with the chance of a Polish or Hungarian tank turning against Soviet forces.

Whether Gorbachev and his colleagues thus feared an outright West-ern invasion, in conjunction with massive unrest in Eastern Europe, or just feared the mutual instability that could arise when each side has to entertain fears of the other side's attacks, this fear would now have gen-erated an additional plausible incentive for the Soviets to be serious about conventional arms control, about a quantitative reduction in the totals of such arms, or especially about a qualitative shift in the nature of armaments.

## A New Soviet Union?

Has the Soviet Union thus changed, or is it merely being exonerated?[9] For decades, Westerners have argued that Stalin and his successors were, at one level of analysis or another, falsely accused of the threats to Europe. Such arguments, often echoed by—or echoes of—official So-viet statements, would have run that the Warsaw Pact did not actually possess any military superiority over NATO (as the totals in the West by some measure, perhaps manpower on active duty, perhaps something else, would be greater than in the East), or that the intentions of the Soviet Union and its allies were entirely defensive or fearful of a return of German aggressiveness.[10] Rather than deploying tactical nuclear weapons as tripwires for escalation, or instead building up the large conventional forces which would reduce the risks of nuclear war (but which would be so much more expensive), such analyses would have advocated simply trusting the Soviets, and by signs of such trust inspir-ing some greater trust in reverse. If all of East-West military tension were thus the result of a fundamental misunderstanding, or was in-stead predominantly the fault of malicious warmongering in the West, this would be a way of breaking out of such traps, reducing the risks of war, avoiding returns of militarism in Germany and elsewhere in the West, and terminating the arms race at last.

The new honesty of Soviet pronouncements on the conventional arms confrontation in Europe cuts at right angles into such disputes about Soviet threats in the past. In some immediate sense, Gorbachev and his colleagues have suddenly looked reasonable and have thus made a favorable impression on the publics in West Germany, Western Europe, and the United States, being seen as even more flexible than Reagan or other Western leaders. If the NATO leaderships are seen as too suspicious of the new Soviet attitudes, or as too slow off the mark in responding to the Soviet trial balloons and proposals, skeptics about Soviet intentions see themselves as the victims of another propaganda offensive.

Yet the very substance of Moscow's new statements about conventional weapons have also amounted to a massive Soviet plea of "guilty" to what has been charged for decades in the West, an admission that countries west of the Elbe have had some serious reason to feel threatened, an admission that Soviet statements about peaceful intentions in the past were not as reassuring as they should have been, accompanied as they were by Soviet maneuvers stressing armored warfare thrusts and the attack in any conventional battles. Gorbachev and his colleagues may still be engaged in a propaganda contest with the West, but the nature of all that is being said surely totals more than a contest, for it seems in part also to be a major dialogue within the Soviet decision apparatus, as those who see what has really been bothering the West Europeans lay it out clearly for those Soviets who have not been able to make this out.[11]

### Western Needs and Interests

Why would the West want a reduction in conventional arms? We have thus far only explored plausible explanations for why Gorbachev and his associates would be moving down this road, in effect taking it for granted that this movement must be of interest to the West.

Our basic premise has indeed been that the NATO countries have been status quo-oriented in the decades since 1945, not ever really being intent on liberating Eastern Europe, but always worried that the Soviets might be interested in "liberating" Western Europe. The deployment of nuclear weapons has largely been seen as the kind of move which reinforces the status quo, discouraging any military initiatives by the prospect of the horrendous collateral damage that occurs whenever such weapons get used. Deployments of conventional forces, by contrast, may or may not favor the anti-status quo power, depending on whether they are inclined (like the tank) toward motion and the offense, and such conventional weapons certainly tend to be expensive.

Virtually any reduction in conventional forces would cut military expenditures (although this may be true only with some time-lags), but not all such reductions will reduce the threats to the political status quo, the threat to peace. Rather than focusing exclusively on quantitative disarmament, if one really wished to enhance crisis stability, one might thus rather have needed to consider the distinctions of qualitative approaches to armaments, retaining those weapons which tend to stop attacks (perhaps even adding to the totals in these weapons), while getting rid of the kinds of weapons which encourage one side or the other to strike first.

Yet, as a last searching question on the Western perspective, we must ask whether the NATO countries would always be truly committed to the status quo for all the scenarios one could have foreseen. If it is correct that NATO has been inclined toward the status quo ever since it was founded, perhaps this has only been because the costs of liberating East Germany and Eastern Europe have seemed too high, or because the odds in the comparisons of the two military alliances seemed too stacked in favor of moves westward, so that the status quo was the best that anyone in the West could hope to attain.

Even if all the earlier Soviet allegations about West German revanchism and American imperialism were basically propaganda, might not many Americans, and many very democratic West Europeans, have been inclined all along to sanction conventional military interventions eastward if only they could be effective and kept low enough in human and economic cost? And if Eastern Europe were to boil over in the aftermath of Soviet glasnost, with an armed resistance to any reimpositions of Soviet and Communist party control and with Hungarians or Poles begging for Western help in face of a Soviet intervention, some in the West might not really be so glad that conventional weapons had been reduced in number, or qualitatively reconfigured toward the defense.

Was our goal thus simply steering the confrontations of NATO and the Warsaw Pact so that neither could threaten the other with a tank invasion? Or do we have to aspire also to making Hungary and Czechoslovakia secure against a Soviet invasion?

These last considerations, many would respond, are only to be introduced as an extreme case, as the testing outer limit of whether Americans and West Germans have really been so against conventional warfare threats in Europe. Most such people might indeed have been happy to relinquish any last hopes of coming to the aid of Solidarity in exchange for extirpating the last fears of the Red Army coming to the aid of Maurice Thorez.[12] Yet our task here is to speculate about the future, as generations replace each other and as the surprises on the Soviet side mount and interact.

## The Offense versus Defense Distinction

There are clearly some important and tangible advantages to a stress on qualitative approaches to conventional armaments, that is, a stress on weapons which favor whomever sits still and lets the other side's attack come at the outbreak of a war (the defensive), compared with weapons which reward whoever has struck first, whomever is on the move into the other side's preexisting positions (the offensive).[13] The phraseology of offense and defense has been abused for purposes of national political propaganda, with every side claiming to have only a "Ministry of Defense" and "defensive forces," but the distinction is nonetheless real. Analysts who see a serious difference have sometimes tried to cut through the euphemisms by referring to "defensive defense." Because everyone will claim that everything underway militarily is defense, why not sort this into the weapons that are really defensive, and those that only pretend to be? This is also what is meant by "nonprovocative defense."

The dichotomy is sometimes phrased in terms of "active" military tools (offensive) and "reactive" tools (defensive), the weapons that initiate combat versus the weapons that come into use only when the other side has taken the first step. Is not a Nobel Peace Prize in order for the invention of a weapon which becomes effective only when the other side has taken the military initiative, the kind of weapon which makes it folly to strike first and leads each side to sit back and do nothing in a crisis, hoping that the other side makes the military blunder of beginning the war?

Yet another set of phrases would separate the categories into preemptive and nonpreemptive, with the former (offensive) category being a major culprit in "wars nobody wanted," the kind of weapon that brings victory to whomever strikes first against whomever waited to strike second. Yet another form of the nomenclature of this distinction would speak of "crisis stability," with the "defensive defense" being stabilizing in that rumors of war would not cause wars to happen, and with offensive weapons being destabilizing, precisely in that rumors of impending wars would tend to become self-confirming. We can indeed define a crisis as a perceived increase in the likelihood of war, with the most important question being whether such a perceived increase then pushes one side or the other over the line into seizing the military initiative.

All of what is described as "defensive" or "reactive" or "nonpreemptive" or "stabilizing" amounts to an antidote to what professional military planners are often accused of—worst-case analysis. Where the attack is favored, each side has to prepare to be attacked whenever political stakes get high, whenever doubts and rumors begin to circulate. When the attack is favored, each side moreover has to compensate for every last augmentation of the other side's forces. This causes arms races nobody wants, even if we can avoid "wars nobody wants."

Discussions of "superiority" fill the air, a concept which by its logical essence can only go to one side at a time. If neither side is to have such a superiority, the best we can attain as an alternative is then "parity," or "essential equivalence," concepts which then torture us with a need for careful measurement and precise definition, and with enormous burdens of verification.

By contrast, when the defense is favored, either side can shrug off and relax about a fair number of force augmentations on the other side, or can match such augmentations only partially. Each side, in a world of weaponry discouraging the attack, has a large range of elbow room, of room for error, and the talk can then be of sufficiency instead of parity or superiority. The advantages of such a turn to the sufficiency phrase are great, because this is something both sides can have at the same time, with neither having to impose an unacceptable inferiority on the other. At the same time, it does not require endless measurement amid anxiety about whether the other side is cheating or whether the measures of the comparisons have been miscalculated.

"It is no accident," therefore, that the same Soviet statements which admit the problems caused by Soviet conventional offensive capabilities (arguing that any offensive capabilities in Western conventional military forces must also be eliminated) have also hit upon sufficiency as the proposed new goal for Soviet (and any other) military forces. This is an interesting echo of the short period in the 1970s when this phrase was endorsed by the Nixon administration, all too quickly to be dropped for the much more troublesome parity and essential equivalence.[14] Critics of sufficiency complained that it was too vague, that it can mean whatever anyone wants it to mean, but there are answers to such criticism. The sufficiency phrase implies two things at once: a satisfaction with the state of one's defenses against the backdrop of a range of possibilities allowing for solutions satisfactory to the opposing side as well. In short, the phrase means that one has spent enough on weapons, in the presence of a nature and state of technology which generates crisis stability and a tilt toward the defensive.

In a manner which could cause confusions, or produce clarifications, Soviet military spokespersons endorsing the formulations advanced by Mikhail Gorbachev have referred to "defensive sufficiency" or "reasonable sufficiency." These could be useful formulations in stressing the sources from which any move toward such a noncontentious military face-off would stem, *or* they could be a troublesome quibble and qualification, almost in the nature of "sufficient sufficiency," arguing that great cautions are in order before the Soviet armed forces let their guard down in the protection of the motherland.

## Sorting the Weapons

What kinds of weapons could one then catalogue as objectionable because they favor the attack, and what kinds would instead be desirable because they discourage it? Tanks and armored personnel carriers are troublesome as are self-propelled artillery and combat-engineer bridging equipment. It might be an elementary intuition that the Soviets have no business getting ready to rebuild Western bridges. What do they know about whether the bridges will have to have been destroyed, and hence be in need of replacement?

Moving back a little further from the cutting edge of weaponry, any substantial logistical preparations for a mobile military operation are a source of worry. By contrast, confrontations where such a logistical tail is less prepared are less tense. Proposals are thus on the table for reductions of ammunition stockpiles and for the fuel concentrations necessary for a sustained armored offensive.

On a slightly different argument, any military systems that depend heavily on mobilization are bad for crisis stability; they tempt the side that has completed such mobilization to strike immediately, when the adversary is still some days away from a parallel enhancement of its forces. The year 1914 is the model of the tension that can be caused by such a confrontation of forces which can not remain forces-in-being for very long. If either side, once mobilized, then dared to demobilize rather than striking, would it not be leaving itself dangerously open to an attack by the other side, which might have held back from releasing its reservists to civilian life?

There are assuredly varying kinds of reserve systems. Those which mobilize a territorial militia to defend specific locations are less threatening to the other side and to crisis stability. Much more worrisome are those which generate maneuver battalions and forces capable of striking deep into the heart of an enemy's territory. Similarly troublesome are troop-carrier aircraft and amphibious landing ships, the transportation systems that can allow either side or both sides to move forces rapidly into some supposed vacuum. Such systems could amount to the functional equivalent of what everyone expected railroads to be able to accomplish at the beginning of World War I, causing side A to move because it felt it necessary to preempt side B, and vice versa.

It is somewhat more difficult to identify the offensive or defensive tilt of fighter-bombers and of helicopters. The Soviets point to these as categories in which NATO is supposed to have a predominance, claiming that these are also preemptive, offensive, and destabilizing. There are at least two important kinds of analytical problems. In confrontations of such systems with their opposite numbers, do they favor the attack—or do they suggest that one would do better militarily by being patient and letting the other side pay the price of being the first to attack? Second, as accessories to battles fought out between the ground forces, would such aerial instruments open the gaps through which offensive columns could pass—or would they rather be gap-fillers? Air forces, after all, can still not capture and hold territory by themselves. If this remains the supreme goal of warfare, infantry and tanks may remain indispensible, with their tendency toward forward motion or toward stalemate thus remaining crucial.

Are there weapons which correspondingly can be seen as aiding the defense, thus weapons not to be reduced at all? Anti-tank weapons are generally desirable, precisely because they reduce the incentives of lunging forward into armored warfare. Any weapons which are specific to a particular piece of terrain in their effectiveness are similarly reinforcements for crisis stability. They give the advantage to whomever was already in the area over someone trying to move in. Fixed fortifications fit into this category, as would training systems which make a militia territorially based. Mountain ranges reinforce the defense but are not generated by human decision. Yet training troops specifically for mountain warfare can mean that such troops are more effective on their home ground than on someone else's home ground.[15]

Mobility might generally seem to favor the attack, whereas immobile weapons favor the defense, but there are some complications. World War II saw the deployment of something called a "tank destroyer," a vehicle which looked very much like a tank but carried considerably less armor, and thus could move at higher speed. Such vehicles thus excelled at strategic mobility (i.e., mobility when not within firing range of the enemy), but were deficient in tactical mobility (the ability to move while engaging an enemy). As such, they were useful for racing around an enemy advance to blunt it but were not good for undertaking an advance themselves. They fit the description of defensive weapons.

Such weapons thus might approximate what was the *true* impact of railroads in 1914, rather than the expected impact. Military planners had anticipated that such railroads would facilitate the rushing forward of tremendous reserve armies, giving victory to whomever mobilized their forces and got them aboard the trains first, with such anticipations indeed very plausibly causing World War I to happen. Yet the real impact was that such railroads offered only strategic mobility and not tactical; the retreating French and Belgians destroyed the railroads in the path of the Germans. The French thus had the lateral rail connections intact to blunt subsequent German advances, while the Germans did not have the same lateral rail communications lines to move their forces for offensive advantage.

With regard to air versus air combat as an auxiliary to ground combat, anything that makes airbases less vulnerable to the other side's fighter-bombers' preemptive attack is stabilizing and welcome. Vertical take-off "jump-jets" may be of great value because they can be dispersed to so many separate locations, thus making it much harder for an attacker to win a sweeping victory. Reductions of range, as in the interceptors that the Soviets have tended to procure, compared with the West's fighter-bombers, have been also more inclined to discouraging attacks.

Yet the same fighter-bomber that is such a threat to opposing fighter-bombers may also be a serious threat to tanks, serving to blunt armored force attacks that might otherwise have produced some major breakthroughs on the ground.

## Some Sensible Exchanges

We come now to speculating about the kinds of trades that might be possible in the European confrontation between NATO and the Warsaw Pact, and the trades that we might actually regard as desirable.

As illustrated in the "zero option" INF agreement, the public at large tends to think too much in terms of symmetrical exchanges concluding too easily that a nuclear-for-nuclear trade makes sense. Actually, it may not. For example, how many theater nuclear weapons would we want NATO to retain if the Soviets had retained all their tanks and had unilaterally gotten rid of all their SS-20 missiles, the nuclear-armed missiles that have the range only for attacks on Europe and not on the United States? The answer is that we would have wanted to retain a great deal. How many of such theater nuclear weapons would we have felt it necessary to retain if the Soviets had instead retained all their SS-20s but had unilaterally gotten rid of their tank forces? In such a case, we could have gotten rid of all our nuclear weapons deployed as trip wires, for the menace they were redressing would have been removed.

One could thus easily enough, in terms of the real strategic impacts of the various kinds of weapons, propose that the remaining nuclear weapons deployed into the center of Europe be traded as serious bargaining counters for the reduction of Soviet armored forces in this sector. Indeed, all of the discussion herein has been nothing more than a rounding out of the arguments for such a trade.

Yet the political imagery we have noted will probably still dictate that some symmetry be offered as well, even after one of the more important Soviet verbal concessions has been to admit that asymmetrical reductions are indeed in order. To save face for Gorbachev and for other reasonable Soviets, to spare them from too abjectly having to admit that their country's negotiating positions of the past three decades have been wrong, and to strengthen them in the inevitable confrontations with the professional Soviet military, some kinds of Western conventional disarmament may thus have to be pushed forward as quid pro quo for Soviet disarmament in this category.[16]

It is not just that Gorbachev may need one kind or another of Western arms reductions to persuade his constituents that he should make concessions. The Soviet leader has probably indeed needed the very process of formal negotiations on arms control and disarmament to ensnare his military into moving ahead with any and all of such a reconfiguration of the Soviet conventional threat to Western Europe. If the feeling around Moscow is that a failure to go through with the elimination of offensively inclined weapons will set back political relations with the outside world and disappoint Americans and West Europeans and neutrals about the nature of the Soviet world outlook, then Gorbachev will have more of the leverage he needs to push his changes through.

Why not then throw in Western tanks in exchange for Soviet tanks, or Western fighter-bombers for Soviet tanks because the Soviet commentaries have claimed that the West has an advantage in such an aircraft? One could even follow on, as some Soviet commentaries have suggested, with Western reductions in antitank weapons, another category in which Moscow claims that NATO is ahead, in exchange for Soviet reductions in tanks.

Yet, here we reach the point where the imagery of political fairness gets in the way of a serious pursuit of the goals of arms control. Antitank weapons, fixed fortifications, and other defensive "platform-stoppers," may be precisely the weapons we do not want to reduce or limit on either side. And, as noted, it is even debatable whether the fighter-bomber is a destabilizing threat to peace or a defensive reinforcement for the status quo.

Because we live in such a political world, it may indeed have been necessary to design exchange packages and ratios with a care for imagery. Yet the concern for the Soviet leader's image problems should also not be taken to excess. The USSR started this process with a tremendous numerical advantage in tanks, armored personnel carriers, and mobile artillery, an advantage it *elected* to create, and which (if it truly wishes any gains) it must do the bulk of the work to eliminate.[17]

We may never be finally and definitively able to sort out whether the risks of war in Central Europe were caused mainly by political frictions or by military temptations. Each has played a role, and each can aggravate the other. Those favoring formal agreements might argue that the political frictions are the main problem, and even a substantively objectionable arms control treaty might be worth signing for the political détente it would produce. Yet the opposite kind of linkage cannot yet be totally dismissed. An important part of tensions since World War II have been caused by the mere possibility of a Soviet armored advance into Western Europe, aggravated by the enormous Soviet investment in armored vehicles.

If West Germany were as immune to Soviet conventional attack as Ireland, could not its political relations with the USSR be as relaxed as Ireland's? A substantively poor disarmament agreement, one removing stabilizing weapons more than it removed the destabilizing, might thus yet increase the likelihood of war rather than decrease it.

## Some Conclusions

A few final cautions are necessary about such a process of stabilizing the conventional military confrontations in Europe. Such a process would make conventional war less likely, a clear gain by all of what we stand for (one should not forget how terribly destructive even a conventional war can be). Such a process can also let us edge into eliminating our reliance on nuclear escalation threats, thus reducing our worries about far, far, worse destruction.

Yet our values are not limited simply to reducing the likelihoods of war, however important this may be, for we care also about human freedom. We care about keeping Western Europe from being intimidated in any of the more bothersome senses of Finlandization. We presumably also care about supporting the freedoms accorded to East Europeans. The question was posted earlier on whether we would regret the stabilization of the conventional balance in Europe, if it might keep us from ever sending help to Czechs or Poles or Hungarians should the USSR seek to reimpose its dominance over them.

One small accessory argument would then need to be introduced. In a situation where NATO had become the anti-status-quo power, any remaining deployments of nuclear weapons in the theater would be a great embarrassment and obstacle for the West, and, paradoxically, an asset—a link of flexible response and extended deterrence—for the Soviet Union. Will we see the day when the Rapacki Plan and other nuclear-free-zone and no-first-use proposals are pushed energetically by Washington and rejected by Moscow?

Nuclear escalatory threats would fade from significance on either side whenever a conventional balancing had finally set in. There would be no more preemptive conventional temptations to be deterred by the prospects of massive countervalue punishment. If the tank has not been eliminated on both sides, however, nuclear escalation may remain important. But who finds it helpful and who sees it as an obstacle may be the reverse of what we have been accustomed to.

# CHAPTER 9 ■
# EAST AND WEST IN
# EASTERN EUROPE
## Charles Gati

"The most dangerous time for a bad government," according to Alexis de Tocqueville, "is when it starts to reform itself." His time-honored observation has come to apply to Mikhail S. Gorbachev's Soviet Union. But for Moscow's imperial domain in Eastern Europe a variation on de Tocqueville's theme is closer to the truth: For bad governments, whose survival depends on a foreign protector, the most dangerous time is when their protector has begun to retreat.

In 1988 the Polish and the Hungarian regimes began to respond both to growing domestic challenges to their rule at home and to changing signals from Moscow. By July of that year Zbigniew Brzezinski, the former National Security Adviser to President Carter, identified the region's condition as "prerevolutionary."[1] Phrasing more cautiously, I also noted at the end of 1988 that as the ideological "foundation of the East European alliance is sinking [and as] the edifice of its socialism is cracked," the Soviet bloc has turned into "a shadow of its former self." Even "the term 'Soviet bloc' is becoming a political misnomer," I added.[2] Gorbachev's speech at the United Nations in December 1988, announcing that Moscow would unilaterally withdraw some of its forces from Eastern Europe independent of any corresponding measures by NATO, was a particularly telling sign, illustrative of the fading of Moscow's imperial aspirations.

The Soviet military decision to retrench contained a critical political message to the region's communist leaders: The Soviet Union would no longer protect unpopular East European regimes against their own peoples. Once that message was conveyed and absorbed, reformers and diehards alike were left with the choice of either making the best deal they could with their own populations or using force to break the people's will.

The Romanian, Bulgarian, Czechoslovak, and East German regimes of Nicolae Ceauşescu, Todor Zhivkov, Miloš Jakeš, and Erich Honecker —the region's "gang of four"—opted to maintain repressive, one-party rule. Their decisions were based on their desire to stay in power. Mistakenly, they believed they had greater popular support than they actually did; they regarded the political situation in their countries as less than explosive or indeed "prerevolutionary." They assumed that, even without Soviet protection, they could handle that "small minority" of oppositionists seeking radical change. Perhaps they also expected Moscow to change its hands-off position if it were faced with an anticommunist revolution. Wouldn't Gorbachev or his successors revert to the principles of the Brezhnev Doctrine in the end rather than permit large-scale defections from the communist fold?

The less rigid Polish and the Hungarian communist regimes interpreted the Soviet message to mean that, like Gorbachev, they should reassess the past, blame current problems on their predecessors, and proceed toward the implementation of radical, if unspecified, reforms. Unlike Gorbachev, however, they entered into formal discussions, first in Poland and later in Hungary, with leaders of the democratic opposition. Although their original intention was no doubt to coopt the opposition into the existing governments and thus create the appearance of power-sharing, the roundtable discussions eventually produced the transformation of one-party rule under peaceful, if often contentious, conditions. Hence the changes brought about by these reform-minded communist regimes ultimately turned out to be far more extensive than the ones they had intended.

## The Question of Soviet Motives

Gorbachev's motives to let his East European allies fend for themselves remain unclear. According to the dominant Western view, which I largely share, his preoccupation with Soviet domestic problems was undoubtedly a compelling factor. Other factors included his desire to reduce the Soviet military budget, and, to further that goal, withdraw Soviet forces from the region. Add to these eminently sensible and rational reasons Gorbachev's personal frustration with the gang of four and their resistance to his own perestroika and glasnost. As the ambitious Soviet leader of a huge empire, Gorbachev, in this view, could ill afford to tolerate an uncooperative and irritating Ceauşescu, Zhivkov, Jakeš, or Honecker forever.

Whether Gorbachev fully understood the likely consequences of his decisions is doubtful. It appears that he misjudged East European popular sentiments by assuming that his version of reformist communism would take root in the region. Deluded by shouts of "Gorby! Gorby!," he seems to have confused the East Europeans' genuine respect for his personal courage and for what he was doing in the Soviet Union with support for reform-communism in Eastern Europe. Expecting his policies to prompt the reform of the region's orthodox communist regimes, he did not foresee revolutions against communism itself. In short, Gorbachev assummed that the East Europeans would stop at perestroika or, indeed, at "socialism with a human face."

In the end, most of Eastern Europe experienced stunning revolutionary changes rather than step-by-step reforms. The changes came about in this manner not only because the old regimes had delayed making the concessions necessary to appease their peoples. In addition, both Moscow and the East European regimes had seriously underestimated the passions emerging among the East European peoples, mistaking their past apathy for permanent acquiescence. The Soviet leadership, in particular, failed to anticipate that the East Europeans would interpret Soviet military retrenchment as political retreat and would press for a change of the system rather than only of the current regimes.

Although it does not speak well for Gorbachev's prescience that he failed to discern the region's anticommunist, prerevolutionary condition, it is to his credit that he refused to fight fire with fire. Indeed, when East Germany's Honecker recognized that only massive force could stem the tide against communism in his country and directed his security forces to shoot the demonstrators if necessary, it appears that Moscow—with almost 400,000 of its well-equipped troops standing by—encouraged Egon Krenz, the second in command in East Germany, to countermand Honecker's order. At this critical juncture, Gorbachev allowed the reform he had hoped for to turn into revolution. Elsewhere, too, Gorbachev refused to be drawn into a costly and potentially dangerous effort to save his dominion. Even when the Berlin Wall was breached and thus the most vital of all Soviet geopolitical interests was threatened, Gorbachev did not use force. He may have believed that in the end the East European revolutions would not damage his country's long-term interests and, indeed, they might even improve his own position.

This interpretation of Gorbachev's motives, which reflects the dominant view among Western scholars and policymakers alike, is rooted in the assumption that Moscow was too weak to defend its East European dominion.

According to a far more skeptical, indeed conspiratorial, interpretation,[3] Gorbachev's new East European policy was more purposeful than it appeared to be. In this view, the policy had *intended* to erase the Soviet Union's threatening image in the West and thereby prompt the eventual withdrawal of the United States from Europe and the neutralization of Western Europe. Accordingly, Soviet retreat from Eastern Europe was but a grand, strategic gamble, a response by Gorbachev to the failure of his predecessors—as in the 1983 INF fiasco—to intimidate the West Europeans, divide NATO, and compel the removal of U.S. forces from the continent. The argument was summarized by Edward Jay Epstein as follows:

> By projecting an image of such weakness abroad, the Soviet Union could hope to undercut the rationale for maintaining the NATO alliance, as well as to weaken public support for the stationing of U.S. forces in Japan, West Germany, Korea, the Philippines, and other countries. The idea that the Soviet economy is in such dire straits, if not a total basket case, also provides a basis in the West for believing that the Soviet Union will make concessions in negotiations in order to get Western help to restructuring it. It is a tactic no different from a retail store feigning an "out of business sale" to make customers believe that they are getting bargains, or airlines pretending to be on the verge of bankruptcy to win concessions in their labor negotiations. . . .[4]

In this view, then, the Soviet goal toward Europe has not changed; only the method is novel.

There is no way to reconcile these two interpretations of Soviet motives; they are mutually exclusive. Reflecting Soviet economic conditions that keep worsening and Soviet political conditions that point toward anarchy, the dominant view states a reality few can deny. To the extent the second view has any merit, it is instructive as a corrective and a warning: Russia is and will remain a critical factor in European politics. Although public evidence to this effect is lacking, it is also possible to imagine that some Soviet politicians have *subsequently* explained—rationalized—recent losses in Eastern Europe in terms of future gains in Western Europe.

In my judgment, Gorbachev had certainly not intended to "lose" Eastern Europe as part of a grand, strategic gamble to undermine NATO. The original Soviet intention (as of early and mid-1989) was to press for Gorbachev-style reform communism in order to bring Eastern Europe in line with Soviet patterns and policies. Such an Eastern Europe was expected to be more prosperous as well as more stable, and thus it would have allowed Moscow to gain time and thus to focus on pressing domestic concerns.

It appears, however, that at least some Soviet policymakers did flirt with the idea of making a "separate deal" with Hungary that was to entail that country's eventual neutralization. In February 1989 Academician Oleg T. Bogomolov, a leading Soviet expert on Eastern Europe, stated that such a Hungary would represent no threat to Soviet security interests. As he made this comment at a press conference held at the

Soviet Foreign Ministry, he is unlikely to have spoken only for himself. If Moscow was indeed contemplating a special arrangement for Hungary, a small and strategically unimportant country, Gorbachev must have hoped to be able to contain the "Hungarian disease" within Eastern Europe, expecting that the Warsaw Pact would remain largely intact while the peace movement would gain new adherents in Western Europe.

If this was the initial Soviet objective, it failed. In the fall of 1989 Hungary opened its Western border to East German refugees, sparking the spirit of pluralism rather than perestroika in East Germany. In a few days democracy came to Czechoslovakia as well. To all intents and purposes the Soviet empire had collapsed. Gorbachev could not have intended all this to happen.

### Illustration: Gorbachev and Czechoslovakia

Until its stunning and successful transition from dictatorship to democracy in November 1989, Czechoslovakia was an anachronism in Gorbachev's world of reform and renewal.[5] In political, cultural, and economic matters, orthodoxy had long prevailed. The main roadblock was the leadership's need to defend and justify its old policies. Before he retired in 1988, for example, Politburo member Vasil Bilak spoke for the entire leadership when he stated that the only policies that should be adopted are those which demonstrate "the strengths and advantages of socialism." He repeatedly warned against what he termed the "opportunistic" emulation of Gorbachev's program, emphasizing the lessons of the "the struggle against the enemies of socialism in the 1960s." In an earlier speech, he had reaffirmed the validity of a resolution, adopted by the Czechoslovak Central Committee in December 1970, that had defined the country's harsh, oppressive course since the 1968 Prague Spring. "There are those," said Bilak, alluding to Gorbachev, "who would like to have that document nullified, but this will not be done."[6]

As early as 1987 Moscow sought to discredit and perhaps even to dislodge the very leaders it had put in power after the 1968 Soviet intervention. When Gorbachev visited Prague in the spring of 1987 and was asked by Western reporters to clarify the difference between Dubček's Prague Spring and his own perestroika and glasnost, his spokesman, Gennadi Gerasimov, replied in two memorable words: "Nineteen years." But Gorbachev himself shied away from openly criticizing Brezhnev's protégés in Prague. At that time he was guided by the belief that the extension of his process of renewal to Czechoslovakia might destabilize that country. This is why Gustáv Husák, who resigned as party leader in December 1987, remained the country's president, and his replacement as head of the party, Miloš Jakeš, was Husák's younger but equally hard-line replica.

Not until the summer and early fall of 1989 were there any overt signs of increased Soviet concern about the Czechoslovak leadership:

On August 8, *Izvestia* carried a long interview with Rudolf Hegenbart, then head of the Czechoslovak Central Committee's Department for State Administration and thus the party's direct supervisor of the secret police. The interview was unusual in that Hegenbart had taken a most critical view of Czechoslovak conditions. Because they did not reflect the party line, Hegenbart's remarks were not published in the Prague press, as would have been customary, and he was reprimanded by his Politburo superiors. Because Hegenbart's position in the Czechoslovak party suggested that he was closely associated with the KGB, and because the interview appeared in the Soviet government's official daily, it is quite likely that he was encouraged by Soviet officials to state the views he voiced.

In an interview that was broadcast on September 4 on Hungarian television, Kiril Mazurov, a former candidate or associate member of the Soviet Politburo, expressed regret over the 1968 Soviet intervention. This was another extraordinary interview, because Mazurov also revealed that, under the pseudonym "General Trofymov," he himself had led the Warsaw Pact forces against Czechoslovakia in 1968. Mazurov also stated that, "In my view, the old guard [in Prague] should, without any special fuss, step down from the stage of politics."

On September 17, *Izvestia* published a letter to the editor from Jiří Hajek, Dubček's foreign minister, doyen of the Czechoslovak democratic opposition since 1968, and a political persona non grata in Prague. In his letter, Hajek clarified Dubček's role during the Prague Spring. In Czechoslovakia itself, even the publication of the author's name had been forbidden since 1968.

In the second half of September a Soviet television crew appeared in the Slovak capital of Bratislava to tape a long interview with Dubček, hero of the Prague Spring. Although Czechoslovak authorities were said to have protested the crew's presence, excerpts from the interview were nonetheless broadcast on Leningrad television in October.

Such evidence on the public record thus demonstrates that Moscow began a persistent campaign in August 1989 against the post-1968 leadership in Prague. By the end of September, it was clear to leaders of the opposition and to party officials as well that the country's old guard did not have Moscow's support. As Jiří Dienstbier, a leading opposition figure who was to become Czechoslovakia's foreign minister in December 1989, said in a private conversation at that time: "The party is dead, but we don't know yet when the corpse will be buried."

The corpse was buried far sooner than anyone, including Dienstbier, had ever expected. By October the party found itself caught between its habit to use force and its fear of confrontation without Soviet backing; it appeared divided and hesitant. With the danger of being arrested or hurt thus lessening, the people took to the streets in ever greater numbers. They were also encouraged by the sight of so many East German refugees in their midst and, especially, by the breaching of the Berlin Wall. If even the East German regime was as vulnerable as it was proving to be, then surely the Czechoslovak regime could not last much longer either.

In the new, postrevolutionary political order that emerged after November 1989, one that was to be led by the dissident playwright Václav Havel, the communists still retained a few government portfolios. But they were divided, discredited, and defeated. The support they had counted on from the working class never materialized. In a pathetic attempt to gain a measure of respectability, they quickly reversed their long-standing condemnation of the Prague Spring and chose (or pretended) to welcome democratic change. Refusing to use force, Moscow also welcomed developments in Prague by endorsing the Czechoslovak party's latest position regarding the Prague Spring and thus, finally and formally, renouncing the Brezhnev Doctrine:

> In 1968, the Soviet leadership of that time supported the stand of one side in an internal dispute regarding objective pressing tasks. The justification for such an unbalanced, inadequate approach, an interference in the affairs of a friendly country, was then seen in an acute East-West confrontation. We share the view of the Presidium of the Central Committee of Czechoslovakia and the Czechoslovak Government that the bringing of armies into Czechoslovak territory in 1968 was unfounded, and that that decision, in the light of all the presently known facts, was erroneous.[7]

All in all, the evolution of Gorbachev's approach to Czechoslovakia demonstrated a few of the general features of Soviet policy in Eastern Europe prior to and during the momentous 1989 revolutions:

For several years, Gorbachev had a preference but not a policy toward the region. Unwilling to lean on the "gang of four," he tolerated their opposition to perestroika while largely limiting himself to expressions of hope that the East European communist regimes would eventually embark on a reformist course.

Only in the late summer and early fall of 1989 did Moscow decide to increase pressure on the East European diehards to fall in line. "Falling in line," however, meant adoption of Soviet-style perestroika, not Western-style pluralism. Positive signals were sent to Dubček, not Havel, which showed "Gorbachev's apparent lack of vision or even ignorance of the real forces at play in this important allied nation"[8] and indeed everywhere else in Eastern Europe.

It should be stressed, then, that "at no point in the preceding four years [since Gorbachev's rise to power in 1985] did Soviet authorities plan, anticipate or even imagine their policies would eliminate communist rule" in Eastern Europe.[9]

Why the Soviet Union in the end accepted defeat is self-evident: overwhelmed by an extraordinary domestic crisis in 1988 and 1989, Moscow lost its ability to sustain its imperial domain in Eastern Europe. To have resorted to the use of force under the circumstances would have brought into question the very survival of the Soviet Union. On the other hand, the indication that it would not use force on behalf of its allies effectively undermined the region's communist regimes, members of the gang of four, especially, but the reformist contingent as well, thus revealing that all East European communist regimes lacked legitimate authority.

Moscow's inability to use force unwittingly sparked the fire next door. "Unwittingly," because the Soviet Union could not have wished to reduce its role in Eastern Europe to that of an interested bystander; his colleagues did not choose Gorbachev to preside over the dissolution of the Soviet empire. Indeed, the Soviet goal was to replace orthodoxy by reform and to trade its sphere of domination based mainly on sheer force for a sphere of influence based mainly on mutual interests. To have failed so completely to achieve this goal suggests that it was unrealistic, the result of a historic miscalculation in Moscow about East European conditions and aspirations.

## Prospects for Finlandization

Can the Soviet Union recapture some or all of its influence over Eastern Europe? Can it put Humpty-Dumpty together again?

The question is more important than it may seem at first glance. For if it is true, as I think it is, that Moscow did not plan the dissolution of its empire—that a *weak* Soviet Union, facing an immense crisis at home, only grudgingly accepted the eventual consequence of a policy based on serious errors of judgment—then it stands to reason that a *strong* or stronger Soviet Union of the future would attempt to reestablish Moscow's presence in the region. Would not such a policy provide a common platform for Gorbachev's critics and opponents? Could not the army, the KGB, orthodox communists, and Russian nationalists accuse Gorbachev with the loss of Eastern Europe and unite against him?

As Eastern Europe enters the constructive stage of its revolution—as it begins to build new institutions of economic and political pluralism, ones that will resemble those created in Western Europe after World War II—the Soviet Union finds itself with nothing of significance to contribute to the region's emerging order. Its political system is in disarray. Its economy has become bankrupt. Its ideology, discredited at home, has lost its appeal even in the Third World. It has retained the means to remain a military power, but military power by itself will not readily translate into political influence. Most East Europeans seem to have concluded that they need not fear Moscow's wrath.

With little leverage left, the Soviet Union may have missed the opportunity to do what it should have done and could have done earlier and what most East Europeans would have gladly accepted in the past: to transform its sphere of *domination* into a sphere of *influence*.

A traditional sphere of influence requires an exchange of concessions. Both sides must be ready to agree to less than what they want. Specifically, the strong state must settle for being influential rather than dominant because the price for hegemony, which normally entails the use of force, is far too high. The weak state, in turn, must agree to be influenced rather than be fully sovereign because the price for full independence, which normally requires armed resistance, is too high.

Thus, steering carefully between that which is desirable (full sovereignty) and that which is unacceptable (domination), the weak state seeks to obtain and then settle for some of what it wants. It accepts only some of what it wants and thus accommodates itself to being in a sphere of influence because it fears that the strong state may one day decide to use force to become dominant. In the end, it is that fear of being dominated rather than influenced—the fear of losing all of its independence—that propels the weak state to acquiesce to a subordinate status.

Although Finns strongly resent the word, and deny that they have such a relationship with the Soviet Union, the term Finlandization is often used to identify Moscow's implicit understanding with its small northern neighbor.[10] In practice, Finlandization has come to mean a Finnish political order that is free and an economy that is privately owned, while Finish foreign policy, irrespective of which political parties make up that country's coalition government at the moment, is guided by a firm, national commitment to harmonious relations with the Soviet Union. On the whole, despite a few irritating incidents over the years, the formula has worked. Finland has retained some leeway in foreign affairs, while its domestic order has remained free of Soviet interference.

Moscow has been satisfied by the situation, as well. During his visit to Helsinki in October 1989, Gorbachev praised the Soviet-Finnish relationship and implied that it might become a model for Soviet ties with Eastern Europe. *The New York Times* on November 1 interpreted his comments to mean that "'Finlandization' [for Eastern Europe] is OK." Yet, despite Gorbachev's endorsement, the Finlandization of Eastern Europe was by then an idea whose time had passed. In Eastern Europe, the choice was no longer seen as between being in the Soviet sphere of domination or a Soviet sphere of influence, but between domination and independence. As Soviet troops withdrew from the region and as Moscow, anxiously attending to disorder at home, was so deeply preoccupied with the very survival of the Soviet Union itself, East Europeans saw no reason to exchange subservience for subordination. Thus, with the lessening of the old, pervasive fear of Soviet intervention, Finlandization, once seen as a respectable formula for a relationship based on mutual concessions, has come to be regarded in Eastern Europe as a needless compromise. In their present mood, at the beginning of the 1990s East Europeans have no use for communism, socialism, "reforms," or indeed the Soviet Union.

Yet, when their passions subside, East Europeans will come to realize that, if only for one reason, their dependence on the Soviet Union must continue for years: the reason is the region's need for energy. As long as Eastern Europe cannot afford to buy energy with hard currency, there will be no alternative to its reliance on Soviet supplies. Hard currency, in turn, will be unavailable until the generally poor quality of East European goods improves sufficiently to make them competitive in Western markets.

Yet even when the East Europeans succeed in improving the quality of their products, another problem will confront them. The Soviet Union, which is by far the largest market for East European manufactures, does not demand—and in most cases prefers not to purchase—high-quality products because it cannot put them to effective use. Under the circumstances, the East Europeans will find it difficult to assemble small quantities of high-quality goods for Western consumption while at the same time producing large quantities of the same goods of lesser quality for the vast Soviet market. Given limited resources and relatively small productive capacities, the East European economies cannot efficiently serve two very different markets because of the initially prohibitive cost that the development of high-quality products will entail.

If the East Europeans were to adopt a Western-oriented economic strategy, they would eventually achieve independence from Soviet energy. They would also pay a high price for their efforts. During the long process of transition they would risk losing the Soviet market for their traditional products while seeking, perhaps in vain, Western markets for their new ones. For this reason, most East Europeans are likely to opt to continue trading some or most of their food and manufactures for Soviet energy.

Still, such continuity in the Soviet-East European economic relationship will begin and end with bilateral trade. There will be no Soviet-dominated coordination of one-, two-, or five-year plans among members of the Council for Mutual Economic Assistance (CMEA), because, by then, there is unlikely to be either a CMEA or any all-encompassing planned economies in the region.

With energy as its sole, albeit compelling, source of leverage, Soviet policy in Eastern Europe is not going to be reversed in the foreseeable future. Soviet domestic conditions, in particular, militate against the reemergence of an assertive Soviet foreign policy. With Stalinism condemned, Leninism rebuked, and West European-type social democracy the only reasonable prospect for a *stable* economic and political order, Moscow may permit institutionalized, if limited, pluralism, and may eventually allow the transformation of the Union of Soviet Socialist Republics into something closer to an Association of Semi-Independent Soviet Republics.

Even with Gorbachev at the helm, it is nonetheless reasonable to expect major setbacks in the Soviet Union during the long decade of transition in the 1990s. Although it is unclear where or when, it is certain that Moscow will draw the line *somewhere* in order to save the unity of the Soviet Union from nationalist pressures. Yet even if massive force were used to restore *domestic* law and order, the application of sanctions against an East European country is still unlikely. After all, even under Gorbachev's predecessors Moscow consistently refrained from using economic sanctions against recalcitrant East European regimes. (Stalin learned during the Yugoslav crisis of 1948 and 1949 that the harsh sanctions he applied only intensified Yugoslav resistance and were thus counterproductive.)

There are, therefore, many in the West as well as in Eastern Europe who belittle the Soviet Union as a "pitiful giant." The available evidence suggests that, as long as it continues to experience such acute difficulties at home, this view may be correct. Confused about its values, overwhelmed by extraordinary pressures from within, and exhausted economically, the Soviet Union appears to have lost its will to pursue its old ambitions and defend its traditional interests. Having withdrawn from Afghanistan, it has retreated both militarily and politically from Eastern and Central Europe as well. Therefore, the immediate prospects for Moscow to transform its sphere of domination into a sphere of influence are not promising. For the time being, the opportunity for Finlandization appears to have been lost.

In the longer run, however, a reassertion of Soviet interest in Eastern Europe cannot and should not be excluded:

When its domestic crisis abates, perhaps later in this decade or at the beginning of the next century, the Soviet Union may well attempt to rebuild its military grandeur and corresponding global role in world affairs. In that case and at that time, regaining its presence in Eastern Europe would be at the top of Moscow's agenda.

If a united Germany extends it economic, political, and possibly military reach into Central Europe and the Balkans, the Soviet Union, feeling threatened, may well counter German policy—peacefully or otherwise.

If, in the years ahead, Eastern Europe experiences a violent nationalist upsurge with a decidedly anti-Soviet and even anti-Russian edge, it is possible to imagine a strong and possibly equally violent Soviet reaction.

Finally, as mentioned earlier, if the Soviet crisis of the 1990s produces an anti-Gorbachev coalition, it would undoubtedly blame Gorbachev for the loss of Eastern Europe and commit itself to restoring Moscow's old dominion.

At the moment these are distant prospects indeed. As this chapter is written, the Soviet bloc has passed into history. Its multilateral institutions—the Warsaw Pact and CMEA—can no longer make binding decisions. Moscow has agreed to withdraw its forces from Czechoslovakia and Hungary. The communist parties in Central Europe (Germany, Czechoslovakia, Poland, and Hungary), competing in free elections, have been shown to lack any significant popular support and genuine democrats are in power; although communism and authoritarianism remain stronger in the Balkans (Romania and Bulgaria), chances are that the governments will seek to treat Moscow cordially. They will do so both before the Soviets leave the region completely—mainly to ensure that they actually do leave—and also after they are gone—to ensure that they will not return.

### East European Security Issues

As even the Finlandization, let alone the Soviet domination, of Eastern Europe is now a distant prospect, the Cold War appears to be over. This is so because, arguably, no other single issue was so central to the Cold War between East and West as the extension of Moscow's reach into the heart of Europe. "[The] Cold War began in Eastern Europe," President Bush noted several months before the 1989 revolutions had swept the region. "If it is to end it will end in this crucible of world conflict."[11] Writing at about the same time, Michael Mandelbaum explained:

The core of the cold war in Europe is the Soviet domination of Eastern Europe. Moscow has imposed unwanted and illegitimate communist regimes on countries that, if free to choose, would have governments much more like those in Western Europe. This is an affront to American values.

More important, Soviet domination of Eastern Europe threatens American security. The American military commitment to Western Europe is based on the fear that without it the Soviet Union would do to France, Italy, the Benelux countries and West Germany what it has already done to Poland, Czechoslovakia, Hungary and East Germany. The threat of Soviet aggression against Western Europe is credible because it has already taken place . . . against Eastern Europe.

Ending the cold war requires ending the Soviet threat to Western Europe, which requires ending Soviet subjugation of Eastern Europe, which means allowing the people of that part of the world to decide freely how to govern themselves. The principal requirement for the end of the cold war, in short, is self-determination for Eastern Europe.[12]

Since Mandelbaum made these astute observations, the countries of Eastern Europe have regained their independence. Once all Soviet troops leave the region and the complex problem of German security is resolved (a subject beyond the scope of this chapter), the Soviet conventional military threat to Western Europe will have diminished, if not altogether disappeared. To all intents and purposes, the East-West confrontation in Europe will have turned into political and economic competition.

Security issues in postcommunist Eastern Europe will likely revolve around old-fashioned ethnic and nationality tensions and conflicts. How serious they will be remains to be seen, but they are not expected to be as divisive as in the Soviet Union. Moreover, if strong democratic governments emerge everywhere in Eastern Europe and if economic conditions improve, it stands to reason that some of the nationalist claims and counterclaims will lose their pervasiveness and some of the ancient animosities will abate. Conversely, poor economic conditions may prompt weak governments to divert attention from their own performance by encouraging nationalist agitation.

The possibility exists for high tension between Hungary and Romania over the Romanian treatment of the Hungarian minority—the largest in Europe—living in Transylvania. Romanians are concerned about conditions for Romanians in Soviet-controlled Moldavia. Bulgarians may renew old claims about Macedonia, which is part of Yugoslavia. Inhabited by ethnic Albanians, Yugoslavia's volatile Kosovo region has already required military intervention. In addition, several East European countries may experience intraethnic conflict—as between Serbs and Croats in Yugoslavia and between Czechs and Slovaks in Czechoslovakia.[13]

In the past the Soviet presence in Eastern Europe tended to inhibit public expressions of both inter- and intranational antagonisms. With the demise of the Warsaw Pact, however, there is presently no mechanism for mediating or controlling nationalist rivalries. Thus the potential exists for the Balkanization of Eastern Europe—for the region to become Europe's Middle East. In that case, history—particularly the history of interwar Eastern Europe—suggests the possible involvement in the region of either Russia or Germany or both, as they would attempt to settle festering disputes either by dividing the area among themselves (as they did in 1939) or by resorting to force (as they did in World War II). Two ambitious and possibly dissatisfied great powers would find an Eastern Europe made up of a series of weak and defenseless states a tempting target.

Although the region's nationalist passions and conflicts might revive Russia's imperial urge and spark excessive German involvement, it is far more likely that nationalism would have the effect of retarding Eastern Europe's democratic evolution. It is difficult to see how political tolerance, for example, would take root and flourish under conditions of intense national rivalries.

The new, post-Cold War security problem of Eastern Europe should be met by movement toward the creation of a confederation for as many of the region's states as possible.[14] The purpose of such a confederation would be to provide a forum for the resolution of national differences and conflicts, enhance economic and political cooperation, and reduce excessive competition among the individual East European states for Western favors. Steps toward unity in Eastern Europe would also pave the way toward the region's eventual entry into a united Europe. What Eastern Europe needs in the 1990s, then, is precisely what Western Europe needed in the late 1940s.

## Western Concerns

The East European revolution has caught the West by surprise. Past West German statements in particular, predicting the inevitability of change in Eastern Europe, have turned out not to reflect official expectations; they were apparently meant to keep hope alive. When change did occur—when instability turned into revolution, and when it became evident that Moscow would not intervene and communist rule would thus end—there was both incredulity and concern.

There has been and will continue to be concern in the West about three related issues.

The first concern involves the extent of Western economic assistance to Eastern Europe. Financial constraints will be the first obstacle. The problem is not that Washington, for example, is not sympathetic to East European needs; it is and it will be. The problem is how to determine the criteria for the allocation of limited resources. So-called humanitarian aid aside, is Poland more important to the United States than the Philippines?

Assuming Poland will continue to receive Western assistance, it will remain a subject of heated political debate whether assistance should include what that country needs most, which is debt relief. For if the West decides to give preferential treatment to Poland, will not other indebted nations in Latin America and elsewhere ask for and expect similar concessions? Will not Poland itself conclude that its future debts will be forgiven as well? The choice for the West is between financial prudence and political opportunity.

Nevertheless, the West will play an important role in attempting to make the changes that have occurred in Eastern Europe permanent, because these changes serve Western interests and because they conform to Western ideals. Western Europe (more than the United States) and Germany (more than any other West European state) can be expected to support those countries that will initiate radical economic and political measures. East European countries with a free enterprise system will easily persuade private Western firms to invest and do business there, especially if the profit they will make is available in hard currency. East European countries that practice political democracy will persuade Western governments to encourage such business activity and also to remove existing barriers from the free flow of goods, including products that contain advanced, although probably not the most advanced, technology.

The second concern involves the Soviet Union. The problem is that the West does not and will not have sufficient influence to make a significant contribution to the Soviet Union's democratic evolution. For the sake of Western security interests as well as Western ideals, the West has a stake in what Gorbachev stands for and, indeed, in the rise of an increasingly democratic Soviet political order. Given the limits of outside influence on the Soviet domestic scene, however, the West can do no more than to applaud Gorbachev's efforts, conclude arms control agreements that serve both countries' interests, ease trade restrictions, and assist Eastern Europe so that its success serve as an example that Soviet reformers can emulate.

Whether these otherwise important steps will make a difference for Soviet domestic developments are highly doubtful. Almost irrespective of what the West will do, it appears that the Soviet Union will encounter greater convulsions in the early 1990s than what Eastern Europe experienced at the end of the 1980s. For the West, the issue is how to prepare for the international consequences of Gorbachev's probable failure to implement his ambitious objectives.

The third concern is the future of European security. That it is a concern is the paradoxical result of the end of the Cold War: as the dangers associated with the cold war disappear, the sense of clarity it offered will disappear as well. Being somewhat removed from the scene, Americans, in particular, will no longer be able to distinguish between friends and adversaries, NATO and the Warsaw Pact, democrats and communists. The end of the Cold War is a concern, then, because there will be no alternative in the 1990s to exchanging the simplicity of a divided Europe for the complexity of a united Europe. Without the Iron Curtain and the Berlin Wall, novel security arrangements will have to be created that take into account both the new geopolitical reality and the possibility that a convulsive Soviet Union will become an unpredictable Soviet Union.

Although American influence over Soviet domestic developments will be marginal, and although its role in Eastern Europe will be important but less than critical, the United States will have to *lead* the West in the search for a dependable and lasting security formula for Europe. As the only superpower in the world of the 1990s, the United States can no more abdicate its responsibility for the future of Europe than it can relinquish its own security interests.

What, in the end, will replace NATO and the Warsaw Pact cannot be predicted. Yet it is clear that, despite Soviet retreat, the new European security formula for the 1990s and for the next century will have to be more than NATO in a new guise. It will have to provide stability for a new Europe, West and East. To devise such a formula and thus to pave Eastern Europe's reentry into the European community of nations is a task that is worthy of the legacy of the East European revolutions.

# CHAPTER 10 ■
# SOVIET POLICY IN
# EAST ASIA: THE QUEST FOR
# CONSTRUCTIVE ENGAGEMENT
Donald S. Zagoria

Since the election of Mikhail Gorbachev as leader of the Soviet Communist party in March 1985, the Soviet Union has greatly increased its efforts to improve relations with all the countries of East Asia, particularly China, but also with Japan, South Korea, the Association of Southeast Asian Nations (ASEAN) countries, and Australia and New Zealand. There has been a new diplomatic flexibility, frequent visits, a drive for better trade links, an effort to join Asian economic organizations such as the Asian Development Bank (ADB) and the Pacific Economic Cooperation Council (PECC), a number of arms control proposals, a unilateral reduction of two hundred thousand troops east of the Urals, and a determined effort to change the poor image of the Soviet Union in East Asia. In several speeches at Vladivostok in July 1986 and at Krasnoyarsk in September 1988,[1] Gorbachev said that he wants to lower the level of military activity in the Pacific, to help resolve regional tensions, to improve Moscow's bilateral relations with all the countries in the region, to advance multilateral cooperation, particularly economic cooperation, and generally to create a "healthier" situation. To those who call his proposals propaganda, Gorbachev said, "we are prepared to consider any alternatives if some of the Soviet proposals are found to be unacceptable."

Although there is no euphoria about Gorbachev in Asia, as there may be elsewhere, his initiatives have had an impact, not only on China and South Korea, but also on the ASEAN countries. A summit meeting between Gorbachev and Deng Xiaoping was held in May 1989, the first such meeting between top Soviet and Chinese leaders in thirty years. A dialogue between Moscow and Seoul has begun; Gorbachev and South Korea's president have met (much to the distress of North Korea), and the two countries have opened trade offices in each others' capitals. These offices will be staffed with high-ranking foreign service officials and thus represent an important step toward mutual diplomatic recognition, something that Seoul has been urging on the Soviets for many years.

Moreover, it seems likely that Moscow and Tokyo will also reach some sort of modus vivendi despite their territorial dispute over the four islands north of Hokkaido. And, now that Vietnam, under a considerable degree of Soviet pressure, has withdrawn from Cambodia, a major constraint on Soviet relations with the ASEAN countries has been removed. In sum, the Soviet Union may well succeed in normalizing its relations with East Asia during the 1990s.[2]

Even if Moscow does succeed in improving its relations with the Asia-Pacific countries, it will remain at a considerable disadvantage in the Pacific region for a long time to come. The United States is the predominant power in the Pacific. It is both a military and an economic heavyweight, and its cultural influence is also significant. A substantial number of East Asian government officials and intellectuals have been educated in American universities, and English is the lingua franca of the Asian business community.

The Soviet Union, by contrast, has only military power in the region; its economic relations are minimal, and there is little chance of any significant increase in business dealings in the foreseeable future. The United States also has a loyal and highly effective ally in Japan, and the two countries have a compelling interest in strengthening the alliance, in improving growth prospects worldwide, and in maintaining the web of security and economic ties that sustain an open world economy and the defense of Western interests. The United States also has a number of other allies and friends in the Pacific, several of them bound by treaty commitments, and all of them sharing an interest in in maintaining a robust American presence in Asia in order to balance other "close-in" powers which they fear most. By contrast, the Soviet Union has only a few allies in East Asia and they are poor, politically isolated, and without much influence.

Moreover, the failure of Stalinist economics, which has become increasingly evident all over the communist world, has made the Soviet Union virtually irrelevant as an ideological model in a region consisting of the fastest-growing market economies in the world.

There is also a basic contradiction in Moscow's new effort to woo East Asia through flexible diplomacy. In the past, the Soviet Union's principal method to expand its influence was through its military power and aggressive behavior. If Moscow now seeks to woo East Asia largely through diplomacy and trade, its leverage will be small because it has little to offer on either count. If, on the other hand, it reverts once again to employing its military power—as it did in the 1970s, when it deployed ss-20s, invaded Afghanistan, and supported Vietnam's invasion of Cambodia—it will again help to mobilize a coalition of powers against it.

Despite these difficulties and dilemmas, Gorbachev's diplomancy in the Asia-Pacific region sharply contrasts with Gromyko's rigid and overmilitarized approach and has already scored some successes. Gorbachev has laid the groundwork for better relations with China by showing more flexibility than any of his predecessors. He virtually accepted the Chinese position on the Amur River border, and he systematically addressed all three of China's obstacles to normalization: Soviet troops on the border, the Soviet occupation of Afghanistan, and the Soviet support of Vietnam's occupation of Cambodia. Three-quarters of the Soviet troops have been withdrawn from Mongolia, and substantial numbers of Soviet troops are to be removed elsewhere along the Sino-Soviet border; the Soviet army has withdrawn from Afghanistan; and Moscow is negotiating directly with China, as well as with other major powers, on a solution to the Cambodia problem. Trade has been accelerated and reached more than $3 billion in 1989. The two countries have agreed to establish a committee to draft a comprehensive plan for a TVA-like project to develop the water resources of the Amur and Argun rivers, and there are plans for five or six hydroelectric plants along the Amur. The Soviets are also helping to refurbish seventeen plants which they built in the 1950s.

In sum, the deep freeze in the Sino-Soviet relationship since the mid 1960s has ended, and a new stage in Sino-Soviet relations is beginning. The process of normalization is likely to continue in the 1990s because powerful motives exist on both sides to improve the relationship. Both Moscow and Peking believe that their most urgent priorities for the next decade or longer is to modernize and reform their economies. To do this, both require a peaceful international climate, sharply reduced defense spending, and calm along their 4,500-mile border. They both also hope to preserve their flexibility and maneuverability in the Great Power triangle involving the United States. By improving relations with Moscow, Peking also hopes to pressure Moscow's client state, Vietnam, to accept China's preferred solution to the Cambodian problem—a dissolution of the existing pro-Hanoi PRK government and its replacement by a genuinely neutralist four-party coalition led by Prince Sihanouk. Most important, now that Gorbachev has withdrawn from Afghanistan and is concentrating on improving Russia's stagnant economy, the Chinese see a much-reduced Soviet threat for some time to come. By the mid-1990s it is therefore conceivable that there will be a border settlement and a substantial mutual withdrawal of both Soviet and Chinese forces from the border.[3]

Although a continuing normalization of Sino-Soviet relations is probable, a return to a 1950s-type alliance seems out of the question. Even the development of an intimate and trusting, much less cooperative, relationship seems highly unlikely. For years to come, China's two major concerns are security and development, and in each area Peking has much more to gain from the West than from the Soviet Union. In the strategic realm, so long as the Soviet Union has the most powerful army on the Eurasian continent, keeps one-third of its total forces in the Far East, maintains a huge Pacific fleet off China's coast, and supplies arms to two of China's adversaries, India and Vietnam, the Chinese will want to maintain stable relations with the West to balance Soviet power. China's view of the United States as a crucial counterweight to the Soviet Union in Asia is implicit in a variety of Chinese writings and explicit in informal conversations with Americans.[4]

Still another constraint on any Sino-Soviet rapprochement will be the continuing geopolitical rivalry between Moscow and Peking in Asia. Geopolitical rivalry between the two great continental land powers is likely to be an enduring feature in the Asia-Pacific region. As a result, the two powers are bound to be wary of each other's policies in several critical regions such as the Korean peninsula, Indochina, and the Indian Ocean. In Indochina, the Chinese are already developing a close military relationship with Thailand in order to balance the Soviet-Vietnamese alliance and have set up a war reserve stockpile on Thai territory. In Korea, which borders on China's strategic province of Manchuria, the Chinese are concerned about growing military ties between Moscow and Pyongyang which allow overflight rights to the Soviets. And in South Asia the Chinese are worried about the Soviet-Indian connection and continuing Soviet pressure on Pakistan.

Moreover, in the long run, a strong China will not reconcile itself to the Soviet domination of Mongolia, a crucial buffer state that the Russians wrenched away from a weakened Chinese empire in the 1920s. Mao raised the question of Mongolia's status with both Stalin and Khrushchev. And the Chinese continue to demand a total Soviet withdrawal from Mongolia, not just a partial withdrawal.

Furthermore, Moscow and Peking maintain deep suspicions about each other's long-range goals. Many Soviet and Chinese analysts see the other country as a long-range adversary now engaged in buying time for strengthening its economy so that it can become a more formidable rival in the next century.

Since the post-Tiananmen Square Chinese crackdown on the democracy movement and the collapse of communist regimes in Eastern Europe, new ideological conflicts have also appeared between Moscow and Peking. The Chinese are accusing Gorbachev of contributing to the collapse of socialist regimes in Eastern Europe and of endangering socialism elsewhere.

Finally, and not least important, despite the downturn in China's relations with the United States and Japan, China's economic relations with the West are almost certainly going to continue to be much more important than its economic relations with the Soviets. China conducts less than 5 percent of its trade with the Russians, whereas its trade with Japan, the United States, and other Pacific countries constitutes about two-thirds of its total trade.[5]

Thus, although the Chinese will probably improve their relations with Moscow during the next few years, it will be normalization without trust or intimacy. The West should not fear such a development. Indeed, if it leads to a general reduction of tension in Asia, such a détente between the two great Asian land powers is in the Western interest.

Gorbachev's greatest single challenge in East Asia will be reaching a modus vivendi with Japan. He wants technological assistance from Japan in order to develop Siberia, and he needs Japan's support if the Soviet Union intends to join the dynamic Pacific economy. Gorbachev has taken a number of small steps to improve relations with Japan. Soviet Foreign Minister Eduard Shevardnadze has resumed regular exchanges with his Japanese counterpart after a lapse of a decade. In contrast to earlier Soviet comments, which dismissed Japan as a stooge of the United States, Soviet media make positive statements about Japan's growing role and importance in global diplomacy. And in contrast to their former rigid and unyielding manner, Soviet diplomats have adopted a new style which the Japanese press refers to as "smile diplomacy."

Even on the territorial issue of the four islands north of Hokkaido, Moscow is displaying new flexibility. While Soviet officials used to say that the issue was closed and there is nothing to talk about, they now concede that a problem exists that needs to be resolved. Moreover, a number of formulas to resolve or to put aside the issue are being considered both in Moscow and in Tokyo. One such formula would be for the Soviets to return the two smaller islands while demilitarizing the other two, pending a final solution of the problem.

Most important, Gorbachev has expressed a desire to visit Japan, the first such visit ever by a Soviet or a Russian leader. To make the visit successful, Gorbachev will display new initiative on the territorial issue.

Both Moscow and Tokyo have strong incentives to compromise. For the Soviets, easing relations with Japan is essential to gaining entrance into the Asian Development Bank and the PECC and to achieving access to Japanese technology, objectives high on Gorbachev's agenda. For its part, Tokyo will not want to be left out of the worldwide rapprochement with the Soviet Union. Moreover, if European and American businesses step up trade with Moscow, the Japanese private sector will also want to do the same.

But even if Gorbachev is able to reach a modus vivendi of sorts with Tokyo, there will be substantial limits to any Soviet-Japanese rapprochement. The first major constraint on Soviet-Japanese relations is Japan's firm alliance with the United States. Although the U.S.-Japanese marriage is troubled by trade imbalances, a divorce between the two countries is unthinkable. The United States and Japan have interests in common to a degree that is probably unparalleled in world history. The United States needs Japanese capital to finance its own industrial renovation; to provide financial and economic assistance to a variety of geopolitically important but unstable Third World countries in which the West as a whole has important strategic stakes; and to maintain a stable and open international system.

Japan, for its part, needs American security protection for the homeland and for its sea lanes of communication; it needs continuing access to the world's largest market, and through cooperation with America, secure access to a stable and expanding world market; and it needs continuing entry into America's vast research establishment that is central to Japan's own technological innovation.[6]

Second, the limitations of the Soviet economy combined with structural changes in the Japanese economy make it unlikely that economic relations between the two countries will improve rapidly. In the 1970s Japan was one of the top three capitalist countries in trade with the Soviet Union. But by 1981, Japan had fallen to fifth among the capitalist nations trading with Moscow. Most Japanese enthusiasm for getting involved in large Siberian development projects has evaporated. Since the 1970s Japan has established a more fuel-efficient production method for its industries and greatly diversified its sources of oil supply. At a time of plentiful oil and relatively low energy prices, the Japanese have lost much of the appetite they once had for exploring Siberian coal and gas reserves. Of several hundred joint ventures the Soviets have signed recently, Japan's share is a meager five.

The third, perhaps most important constraint is a historically rooted legacy of mistrust existing between the two countries that is bound to inhibit any substantial warming of relations. They have been at odds for most of the twentieth century and have yet to sign the peace treaty ending World War II. Japan and the Soviet Union have fought four times in this century, the last in 1945 when the Red Army entered Manchuria, an invasion that the Japanese still regard as a stab in the back which violated the Soviet-Japanese treaty of neutrality of 1941. Moreover, the Soviets kept more than half a million Japanese prisoners in the Soviet gulag, many of whom never returned. As a result of this history, Japanese public opinion polls regularly show that the Soviet Union is the least liked and most distrusted of all foreign countries. Even among the Japanese elite, particularly those of Japan's professional diplomats who are Soviet specialists, dislike of the Soviet Union is deep. It stems in part from the crude and condescending behavior that the Russians displayed toward Japan during the Gromyko era. Thus, the Japanese are perhaps more cautious and skeptical than any country in the Western alliance about the changes in the Soviet Union under Gorbachev.[7]

In Korea, the Soviets are playing a new game designed to have the best of both Koreas. They are increasing their strategic relations with North Korea while demonstrating new flexibility toward South Korea. Since Kim Il-sung's visit to Moscow in 1984, there have been exchanges of naval port calls between the Soviet and North Korean navies, and the Soviet Union has gained overflight rights over North Korean territory. Soviet and North Korean negotiators have met to discuss the extension of broad-gauge railroad tracks from the USSR to the North Korean ports of Najin and Chongjin to facilitate the delivery of military equipment. The Soviets have also supplied Pyongyang with new military hardware, including su-25 ground-attack aircraft, the most effective of their attack planes; mig-29 Fulcrum aircraft, one of the most sophisticated planes in the Soviet arsenal; and sa-5 Gammon surface-to-air missiles along with the advanced Tin Shield early warning radar network, the first time the Tin Shield system has been deployed outside the Soviet Union. All of this contrasts with Moscow's earlier reluctance in the 1970s to supply the volatile North Korean dictator with advanced weapons.

The Soviets are actually pursuing a de facto "two Koreas" policy and Moscow is holding out olive branches to the ROK, too. The Soviets attended the Seoul Olympics in 1988, despite Pyongyang's boycott; in his speech at Krasnoyarsk in October, Gorbachev signaled his intention to expand economic relations with South Korea; and quasi-diplomatic relations have begun with the establishment of the trade offices. Seoul is responding favorably to Soviet overtures. It wants to reduce its excessive trade dependence on the United States and to prod North Korea into negotiation. President Roh Tae Woo has authorized top ROK business leaders to visit Moscow and scout the possibilities for trade, investment, and joint ventures. He has also formally proposed a six-power conference, including the Soviet Union, to help resolve the Korean issue.

Over the longer run, however, Seoul's enthusiasm for its new Moscow connection may wane once South Korean business discovers the realities of commerce in the Soviet Union. South Korea's leading firms are seeking Japanese coparticipation in Siberian joint ventures and receiving only a lukewarm response. Moreover, Seoul may discover that Moscow's influence in North Korea is limited. Finally, since South Korea is surrounded by communist states and its former colonial master, Japan, these geopolitical realities will dictate a continuing South Korean interest in a strong alliance with the United States.

In Southeast Asia the Soviets are also trying to have it both ways by seeking to court ASEAN without jeopardizing their ties to Vietnam. In sharp contrast to their behavior during the Brezhnev era, when Moscow denounced ASEAN as an imperialist block, Foreign Minister Shevardnadze toured Indonesia and Thailand in 1987, the first such visit by a Soviet foreign minister in twenty years. The prime ministers of Malaysia, Australia, and Thailand have all visited Moscow with their foreign ministers, and the presidents of the Philippines and Indonesia are expected. Moscow is also seeking to become a "dialogue partner" of ASEAN, along with the United States, Japan, and the European Economic Community.

But although a more positive image of the Soviet Union is beginning to emerge among the ASEAN countries, as is a growing acknowledgment that the USSR can play a constructive role in the region, acceptance of the Russians is still conditional and not uniform. Indonesia and Malaysia are the most positively disposed toward Moscow, Thailand and the Philippines are becoming more open to relations, and Singapore and Brunei are the most conservative.

Throughout the region, however, there is a historically rooted deep fear of communism. Communist parties are illegal in all the ASEAN countries, where most of the ruling parties fought communist insurgencies for decades. The Philippines is still engaged in a struggle with a serious communist insurgency.

Moreover, continuing concern exists throughout the region over Soviet espionage. For example, when the Thais arrested two Europeans, allegedly spying for the Soviet Union, the Thai National Security Council stated that approximately 50 percent of the eighty-seven Soviet officials in Thailand are disguised intelligence officials who have as their main tasks the recruiting of Thai nationals and the monitoring of American and Chinese activities in Thailand.[8] Fear of subversion and infiltration is even more acute in Indonesia. On one occasion, a Soviet ballet company was refused permission to enter Indonesia because of restrictions imposed by the Indonesian security agencies.

Another factor that will limit Soviet-ASEAN relations is the paucity of trade, although ASEAN leaders have responded favorably to Soviet calls for improved economic relations, and many trade ministers and officials have visited the USSR. Trade conferences and exhibitions also have been organized by the Soviet Union in the ASEAN countries; the volume of trade remains minimal, however. The two main barriers to trade as identified by ASEAN officials are the inconvertibility of the ruble and the unattractiveness of Soviet goods, which have to compete with Japanese and Western products.

Improving its bilateral relations with all the countries of the region is one general Soviet objective in East Asia. Another is to increase Soviet trade with, and involvement in, the dynamic Pacific economy. While most of the Asia-Pacific countries, including China, have become increasingly integrated into the Pacific economy, the Soviet Far East has been isolated from it. Not only has there been a general stagnation of the Soviet economy, but Moscow, because of its past obsession with military secrecy, has also closed off the Soviet Far East, including Vladivostok, the capital of the Maritime Province and the Soviet Union's main naval base in the Pacific. However, the Soviets say that they intend to open Vladivostok and to turn parts of the Soviet Far East into a special economic zone designed to attract foreign investors, joint ventures, and tourists. At a conference in Vladivostok, the Soviets indicated that they wanted to triple their Pacific trade within twelve years, in principle an objective that should not be too difficult to achieve. Soviet trade with the Pacific region amounts to only 6–8 percent of total Soviet trade; of this volume, the largest amount is carried out with other socialist countries such as China, Vietnam, Mongolia, and North Korea. Soviet trade with most of the market economies in the region is minimal and unbalanced. That is, the Soviets import far more than they export because their exports are simply not competitive, either in terms of price or quality. Soviet trade with the ASEAN countries, for example, has declined by half to less than $500 million since the mid-1980s, and only some 20 percent of that tiny trade consists of Soviet exports.

The obstacle to expanded Soviet trade with East Asia is structural. For reasons that stem from the very nature of the command economy, Soviet enterprises do not have much incentive to export. They are not in competition with each other or with foreign companies; they have little interaction with foreign customers or foreign competitors. They have an assured domestic market for their goods, and they do not have the "survival motive" that is so important in the Western market economies because the state makes sure that the Soviet enterprise does not go under.[9] Even if all of these problems were resolved by a dramatic move toward market reforms, Soviet enterprises would have to start producing high-quality, reasonably priced manufactured goods that could compete with Western, Japanese, and other East Asian goods on world markets—an unlikely event in any foreseeable future.

Moreover, despite a good deal of rhetoric about a new economic policy in the Soviet Far East, economic realities dictate that Siberian development will be put on the back burner because of its enormously high cost and difficulty. Any new large increments of investment will almost certainly go into the European regions of the USSR, where the cost of labor is much lower and the infrastructure is more highly developed.[10] The Soviet military desire for continuing to limit Western access to the Soviet Far East will also be an inhibiting factor in opening that vast region up to commerce. At this writing, some three years after Gorbachev first announced his intention to open Vladivostok, that city remains closed.

There will also be severe obstacles to attracting substantial numbers of foreign investors to participate in joint ventures in the Soviet Far East. The Soviets must make conditions for doing business and repatriating profits more attractive and also develop the Far East by putting substantial new investments into roads, railways, and ports. Even if these things are accomplished, foreign companies still must to do business in a Soviet economy that remains notorious for its bureaucratic rigidities, shortages of raw materials, and general inefficiency.

Yet another professed Soviet objective in East Asia is to begin a discussion on regional arms control and reductions. In his speech at Krasnoyarsk, Gorbachev made a seven-point proposal: to freeze the level of nuclear weapons in the region; to invite all naval powers in the region for consultations on freezing naval forces; to have a multilateral discussion on reducing military confrontation in Northeast Asia; to eliminate U.S. military bases in the Philippines in exchange for Soviet withdrawal from Cam Ranh Bay; to discuss ways to prevent incidents in the open sea and in the air space above it; to have an international conference for turning the Indian Ocean into a peace zone; and to develop a negotiating mechanism to examine these and other proposals.

So far, the dominant reaction in the West to Gorbachev's arms control initiatives has been one of skepticism. Two American officials, Richard Armitage and Gaston Sigur, have observed that the Soviet proposals were one-sided. Capping naval force levels, they said, would inhibit Japan from making greater contributions to its own defense. Freezing naval and air deployments in the region, they argue, makes more sense for the Soviet Union, a land-based power, than it does for the United States, a naval power which relies on a strategy of forward deployment. As they point out, "sea lines are to America what railroad lines are to the Soviet Union. We cannot imagine the Soviets agreeing to constrict their own vital arteries."[11] If the Soviets really want to eliminate tensions in Asia, say the American officials, they must reverse the growth in Soviet land, naval, and nuclear forces which threaten Asia. One-third of all Soviet forces are stationed in the Pacific, with particular concentration on the Sino-Soviet border, the Kamchatka Peninsula, and the Sea of Okhotsk.[12]

Some Chinese newspapers are also skeptical about Gorbachev's proposals. They suggest that his proposal was designed to weaken the American naval superiority in the region and to preempt a Japanese naval buildup. The Japanese are even less enthusiastic. They insist that the Soviet Union should adopt a more defensive posture in the Soviet Far East, recognize Japan's legitimate security interest in its alliance with the United States, and move toward some settlement of the territorial dispute if Moscow is really interested in defusing tensions in the region. Japanese officials also point out that arms control is not an end in itself, but merely a means toward achieving stability. In Europe, a German settlement preceded the Helsinki Conference on European security. In Asia, they argue, the first task is not arms control, but an effort to resolve the political conflicts over Korea, Cambodia, and Japan's Northern Territories.[13]

There is a good deal of merit in all of these objections to Gorbachev's proposals. The fact is that the Soviet Union seeks to overcome American naval superiority in the Pacific through naval arms control, but the United States has little incentive to rectify this imbalance in the Pacific. Even in the new global environment, in which there is a substantially reduced Soviet threat, the United States has a vital interest in maintaining a robust naval presence in the Pacific in order to reassure its allies of its credibility and to help maintain regional stability. The United States is under no pressure from any of its friends or allies to reduce its naval presence in the region. On the contrary, as long as the Soviet Union, North Korea, and Vietnam retain huge land armies in Asia, China remains politically unstable, and as long as potential threats remain to Western oil supplies from the Persian Gulf, America's allies will want it to maintain visible naval and air superiority. Nor will the Japanese or Chinese have any interest in freezing naval deployments when they both perceive themselves to be at a great disadvantage to the Soviet Union.

Moreover, many of Gorbachev's arms control proposals are so patently one-sided that they inspire the belief that they are largely intended for propaganda. One example is the proposal to establish nuclear-free zones in Korea, Southeast Asia, and the South Pacific, where American naval forces are stationed, while omitting any mention of the Sea of Okhotsk, the Kamchatka Peninsula, and the Soviet Union's own Maritime Province, where Soviet nuclear forces are stationed. The offer to trade a Soviet withdrawal from Cam Ranh Bay for an American withdrawal from the Philippines is yet another example. American bases in the Philippines are much more important to the geostrategic position of the United States than are the Soviet bases in Cam Ranh Bay to the Soviet position.

Still, an appropriate Western response to Gorbachev's Krasnoyarsk proposals would be to point out precisely why his proposals are one-sided and then suggest some ways that are in everyone's interests to reduce tension in the Pacific.

Although it is appropriate for the West to remain cautious about the concrete proposals that Gorbachev has advanced to reduce tensions in the Pacific, it is not wise to yield the initiative to the Soviet leader as the self-appointed Asian peacemaker. The United States needs to respond with its own agenda for constructing a healthier situation in the Pacific. This should be done not only for reasons of public relations, but also more important, not to miss opportunities to test Gorbachev. The strategic environment is quite favorable for a general reduction of tensions in Asia. By the early 1990s, for the first time in postwar history, a major reduction of tensions between all four of the major powers in the Pacific was taking place. The United States and the Soviet Union, after five summits, an INF accord, and a Soviet withdrawal from Afghanistan, were at the verge of a new détente; Sino-Soviet relations were improving; and Soviet-Japanese relations seemed likely to take a turn for the better.

While major power relations in Asia are improving, prospects are opening for easing regional tensions in Korea and Cambodia. In the Korean case there are two encouraging new factors. First, ROK President Roh Tae Woo is adopting a more flexible policy toward North Korea than any previous South Korean leader has dared. He is wisely encouraging the United States and other Western countries to be more flexible toward Pyongyang in an effort to end North Korea's long isolation. The second promising new development is that both China and the Soviet Union, Pyongyang's two allies, are holding out olive branches to South Korea. In the meantime, the Vietnamese have withdrawn their forces from Cambodia and—despite the resumption of the civil war between the contending Cambodian factions—intense international pressure is evident for a political settlement.

To be sure, there are many uncertainties in the rapidly changing strategic situation in East Asia—not least of which is China's future course—and there will be many barriers toward a more peaceful and stable environment. Suspicions among the powers are strong after forty years of Cold War, several decades of Sino-Soviet hostility, a century of mistrust between Russia and Japan, a colonial relationship between Japan and Korea that left bitter scars, and a long history of Sino-Vietnamese enmity.

Still, the prospects for breakthrough in easing tensions in the region has not been better since the end of World War II, and the unfolding opportunities—particularly the new flexibility in Soviet diplomacy in the region—should be explored.

If a stable post-Cold War world is to be brought into being in Asia, it will be necessary to realize that the situation there is quite different from that in Europe, and that the patterns of accommodation in Europe cannot be mechanically transplated to the Pacific. Whereas there are two multilateral alliance systems in Europe, NATO and the Warsaw Pact, there are no such multilateral security arrangements in the Pacific. Whereas in Europe regional economic integration is far advanced via the European Economic Community and other organizations, in Asia the forces of regional integration are still rather weak. Whereas in Europe it is possible to make arms control trade-offs because of the symmetries in NATO and Warsaw Pact force structures, both of which are largely ground forces, in Asia the asymmetries in the force structure of the United States and the Soviet Union make arms control much more difficult.

To reduce East-West tension in the Pacific, a formula quite different from the one applied in Europe will need to be employed. Several conditions will need to be met. First, the United States and the Soviet Union will need a realistic sense of strategic direction that takes into account the peculiar political, cultural, and geopolitical circumstances of the region. Second, continuing improvement is necessary in bilateral relations between the major powers with intersecting interests: the United States, the Soviet Union, China, and Japan. Third, a radical breakthrough must occur toward a political resolution of the outstanding regional conflicts in Korea and Cambodia and of the territorial dispute between the Soviet Union and Japan. Fourth, continuing progress must be made toward regional cooperation, including the establishment of viable regional institutions. Fifth, continued movement is necessary toward political and social pluralism throughout the region. Finally, a variety of efforts is required to reduce the military confrontation between the superpowers in the region, between China and Vietnam, between North and South Korea, and between the Soviet Union and China.

As far as the superpowers' strategic direction is concerned, it should be recognized that the traditional Soviet approach to Asian security, which envisages the creation of a broad, comprehensive security dialogue modeled on the Helsinki Conference in Europe, is premature. Few countries in Asia have been attracted to Moscow's pan-Asian security proposals, either in their Brezhnevian or Gorbachevian forms. Economic, political, and cultural differences in the region are simply too great to allow for the creation of a broad, collective security system at this time.

A second important reality that must be taken into account is that the U.S. bilateral alliance system in the Pacific, and the U.S. system of forward deployment which supports these alliances, have helped preserve the peace and to stabilize the military, political, and economic environment. Without the stability brought about by the American presence, it is doubtful that the region would have achieved such extraordinary economic and political success in recent decades. Moreover, all of noncommunist Asia, and China as well, continues to look to American naval power as a necessary counterweight to the land-based military potential of the Soviet Union and to the military power of other countries in the region. None of America's allies and friends in Asia are calling for a reduction of the American military presence in the Pacific.[14]

Yet a third crucial reality is that existing military and political status quo in the region strongly favors the United States and is therefore more acceptable to Washington than to Moscow. Unlike the situation in Europe, the United States is under no great pressure from allies in Asia to respond to Gorbachev's various initiatives.

The Soviet Union's unsatisfactory position in Asia is largely attributable to its economic weakness, which inhibits economic interaction with the dynamic market economies of the region, and to unwise policies of the past. To the extent that Gorbachev succeeds in changing these policies—and he has already gone some way in this direction—the Soviet Union will be able to normalize its relationship with most countries of the region.

The single most important way to begin laying the foundations for a more stable system of international relations in the Pacific is not through premature calls for pan-Asian security schemes, but rather by improving bilateral relations among the major powers. There are already many encouraging signs of progress in this direction. For example, the United States and the Soviet Union are making progress on a new START agreement and on conventional and chemical weapons agreements. They are also discussing a variety of other ways to improve their bilateral relations. Soviet relations with China have been normalized, and Soviet-Japanese relations are also improving, as are Chinese-Indian relations. Rajiv Gandhi, the former Indian prime minister, visited China in 1988, the first Indian leader to do so since Nehru went to Peking in 1954.

This improvement in relations among the major powers has been accompanied by a variety of measures to increase transparency and mutual confidence. Soviet and American military leaders are beginning to exchange data and to visit each others' military installations. The Soviet Union has announced its intention to remove twelve divisions from the Chinese border and to withdraw the majority of its forces in Mongolia, while China has already demobilized a million men from its armed forces. A joint Sino-Soviet military-political commission is considering how to implement mutual force reductions along the border.

The revolution in Soviet foreign policy under Gorbachev is an important factor that has led to the improvement of major power relations in East Asia. Several important factors are driving this revolution; the first is tactical, but the other two are more fundamental. The tactical explanation is that Gorbachev inherited from Brezhnev a policy in Asia that was extremely counterproductive. Brezhnev's rigid, U.S.-centered, and overmilitarized foreign policy was leading in the early 1980s to a united front of all the major powers against the Soviet Union. Any post-Brezhnev Soviet leader would have reevaluated Soviet policy in Asia.

Second, and more fundamental, is the fact that as long as Gorbachev's highest priority is to reform and to modernize the stagnant Soviet economy, he will need a peaceful international environment, stable relations with all the Western powers, especially the United States, and arms control agreements that will enable him to justify the drastic reductions in the Soviet military budget that he needs to revitalize the civilian economy. Gorbachev has also come to understand the limits of military power in the modern world and the fact that the very nature of power is changing. In the world of the information revolution, the progress of science and technology, not the expansion of arms and territorial aggrandizement, is the key to power and influence.

There are thus some encouraging trends in the relations among the major powers in East Asia. A strategy designed to develop a more stable and secure structure of international relations in the region should build on these trends.

Two sets of bilateral relations among the major powers need to be improved: Sino-American relations and Soviet-Japanese relations.

Sino-American relations suffered a sharp deterioration after the brutal crushing of the pre-democracy movement in Tiananmen Square in June 1989. As a result of the Tiananmen massacres, the Bush administration imposed a number of sanctions on China, and the U.S. Congress wants to go even further. By sending National Security Advisor Brent Scowcroft to China in December 1989, the Bush administration signaled its interest in preventing a further deterioration in the relationship, and the Chinese leadership made some modest response. Neither side wants to see a further downturn in a relationship built up so painstakingly since the late 1960s and based on a variety of common interests. But the harsh crackdown on the students, the executions and arrests that followed—as well as efforts by the new, hard-line leadership in Peking to restore central control over the economy and to reimpose a more orthodox ideological line—contributed to a negative image of China in the United States. President Bush came under fire from Congress and the media for allegedly kowtowing to China by sending the Scowcroft mission.

China, for its part, blames the West in general and the United States in particular for fostering the democracy movement in China. The

United States is accused of trying to subvert socialism in China and of intervening in China's internal affairs. Complicating the issue is the fact that China is entering a period of political instability. Deng Xiaoping and many other leaders are in their eighties, and a new generation of leaders was not yet in place by the early 1990s. It is questionable whether Deng's heir, Jiang Zemin, would be able to get the support of the military and the party after Deng's demise. More likely is a protracted struggle over power and policy. Under these circumstances, it is difficult to be sanguine about the immediate future of Sino-American relations. Over the longer run, however, the underlying forces for reform in China remain strong, and the common interests that bind the United States and China together are powerful. It is likely, therefore, that these two Great Powers will seek at some point to restore their relationship.

Soviet-Japanese relations remain strained for reasons I have discussed. The difficult heritage of the past cannot be altered; a breakthrough will be possible only if Gorbachev finds some way to resolve the territorial dispute.

In addition to improving relations among the major powers, a second condition for a more stable Pacific is the need to achieve a breakthrough in resolving the outstanding regional conflicts in Korea and Cambodia. The stark facts of life in the Korean peninsula are that more than a million armed men face each other across the narrow waist of the 38th Parallel, and little genuine progress has been made in moving toward a North-South Korean détente. The principal obstacle to peace in Korea is the unreconstructed, Stalinist regime in Pyongyang, which refuses to accept the legitimacy of the government in the South and continues to try to reunify Korea on its own terms. North Korea remains one of the most highly militarized, secretive, and isolated countries in the world, and it is led by a dictator who may not be in touch with reality. Until and unless North Korea moves toward glasnost and perestroika, it seems unlikely that any substantial diminution will occur in tension on the peninsula. Developments in Eastern Europe, where communist party monopolies on power have been overthrown, must be strengthening the North Korean dictator's resolve to take a harder line.

Still, the Great Powers must do what they can to encourage and pressure North Korea to come to an accommodation with Seoul. The immediate objective should be a new dialogue between the Koreas which leads to a substantial drawdown of forces along the 38th Parallel, family reunification, the beginning of trade, and a variety of contacts between Seoul and Pyongyang. A later goal is a peace treaty between the Koreas and the entry of both into the United Nations. In Korea, as in Central Europe, mutual security can be improved by the opposing sides restructuring their armed forces into a mode of "defensive defense," an appropriate form of mutual threat reduction for the peninsula.

In Cambodia, the Great Powers should increase their efforts to arrange a political settlement among the four contending Cambodian factions. There are encouraging developments. The five permanent members of the United Nations Security Council, the United States, the Soviet Union, China, Great Britain and France, meeting in Paris, have agreed on a plan, the core of which is an enhanced role for the United Nations, to bring peace and free elections to Cambodia. It would require that the existing Vietnamese-backed, Hun Sen government surrender the top reaches of the administration to UN officials. A cease-fire, to be policed by the UN, would then come into effect between the Hun Sen regime and the three-party opposition coalition headed by Prince Norodom Sihanouk but militarily dominated by the Khmer Rouge, which has been fighting it. The United Nations would run Cambodia for a year or so, during which it would organize and oversee elections. It would then withdraw, leaving the elected government to rebuild Cambodia.

Such a UN operation will be expensive, but Japan has already promised to underwrite much of the cost. A more serious question is whether China, the principal external supporter of the Khmer Rouge, will be able and willing to strangle the Khmer Rouge's ability to wage war. If the Khmer Rouge go on fighting, the big powers and the United Nations will be forced to muster a real peacekeeping force in Cambodia, not just an election-watching operation.

A third condition for moving toward a more stable Pacific is to foster the development of regional political and economic organizations such as ASEAN, the Asian Development Bank, the Pacific Economic Cooperation Council, and the newly created regional economic organization which brings together most of the market economies in the region.

Once there is a political settlement in Cambodia, Vietnam may be invited to sign the Bali Treaty which led to the creation of ASEAN. Following this, there could be an increase of political and economic relations between Vietnam and the noncommunist countries of Southeast Asia. The prime minister of Thailand has outlined a plan for turning all of Indochina into a market place, and there is a considerable potential for the development of economic relations between Vietnam and the ASEAN countries and between Vietnam and the other market economies of the Pacific Rim.

For some time to come, Pacific economic organizations will be largely confined to the market economies, but the Soviet Union has already become an observer at PECC and ADB meetings and, over time, as the Soviet Union and other socialist countries in the Pacific move toward market reforms, these ties to regional economic organizations can be expanded.

Any stable security structure in the Pacific will also require continuing progress in the region toward political and social pluralism as a political principle respected within each country. The attempts by the new hard-line leadership in China to turn the clock back on reform, and the continuation in Pyongyang of an anachronistic Stalinist regime are incompatible with any genuine progress toward regional security and stability. By the same token, much will depend on the continuation of political and economic reform in the Soviet Union.[15]

Finally, there need to be some efforts to reduce the military confrontation in the region between the United States and the Soviet Union. There is, however, no need for formal arms control negotiations of the type that are taking place in Europe. The severe asymmetries in the military forces of the two sides rule out the approaches of common ceilings or equal percentage reductions that arms control politics almost inevitably demand. The Soviet Union is a land power, while the United States depends upon maritime power, and the military forces of other countries in the region also play an important role.

There are some possibilities for a selective development of confidence-building measures, but these measures should be chosen with care so that they do not benefit one side more than the other. Many of the confidence-building measures proposed so far by the Soviet Union are likely to be counterproductive because many Western analysts consider them self-serving and designed to hamper the access of the United States navy to the Pacific. As a maritime nation, dependent on the seas for its economic health, and with critical alliances across both oceans, the United States will always be reluctant to enter into any agreements that interfere with its navy's freedom of movement.

This does not mean, however, that nothing can be done to reduce the level of military confrontation between the two superpowers in the Pacific. Some reduction of Soviet and U.S. military forces are almost certainly going to be brought about by defense budget constraints on both sides. Some of the existing forums, such as the incidents-at-sea talks between the Soviet Union and the United States (among the most successful of the various Soviet-American dialogues) could be expanded to include China and Japan. All four of the major powers could begin to exchange data on their respective defense budgets and defense plans. High-ranking naval officials from all four countries could enter into regular exchanges to discuss their respective naval doctrines and their future force projections. Military exercises could be reduced and made less provocative, and there could be pre-notification of all naval exercises over a certain size. In addition, because it is in the common interest of all of the major powers to discourage nuclear proliferation and the spread of ballistic missiles and other advanced military technologies in the region, talks might begin on this subject.

It will also be necessary for both the United States and the Soviet Union to reassess their military strategy and their military deployments in the Pacific. On the Soviet side, there could be a substantial reduction in aircraft, which number more than 2,400 and in submarines, which total about 140.

As far as the American side is concerned, if there is a CFE treaty that substantially reduces Soviet forces in Western Europe, and if the East European countries continue to move in the direction of political pluralism, the danger of a Soviet attack on Western Europe will be greatly diminished. As a result, the U.S. strategy of deterring a Soviet attack in Europe by posing a threat of horizontal escalation in the Pacific will lose much of its credibility. The United States will therefore need to develop a strategy in the Pacific that focuses less on the threat from the Soviet Union and more on the multiple threats from other sources that can be expected to continue in the 1990s: threats to secure oil supplies from the Persian Gulf, threats of maritime interdiction, and, above all, threats from several flashpoints which could involve the United States in conflict at lower levels. Any U.S. strategic reassessment in the Pacific should, however, bear in mind that for some time to come a substantial U.S. presence in the Pacific will be necessary, not just to shore up or protect threatened allies but to underpin U.S. political and economic policy.

In sum, security and stability for the two superpowers in the Pacific, as well as for other nations in the region, could be considerably enhanced if these nations progress along six paths. The superpowers in particular need to take realistic account of the particular political, cultural, and geopolitical circumstances of the region. Further improvement is needed in all the bilateral relations involved, and especially in U.S.-Chinese and Soviet-Japanese relations. Resolutions must be found to the serious confrontations in Korea and Cambodia. Progress toward economic and other cooperation within the region needs to continue, as must progress toward political and social pluralism. And finally, efforts are needed to reduce the military confrontations in the region, especially the U.S.-Soviet confrontation. Progress in all these directions is certainly possible and, if made, will produce real grounds for hope that all the nations in the region can enjoy greater security.

Timeo Danaos et dona ferentes.—Virgil

The contemporary discourse of human rights is based on an insurmountable contradiction between political sovereignty and moral absolutism. Sovereign states cannot accept the terms on which the absolutist regime of human rights demands that they be implemented—universality, comprehensiveness, and unconditionality—because bowing to these conditions would undermine state sovereignty and the stability of the international system of states. But because states must speak the language of human rights lest international opprobrium ensue, the human rights discourse of states has all the earmarks of an elaborate theatrical ritual—a complex set of signs, words, and motions that pay ceremonial homage to putative moral commands while concealing less lofty political ambitions and material interests. Although the ritual language of human rights suffuses interstate relations, human rights concerns do not actually inform them, most visibly so when great powers are involved. Quite the contrary, the Soviet-American human rights ritual bears witness to the fact that human rights become bones of contention only as epiphenomenal manifestations of underlying conflictual relations.

The contradiction between states and human rights flows from the "conceptual essence" of both.[1] The concept of human rights is based on that of natural rights, a theologically derived notion that attributes to all human beings, as children of God, certain inalienable prerogatives that precede and transcend the claims of earthly authorities.[2] Regardless of whether or not contemporary understandings of human rights recognize the religious origins of the concept—and for the most part they do not (a reason, perhaps, for the logical incoherence of many human rights debates)—the human rights discourse continues to emphasize the primacy of the sovereign individual over the state.[3] In the world of human rights, human beings possess rights simply by virtue of their being human, not as a result of their involvement in some human association. The world of human rights rejects outright Aristotle's claim that, logically, the political association precedes the individual.[4] Instead, the human rights world reverses the relationship and derives all human associations, political or otherwise, from the sovereign human being, who is sovereign, simply and well-nigh magically, by virtue of being human.

The world of human rights is, and must be, an absolutist world. Somewhat in the manner of Kant's categorical imperative, the world of human rights both arrogates to human beings the exclusive right of determining their own rights and brooks no violation of this claim, as doing so would undermine its ethical and logical foundations.[5] Because the exact content of human rights is less important than the principles of self-generation and absolute obedience on which these rights claim to be based, the first and foremost human right is, quite simply, that only individual humans, alone and unencumbered, are empowered to determine what their rights are.

The world of human rights is absolutist in another sense as well. Like the categorical imperative, it insists that only a universal, comprehensive, and unconditional extension of human rights is consistent with the logic of human rights: that is, *all* human beings must have *all* of the same human rights to the *same* degree. Human rights, if they are truly to be the rights of humans, must be as indivisible, indestructible, and incorruptible as St. Augustine believed the human soul to be.[6] To ascribe any lesser status to human rights is to pay homage to expedience, to demote them from the sovereignty and primacy they demand, and to establish as a first principle some other notion.

This point bears emphasizing because it illuminates the confusion surrounding much of the contemporary human rights debate. Although the partial, marginal, and conditional application of human rights standards obviously benefits the people or peoples concerned, the guiding principle of such particularistic behavior decidedly is not human rights, but compassion, self-interest, or hostility. To claim, in other words, that certain humans deserve to have certain rights is fine, but it is not the pursuit of human rights. Once selectivity comes into play, once one begins to choose between individuals and between nations and to emphasize some rights while neglecting others, then the motivation is no longer respect for human rights, but a—perfectly legitimate—concern for particular individuals, who, naturally, happen to be human.

These nuances notwithstanding, states logically cannot accept an absolutist principle that denies them the sovereignty they demand, both as instruments of coercion and as repositories of absolute authority in some territory. Autonomous or beholden to the ruling class, self-centered or benign, aggressive or pacific, the state as instrument of coercion is logically antithetical to the primacy and inviolability of the individual. State coercion—indeed, coercion of any kind—is incompatible with a view of the world in which human beings are presumed to be totally free agents whose decisions are theirs alone. Coercion represents an unwarranted intrusion into the individual's holy sphere of autonomy. State coercion is the ultimate such intrusion because it emanates not from autonomous individuals presumably exercising their freedom, but from abstract associations that are secondary to human beings.

The state also claims to possess absolute authority in some defined territory. Although human beings claim not territorial sovereignty but personal sovereignty, their pretensions inevitably clash with those of the state. Two or more sovereignties cannot coexist for long if the claimants are states and their opponents. The claims of states and human beings can, and obviously do, coexist because the objects of their claims —here the individual, there the territory—are formally distinct. Nevertheless, tension is unavoidable, as two sets of sovereign claims overlap and a condition of "multiple sovereignty" arises.[7]

The contradiction between the world of the state and the world of human rights is, if anything, only aggravated when more concrete forms of both are investigated. The international documents that form the basis of contemporary human rights interpretations—the United Nations Charter, the Universal Declaration of Human Rights, the International Covenant on Economic, Social, and Cultural Rights, the International Convention on the Elimination of All Forms of Racial Discrimination, and countless others—paint a vision that extends well beyond claims to freedom from coercion and to personal sovereignty. By extending the realm of distinctly human rights to include individual socioeconomic and group rights of self-determination, international documents not only challenge states' claims to coercion and authority, but also obligate them to sacrifice self-interest to philanthropy and self-preservation to nationalism.[8] It is as if a theoretical challenge to sovereignty were not enough: socioeconomic and national rights proceed to undermine actual viability and continued existence. As noble as such extended human rights sentiments may be, they place the state that pretends to share them into a serious *and* hopeless predicament.

It makes little difference what kind of state is involved. The degree to which the claims of human rights subvert states is virtually identical, regardless of whether states are as different as, say, the Marxian, Rousseauian, Hobbesian, or Lockeian. The Marxist image of the state as a dictatorship of the ruling class clearly rules out any consideration for the human rights of the ruled.[9] Rousseau's normative vision of a social contract that expresses equally the rights of individuals and of the community reveals its hostility to human rights by purporting to possess the right to force individuals to be free. Such coercion, however well-intentioned, is incompatible with the human rights vision of sovereign human beings.[10] The Hobbesian state—the most autonomous and self-centered of all the varieties under discussion—is least concerned with the panorama of rights that claim to be human. Once protection and preservation are guaranteed, the Hobbesian state admits of no further responsibilities with respect to its subjects.[11] Contrary to one's expectations, the Lockeian state fares no better than its counterparts. Although its contract with the citizenry appears to mitigate the extent of their differences regarding coercion and sovereignty, such harmony ensues at the cost of ignoring the state's putative socioeconomic obligations. By tolerating the institution of private property, indeed, by making private property the raison d'être of its foundation, the Lockeian state can but tolerate resulting socioeconomic inequalities. Indeed, as such inequities are largely outside its domain, the Lockeian state can, without undermining its own character, at best take only partial measures to alleviate them.[12]

Group rights, as embodied in the right of nations to self-determination, are equally problematic for all four types of states. The Marxian state's class character results in disregard for, if not hostility to, the aspirations of ethnic groups. The Rousseauian state rejects all particularistic associations that disturb the delicate mechanism of the General Will. The Hobbesian state cannot rightfully be challenged for not recognizing such pretensions on the part of its subjects as long as it fulfills its primary task, protection. Nations might fare somewhat better in a Lockeian setup, as they could arguably claim that life, liberty, and their possessions—the three things Locke subsumed under the concept of property—were being violated by the state and, thus, that they were justified in annulling the social contract and seeking a new sovereign. Yet here, too, a conunudrum exists. On the one hand, a minority is unlikely to sign a social contract if it does not believe that the resulting political arrangement will be favorable to its ends. On the other hand, if it comes to view the sovereign as tyrannical *after* having joined the community, its minority status is a sure guarantee of its incapacity to go against the wishes of the majority and break away. Appeals to heaven, no matter how insistent and loud, are unlikely to help.[13]

In theory, therefore, states and human rights are logically incompatible institutions. To make this argument is not to suggest that states must, or can only, be crass violators of human rights. Although states need not, and in fact do not, act in so vicious a manner, they can pursue what is at best the partial, marginal, and conditional application of human rights—which is to say that states do not and cannot interpret human rights in the manner that human rights demand to be understood, as a comprehensive, universally applicable, and rigorously unconditional first principle.[14] Of course, to recognize states' innate reluctance to pursue human rights in good faith is no reason for despair. A neorealist perspective on international behavior should lead the tiny band of genuine defenders of human rights to the sobering conclusion that their struggle is bound to be difficult and that, even though complete success is impossible as long as states exist, progress can be made if norms of behavior are forced upon states. Naturally, this is a tall order for such potential human rights constituencies as idealistic leaders, nongovernmental organizations, and popular movements, yet history suggests that states are not as immune to pressures from within or from without as their claims would have us believe.

Although the proposition that all states are in conflict with human rights may be persuasive in light of the competing sovereignties involved, not all states and not all types of states are completely or equally impervious to demands for human rights. At least four factors account for the variation in state behavior with respect to human rights. The first, which is intrinsic to all states, even those that are most open to influence from civil society, is their relative autonomy as political organizations presiding over territorially bounded populations.[15] To some degree independent of dominant economic, ethnic, and other social interests, states can and do adopt policies whose intent is neither the oppression of the masses, nor the dictatorship of the bourgeoisie. States also pursue their own interests; in so doing, they frequently adopt stances and implement policies that appeal to key constituencies at home and abroad, marshall their support, and thereby enhance state reserves of legitimacy and stability. Human rights are tailor-made for such purposes, and it is no surprise that all types of states, from dictatorships to democracies, resort to such slogans, appeals, and rallying cries.

Leaders are the second factor. Despite certain differences, all contemporary states have some type of leader at their helm, and leaders, regardless of the set ways of state bureaucracies, do make a difference in the behavior of states.[16] Just as weak and vacillating leaders can help destabilize their own states, so, too, strong, willful, or charismatic leaders can radically, if perhaps only temporarily, affect state policies as well as state relations with society, economy, and the world. Naturally, the appropriate circumstances must be on hand for the message to be heard and acted upon, but if they are, then such idealistic leaders as, say, Jimmy Carter—and charismatic ones, such as, perhaps, Mikhail

Gorbachev—can impose at least a semblance of a human rights commitment on states. By the same token, leaders can reverse such a course,
an action that is eminently easier in light of the state's "innate" reluctance to meddle with moral absolutism.

The third factor, one that probably accounts for the most variation
among types of states, is the vitality of civil society.[17] Of all states, it is
the Lockeian that confronts the strongest civil society and is therefore
most susceptible to penetration by societal forces. In contrast, Marx's
state rejects civil society as a bourgeois creation, Rousseau's sees in it
an obstacle to the formation of a genuine General Will, while Hobbes's
claims to be responsible for its very emergence. Only the Lockeian state,
or, in everyday terms, the democratic state, is signatory to a contract
with, and therefore formally recognizes, a more or less equal and organized societal partner. No wonder, then, that Lockeian citizens can make
a relatively large input into the workings of the state. If organized, committed, and resourceful, such citizens can even pressure the Lockeian
state into making concessions on issues they deem important. One
such contemporary issue, clearly, is what passes for human rights. Popular movements and nongovernmental organizations use human rights
terminology for their own causes—most of which rarely involve a genuine commitment to the rights of humans—and Lockeian states frequently act against their own best judgment by succumbing to these
groups' irresistible incantations.

The final intervening variable is the direct and indirect influence
of other states, acting alone or in concert. Hegemons, alliances, and
international or regional organizations often attempt to impose their
preferences on other states as the price for continued support or for
diminished hostility. States act in this manner, not, as I suggested above,
out of a genuine concern for human rights, but because powerful constituencies or influential leaders compel them or because it is in their
interest to do so. Accusations of human rights violations serve state
interests if they cause adversaries to lose face internationally or undermine their legitimacy with elites at home. Confronted with such assaults, weaker states may actually alter their behavior; equals, on the
other hand, generally lash out with their own, equally self-interested,
counteraccusations. In both instances, human rights serve as weapons,
but—and this point is crucial—only as those of a tactical kind. In
normal circumstances states will not launch massive human rights'
strikes—universally, comprehensively, and rigorously unconditional
charges—because such strategic assaults could result in their own
delegitimation as well as destabilization of the international system of
states.

Because states regard human rights as purely tactical weapons, the pursuit by states of human rights becomes, to extend von Clausewitz's insight, the continuation of politics by other means. But this proposition suggests that, barring the intervention of such variables as powerful interest groups or leaders, human rights rattling will be employed only if states are already in conflict, and not if they are inclined to cooperate. That is, states will highlight human rights violations only if violator states are adversaries; conversely, allies will tend to remove human rights from their joint agendas. And, indeed, this conclusion tallies with the behavior of real states. Western democracies generally find fault only with socialist and certain Third World countries—and vice-versa—although the democratic record on the full panorama of human rights, like that of their adversaries, is hardly above reproach. By the same token, human rights are of slight importance to intra-Western or intra-socialist relations. American criticism of the Shah of Iran or of Anastasio Somoza was due largely to President Carter's initiative and is, thus, the exception that proves the rule.

Human rights rattling is useful in international conflicts only because the language of human rights currently exerts a hegemonic influence on international discourse. We sense that this must be so, not so much because a myriad of international human rights covenants have been signed, as because even dictators now claim to be ardent defenders of human rights. That human rights have come to dominate the language of states is clearly attributable to far more than President Carter's personal commitment to the cause. Rather, the human rights zeitgeist appears to be the product of two concomitant processes: the growing modernization of the world's population and the "crisis" of the modern state.[18] Popular education, widespread professionalization, and individual self-assertion have combined with the state's growing incapacity to execute properly its assumed functions in the economic, social, cultural, environmental, and virtually all other spheres to produce citizen demands for greater individual autonomy and reduced state interference. Not surprisingly, modernized elites, as best typified by East European and Soviet dissenters and the supporters of Amnesty International and the American Civil Liberties Union, are in the forefront of human rights struggle. It is surely testimony to their scientific, intellectual, and cultural indispensability to the modern world that the language of human rights, which above all is their language, has come to permeate the language of interstate relations. Indeed, support for human rights has become de rigeur for all states.

It is in the conflict between the raison d'être of states and the demands of modern society that we find the origins of the human rights ritual. Although necessarily regarded by states only as tactical weapons without strategic value, human rights are—and, indeed, must be —touted as a strategic goal, the alpha and omega of international relations. States cannot act otherwise, because to avoid raising human rights to the level of a categorical imperative is to challenge a hegemonic discourse and all its associated symbols, images, and meanings and, thus, to ostracize oneself from the international community of self-styled humanitarian states. The contradiction between the actual tactical utility of human rights and their stridently proclaimed strategic indispensability gives rise to ceremonial behavior that closely resembles political ritual. As in the nineteenth-century Balinese theater-state, the *Negara*, political rituals, of which human rights are an excellent contemporary example, are the form that political relations assume once their material underpinnings are mediated by a complex set of what are claimed to be obligatory norms, values, and beliefs.[19] Political rituals, like all rituals, structure behavior, but they do not cause it: they provide a stage for the acting out of preexisting tendencies to conflict or cooperation.

The human rights discourse of states thus represents an acting out of human rights disagreements. The human rights discourse is, in a word, grand theater: the actors play assigned roles and mouth preset phrases, the plot is known to all, and the denouement represents both the end of one play and the beginning of another. Like all theater, human rights theater revolves about a conflictual relationship between the leading characters. But, unlike real theater, the conflictual relationship at the center of human rights theater has its origins in real, extra-theatrical relationships. The very real adversarial relationship between the United States and the Soviet Union, for example, inevitably casts the two sides as protagonist and antagonist on the human rights stage. The nature of the parts played by both actors is, thus, a function less of a genuine human rights plot than of the political, economic, and social pressures that surround the staging of any theatrical work.

The nature of the human rights ritual is especially evident in the human rights tug-and-pull between the United States and the Soviet Union, as their status as superpowers impels them to act as paragons of virtue on the one hand and to be particularly sensitive to the distinction between tactical ploys and strategic assaults on the other. Significantly, the human rights debate between the United States and the Soviet Union did not get under way until the middle of the 1970s. For more than thirty years, neither side was overly enthusiastic about the documents both had been signing on a regular basis since the end of World War II. Both paid scant attention to human rights in their respective spheres of influence, and both used a different language in criticizing aspects of the other's political and social system.

Things changed in the 1970s. The Soviet dissident movement, the American civil rights movement, Western Jewish groups, nongovernmental organizations such as Amnesty International, and, ultimately, states themselves appropriated human rights terminology and transformed human rights records into touchstones of state legitimacy. The Great Human Rights Debate began with a vengeance during the Carter administration, but, ironically although not surprisingly, the nature of human rights criticisms was reflective of the self-perceptions and self-interests of both sides. Both the United States and the Soviet Union generally exercised the kind of criticism to which they perceived themselves as being immune, and both sides were selective even within the narrow confines of the criticism they expressed.

American criticism of the USSR, for example, was typically focused on violations of civil and political rights, in particular the rights to free speech, press, and assembly. Washington's charges rarely extended to economic and social violations, because the USSR was perceived as standing on somewhat firmer ground in this respect. In addition, placing these issues on the agenda could expose the United States to criticism of its less than exemplary record on unemployment, urban blight, and the like, as well as violate the American government's determination not to trespass on the rights and duties of private enterprise. No less surprisingly, the right of nations to self-determination seldom found a place on Washington's list of human rights criticisms—although it figured highly in the anticommunist rhetoric of the 1950s and early 1960s[20]—inasmuch as America's own ethnic problems and the perceived undesirability of dismembering a superpower militated against so destabilizing a rallying cry. Conversely, the Soviet Union generally downplayed civil and political rights, while emphasizing the priority of socioeconomic ones—areas in which it felt weak and strong, respectively. Moreover, the Soviets were far more inclined to invoke national self-determination, both with respect to the United States and other countries of the world, on the rationale that their own formally federal solution to the national question represented a theoretical model for other countries to emulate. Whether this was in fact the case, which it obviously was not, is of course besides the point.

Even within this circumscribed vision of what human rights entail, the United States was decidedly selective in its choice of human beings whose rights it claimed had been violated. The American penchant was for championing those dissidents that the media had transformed into stars, such as Aleksandr Solzhenitsyn, Andrei Sakharov, or Anatoly Shcharansky. Lesser dissidents, or those living outside Moscow, generally did not receive the attention that they, as human beings, would have been entitled to by a genuine commitment to human rights. To be sure, Washington's actions did improve the lot of many repressed individuals. Nevertheless, by focusing attention on individuals, the United States sent the Soviets the unmistakable signal that selective leniency, and not systemic change, would suffice to alleviate American concern, as indeed it usually did.

By the same token, American—or, for that matter, West German —concern for freedom of movement had little in common with human rights, and far more with the importance of catering to domestic imperatives. Not just Soviet Jews and Germans wished to emigrate from the USSR, yet only they received the undivided attention of Washington and Bonn. A genuine concern for freedom of emigration would have extended to all of the USSR's 285 million inhabitants and the more than one hundred nationalities they represent. As states appeared to realize, however, such a commitment would have required a revolutionary transformation of the Soviet system while resulting in the inundation of the West by Soviet immigrants. Understandably, few of the USSR's international adversaries were ready for so radical a course before Gorbachev made the issue moot.

It is no tribute to the Soviets that their human rights behavior was somewhat more consistent than that of the United States. Lacking both a popular domestic constituency vitally interested in a certain interpretation of human rights in the United States and a target group—an American counterpart to the dissident movement—willing to listen to Soviet appeals, Moscow lacked the opportunity to particularize and personalize its own socioeconomically oriented human rights message. In addition, the Soviet focus on socioeconomic rights lent itself far more easily to the sort of generalizations that a genuine human rights commitment demands. Inflation, unemployment, racism, and other social ills can be persuasively represented as capitalism's assaults on working people as a whole, whereas political repression, unless on a mass scale, is inevitably tied to personal fates.

Since Gorbachev's accession to power in 1985, the Soviet and American approaches to the human rights ritual have undergone an interesting, although not unexpected, evolution. Not surprisingly, emigration and self-determination, the two human rights that threaten the sovereignty of states most directly, figured as the central issues. Wishing to establish closer economic and political relations with the West, Gorbachev acquiesced in Western human rights demands and loosened travel and emigration restrictions, particularly for Soviet Jews and Germans. The American reaction was consistent with the epiphenomenal nature of human rights theater: Washington responded by placing immigration quotas on Jews while ignoring the momentous implications of Gorbachev's move for other non-Russians wishing to exercise their right to freedom of movement.

The right of nations to self-determination became an issue after glasnost, democratization, and the decentralizing economic logic of perestroika provided an opening for non-Russian national aspirations. The Baltic republics responded immediately by acting as the sovereign states they aspired to be; they particularized a universal principle and argued that their unique status entitled them to secede from the USSR. Lithuania took the argument to its logical conclusion and declared independence in early 1990. In turn, the United States, which has refused to recognize the Soviet incorporation of the Baltic states since 1940, greeted this opportunity to advance so important a component of its own human rights agenda with an awkward amalgam of silence, fear, and embarrassment. Although Washington encouraged Moscow not to respond to the Lithuanian crisis with force, American concern rang hollow in light of the fact that the rejection of force posed no obstacle to Moscow's determination to smother Lithuania with the troops already stationed in the republic. Once again, the human rights discourse was exposed as ritual—as so much window dressing behind which a concern for stability and order could hide.

The United States was not alone in abandoning human rights when its own interests were at stake. West Germany's ritual incantation of the human rights of genuinely oppressed East Germans was put to the critical test in late 1989 and, not unexpectedly, it too, failed. Freedom of emigration was a compelling slogan as long as East Germans actually could not threaten West Germany's living standards. Reunification was imperative as long as there was no chance of reunification. As soon as the Berlin Wall was breached, however, and these impossibilities became certainties, West Germany began speaking the language of stability and prosperity. The strategic pretensions of human rights collapsed, while the principle of their tactical utility asserted itself with a vengeance.

The most notable aspect of the human rights ritual between the United States and the Soviet Union is that it betokens both superpowers' appropriation of the language of the contemporary zeitgeist. Consequently, human rights will remain a source of dramatic tension between the United States and the Soviet Union as long as their relationship remains adversarial and human rights continue to exert a hegemonic influence on contemporary political discourse. The latter condition is likely either to remain unchanged or to intensify in the foreseeable future. Gorbachev's human rights offensive, Western agreement to hold a human rights conference in Moscow in 1991, and the ignominious collapse of East European communist dictatorships should see to that. The prospects for diminished superpower rivalry, on the other hand, are more mixed than the warming in Soviet-American relations would suggest.

Ideologically, a rapprochement of sorts appears to have taken place, with American policymakers abandoning evil-empire terminology and their Soviet counterparts discarding the so-called class approach to international relations. On closer inspection, however, it seems clear that Soviet concessions have been more far-reaching. The USSR's ideological mea culpas are especially striking in contrast to the emerging American sense of ideological and cultural superiority, smugness, and self-righteousness. At some point—and on the assumption that the USSR survives its nationality unrest more or less intact—a Soviet backlash is inevitable. Self-flagellation will cease when Moscow realizes that the ideological legitimacy it derives from its necessary self-identity as some kind of socialist state is being undermined. A return to Brezhnevite rhetoric is highly unlikely, but a hardening of ideological positions is not.

Strategically, the Soviet-American relationship portends a number of uncertainties. Soviet acquiescence in the upheavals in Eastern Europe, Gorbachev's announcement of unilateral cuts in the USSR's armed forces, the signing of the Intermediate Nuclear Force agreement, the Soviet withdrawal from Afghanistan, and many other encouraging developments portend what a variety of analysts, in this volume and elsewhere, suggest is the end of the cold war.[21] Viewed more skeptically, however, these moves may only have eliminated several unnecessarily provocative elements from an inherently adversarial Great Power relationship. Soviet decline to regional superpower status—or, conversely, American adoption of neo-isolationism[22]—might change the equation permanently, but, for the time being at least, the dynamics of great-power relations in an anarchic world should suffice for the Soviet-American relationship to remain inherently contentious. There are more than enough actual and potential problems between the two sides to assure friction for years to come, especially if, say, any of the following not implausible scenarios comes to pass: the West's infatuation with Gorbachev becomes tempered with the realization that the USSR is still, at best, an enlightened dictatorship; Gorbachev is overthrown or retreats from perestroika; economic decline and political turmoil destabilize the newly established democracies of Eastern Europe; non-Russian declarations of independence provoke a violent reaction on the part of Moscow; or chaos, perhaps even civil war, descends on the USSR. As the wise Murphy reminds us, this list of contingencies is hardly exhaustive.

It seems reasonable to suggest that the hegemony of human rights and the adversarial nature of Soviet-American relations will, despite fluctuations, continue more or less unchanged, and that both the United States and the Soviet Union will continue to employ human rights as tactical weapons while proclaiming their unconditional devotion to a vision of the world in which humanity, and not states, is sovereign. Indeed, the ritualistic invocation of the human rights gods may intensify if, as I suggested above, the human rights zeitgeist comes to dominate international discourse completely. In that case, even if the strategic component improves markedly, the play will not end, but become more intricate and more reflective of the high-stakes symbolism involved.

Ironically, Soviet willingness, under the impact of glasnost and perestroika, to adopt Western views of human rights will not change the validity of this proposition. Soviet scholars and politicians now speak of the centrality of the individual, of the validity of universal truths earlier lambasted for being mere bourgeois abstractions, and of the necessity to transform the Soviet state into a *Rechtstaat* based on a clear delineation of the rights and obligations of both citizens and state. Although a healthy dose of skepticism may still be in order, such talk seems to herald the USSR's possible transformation from some variant of a Hobbesian state into a weak approximation of a Lockeian one.

For all their promise, it would be incorrect to think that such welcome changes will draw the curtain on human rights theater. Far more likely, the plot will thicken and ritualistic conflict will intensify. The United States and the Soviet Union used to be engaged in monologs, as the targets of their criticism were so different. If both actors claim to stand for the same kind of justice, if their overall relationship remains adversarial, and if the hegemony of human rights continues, their ostensible human rights disagreements will not diminish, but sharpen. Two contenders for the same prize, two prima donnas, are far more likely to indulge in self-righteousness and critical excess than aspirants to different crowns. In this sense, although Stalin was wrong about the intensification of class struggle, his general maxim may be appropriate for the human rights debate.

Complicating the matter even more is the growing conviction on the party of virtually all sectors of the American elite that the American way of life has triumphed and that socialism is a relic of the past. Such hubris, together with the adoption by the Soviets of certain elements of the American value system and their likely eventual reassertion of pride in socialism, should raise the symbolic stakes of human rights acting and incline both superpowers to aspire to the leading part in the play. In circumstances such as these, the United States will manage to find any number of human rights violations in the Soviet Union, even if—mirabile dictu—Moscow never again arrests political dissenters and opens the country's doors to all Jews. Neutrality, not to mention cooperation, simply is not in the script for great-power contenders in a still-anarchic world.

In the final analysis, human rights theater will remain a spectacle that diverts attention from the Great Power realities that mold the adversarial relationship between the United States and the Soviet Union. And as theater, the human rights ritual can serve a useful function—that of compelling both states to act as if they were committed to humanitarian goals, a fact of no small importance to the lives of many people. Ironically, however, the human rights ritual can retain so beneficent a function only as long as it remains theater. If, under the pressure of idealistic leaders, nongovernmental organizations, and popular constituencies, human rights were to be converted into political programs, the consequences for both states and persecuted individuals and groups would be catastrophic.

Because human rights brook no compromise and demand, not partial measures, but wholesale systemic change, the politicization of human rights would subvert international diplomacy, result in a hardening of positions, reduce the likelihood of interstate détente, and worsen the plight of those whose human rights truly are being violated.[23] The dilemma is tragic, yet inescapable in a world of sovereign states and autonomous human beings. Perhaps, as some might suggest, the solution to the human rights problem is the abolition of the international state system. True or not, as long as states exist—and they are likely to be around for a long time to come—human rights and states will be in direct opposition to each other. And, for better or for worse, the dilemma is unlikely to be resolved in favor of human rights as long as states have more divisions than Amnesty International.

# CHAPTER 12

# THE UN REDISCOVERED: SOVIET AND AMERICAN POLICY IN THE UNITED NATIONS OF THE 1990s
Toby Trister Gati

The Soviets have a new image and a new policy at the United Nations. After forty years of minimal political and financial support, Soviet policymakers have begun to involve the United Nations in conflict resolution from Angola to Afghanistan, called for international verification to monitor disarmament agreements, and proposed new regimes to coordinate the activities of the world community in such diverse areas as the environment, human rights, and terrorism. They have put forward proposals to expand the jurisdiction of the World Court in certain situations, said they would accept international standards as the benchmark for domestic legislation in such sensitive areas as human rights and emigration, and proposed that decisions of the General Assembly be based on consensus rather than voting. As a sign that the rest of the world should take their newfound faith in the United Nations seriously, the Soviets have even agreed to pay approximately $200 million in arrears to the United Nations, including back payments for peacekeeping activities from the mid-1960s.

Whatever the goal and merit of each of these new Soviet proposals, together they present an opportunity for both the United Nations and the United States to close a particularly unproductive chapter in postwar history. The Cold War survived at the United Nations long after East-West relations began to thaw in the 1970s, with the United States and the Soviet Union voting on the opposite side of most issues on the UN agenda. Consultations aimed at improving U.S.-Soviet relations at the United Nations were rare until Moscow signaled a change in policy in mid-1987.

That the Soviet Union intends to use the United Nations to further its political and arms control objectives, rather than just score points with the Third World or isolate the United States, as in the past, is an encouraging sign. It is now possible to talk to Moscow about a strengthened UN, one actively involved in peacekeeping and peacemaking, the environment, arms control, human rights, and development.[1] Because talking is the United Nation's business, what the Russians say does matter; whether there will be progress on any of these issues, however, depends on how words are translated into deeds.

Much also depends on the priorities of U.S. policy and how the United States responds to the new Soviet activism. American policy at the United Nations during the Reagan administration was first uninterested in and then highly skeptical of the transformed world organization General Secretary Mikhail Gorbachev described in his statements on the United Nations in 1987 and 1988. The "new" Soviet diplomacy at the United Nations represented such a rapid turnabout from the previous four decades of confrontation that the United States (and it was not alone) could not accept the change as real. America's priorities at the United Nations in the 1980s were framed largely in reaction to Third World excesses of the 1970s—excesses in budget, in staffing, and in anti-Western rhetoric. There was praise for an ideal world body—a nonpolitical, high-minded group of states devoted to ameliorating international conflict and developing global cooperation—that some would say never existed. This image highlighted even more starkly in the public's mind the contrast between the organization's potential and its poor performance.

Both the tone and the substance of American policy began to change under George Bush, as a new team took over and cooperation with the Soviet Union on specific regional issues began to bear fruit. International organizations have attracted generally positive comments from President Bush. The first guest for dinner at the White House after his inauguration in January 1989 was UN Secretary-General Javier Pérez de Cuéllar, with whom Bush has had a good personal relationship. And the president has followed through on his promise to include payment of back dues in each of his budget requests to Congress.

As a result of changes of both sides, the United Nations has gotten a second lease on life. It plays a more important role in regional conflicts than at any time in its history, and both superpowers are more comfortable dealing with each other at the United Nations than at any time in recent memory. At the 44th General Assembly, an unprecedented joint resolution was submitted by the Americans and Soviets calling for a reinvigorated UN, but it is still a second-order priority for both sides. The U.S. Congress has yet to appropriate the money to pay arrearages (totaling more than $500 million), and those in charge of UN policy are uncomfortable about expanding the UN's role in areas like environment, international law, and economic development. The Soviet Union, for its part, has yet to participate in or pay for many of the UN development programs, the General Agreement on Tariffs and Trades (GATT), the International Monetary Fund (IMF), and the World Bank, among others.

Whether the new spirit can be translated into changes in U.S. and Soviet policies—and whether the United Nations itself can seize the new opportunities before it—will determine the degree and success of UN involvement in regional issues, global problems, and North-South relations in the 1990s.

What are the key elements of the Soviets' UN strategy, and how does it fit into the new political thinking? What role does the USSR envision for the United Nations? And, finally, what opportunities and challenges does the new Soviet policy present for the United States?

## Soviet Policy at the UN

Soviet leaders have often said that the United Nations was important to their foreign policy, but in the past they rarely if ever used it for constructive diplomacy.[2] Rather, it served primarily as a public soapbox to explain or defend Soviet policy, or as a bully pulpit to castigate "imperialist" designs. The disarmament initiatives proposed there (a resolution renouncing the use of force in international affairs, a no-first-use pledge for nuclear weapons, or a call for a world disarmament conference) attracted little attention outside what was the socialist community, although they invariably passed by large margins in the General Assembly. Soviet participation in the economic and development activities of the United Nations remained minimal except for strongly worded support for Third World redistributive schemes addressed to the developed Western states. Moscow always voted with the majority on issues relating to South Africa and the Middle East, including the notorious "Zionism Is Racism" resolution in 1975.

Unable to prevent the General Assembly from adopting resolutions critical of the USSR for the 1979 invasion of Afghanistan and support for the Vietnamese occupation of Cambodia, Moscow sought to downplay their significance by attributing their passage to Western pressure for nonaligned votes. Soviet diplomats also spent a great deal of time and effort keeping Soviet human rights violations off the agenda, to place Soviet nationals in key secretariat positions, and to keep budget growth in line. Never did they sway from their rigid interpretation of the inviolability of the Charter, the "special responsibilities" of Security Council members for preserving the peace, and the sanctity of the veto.

Soviet experience with an activist secretary-general during the 1960s had both political and financial repercussions on their UN policy. After the Congo peacekeeping force, the Security Council authorized fewer and fewer peacekeeping operations, and those that it did were controlled more strictly by the council at Soviet insistence and given a shorter mandate.[3] Moscow's refusal to pay assessed contributions for the Congo operations caused a financial crisis that almost paralyzed the organization. It has proven impossible to agree on rules and procedures in advance for peacekeeping operations authorized by the council or to agree upon a uniform method for financing peacekeeping.

During the 1970s, Soviet strategy at the United Nations took advantage of the growing hostility between the industrialized West and the developing South. Although the Soviet Union never assigned a high priority to the economic side of the UN's work or gave financial support to its development efforts, the USSR encouraged politicization of the economic and functional bodies and offered rhetorical support to the demands of radical Third World countries for a New International Economic Order (NIEO). This enabled the USSR to present itself as the "natural ally" of the Third World without having to pay any of the bills.

In the early 1980s Moscow shifted its focus and turned to the United Nations as a forum for advancing its global disarmament agenda, first and foremost for heightening international concern about the risk of nuclear war. Each vote on disarmament was touted as a referendum on Soviet and American policies, one in which solid majorities of the world community almost always sided with the USSR. At the 1980 Nuclear Proliferation Treaty (NPT) Review Conference, for example, the Soviet Union strongly criticized the United States for failure to negotiate in good faith on nuclear arms reductions under Article VI of the NPT treaty, even as Moscow asked other states that had earlier used this as an excuse for not signing the treaty to ratify it now.

Soviet attitudes and policies began to change under the impact of three disparate events, each traumatic for Soviet foreign policy in its own way and each reinforcing the sense among at least part of the leadership that something was fundamentally wrong with the way policy was carried out: growing international criticism of the invasion of Afghanistan, the shooting down of the Korean airliner over Soviet airspace, and the nuclear accident at Chernobyl. The changing nature of Soviet-American relations and a changeover in Foreign Ministry personnel also contributed to the reassessment.

It is unlikely that the Soviet Union anticipated the persistence or cohesion of the nonaligned and Islamic groups' opposition to the presence of "foreign troops" in Afghanistan. Year after year, the number of states registering disapproval of the invasion grew, providing several weeks each year of embarrassing public debates at the United Nations and deflecting attention from other regional issues high on the Soviet agenda. Perhaps to defuse Third World (particularly Islamic) criticisms, perhaps to undercut outside support for the resistance, the Soviet Union agreed to the appointment of a personal representative of the secretary-general to discuss the question of Afghanistan in early 1981. Although few believed in the beginning that the prospects for withdrawal were promising, the experience of the proximity talks seems to have left Moscow with a more positive assessment of UN mediation efforts. When the first personal representative, Pérez de Cuéllar, became secretary-general in January 1982, there was for the first time in many years a man at the helm whom Soviet diplomats had come to know and trust, one who understood the limits of Soviet flexibility. The Geneva accords, signed in April 1987, could therefore build on the UN's earlier diplomatic effort. Because the Soviets completed their withdrawal in February 1989, UN observers and refugee relief workers are playing an increasingly important role in the reconstruction of Afghanistan. By mid-1989, more than $992 million had been pledged to aid the UN reconstruction effort in Afghanistan; the USSR provided 400 million rubles ($600 million at the then-official exchange rate). The United States has resisted any role for the United Nations in forming a new government for Afghanistan, despite Gorbachev's request in December 1988 that the UN place a peacekeeping force in Afghanistan.

After the shooting down of a Korean civilian airliner in September 1983, the International Civil Aviation Organization (ICAO) was called into extraordinary session at the request of South Korea and Canada. In a highly public and political manner, the United States proposed a resolution (seconded by the Japanese) condemning the use of armed force against civilian aircraft and the Soviet noncooperation with the search and rescue operations and subsequent ICAO investigation. Only after this resolution passed and the heat was off the Soviet Union did the Soviets give ICAO the green light to begin the quiet international negotiations necessary to strengthen air communications in the Pacific air corridors. At this second stage, the Soviets worked closely with the United States and Japan to ensure that such an event would not reoccur.

After the nuclear accident at Chernobyl in April 1986, the International Atomic Energy Agency (IAEA) was the center of Soviet diplomacy aimed at recouping the bad publicity engendered by the initial policy of denial and subsequent delay in providing surrounding states and Soviet diplomats abroad with relevant information on the extent of damage caused by radioactive contamination. By inviting the IAEA director general and an international team to the site, by providing an unexpectedly detailed account of the consequences, if not the causes, of the accident to a special session of the IAEA in September, and by becoming one of the first states to sign and ratify two new international conventions dealing with early notification and assistance in the event of a nuclear accident, the USSR attempted to gain the initiative and a new international image. At the same time, the USSR took the lead in setting the agenda on nuclear safety for the practical follow-up work of the agency to the applause of the international community.

Improved relations with the United States, particularly the resumption of a serious arms control dialogue in early 1985, also contributed to a reassessment of Soviet policy at the United Nations. Loud condemnation of U.S. recalcitrance no longer fit with broader Soviet objectives. At the 1985 Nuclear Proliferation Treaty Review Conference, for example, the focus was again on the importance of the nonproliferation regime, not on U.S. responsibility for the slow progress on arms control. U.S. support for a chemical weapons treaty coincided with Soviet interest in pursuing a multilateral ban on these weapons. True, Moscow continued to use the United Nations to highlight concern over SDI and space defense in resolutions calling for the prevention of an arms race in space and the creation of an international space inspectorate. But it also sought to mobilize international support for Soviet policy by providing a "carrot"—the creation of a World Space Organization (WSO) to assist all nations in the peaceful use of outer space sometime in the distant future—as well as an anti-U.S. "stick."

By 1986, then, the Soviets had discovered individual parts of the UN system. Their overall attitude toward the organization, however, remained unchanged: the United Nations was useful to the extent that it passed Soviet arms control initiatives and allowed important regional issues to be managed by the great powers. Meanwhile, Moscow paid lip service to economic and social issues. Only since 1987 have the Soviets addressed in a coherent manner the relationship of parts of the central UN to each other and the Soviet role in each.

## "New Thinking" for a New UN: Soviet UN Policy Under Gorbachev

Language has always mattered at the United Nations. Now the language of the USSR is the language of the new political thinking: global interdependence; the interconnection between military, political, and economic security; an emphasis on nuclear disarmament, global environmental issues, and human rights; and the primacy of international law. The packaging of Soviet UN initiatives, however, has been influenced by the particular way issues are debated at the United Nations, with its emphasis on resolutions and bloc voting.

An entire series of speeches and articles has appeared and advanced the new principles behind Soviet policy, beginning with Mikhail Gorbachev's September 17, 1987, *Pravda* and *Izvestia* article, "Realities and Guarantees for a Secure World," continuing in four years of First Committee debates on the 1986 Soviet proposal to create a Comprehensive System of International Peace and Security, in speeches by Deputy Foreign Minister Vladimir Petrovsky and by Head of the International Organization Department Andrei Kozyrev, and culminating in Gorbachev's address before the 43rd General Assembly on December 7, 1988; details of the proposals are given in the Appendix.[4] The new emphasis represents radical change.

The Soviets first signaled their new view of the United Nations by proposing a new agenda item at the 41st General Assembly based on Gorbachev's previous statements about the changed nature of international affairs. In this initiative he proposed a "comprehensive" examination and updating of the Charter in the political, military, economic, humanitarian, and environmental areas.[5] Convinced that nations must change the way they manage conflict, Soviet leaders have since spoken of the need to shift the world body's attention from crisis management to crisis prevention; to substitute policies based on a balance of interests for those based on national interest; and to encompass all aspects of international activity under the rubric of security.[6] Comprehensive security, for all its faults, represented a significant evolution in Soviet policies toward the United Nations. Whereas its own past interpretation of the Charter had been narrow and legalistic—everything not specifically in the Charter was to be brought to the UN only at the indulgence of the Soviet Union and the other permanent members of the Security Council—the new approach outlined in 1987 was broad and inclusive. The Soviet Union was calling for a strengthened UN system in which all questions of international concern, even those that the USSR had long fought to keep *off* the UN agenda, would be legitimate topics of discussion by the world community. As part of the new policy, Soviet diplomats were welcoming, even soliciting, suggestions on the form and content of the new initiative.[7]

Comprehensive security also provided the conceptual basis for Soviet acceptance of interdependence, an idea earlier seen as a ploy by the developed West to subjugate the less-developed nations and to create a moral equivalence between the policies of market and socialist states toward the third world. Now interdependence is viewed as the only logical approach to the nuclear and ecological threats facing the planet.[8]

During the 1980s there was also an about-face in Soviet attitudes toward international action to protect the environment. Earlier, criticism of Western environmental practices, particularly the exploitation of developing countries, was combined with a self-congratulatory tone about Moscow's own concern for the environment. The first UN conference on the environment, held in Stockholm in 1972, was not even attended by the Soviet Union, which at that time was protesting the exclusion of East Germany from the meeting. By the early 1990s, Moscow was actively engaged in plans for the 1992 Conference on Environment and Development and on several occasions expressed concern that cooperative efforts were not moving fast enough. The right to live on a planet free from the threat of nuclear annihilation is given the same urgency in the Soviet mind as the right to an environment free from deadly pollutants.

The life-or-death nature of these two themes has provided the Soviet Union with a rationale for adopting an increasingly nonconfrontational policy at the United Nations. Trying to free itself from its past position as outsider and spoiler, the Soviet Union has joined more fully in the give-and-take of multilateral diplomacy that is the lifeblood of the UN. Its willingness to compromise and accommodate other points of view through an exchange of ideas has also made Moscow a more reasonable partner for bilateral or multilateral negotiation. Soviet diplomats are particularly pleased that their leaders are viewed as forward-looking statesmen at a time when "others" appear to have lost interest in the United Nations and in global issues.

Rhetoric aside, Soviet diplomacy at the United Nations under Gorbachev continues to focus primarily on the political issues before the General Assembly and the Security Council, on the role of the permanent members in resolving regional conflict, and on human rights activities. Gorbachev's December 1988 statements on enlarging the UN's role in debt relief aroused little enthusiasm among the main creditor nations; other Soviet proposals (i.e., suggestions that foreign aid be "depoliticized" and multilateral forms of ODA expanded) have not been followed up with any concrete offers of cash. Because it contributes so little to voluntary programs such as the United Nations Development Program (UNDP),[9] and because it does not yet belong to several specialized agencies—the Food and Agriculture Organization (FAO), or the International Fund for Agricultural Development (IFAD)—or to the international financial institutions (the World Bank, GATT, or the IMF), the Soviet Union has yet to have a major impact on the UN's economic agenda. The fact that many of the countries which have followed the Soviet economic model are among the poorest performers today has also limited Moscow's appeal.

This new global perspective does not mean that the Soviet Union has forgotten the concept of national interest. In the Soviet view, the United Nations is still a collection of independent nation states, and national sovereignty must be defended, particularly in those nations where a foreign (read Western) military presence remains or whose weak domestic economies are dominated by transnational corporations and distant (read Western) banks. At the same time, however, a more internationalist trend is gaining momentum. As Foreign Minister Eduard

Shevardnadze put it, "The interrelationship of events in an inter-dependent world increasingly compels us to delegate some national pre-rogatives to an international organization. In fact, this is already happening."[10]

Now that it claims to be willing to cast its lot with other nations, the Soviet Union maintains that it is prepared to accept in theory and in practice the primacy of international law and to apply uniformly and in all cases the rules and procedures by which international organiza-tions function.[11] Admitting that past decisions not to pay assessments for peacekeeping were errors, Moscow insists that in the future such selective enforcement of Charter obligations will not occur. Soviet spokespersons are eloquent about the rule of law as the guiding princi-ple for their nuclear-free world of the twenty-first century. In the nearer term they call for the harmonization of domestic law with interna-tional standards in such traditionally off-limit areas as terrorism and human rights. They have even rediscovered the International Court of Justice (World Court), proposing that it advise the Security Council and the General Assembly on a regular basis and that all UN members, par-ticularly the permanent members of the Security Council, accept its mandatory authority by mutual consent.[12]

Soviet diplomats have made such promises before—implicitly when they first signed the UN Charter and explicitly under the Helsinki Agree-ments and the various UN Human Rights Covenants. Yet, although a Soviet judge sits on the World Court, the Soviet Union until this year would not accept World Court compulsory jurisdiction and refused to sign optional protocols which would permit World Court adjudication of bilateral or multilateral agreements.[13]

Meanwhile, Moscow has provided new support (both political and financial) for peacekeeping forces and has taken a positive approach to the creation of new forces in other conflict areas. It has outlined new functions for these forces, such as the supervision of elections, observa-tion of hot spots, and possibly naval peacekeeper in areas like the Persian Gulf. It has indicated its support for an active UN role in preventive diplomacy and early warning of crisis situations, a more independent secretary-general, and the reactivation of those parts of the UN system that atrophied through disuse (the Military Staff Committee and the World Court) during the Cold War.

New thinking at the top has thus expanded the Soviet vision about *what* the United Nations should do. The practitioners of Soviet UN policy, for their part, have taken their cue from the secretary-general's own yearly reports and begun to suggest *how* the UN might reorganize its decision-making and voting processes to improve its performance. In addition, serious thought is being given to how the Soviet Union should change its national legislation and domestic decision-making processes to comply with its new international obligations. This focus on specifics marks the emergence of a second stage in Soviet thinking about the United Nations.

In the Soviet view, existing peaceful settlement machinery is not adequate to the new tasks before the United Nations. Thus, those Soviet proposals which address the political activities of the organization usually call for an expansion of the UN's capabilities or the taking on of new functions, especially in the area of preventive diplomacy. These include greater reliance on fact finding by the General Assembly and the secretary-general, establishment of observation posts in explosive areas under Security Council auspices, and a multilateral verification center to facilitate monitoring of the military preparedness of states in crisis areas. The Soviets have said they are willing to take on additional responsibilities for peacekeeping, including the training of peacekeeping forces and the supply of Soviet forces for these operations. Some Soviet proposals are simply procedural (holding closed meetings of the Security Council or allowing the secretary-general to request meetings of the council and to submit reports to it on particularly important issues on his own initiative), while some are structural (universalization of the Conference on Disarmament and the UN's Economic and Social Council [ECOSOC] and elimination of some of the latter's subsidiary bodies). Others are aimed at bolstering the capabilities of the UN (establishment of a Center for Emergency Environmental Assistance, the opening of a "hot line" between UN Headquarters and certain member states, the deployment of a naval peacekeeping force). One particularly interesting Soviet suggestion is that, to the extent possible, General Assembly decisions be based on consensus rather than voting in order to assure balanced and nonconfrontational outcomes that serve to resolve rather than exacerbate problems.

## U.S. Policy at the UN

Underlying support for UN goals and objectives, combined with strong criticism of the organization's specific policies, is not new to American foreign policy. For much of the postwar era there as been broad although diffuse support for the organization, based in large part on a perceived congruence between the principles of postwar U.S. foreign policy and the UN Charter's commitment to political freedom, economic development, and human rights. The organization's inability to live up to these goals, combined with its sloppy administration and ineffective management, have been the primary source of U.S. disillusionment with the United Nations.[14] U.S. policies and perceptions are also very much influenced by world events: the ability to use the United Nations constructively continues to depend in large part on the state of relations with the Soviet Union and the Third World.

Most of the UN institutions established after World War II were compatible with U.S. foreign policy interests and indeed, until the era of "automatic majorities" in the General Assembly ended in the late 1950s, the United Nations was seen as a relatively safe haven in which to discuss global political, economic, and security problems. The United States had a great interest in decolonization and the economic development of the Third World, despite the tensions this sometimes caused with its closest allies (for example, during the 1956 Suez crisis).[15] A slight warming of East-West relations also permitted some early progress in multilateral arms control. The IAEA was created in 1957, and the Antarctica Treaty (1959), the Limited Test Ban Treaty (1963), the Latin America Nuclear Free Zone and Outer Space Treaty (1967), and the Non-Proliferation Treaty (1968) were all negotiated or signed at the United Nations during this period.

Early UN peacekeeping operations were strongly supported by the United States, even as the Soviet reluctance to expand this role grew after the Congo operations. But the UN's role in regional issues was not really greater during this period of hegemony than it was when U.S. influence diminished. In any case, the United Nations was strongly identified in the American public's mind with its development efforts and the programs of the "other" UN: the World Health Organization's campaign to eradicate smallpox, UNICEF's fight against infant mortality, the alleviation of world poverty and hunger through the technical assistance program of the UNDP, the establishment of international safeguards on nuclear reactors by the IAEA, the provision of food aid through FAO's World Food Program, and UNESCO's literacy campaign.

Growing Third World radicalism in the 1970s left the United States isolated and increasingly hostile toward the organization. Through virulent debate and lopsided votes, the Third World managed to alienate vital American constituencies systematically, such as business, Jewish groups, the media, human rights activists, and the labor unions, all of whom had been supporters of the United Nations. The Third World pushed for the creation of a new international economic "order" which would require the redistribution of (Western) resources to the less developed nations and a New World Information and Communications Order (NWICO) which would restrict the flow of outside (Western) news to and from the Third World. In addition, the Third World majority applied a double standard to the organization's consideration of human rights, criticizing countries close to the United States while ignoring abuses in any country belonging to the socialist or nonaligned bloc.

Criticism of Israel grew, and in 1975 the General Assembly passed the Zionism Is Racism resolution, perhaps the one single step most harmful to the image of the United Nations as an impartial force for peace. American public support for the United Nations reached an all-time low in that year.

The balance between cooperation and conflict at the United Nations shifted toward systemwide North-South confrontation at about the same time that East-West relations outside the UN were improving. However, this détente was not reflected in the corridors of the United Nations. Soviet support for radical Third World states did not waver —the Third World was viewed as a "natural ally" of the USSR and its anti-imperialistic drive—and Soviet disarmament positions continued to be aimed at isolating the United States. U.S. officials at that time described the United Nations as "a dangerous place" where "lies are told" and "the tyranny of the majority" held sway.[16]

All during this period, the United States remained the chief financial supporter of the United Nations, paying 25 percent of the regular UN budget and about 25 percent of the assessed contributions to most specialized agencies.[17] No conditions were attached to U.S. contributions, despite the rhetorical pounding the United States was taking. But the seeds for massive financial withholding in the next decade were being sown, as U.S. Ambassador to the UN John Scali indicated in 1974, when he said that the continuation of irresponsible conduct in the United Nations could cause the American people and the Congress to be less generous toward the UN in the future.

The Carter administration came into office with a view to relying more on the United Nations as an option for American foreign policy. Carter's permanent representatives to the United Nations, Andrew Young and Donald McHenry, adopted a more conciliatory posture toward the Third World and sought to work with the General Assembly's majority to reach compromises on issues important to both the United States and the Third World. President Carter supported efforts to ratify the international covenants on human rights, racial discrimination, genocide, and forced labor. The United States took a stronger stand against apartheid, supported majority rule in Namibia and Rhodesia, and repealed the Byrd Amendment, which had permitted chrome imports from Rhodesia. The administration supported increased development aid, enlargement of IMF quotas, and looked more favorably on International Commodity Agreements. President Carter also placed greater emphasis on multilateral arms control measures, sent Vice President Walter Mondale to address the First Special Session on Disarmament (which led to an enlargement and reinvigoration of the UN's principal negotiating body on disarmament, the Conference on Disarmament), initiated trilateral talks on a Comprehensive Test Ban, and acknowledged the nuclear weapon states' obligation to disarm, as stipulated in Article VI of the Non-Proliferation Treaty (NPT).

In the final analysis, however, the Carter administration was constrained by the political realities of the UN's bloc structure and the Soviet Union's intransigence. One of Carter's major foreign policy successes, the Camp David Accords, did not receive any support from the United Nations, and U.S. rather than UN forces were sent to the Sinai to monitor the Israeli-Egyptian disengagement. The recriminations and demands of the developing nations continued unabated, as the Group of 77 and the non-aligned movement remained highly cohesive and inflexible. Soviet-supported conflicts in Angola, Southeast Asia, and Afghanistan placed new items on the UN agenda, but the organization made little progress toward settling any of them. The Security Council was able to agree on a broad framework for a future Namibian peacekeeping operation (Security Council Resolution 435), but unable to get the parties on the ground—each supported by its superpower ally—to talk.[18] During the Carter administration, American tolerance for the politicization of the specialized agencies reached its limit, and the United States made good on President Ford's announcement that it would withdraw from the International Labor Organization (ILO) because of the actions of Soviet and East European state-controlled labor unions.[19]

The Reagan administration made no claim to use the United Nations as an important tool for U.S. policy. The foreign policy goals outlined by President Reagan—to reassert American strength in the international system, to get tough with the Soviet Union, and to redefine and curtail the global agenda put forth by the Third World in the 1970s—did not require active multilateralism. As a result, the UN became marginal to U.S. diplomatic efforts.

During the Reagan administration, the United States signaled its displeasure not only in words, but also through a series of concrete steps that put it in opposition to a majority of UN members. The United States withdrew from UNESCO, refused to sign the Law of the Sea Treaty, refused to participate and would not accept ICJ (World Court) rulings on Nicaragua, threatened to withdraw from the IAEA over the issue of Israeli representation, tried to close the PLO observer mission, denied Yasar Arafat a visa to address the General Assembly, and chose not to participate in the 1987 Special Session on Disarmament and Development. U.S. delegations used the United Nations to denounce Soviet human rights abuses and repeatedly stressed its dissatisfaction with Soviet personnel policy (particularly the practice of secondment) and the improper use of Soviet secretariat and diplomatic officials for intelligence purposes. Ambassador Jeane Kirkpatrick aggressively used the right of reply and sought to make other countries accountable for their votes in the United Nations.[20]

President Reagan used the UN as a global pulpit, addressing the world body more often than any other American leader. He used these speeches to castigate Soviet foreign policy, particularly the Soviet invasion of Afghanistan and trampling of human rights. At the same time, he expressed his belief in the fundamental correctness of UN Charter ideals and called for the United Nations to return to its original principles, placing the blame for UN inadequacy primarily on "the emergence of blocs and the polarization of the United Nations [which] undermine all that the Organization initially valued."[21] Rhetoric aside, however, no American initiatives were advanced to improve UN ability to solve regional disputes, enhance global security, or expand cooperation on global problems. And it is unlikely that if there had been, the Soviet Union would have reciprocated.

During this period the only area of open Soviet-American agreement was the desire of both countries to keep the UN budget in check. The United States and the Soviet Union joined consensus resolutions on the budget and supported the Group of 18 efforts to reform the budget process. However, even here, there was little discussion of and no agreement on priorities for UN spending.

As several major regional crises moved from the battlefield to the negotiating table, the search for a way to end the fighting led both superpowers to the United Nations. The United States supported the efforts of the special representative of the secretary general on Afghanistan —an issue of great importance to the Soviet Union. After the U.S. Sixth Fleet was dispatched to the Persian Gulf to keep the oil supply lines open (followed by Soviet ship deployments in the Gulf), the United States lent full support to the secretary general's efforts to secure a ceasefire in the Iran-Iraq war (Security Council Resolution 598). Both countries worked with other Security Council members to implement the independence plan for Namibia agreed upon in the late 1970s, including the deployment of peacekeeping forces.

## Bush and the UN

The relative success of ongoing reform, indications of political moderation in the Third World, and the upturn in U.S.-Soviet bilateral relations presented the Bush administration with new possibilities for strengthening the role of the world body. The appointment of a highly respected career diplomat, Thomas R. Pickering, as U.S. permanent representative to the United Nations was warmly welcomed at the UN, despite some concern that he would not hold the cabinet-level status accorded every UN permanent representative since Henry Cabot Lodge. In short order, discussions of regional conflict broadened to include a first-time-ever UN role in the Central American peace process and the monitoring of the February 1990 elections in Nicaragua, as well as a series of consultations and conferences on a possible UN administration and election monitoring role in Cambodia.[22] The administration also hinted at new functions for the United Nations on a variety of global issues, but few concrete proposals have been advanced.

President Bush's speech before the 44th UN General Assembly on September 25, 1989, was a "coming home" event eagerly awaited by the delegates, some of whom had known Bush when he was ambassador to the United Nations in 1971 and 1972. Bush spoke in affectionate terms about the people he had known at the UN and expressed general support for efforts in the peaceful settlement of regional conflicts, in combating the international traffic in illegal drugs and in organizing preventive action against terrorism. By jettisoning the rigid ideology and aggressive moralizing of the Reagan years for a more cautious, pragmatic, and guardedly optimistic approach, he appeared to open new opportunities for dialogue with all countries, in particular with the Soviet Union.

President Bush was most specific in his proposals for dealing with chemical weapons, a subject in which he has taken a strong personal interest. Indeed, Bush has said that he would like to be known as the president who outlawed chemical weapons. (As vice president, he submitted a U.S. draft treaty in 1984 to the Conference on Disarmament in Geneva, where discussions of a global ban on chemical weapons have been underway for years.) In 1989 the United States accepted Soviet proposals for a strengthened role for the secretary-general in the investigation of chemical weapons use and offered new proposals of its own throughout the year to speed the conclusion of international treaties dealing with chemicals weapons and the proliferation of ballistic missile technologies. Missing from Bush's speech was a political commitment to reassume America's traditional leadership role in multilateral diplomacy. Also disappointing to his audience was his failure to mention what his administration intended to do about growing U.S. arrearages.

The nearest approximation to an overall UN policy is the concept of a "unitary UN" put forward by Assistant Secretary of State for International Organization Affairs John Bolton in June 1989.[23] The unitary UN idea seeks to encourage the establishment of priorities in program planning and the maintenance of zero real budget growth by stipulating that proposed expansions in the responsibilities of any one UN component be matched by proportional cuts elsewhere in the system. Through this strategy, closer tabs can be kept on the budgets of various UN bodies. As outlined, however, it is more a bookkeeping device than a guide to policy, for it does not offer any suggestions about what should be expanded and what should be cut. In the light of congressional action to force changes in UN practices, it could be a useful tool to pressure the United Nations for internal reforms, especially in its developing economic and social activities, where most of the money is spent, *if* it were combined with a broader vision of what the United States wants the United Nations to do.

American policymakers are showing an interest in defining a UN role on such "transnational" problems as narcotics, terrorism, environmental degradation, AIDS, and refugees. A major expansion in UN activities is not in the offering, but improvements in Soviet-American relations and ongoing collaboration among the five permanent members of the Security Council make it possible to consider multilateral cooperation as complementary to bilateral foreign policy initiatives. At the Special Session on Narcotics in February 1990, for example, Secretary of State James Baker called for improving multilateral structures to complement domestic anti-drug efforts and for broader ratification of the international drug control treaties.[24] In preparing for the 1992 Conference on Environment and Development, the administration has ample opportunities to consider whether new international mechanisms are required to deal with global warming, the greenhouse effect, and acid rain. In the area of human rights, the administration has put the Convention on Torture before the Congress (the Genocide Convention was ratified in 1989).[25] This follows a successful campaign to place Cuban human rights abuses on the UN agenda and the positive support other UN members have given to the U.S.-sponsored draft resolutions on democratic concepts such as the right to own property and to hold free elections.

Strict oversight of UN budgetary practices continues to be guided by restrictions put in place by Congress since 1985. These determine the conditions under which full funding can be appropriated and what the president must certify to release funds. Mindful of the congressional role and of domestic financial pressure, President Bush has nonetheless made it clear that the United States accepts its financial obligations to the world body, and in his budget requests has included full funding and authorization for full payment of U.S. arrearages over five years.[26]

As each important issue comes to a vote, the Soviet Union is still challenged by one or another administration spokesperson to "prove" it has changed its attitude toward the UN by voting with the United States.[27] But open clashes between the superpowers on the important political issues before the UN are now rare.

In true UN fashion, the formal truce in the forty-year war of words between the United States and the Soviet Union was marked by the introduction of a General Assembly resolution—a joint resolution sponsored by the United States and the Soviet Union on "Enhancing international peace, security, and international cooperation in all its aspects in accordance with the Charter of the United Nations."[28] (The Soviet Union then agreed to drop the comprehensive security initiative.)

The draft, adopted in plenary session without a vote and without debate, calls for intensified practical efforts toward ensuring international peace and security, reaffirms the "validity and relevance" of the Charter, and encourages all member states to find "multifaceted approaches" within the UN framework to implement and strengthen Charter principles. The resolution is ingenuous for reconciling what for four years had seemed irreconcilable. Incorporating the concept of a "multifaceted approach" to the United Nations allows the Soviet Union to say that the core of its comprehensive security initiative has been preserved; the emphasis on strict adherence to the Charter allows the United States to say that nothing has changed.

The significance of the resolution goes beyond its three brief operative paragraphs, however. Its joint U.S.-Soviet sponsorship alone gives it a special significance in UN politics, for the superpowers have never before collaborated in drafting and introducing such a General Assembly resolution. And, as the identical statements issued by both governments indicate, the most important thing about the resolution is not what it commits each side to do, but its symbolism as a "new beginning" at the United Nations. Both sides pledge to work together in a "new spirit of constructive cooperation," to preserve the peace and promote budgetary reform, and to depoliticize UN proceedings, promote an atmosphere of realism, and agree to "set aside the tendentious polemics that have been too common in the United Nations in the past." And at the UN, words are often a prelude to action.

## The Impact of Soviet UN Initiatives on the Domestic Policy Debate

Some Soviet diplomats have argued that the acceptance by the international community of the comprehensive system of international security will foster a process of internal change in the Soviet Union,[29] a change in both the substance of policy and the process of Soviet decisionmaking. In their view, changes in Soviet policies at the United Nations can complement and reinforce ongoing processes at home. The link between the two is not always direct, but Soviet UN policy seems to have had some impact on Soviet domestic policy in the areas of human

rights, the environment, military glasnost, and public access to information on Soviet foreign policy.

In a major shift in policy, the USSR has said that it will accept international human rights standards as a yardstick for Soviet performance
and allow the United Nations Human Rights Commission to play a
larger role in the investigation of human rights abuses. The Helsinki
process had allowed Soviet citizens to become familiar with external
criticisms of their government's human rights policies, but the publication of the UN Declaration of Human Rights in the Soviet Union for the
first time in December 1988 (the occasion being the fortieth anniver-
sary of the signing of the declaration) gave Soviet citizens the opportunity to compare directly the human rights guarantees in their own legislation with international standards. This may have added additional
pressures to rewrite Soviet domestic legislation in such sensitive areas
as emigration, the right to information, and the status of political prisoners. As one Soviet member of a UN Human Rights Commission noted:
"Many experts believe that participation of a state in international mechanisms of control over the observance of human rights facilitates the
performance of national bodies, makes them improve internal rules and
regulations, [and reduces] the time for examination of complaints."[30]
One Soviet diplomat suggested that one unintended, but desirable, effect of making domestic laws correspond with international norms might
be that pressure will now be applied to the process of legal reform and
human rights protection in socialist states that have even worse human
rights records than the Soviet Union.[31]

Other instances can be cited as well. Many new informal Soviet
environmental groups have found recent Soviet government statements
that the USSR will abide by international environmental standards to
be an important tool for pressuring local officials and plant managers to
upgrade local pollution controls. And Soviet invalids have begun to assert their rights to education and full integration into society based on
the provisions of the UN Declaration on the Rights of Disabled Persons.

In May 1989 the Soviet Union made good on a two-year-old pledge
to make its military budget public after previously stating at the United
Nations that it would begin to comply in 1990 with UN resolutions
calling for the publication of information on military budgets and on
conventional arms transfers using the agreed-upon reporting system.[32]
Soviet diplomats also began to stress the need to provide more information on military activities at meetings of a UN Study Group on international verification. Yet, as Foreign Minister Shevardnadze himself noted,
it is not so easy to translate a political decision into action—especially
when it concerns matters of state security under the jurisdiction of the
Ministry of Defense.[33] Having assented to a broader flow of information

on these subjects before an international audience, the Soviet political leadership may be better armed to do battle with those who have resisted such disclosures.

The way policy is implemented is also affected by the glare of international attention. Because the tendency of the bureaucracy is to mouth the new words but stall over changing administrative methods, international pressure can prod bureaucrats to effect changes that the political leadership desires. The certainty of international scrutiny may, for example, prompt a quicker response to human rights complaints or extract the information the Ministry of Foreign Affairs has promised the world would be forthcoming. The Supreme Soviet is likely to increase pressure for openness and accountability, using the commitment of the Soviet government to greater exchange of information and to adherence to international norms in order to assert its own "right to know."[34]

These changes have already had an impact on the style of Soviet diplomacy and on the amount of information available to Soviet citizens about the United Nations and Soviet policy at the United Nations. For many years the Soviet public was kept in the dark about the extent of international opposition to the Soviet intervention in Afghanistan, as the negative vote tallies in the General Assembly went unreported or were glossed over. This "veil of secrecy" at home and abroad is now viewed as having hurt Soviet interests, for it contributed to the perception that the Soviet Union was an unreliable negotiating partner.[35] The harmful effects of self-imposed isolation, particularly in the economic and humanitarian spheres, was best expressed by Foreign Minister Shevardnadze in an interview appearing just after the earthquake in Armenia: "From the positions of our day we see as unjustified our non-participation . . . in the activities of the UN Disaster Relief Office. There was a time when we even voted against strengthening the financial basis of its operations. Now tragedy has come to our home and the Office has extended a helping hand to us, offering to coordinate international efforts aimed to relieve the lot of the earthquake victims in Armenia. What else except shame can we feel today for the shortsightedness of our previous position?"[36]

International forums also provide a good opportunity for signaling shifts in Soviet foreign policy both at home and abroad. The Soviet decision to support a compromise resolution at the May 1989 World Health Organization Assembly to postpone consideration of the application for full membership by the "state" of Palestine was a clear signal to all Middle East states (and to the United States) of the Soviet desire not to put new obstacles in the way of a Middle East peace. It also highlighted a new Soviet interest in protecting the specialized agencies from unnecessary politicization. As of yet, however, this new spirit does not yet extend to the discussions of Middle East issues in the General Assembly, where the Soviet Union has so far refused to support American efforts to repeal or in some way supercede the 1975 Zionism Is Racism resolution.

## The UN in Soviet Foreign Policy

Looking at the UN's role in Soviet foreign policy more broadly, a USSR preoccupied with its internal restructuring would have good reason to want a breathing space during which international crises were handled in a more predictable way. By calling on the Security Council to act rather than seeking military solutions to political problems, the Soviet Union can minimize the potential for conflict with the United States and avoid the huge financial or military commitments that follow unilateral interventions.

Under these circumstances, the Soviet Union has little interest in pursuing policies which would foster a very strong American hostility toward the United Nations or cause the United States to ignore or withdraw from the UN. Indeed, since 1987 the Soviet Union has gone out of its way to address several issues of importance to the United States, including the long-standing American complaints about the anti-U.S. bias of General Assembly votes to the Soviet policy of placing their UN employees on short-term contracts (secondment) and the need for reforms in the UN's budgetary process.[37] One particularly important Soviet gesture was the decision to abstain when an Arab-sponsored effort to challenge Israeli credentials in the 44th General Assembly came to a vote.

There is nothing altruistic in these moves. The U.S. withdrawal from various UN bodies, its unwillingness to participate in special UN conferences, and its failure to pay assessed dues give the Soviet Union a better image but it does not help get things done. The "opinion of mankind" cannot influence policy if the United States is not listening. The USSR is willing to let the United Nations take the lead (and the heat, if things go badly) when crises do develop, in part in order to reduce the likelihood of unilateral action by other countries, particularly the United States. From the Soviet point of view, a UN multilateral presence, rather than a U.S. military presence, should be available to fill any regional power vacuum.

## Americans and Soviets at the UN:
## A Look Ahead

As in 1945, the nature of Soviet-American interactions at the United Nations largely defines the art of the possible. Without both Soviet and

American participation, the United Nations cannot significantly expand its role in any area of human endeavor. The other side of the coin is less well understood: even with active collaboration by the two superpowers, it will not be as easy to shape the post-Cold War world as it was for either side to dominate the UN during the Cold War years.

At every stage in the Cold War the United Nations was held hostage to U.S.-Soviet rivalry. As long as the Soviet Union was on the outside looking in, the UN was limited in what it could do—and what it undertook to do was largely defined by America's UN agenda. The United States can no longer dismiss the potential for using multilateral mechanisms on the assumption of Soviet intransigence. Nor can it be assumed that when the UN acts it will take as its starting point American objectives and preferences. If the Soviet Union is actively engaged at the UN, then the United Nations will have to be responsive to Soviet as well as American priorities.

Having voluntarily abdicated a leadership role during the Reagan administration, the Bush administration finds that others—Soviets and Third World states—have filled the gap with a new UN agenda of their own. The breakdown of coalitions—the fragmentation of the Group of 77 Third World states and the collapse of the socialist bloc—has also an impact on the UN. For the first time in its history the UN is a truly multilateral organization, which responds to but cannot be controlled by the Soviet Union or the United States, acting alone or together.

Those who know the UN realize that it may be possible to deideologize it, but it will never be possible to really depoliticize it. In the future, the American and Soviet political agendas at the UN may overlap in important ways, but they are never going to be identical. Each country has its allies and friends, and each sees the world's problems and its own national interest in different ways. The USSR is still quite edgy about the appearance of collusion among the great powers even as the Soviets work to strengthen their special relationship with the United States and the three other permanent members of the Security Council, all of whom have the veto. The United States is still smarting from the many years of sharp criticism by the socialist bloc and the Third World majority. The UN's political culture increasingly stresses consensus and pragmatism rather than confrontation, but the UN remains an unwieldy organization in which 159 states participate, not all of which applaud the more businesslike approach taken by the two superpowers. Complicating the situation are Third World states, many of whom for years talked about the necessity of superpower cooperation but now approach the fact of such cooperation with unease, fearing that they may be shut out of important decisions.

But if the Soviet Union couples some dubious or mischievous proposals with a willingness to have the United Nations send international monitors, peacekeeping forces, and development assistance to places like Afghanistan and Cambodia (where Soviet interests *are* vitally involved) and if the Soviet Union continues to pay its assessed share of UN dues and peacekeeping bills, then its professed interest in the organization must be addressed seriously. The United States needs to press the Soviets on the specifics of their proposals and to come up with some good ideas of its own. If the United States continues to take a backseat at the UN, then the measurement of "progress" accepted by the international community will by default be a Soviet yardstick.

To work well, the United Nations needs an activist United States *and* an engaged Soviet Union. Both the United States and the Soviet Union must be clear about the political requirements and institutional changes necessary to make the UN more effective.[38] Without them there will be no way of knowing if the United Nations can function as it was first intended: as a global forum reflecting both American and Soviet interests and, in the bargain, enhancing international security.

## Appendix

Perestroika at the United Nations
A Summary of Soviet Proposals and Positions
Richard A. Falkenrath, Jr., and Edmund Piasecki

Since the September 1987 publication of Mikhail Gorbachev's *Pravda* and *Izvestia* article "Realities and Guarantees for a Secure World," Soviet diplomats have vigorously followed up on the UN-centered "comprehensive system of international security" sketched out by the Soviet leader. Several dozen specific proposals have been introduced to various UN bodies. Some are reiterations of old positions, both Soviet and non-Soviet; others represent radical departures from Moscow's traditional UN policy. All have been presented in the context of "new thinking" and glasnost.

Soviet proposals in the area of preventive diplomacy, particularly regarding the use of UN peacekeeping forces before hostilities erupt, have found wide support. Soviet suggestions in the area of arms control and disarmament, such as the international verification agency and the world space organization, have been less well received but have engendered lively debate. The process of refining specific proposals based on discussions with other member states is ongoing, and the Soviets have evinced a growing sophistication at presenting a new foreign policy based on national interests but pursued through their formulation of a "balance of interests."

Included herein are the most important Soviet proposals presented at the United Nations General Assembly, various UN committees, and in speeches and statements by various foreign policy spokespersons from September 1987 through March 1990. They may be grouped under four main headings: (1) measures to improve UN conflict control capability; (2) measures to make better use of the main UN bodies; (3) measures to promote economic, social, humanitarian, and ecological well-being; and (4) measures to make international law more comprehensive.

*1. Measures to Improve UN Conflict Control Capability*

*Arms Control and Disarmament*

1. Develop a multilateral verification "mechanism" at the UN, perhaps in the form of an "international verification agency" (IVA) and a multilateral verification center. The agency will verify compliance with arms control agreements, as well as monitor the military situation in regions of conflict. The center will collect data on areas of potential conflict, primarily through fact-finding missions to such areas.
2. Set up a multilateral war risk reduction center under UN auspices and regional centers around the world. The centers are to make the accidental or unauthorized use of nuclear weapons less likely, reduce the possibility of surprise attack, and also help prevent conventional war.
3. Establish a seven-way hotline between the capitals of the five permanent members of the Security Council, the chairman of the Non-Aligned Movement, and the office of the secretary-general, perhaps as part of the risk reduction centers.
4. Establish a UN data bank to compile data on disarmament and verification-related information (originally proposed by Finland).
5. Establish an international satellite monitoring agency (ISMA), perhaps as a first step toward the establishment of the IVA (originally proposed by France).
6. Establish a worldwide seismic monitoring system as a first step toward implementing and verifying a comprehensive nuclear test ban (originally proposed by Japan).
7. Establish an International Space Inspectorate (ISI) to ascertain that objects launched into space are not used for military purposes.

*Peacekeeping Operations*

1. Allow the Security Council to set up special observer stations in potentially explosive areas.
2. Use special missions of the Security Council to evaluate problem areas and make on-the-spot recommendations.
3. Use UN personnel to safeguard member states from external interference by stationing them in one state's territory at the request and consent of that nation alone.
4. Establish a system to train personnel for UN field operations.
5. Create a reserve of UN military observers and peacekeeping forces.
6. Prepare a list of approved experts in advance for peacekeeping missions to ensure the dispatch of such missions without delay.
7. Establish a UN naval peacekeeping force.
8. Use UN peacekeepers in international drug control efforts and to prevent terrorist incidents.
9. Use Soviet personnel in UN operations.
10. Convene an international conference on the elaboration of guarantees to implement the accords achieved on the question of Cambodia and ensure the independence of Cambodia and peace in Southeast Asia.

*2. Measures to Make Better Use of the Main UN Organs*

*Making and Keeping the Peace*

1. Promote greater cooperation between the UN, especially the Security Council, and regional organizations.
2. Have the permanent members of the Security Council become guarantors of regional security and assume obligations to renounce the use of threat of force, withdraw their military presence abroad, and agree not to supply arms to any side in a regional conflict.
3. Hold foreign minister-level meetings of the Security Council at the beginning of each General Assembly session to identify ways to improve the international situation.

4. Hold special, expanded Security Council meetings in the capitals of the five permanent members and in regions of active or potential conflict.
5. Periodically hold meetings between the five permanent members of the Security Council and the secretary-general.
6. Increase the use of informal consultations among Security Council members and parties involved in disputes.
7. Hold closed meetings of the Security Council to discuss sensitive issues.
8. Revitalize the Military Staff Committee by holding consultations between the Staff Committee experts of the five permanent Security Council members and other experts to examine politico-military problems and the status of peacekeeping operations in the field.
9. Adopt more General Assembly resolutions, particularly those concerning security issues, by consensus.
10. Adopt measures and establish mechanisms to monitor the implementation of General Assembly resolutions and decisions.
11. Convene more special sessions of the General Assembly under Article 20 of the Charter on urgent political or disarmament issues, as well as other issues directly relevant to international security.
12. Using Article 22 of the Charter, encourage subsidiary bodies of the General Assembly to submit draft international documents after thorough discussion, for General Assembly approval.
13. At the conclusion of General Assembly debate, have the Secretariat make a list of issues to be discussed in concrete terms in relevant UN organs.
14. Allow the General Assembly to dispatch fact-finding missions.
15. Have the General Assembly consider the secretary-general's annual report on the work of the organization more fully, especially the recommendations on improving the functioning of the organization, and adopt appropriate resolutions and decisions.
16. Recommend that the secretary-general dispatch fact-finding missions to areas of actual or potential conflict, regularly convene and inform the Security Council of developments in those regions, and take more initiatives to prevent and peacefully resolve disputes.
17. Encourage the secretary-general to submit on his own initiative reports to the Security Council on questions regarding the maintenance of international peace and security, including disarmament.
18. Encourage the secretary-general to more frequently use his powers under Article 99 of the Charter to bring to the attention of the Security Council any matter which, in his opinion, may threaten international peace and security.
19. Set up a UN tribunal to investigate acts of international terrorism.
20. Implement the Declaration on the Prevention and Removal of Disputes (General Assembly Resolution 43/51 of 1988).
21. Draft a "General Act of Peaceful Settlement of Disputes," perhaps in the Special Committee on the Charter, and finalize and adopt the draft at a conference of plenipotentiaries, perhaps in Moscow.
22. Conclude a multilateral agreement on the prevention of incidents on the high seas (originally proposed by Sweden).
23. Broaden the mandate of the Special Committee on the Charter to consider: (a) implementing enforcement measures against a state who has violated the peace and is failing to abide by Security Council decisions; (b) taking provisional measures under Article 40 of the Charter to prevent the deterioration of a crisis situation; (c) strengthening the collective security regime envisioned in the Charter; and (d) examining the effectiveness of the UN system as a whole (originally a U.S. proposal).

*Arms Control and Disarmament*

1. Develop a system for continual monitoring for and automatic UN investigation by the secretary-general of alleged use of chemical or bacteriological weapons.
2. Set up a similar mechanism as above to investigate instances of possible violations of the Convention on Inhumane Weapons.
3. Turn the forty-nation Geneva-based Conference on Disarmament into a universal year-round negotiating body.
4. Cut the number of resolutions adopted by the General Assembly's First (Political and Security) Committee and increase the number of decisions taken there by consensus.
5. Streamline the agenda of the General Assembly's Disarmament Commission, and consider the more divisive items on a two-to-three year basis.
6. Implement the ideas of "open skies" (originally a U.S. proposal), and expand it to include "open lands," "open seas and oceans," and "open space."
7. Have the Security Council elaborate an agreement on measures to reduce the risk of nuclear war.
8. Within the framework of the World Campaign for Disarmament hold an international seminar on making the Indian Ocean a zone of peace and an international conference on the implication of disarmament for employment and conversion of military industry to nonmilitary uses.
9. Promote the efforts of the United Nations Institute for Disarmament Research (UNIDIR).
10. Declare the 1990s the "Decade for Building a Nuclear-Free and Non-Violent World."
11. Create a World Space Organization (WSO) through which member states with space capabilities may share information gained from space exploration with other member states.
12. Establish a UN register of international sales and transfers of conventional weapons (originally proposed by Italy).
13. Develop within the UN universally acceptable standards and norms for accounting of national military budgets.
14. Establish a UN body to monitor and assess new technologies for their military applications (originally proposed by India).
15. Undertake a multilateral comparison of states' military doctrines.
16. Limit and reduce national naval forces.
17. Reduce and eventually eliminate all national military forces stationed abroad.

*Administration and Budget*

1. Intensify efforts to strengthen the coordination function of the Economic and Social Council (ECOSOC).
2. Provide data on the geographical distribution of Secretariat personnel in specific posts.
3. Increase the number of Secretariat officials on fixed contracts.
4. Determine UN budgetary assessments using official exchange rates rather than the market-determined rate.

*3. Measures to Promote Economic, Social, Humanitarian, and Ecological Well-Being*

*Economic and Social*

1. Promote the economic welfare of the developing world by reducing interest payments on external debt and providing generous debt relief through programs coordinated by the UN.
2. Convene a special session of the Security Council to discuss the relationship between disarmament and development and establish a permanent special commission on disarmament and development to facilitate international consensus on the issue.
3. Establish a fund for disarmament and development to facilitate the redistribution of resources from the military sector to development activities.

4. Have all states submit plans to the UN on converting industries from military to nonmilitary production.
5. Convene a group of scientists and experts to undertake a thorough analysis of the problem of conversion and report their findings to the UN.
6. Have the secretary-general provide assessments and forecasts of technological progress and its impact on disarmament and peace (originally proposed by the Non-Aligned Movement).
7. Create a World Information Program (WIP) under UN auspices to strengthen through the means of information mutual understanding and mutual respect among all member states.
8. Establish within the framework of the Committee on Information (COI) a group of experts that would function as COI's working body between sessions.

*Humanitarian*

1. Establish a voluntary fund for international humanitarian efforts to be funded through reductions in national military budgets and private contributions.
2. Unify international legal criteria for the reunion of families, marriages, cross-cultural contacts, and visa regulations.
3. Create a worldwide health information network under the auspices of WHO to coordinate the fight against disease.
4. Convene an international conference on global humanitarian problems in Moscow.
5. Create a special unit of servicemen or a voluntary international peace corps to deal with emergency humanitarian problems, particularly in Afghanistan (originally proposed by France).
6. Establish a world consultative council to enrich the spiritual and ethical potential of world politics.
7. Create an international laboratory for the world's scientists (originally proposed by Italy).
8. Establish an international order under UNESCO's supervision to ensure an equitable distribution of the achievements of science.
9. In the context of the World Cultural Development Decade, hold an international symposium in Moscow on "The Common Heritage of Mankind—to the Third Millenium."
10. Develop a long-term strategy for scientific cooperation under UN auspices.
11. In the field of human rights: (a) have the Subcommission on Human Rights develop a generic approach to the issues it considers, rather than spending so much time on individual countries; (b) put more emphasis on maintaining standards in the Human Rights Commission rather than on creating new ones; and (c) emphasize the prevention of abuses through arbitration rather than condemnation in meetings of the commission.

*Ecological and Energy-related*

1. Discuss the problems of environmental security at the level of the Security Council by turning either the Trusteeship Council or the UN Environment Program (UNEP) into an "Environmental Council."
2. Strengthen UNEP's ability to deal with world climate change.
3. Create a UN center for emergency environmental assistance—"International Green Cross."
4. Develop a UN system for early warning of dangerous environmental trends, perhaps including an international space laboratory or a manned orbital space station designed exclusively for environmental monitoring.
5. Establish environmental risk warning centers, akin to the existing U.S.-Soviet nuclear risk reduction centers or the proposed multilateral war risk reduction center.

6. Add an environmental component to the open skies concept.
7. Establish a mechanism for fact-finding and for the prevention and resolution of disputes in the field of ecology (originally proposed by Austria).
8. Convene a series of three international expert- and summit-level conferences to devise a global strategy for dealing with ecological problems.
9. Create a Moscow Energy Club to cooperate with UNESCO on the development of new technologies relating to energy.
10. Strengthen the UN role in providing comprehensive and reliable information concerning the energy resources of the Third World.

*4. Measures to Make International Law More Comprehensive*

1. Have the General Assembly and the Security Council approach the International Court of Justice (ICJ or World Court) for advisory opinions more often and involve the ICJ more in disputes over the interpretation of international agreements.
2. Recognize the mandatory jurisdiction of the ICJ under certain mutually agreed conditions, starting with agreement by the permanent members of the Security Council.
3. Develop and codify a universal approach and set of binding principles regarding international law and the role of the ICJ.
4. Assert the primacy of international law by bringing national legislation and administrative rules on humanitarian issues into accordance with international standards.
5. Develop a legal basis for the exploration and exploitation of outer space, including the delineation of national air and space territory.
6. Make General Assembly decisions adopted by consensus morally and politically binding.
7. Include in future agreements negotiated under UN auspices provisions for ICJ adjudication in the event of disagreement over interpretation.
8. Accept the binding jurisdiction of the ICJ regarding the interpretation and application of human rights accords.
9. Within the context of the UN Decade on International Law, elaborate an international legal strategy to encourage the development of international law.

# CHAPTER 13

# ENVIRONMENTAL PROTECTION
# AND SOVIET-AMERICAN RELATIONS
Glenn E. Schweitzer

## Global and Local Ecological Concerns
## and the Political Agenda

Since the mid-1980s growing awareness in the United States and the
USSR among scientists, government officials, and the general public
over the increasing seriousness of environmental problems has significantly affected Soviet-American political relations. In the USSR, Soviet
investigative reporters, unshackled for the first time, have inundated
the population with revelations about how unbridled industrial and agricultural practices have threatened the health of children and workers
and have ravaged the countryside. With a newfound environmental consciousness, the Soviet government is seeking help from the West in
reversing the past patterns of environmental neglect. In the United States
environmental attention has turned to predictions that air pollution
will cause a rise in the the temperature of the globe. The U.S. government recognizes that cooperation between the United States and the
USSR—the two energy megapowers—can be very important in abating
worldwide emissions of carbon dioxide, sulfur dioxide, and other greenhouse gases that result from energy and other industrial activities.

Worldwide ecological problems became a popular theme during the
Reagan-Gorbachev summits, particularly at the meetings in Washington in 1987 and in Moscow in 1988. Then in early 1989, the topic of
global issues, including environmental issues, was added to the four-
point negotiating agenda previously adopted by the two governments in
the mid-1980s, the others being arms control, human rights, bilateral
relations, and regional issues.[1] Environmental problems will undoubtedly again be high on the agendas of the Bush-Gorbachev summits during the next several years.

In January 1990 General Secretary Gorbachev hosted a large international gala in Moscow devoted primarily to protection of the environment. More than 150 prominent Americans who were in attendance

provided a clear bilateral dimension to this multilateral affair.[2] Not to be outdone, President Bush called a White House conference on global ecological concerns for the spring of 1990, to which the USSR sent a strong delegation to the session.

Meanwhile, by 1990 there were more than forty bilateral projects formally endorsed by the two governments and directed to environmental assessment, environmental control, and environmental research; hundreds of specialists from the two countries were involved. Additional bilateral environmental projects sprang up as components of people-to-people programs and as initiatives by educational and scientific groups in both countries. Soviet and American political and scientific leaders repeatedly call for the two countries to help stimulate collective action of all nations in addressing common environmental problems which some experts assert could, if unattended, lead to catastrophes on a scale approaching the predicted devastation from a global war.

Soviet representatives at international meetings are no longer reluctant to talk about the horrendous environmental problems in the USSR, but when discussions turn to collaborative efforts, Soviets often emphasize the macro problems facing all countries rather than dwell on the seemingly intractable micro problems in their country.[3] This Soviet emphasis on large-scale international concerns is reflected in the following excerpt from a joint statement developed by the U.S. National Academy of Sciences and the Academy of Sciences of the USSR in December 1988:

> The problem of global ecological security that confronts all humankind has increased greatly in its seriousness, and its effects have become widely appreciated and discussed. The consequences of the rapid growth of our population coupled with global economic development now pose a significant threat to our continued existence. Natural resources are being exhausted on land and in the sea, and thousands of species of plants, animals, and microorganisms are becoming extinct. Natural biogeochemical cycles, on which all life depends, are being disrupted; all parts of the environment are being polluted. The global ecosystem is being degraded rapidly, so that its sustainability is being called into question. As a consequence of the exhaustion of land, water, fishery, forest, mineral, and other natural resources, the basis for economic development is being undermined. Indeed, it is calculated that human beings currently consume directly, divert, or waste some 40 percent of total global photosynthetic productivity on land, while our numbers climb rapidly. In these circumstances, urgent action is clearly required.[4]

This awakening within the two countries to the threats to the planet's environmental support system and the appeals for action parallel the broader international clamor over the increasing worldwide indicators of environmental deterioration and the need for more effective responses by all nations. As two of the largest countries, the United States and the USSR are themselves experiencing many adverse effects of trans-boundary pollution problems near their borders. The governments of the two countries are also becoming increasingly sensitive to the contributions of their own industries to global pollution problems. The United States, the Soviet Union, and China are the three nations that lead the world in food production and food consumption; as environmental pollution becomes indicted as a predictable cause of climate changes and consequent future dislocations in the world's food supply, environmental concerns become even more tangible.[5]

While the two nations have committed to work with all countries on environmental topics, Soviet economic problems as well as shortcomings in addressing many pollution problems at home clearly inhibit their positions internationally. For example, the Soviets hesitated considerably before finally signing the Montreal Protocol calling for a 50 percent reduction in the use of chlorofluorocarbons which can degrade the ozone belt around the earth, and they have shown no interest in subsequent international calls for an eventual ban on the use of this class of chemicals. They have only begun to consider seriously the alternatives to chlorofluorclarbons because they have been planning to continue to rely on these chemicals for refrigeration and other uses.

With regard to limitations on emissions of sulfur dioxide, the USSR has joined the "30 percent club" of European nations that have agreed to reduce emissions in the next few years. Given the high levels of Soviet industrial emissions, relatively inexpensive control technologics should be effective in reaching the 30 percent reduction target, but the Soviets will undoubtedly resist efforts to reduce emissions further due to the increasing control costs attendant to more stringent limitations.

The interest of the governments of the two superpowers in working together on environmental issues has received considerable impetus from the burgeoning political détente symbolized by progress in arms control. Arms control accords unfold at a very slow pace, however, and the East-West military confrontation continues. Thus, the two countries and indeed the world are searching for additional paths to peace, and cooperation in the "humanitarian" and critically important field of environmental protection provides a politically appealing counterweight to the often acrimonious debates over the continuing role of military power. Soviet and American environmentalists exude confidence that their collaborative efforts can move rapidly along smoother paths. Cooperation in improving understanding of the causes and implications of the greenhouse effect in particular is at the top of the bilateral agenda.

Glasnost is having a profound influence on environmental awareness in the USSR. The Soviet public understands the consequences of inadequate environmental policies: the Chernobyl disaster, the shrinking of the Aral Sea, the continuing pollution of Lake Baikal, the brown clouds over the Siberian cities, and the toxic fumes from chemical plants in the Urals are close to the personal emotions and daily lives of the Soviet population. Indeed, as in almost all countries, environmental protection is rapidly becoming a people's issue there.

Environmental degradation has also become an ethnic issue, as vocal minorities in some Soviet republics claim they have been short-changed more than others in the national neglect of the environment. Environmental groups springing up in the Baltic republics, in particular, have become rallying points for venting pent-up frustrations over past Russian domination of the region.

Environmental mismanagement is also an economic issue. Soviet journalists are having a field day in calculating the costs from destruction of forests, contamination of drinking water, and decline in sturgeon in the Volga River, for example. As plants are closed by the health authorities, the concept of unemployment takes on meaning for the first time in some locations.

Of course, in the United States environmental protection has penetrated the very fiber of everyday living: the operation of industrial plants and farms, the administration of cities and towns, the use of land and water resources, and even the control of the wastes of individual households. The sources, extent, and solutions of most local environmental problems are reasonably clear, although the political will and the financial resources for correcting the problems are often lacking. However, the possibility of changes in the climate as a result of air pollution and other human activities raises many poorly understood issues, and here and in related areas of global concerns cooperation with the USSR seems to offer the greatest payoff.

The Soviets have lagged behind the West in addressing local environmental problems—by two decades according to Soviet officials, and by a longer period according to many American experts. They are only beginning to realize, however, that prevention of pollution can no longer be put aside and have not yet comprehended the seriousness of many local pollution issues and the feasibility of reducing human and ecological risks resulting from high pollution levels. Consequently, Soviet interest in international cooperation is driven by a newly found desire to improve their own understanding of local problems as well as to participate in international assessments of global issues.[6]

## The Environmental Dimension of Perestroika

Gorbachev's efforts to restructure Soviet society (perestroika)—together with his advocacy of a rapid succession of arms control initiatives, the Soviet withdrawal from Afghanistan and Eastern Europe, and the resolution of many human rights cases in the USSR—have had a dramatic effect on Western policies toward the USSR. In general, Western governments have responded with a much greater interest than in the past in constructive interactions with the USSR and have encouraged a variety of trade initiatives and cooperative programs. "We want perestroika to succeed," proclaims President Bush again and again.

Perestroika has moved forward rapidly on the political front while encountering many high hurdles in the economic sphere. Both thrusts are important for environmental improvement, although many of the relationships between perestroika and protection of the environment are only now becoming apparent. Insofar as the policies of the United States and other Western governments are linked to perestroika, their policies are also tied to Soviet efforts to cope with the extremely serious environmental problems which have been largely ignored for many years.

Effective mechanisms for enforcing environmental standards in the USSR did not exist in the past. Environmental inspectors were organizationally positioned in the production ministries, where they immediately encountered conflicts within the ministries between the demands for higher levels of production and the need to temper production enthusiasm with environmental restraint. Closing dirty plants, modifying production processes to reduce emissions, and diverting investment resources from new production capacity to pollution control have been very unpopular options within these ministries. The executive councils of the districts and towns where production facilities are located have exerted little influence in decisions concerning pollution control even though the councils are nominally responsible for the well-being of residents of the area. Occasionally, a local representative of the procurator general in Moscow has intervened in serious cases of environmental pollution, but such intervention has been the exception rather than the rule.

Now, new Soviet managers who are more receptive to new ideas and different approaches are assuming responsibilities within many ministries and enterprises, and organizational changes are underway throughout the government. Most important, the environmental compliance responsibility which has been diffused in the production ministries is being centralized within a new State Committee for Protection of Nature, which is to have local offices throughout the country. Thus, inspectors will enjoy a degree of independence from the production organizations. They should inject a greater sense of local environmental concerns into the enforcement program. The willingness and capability of the new committee and its inspectors to challenge the major polluters have yet to be tested, but in principle the inspectors seem well positioned.[7]

Efforts to strengthen the local executive councils throughout the country also have important environmental implications. Frequently in the past the production ministries with facilities in a town have developed the associated infrastructure—roads, water systems, electrical networks—simply because they had the only available resources for the job. Consequently, as each ministry developed its sites and used the surrounding territory in accordance with its own needs, the possibility for environmentally oriented town planning decreased. Now, town councils are scheduled to receive increased support from the ministries to help develop the physical infrastructures, and if they do, they should be able to ensure a greater environmental sensitivity in local development.

Overarching these developments are the activities of the Supreme Soviet, one of the early manifestations of perestroika, which has taken a special interest in environmental issues, and a series of resolutions and laws calling for more stringent environmental regulation will probably be passed in the future.[8] Independent environmental groups are emerging, not only in the outlying republics where they address local issues, but also in Moscow, where national approaches to environmental protection are at the center of their attention.[9]

As environmental enforcement becomes more of a reality than in the past, the costs to the enterprises of environmental control equipment must be given greater weight, both in the design of new facilities and in the retrofitting of old plants. These costs will be substantial and are emerging as the Soviet economy staggers from a decade of no growth and an attendant accumulation of an enormous budget deficit. They will presumably affect prices considerably, and at least in the short run may require access to foreign exchange for purchase of equipment abroad since the pollution equipment industry is not well developed in the USSR. But foreign exchange is in extremely short supply, with increases in Western credits the only apparent solution to this dilemma.

At the same time, the concept of internalizing the costs of environmental protection is new in the USSR; enterprises already struggling to adjust to unfamiliar requirements for self-financing will have considerable difficulty accepting their environmental responsibilities.

After a painful educational process during the past several decades, advocates of perestroika finally appreciate the need to supplement the traditional Soviet emphasis on high levels of production using proven technologies with new priorities for improved quality of products and for the use of more efficient technologies. Such an educational process is only beginning with regard to pollution control, and few Soviets recognize clean air or clean water as important indicators of the success of economic reforms.

The financial need to improve efficiency in the use of energy has been widely recognized among Soviet economists. Coal-fired power plants are notorious polluters in the USSR and elsewhere, and reductions in energy use would have significant environmental implications. However, as long as energy is highly subsidized, little incentive exists for significant savings. Until price reform becomes a reality, opportunities for energy conservation in the Soviet power industry, in the design and heating of buildings, and in energy-intensive manufacturing processes will continue to be lost. A final economic concern relates to the high costs of installation and operation of sewage treatment systems and the expense of proper disposal of both municipal and industrial wastes. Such responsibilities loom large before the town councils which have small budgets to support many services.

Thus, these and other environmental problems are not adequately addressed in many communities. In short, many of the interrelationships among economics, energy, and environmental protection have yet to command serious attention in the USSR, and many possibilities for reducing costs in the national effort to reduce pollution have not been widely recognized. GOSPLAN and other agencies at the national level and many institutions at the local level are only beginning to refine their thinking in this regard as an integral part of perestroika. Given the costs of pollution control, all of these organizations have preferred not to address the problems, but they have no choice.

Some Soviet experts repeatedly proclaim that the pollution problems in the USSR will be solved only when the obsolete industrial base of the entire country has been replaced with modern technologies.[10] They are correct, but in the meantime the country must cope with its industrial infrastructure. Pollution abatement simply cannot wait, for the environmental consequences of past neglect are apparent to all. Retrofitting old facilities may be extremely expensive, but in many cases no other alternative exists.

As Soviet policies evolve which are designed to improve the balance of economic development priorities with environmental protection requirements, significant opportunities for bilateral cooperation should emerge. The United States and other Western countries have repeatedly addressed the cost aspects of pollution control and have developed a keen awareness of how important economic assessments are to the planning of projects with potentially adverse impacts on the environment.

## The Benefits and Limitations of Bilateral Cooperation

The U.S.-USSR Agreement on Environmental Protection was signed in 1972, and cooperation has continued. Projects are clustered in air pollution, water pollution, agricultural pollution, the urban environment, preservation of nature, pollution of the marine environment, biological effects of pollution, influence of changes on climate, earthquake prediction, arctic and subarctic ecosystems, and legal protection measures. The agreement is the environmental centerpiece of the bilateral relationship, and its contributions to improved political relations can be considered from several viewpoints.[11]

The Environmental Agreement was one of a number of accords calling for cooperation in science and technology that the two governments signed in the early 1970s. Each agreement was to bring concrete technical benefits to both countries, but much of the impetus for the development and support of the agreements can be traced to political considerations: in the United States in particular, Secretary of State Henry Kissinger was interested in visible manifestations of détente.

In the late 1970s and early 1980s Soviet-American political relations took a downward turn following Soviet intervention in Afghanistan, the suppression of Solidarity in Poland, the Soviet destruction of the Korean airliner 007, and the mistreatment of Andrei Sahkarov and other political dissidents in the USSR. Part of the U.S. response to these developments was a curtailment of cooperation in science and technology; some of the intergovernmental agreements were not renewed, and others became inoperative. The exception was cooperation in environmental protection, and joint activity continued unabated. Collaboration had become popular within several U.S. government agencies, and their scientists presented persuasive arguments about the short-term and long-term benefits to the United States. These arguments outweighed the political pressures for the United States to distance itself from the USSR. In the late 1980s, as political relations improved, many of the other agreements were revitalized. Environmental cooperation expanded dramatically, largely in response to new concerns over holes in the ozone belt, buildup in the atmosphere of carbon dioxide, and other global ecological problems.

Bilateral cooperation in addressing environmental problems has in many ways been similar to collaboration in other fields. The programs are developed in great detail during formal negotiations. Senior scientists, generally of high rank, participate in the activities, and considerable comradery develops among the participants. Unfortunately, young scientists have limited opportunity to take part in the programs. As in all bilateral programs, administrative problems are formidable. Visas are regularly issued at the last minute. Changes in Soviet plans are frequently unannounced until the times for the changes. Promised scientific reports and data sometimes do not arrive from Moscow, preparation of joint documents is usually delayed for many months waiting for Soviet manuscripts, and planned visits are often truncated due to problems on the Soviet side.

Unlike most bilateral programs which are highly compartmentalized within individual Soviet agencies, cooperation in environmental protection has drawn on Soviet specialists from institutions of many different ministries and committees. Also, the environmental sciences have a strong field orientation, and quite a few Americans have traveled to areas of the USSR not normally visited by foreigners. While survey visits and seminars in both countries are commonplace within cooperative programs, environmental collaboration has penetrated far deeper into the working levels in both countries than has been the case in many other programs. Some activities have emphasized joint research projects, with scientists working side by side on ships, in laboratories, and in the field for short periods; others have involved detailed comparisons of results of research projects conducted independently in the two countries. Finally, in contrast to cooperation in other fields of science, often hampered by concerns that cooperation will involve Soviet access to high technologies with near-term military applications, environmental projects have been generally free of technology transfer constraints.

Many scientific publications coauthored by Soviet and American scientists have resulted from the cooperative programs, and a number of American scientists have had access to Soviet data bases that were not previously accessible. Joint surveys of the Bering Sea uncovered unanticipated pollution levels, investigations in the southern areas of the USSR helped classify little-known plant species, scientists from the two countries improved techniques for estimating the probability of earthquakes in California and the Caucasus, and Arctic specialists gained new insights of ecological problems in the Far North. The Soviets have clearly demonstrated their strong mathematical modeling capabilities, the importance of data collected by their extensive monitoring networks covering vast areas, and their considerable expertise in studying ecological changes in disturbed and undisturbed natural settings. Thus, cooperation has advanced international science in many ways, and the outlook for future benefits for both countries is good.

At the same time, the USSR has little to offer in some fields. For example, its pollution control technology is not up to date, its techniques for analyzing pollutants lag, and Soviet concern over secrecy has until recently precluded use of their satellite imagery which could be helpful in assessing ecological changes. The quality of Soviet scientific publications is disappointing. Important details about experimental approaches are frequently omitted from the publications; the quality of the paper, photographs, and graphs is generally poor; and important reports and books may be published in so few copies (e.g., several hundred) that they are soon unavailable even in the USSR. These deficiencies underscore the need to design collaborative programs carefully to help ensure that all participants benefit and that science and not cultural experience remains the principal motivation for participation.

Since the mid-1980s global ecological issues have become prominent in the projects carried out under the Environmental Agreement. Given the sheer size of the two countries as well as their levels of development, they must be central participants in any efforts to reverse adverse impacts on the world's climate or to preserve biological diversity. Bilateral cooperation has been particularly important in encouraging constructive Soviet participation in broader efforts of intergovernmental organizations, including the UN Environmental Program and the World Meteorological Organization, and of nongovernmental organizations within the International Council of Scientific Unions.

### Political Constraints and Overexpectations

As worldwide efforts to cope with the increasing seriousness of global environmental problems intensify, the two governments should be careful not to preempt the role of other countries that also want to participate in setting the international agenda for research and action. More effective mechanisms are needed for disseminating the benefits from bilateral cooperation and for calming international anxieties that bilateral activities could result in undue Soviet-American influence at international meetings. Timely publication of the results of cooperative activities and increased consultations among the Western governments concerning East-West programs of all countries in the environmental field should help.

Another political concern relates to proposals to site bilateral environmental projects in the Third World. For example, American environmental groups have encouraged Soviet scientists to join them in calling for joint U.S.-USSR efforts to help with reforestation efforts in Madagascar. Considerable political symbolism might characterize such efforts of the two superpowers to promote environmental awareness rather than military confrontation in the developing countries. The U.S. government would perhaps like to see the USSR use its influence in Indochina, Cuba, and Central Africa to promote environmental projects.

At the same time, some U.S. officials are skeptical over the Soviet track record in extending foreign aid to the developing countries, foreign aid which could be a mask for political penetration. They have argued that U.S. participation in joint projects in countries outside the Soviet bloc would simply legitimatize Soviet access to areas denied in the past. With regard to joint projects within the bloc, for example, Vietnam, apprehensions exist about scientists from the United States being out in front of official U.S. policy.

For the foreseeable future, many political flash points will punctuate the Soviet-American bilateral relationship, including environmental problems. For example, air pollutants from the industrial city of Norilsk in the north of the USSR continue to feed the pollution cloud circulating in the Arctic, and this blight disturbs Alaskans, who have grown accustomed to relatively pristine environments. As long as the Soviet fishing fleet operates in U.S. coastal areas, frictions with American fishing interests will persist. Soviet readiness to reduce use of chlorofluorocarbons which contribute to ozone depletion and to conform with the European commitment to reduce sulphur discharges is being put to the test at a time of great economic pain for the USSR. It is probable that the control of air emissions will remain a contentious international issue through the 1990s, and the international community will expect both countries to take more aggressive action to reduce emissions.

Meanwhile, problems will continue to inhibit the implementation of bilateral projects. Many ecologically interesting areas and important research centers of the USSR remain off-limits to foreigners, although during 1989 some facilities were opened for the first time. Still, a continued lack of full access will frustrate American specialists. For example, the principal Soviet research center for development of lasers for measuring air pollution is in Tomsk, a closed city. The Soviets have announced that in 1990 an international conference devoted to environmental assessment techniques will be held in the city, but it seems unlikely that the institutes in the city will be wide open to visitors. Likewise, Vladivostok and other areas of the Far East have been closed; while they are gradually opening to Western visitors, constraints on movement in this region will remain.

True cooperation involving high technologies will be difficult. On the U.S. side, export controls and other constraints imposed by government agencies are being felt. In particular, limitations are being placed

on the use of advanced computers and satellite technology in cooperative activities. Presumably, American specialists will be able to share
results obtained with these assessment tools, but more intimate cooperation will probably not be possible. Because modeling and remote
sensing are key technologies for studying global problems, these are
serious constraints. In the field of oceanography, the U.S. Navy will be
reluctant to permit Soviet access to sophisticated navigational equipment on American research ships. Even with regard to land-based monitoring, some U.S. agencies will oppose the sharing of sophisticated elec-
tronic equipment and advanced software programs.

Another caution concerning the future of environmental cooperation relates to financial support in both countries. Environmental projects covering large geographical areas can be very expensive. Whereas
past cooperation has been extensive, the expense has primarily been for
travel and associated living expenses. Now there are many schemes for
joint experimental programs, such as sending icebreakers and research
ships into the Arctic, establishing unmanned monitoring networks in
remote areas, and establishing large central data centers. Despite the
merits of these proposals, both countries will have difficulties making
the transition from simply the support of travel to support of new facilities. However, some facilities already in place or planned for national
programs can be adjusted to take into account interests that emerge in
the bilateral context, and participants should emphasize the use of existing facilities and the fine-tuning of national programs.

Finally, environmental problems are complex and often seemingly
intractable. Many will not be solved quickly, or even in a decade or
more. Thus, measuring the short-term payoff from cooperation will be
difficult, and both governments must recognize that it will require
many years to reap the real benefits of cooperation.

## Environmental Cooperation: A Success Story

Cooperation in environmental protection has the major ingredients for
success; both countries have substantial capabilities to address problems. The boundaries on cooperation are very real, but within these
limits there is considerable room for productive programs; the years of
past cooperation provide an excellent foundation for the future.

Political leaders of the two countries recognize the importance of
cooperation in environmental protection which over time should contribute to the well-being of both countries, and which in the shorter
term strongly supports a positive political relationship. Environmental
cooperation can help build mutual confidence and trust among political leaders, government officials, scientists, and laypersons—all have a
major stake in environmental protection.

# PART III
## SOME
## POLICY
## CHOICES

# AMERICA'S STRATEGIC IMMUNITY: THE BASIS OF A NATIONAL SECURITY STRATEGY
### Eric A. Nordlinger

This essay offers a prescriptive analysis for America's national security posture toward the Soviet Union in the present and into the near future. It is sufficiently general to apply to a future that features a fragmenting USSR, a hostile Russophile nationalism, a military arm-flexing stance reminiscent of the 1970s, an economically rejuvenated socialist or market economy, or a politically dynamic, self-confident leadership with renewed ambitions of striding across the international stage. The underlying reasoning and supportive evidence refer almost entirely to the second half of the Cold War from about 1968 to 1988. As such, this chapter also constitutes a sharp critique of past U.S. security policies —the central policies for safeguarding our territorial integrity, political constitution, economic good health, and physical survival.

The strategy that reverses just about all the policies and doctrinal components of our postwar strategy is commonly referred to as isolationism. Given the prejudicial and distorted meanings that are often assigned to it, some other descriptive labels would seem to be more meaningful. That of a *national* security strategy is appropriate when contrasted with the international strategies of hawks and doves. It may also be called strategic isolationism, nonengagement, disengagement, restraint, or autonomy, as opposed to the conventional strategies of adversarial and conciliatory engagement. A national strategy does not at all entail or imply our literal isolation from the rest of the world, and, as noted in the last part of the chapter, it may actually promote more extensive and effective international policies beyond the national security realm.

A national strategy is first and foremost unilateral and noninterventionist. The security perimeter is strictly limited to the continental and extracontinental United States, Canada, and Mexico, national ships and planes, and people traveling to and from North America. Challenges to, in, and around the core are obviously unacceptable; they are to be deterred and defended against. But beyond the security perimeter there are no allies, defense commitments, or interventions to ward off expansive actions. Washington does not use peripheral issues to maintain its credibility for protecting the core, support the internal and external opponents of Soviet clients, or use carrots to detach and sticks to weaken them. Nor are there any conciliatory efforts to negotiate territorially centered agreements with Moscow involving spheres of interest, mutual limits on military support and interventions, the avoidance and management of crises, and any other rules of peaceful competition. The United States is not actively competing for influence and control. Beyond the core it is not involved in implementing, verifying, and enforcing cooperative Soviet-American accords.

The overall doctrinal rationale for policies of national reserve comes in two parts, with a third constituting a variable or "optional" addition. Activist efforts to safeguard an extensive, quasi-global security perimeter are unnecessary or superfluous, injurious or counterproductive, and possibly unaffordable and unrealizable. The first kind of justification is the most basic. It comes reasonably close to constituting a sufficient argument for strategic restraint and a necessary one for offering the patently consequential claims of the second. The constraining imbalance between our nation's capabilities and commitments, our global overextension, could be part and parcel of the case for nonengagement to the extent that it is, in fact, warranted.

This essay focuses upon nonengagement's most basic justification, which also happens to be the crucial one for all variants of adversarial and conciliatory internationalism.[1] From about 1950 to the present it has been assumed—without question and relentlessly—that unless the Soviet Union were somehow dissuaded from undertaking them, it would carry out great expansionist efforts that other states would be unwilling or unable to deter, defend against, or otherwise ward off. Without our support and guarantees its targets would not be resilient enough to insulate the United States. According to the other crucial assumption, just about all extensions of the Soviet presence, influence, or control would have adverse security consequences for the United States—if not immediately and directly, then over the near term and indirectly, and if not in the geostrategic and military realms, then in the economic, political, and psychological ones. The United States is sorely vulnerable. Each variety of strategic engagement, each point on the hawk-dove policy continuum, derives almost entirely from such assessments of our inordinate susceptibility to Soviet expansionism. It then follows inexorably that Moscow must be dissuaded from acting upon its threatening motivations. Its expansionist aims must be deterred insofar as they stem from hostility and ambition; they must be assuaged and accommodated insofar as they stem from defensive concerns and legitimate security interests.

To suggest that the two doctrinal supports for policies of strategic engagement have been and will continue to be unwarranted is to claim that the United States is strategically immune. Just as an individual's immunity to certain disease germs is inherited or acquired with a few simple innoculations, as opposed to being instilled by expensive medications or painful procedures, so too is the United States immune to the Soviets' expansionist ventures. Our national health or security would not be put at risk by a minimally activist, noninterventionist strategy, and this is based on the premise that Moscow will certainly, probably, or possibly make frequent and exceptionally effortful expansionist attempts, be they motivated by great ambitions, the expansive opportunism of a "traditional" power, or defensive concerns and security fears.

A state that is strategically immune to its rival's expansionist undertakings is either insulated or invulnerable.[2] We are exceptionally well insulated in that nearly all of the Soviets' expansive undertakings would not only fail, but would fail because the "targets" themselves are sufficiently resilient to serve as buffers and barriers. We are exceptionally invulnerable in that nearly all expansionist successes would not have security deflating consequences—militarily, politically, or economically. And this is true without our actively compensating for any Soviet advances. Ranking high on both counts, the United States is doubly immune, which is to say maximally secure, despite minimal security efforts.

Wherever possible, this chapter stacks the cards against the case for nonengagement, as opposed to choosing examples and evidence in some more or less arbitrary, convenient, or otherwise less persuasive manner. Thus the discussions of Soviet expansionism in the Third World give due weight to the 1970s. For it seems least likely to find that we were exceptionally well insulated in the wake of the defeat in Vietnam, the dire predictions of falling "dominoes" and allies "bandwagoning" with Moscow, and the Soviet Union's forceful move into southern Africa, provision of military advisers and weapons to several dozen Third World states, and invasion of Afghanistan, which President Jimmy Carter depicted as the greatest threat to world peace since 1945. On the European side, Washington made its most extensive defense and deterrent contributions during the mid-1980s, and the Warsaw Pact forces were then significantly more advantaged than at any time since the late 1950s. These represent the least likely years in which to demonstrate that Western Europe could stand securely on its own feet or that it was capable of deterring and defending against a Warsaw Pact attack equally well with or without our help. America's overall "decline" is said to have set in during the early 1970s. The turnaround in the political-military spheres during the 1980s did not compensate for the long-run setbacks, while our weakened position in the international economy was most pronounced during the 1980s. In showing the country to be militarily and economically invulnerable it would thus be most telling to concentrate upon the last years of the Cold War.

It would, of course, have been much easier to make the case for America's insulation and invulnerability with reference to the very recent past and present. Even if it is decidedly unwarranted to speak of the Soviet Union's "collapse," there is the near consensus view of a sharp alteration in its capabilities and immediate intentions as they put the security of the Third World, Western Europe, and the United States at risk. This chapter's claims should be especially persuasive precisely because they have been developed under far less favorable conditions. As such, there is also considerable warrant for extrapolating them into the future, for using the 1970s and 1980s to make some inferences about the affordability of strategic isolationism in the 1990s and beyond. And with due regard for the usual caveats and likely rejoinders, this essay might also offer some rough policy guidelines for minimizing the security threat from any potential or newly emergent rival, be it a united Europe, Germany, Japan, China, or Brazil.

The United States is insulated insofar as the USSR's efforts to extend its influence-control are unsuccessful—unsuccessful due to the resilience of third states. They are willing and able to circumvent, offset, buffer, negate, or otherwise neutralize Moscow's more and less forceful, direct and indirect expansionist ventures. The most important insulating conditions include powerful nationalist, ethnic, and religious attachments, political and security interests that are incompatible with Moscow's, and a deep mistrust of its intentions. In addition, third states are not dependent upon Soviet economic or military assistance, their armed forces are able to counter Soviet-supported insurgencies, defend against interventions with the "aid" of a hospitable terrain, and deter and withstand coercive threats and outright attacks in the case of nuclear-capable states.

An examination of Soviet expansionism in the Third World may not appear capable of supporting the case for America's insulation, for by definition the latter must obtain in the absence of activist containment policies. Yet the problem can be circumvented by focusing upon expansionist efforts whose failures and limited successes were largely unrelated to U.S. activism. They are attributable to the immunity-enhancing conditions found among the states of the First, Second, and Third Worlds.

In the mid-1950s, the Soviets did mount a successful ideological offensive in the Third World. An impressive, globe-spanning propaganda machine effectively exploited anti-imperialist and anticapitalist sentiments. Most former colonies expressed an affinity for the Soviet Union in their foreign policies, many adopted a centralized planning model for their economies, and some embraced a socialist political ideology. The Soviets came over to the side of the neutral states, lauding them as a "beneficial and positive" force, and including them in an "extensive zone of peace" along with the socialist states. By the late 1950s these efforts were proving so effective that Nikita Khrushchev announced a bandwagoning movement in enlisting Third World states as Soviet allies.[3]

These successes were soon reversed, long before the Soviet Union was seen to be entirely bankrupt as an ideological model in the 1980s. In the early 1960s the appearance of socialist unity suffered when China openly began to challenge the Soviet Union's ideological preeminence. As the post-independence euphoria waned, the unenviable record of those states that adhered to socialist political ideals and relied upon economic planning models became widely evident. By the late 1970s slow economic growth culminated in a widening Soviet-American gap, followed by unflattering comparisons with the performance of such "undeveloped" countries as South Korea and Brazil. Socialism was increasingly linked to poverty with the acquisition of Soviet clients that were poor even by Third World standards. The continuously expanding recognition of Russia, not as the fervent advocate of peace, self-determination, and socialism, but as just another great power with imperialist designs became widespread in the Moslem world with the invasion of Afghanistan. Currently, only some dozen Third World regimes identify with the Soviet Union ideologically, and for a few it may be a largely symbolic exercise to obtain material support.

Around 1955 Moscow began using economic incentives to expand its influence in the Third World. Those efforts have never overcome the Soviet economy's decided limitations in supporting effective programs of trade and aid.[4] Its autarkic features, inconvertible currency, hard currency shortages, and shoddy manufactured goods continue to preclude extensive economic relations, not to mention trade-based dependencies. In the 1960s the Third World conducted 5 percent of its trade with the Soviet bloc. Some twenty years later it was 6 percent, which also happens to represent 1/15 of its trade with the developed capitalist countries.[5] The visible Soviet presence in some large development projects—notably the Aswan Dam and the Helwan steel complex in Egypt—pales in comparison with that of thousands of Western subsidiaries and joint ventures. Soviet aid programs have been inflexibly tied to second-rate Soviet products and machinery that often take years to deliver. Promises outran deliveries. Over a twenty-five year period only

$8 billion of $18 billion in commitments have actually materialized. Moscow has disappointed friendly regimes, such as those of Salvador Allende in Chile and John Manley in Jamaica, that were desperately seeking aid and trade to offset their dependence upon the West. Clients have been encouraged to look to the West for assistance since the late 1970s.

Starting in the mid-1980s the Soviets gave a new twist to their courting tactics in trying to establish friendly relations with some dozen influential "nationalist" regimes, including Brazil, Argentina, Saudi Arabia, Morocco, Nigeria, Indonesia, and Thailand. Along with the downplaying of communist ideology, they have been courted with trade agreements, cultural exchanges, high-level visits, and effusive commendations so as to gain diplomatic support, put a greater distance between these countries and the U.S., and influence regional conflicts. Bilateral relationships have been warmed up, but beyond that there are no tangible results to date, given the little that Moscow can offer these regimes —they do not need military aid, and its economic offerings do not usually compare with the West's. Soviet-Indian relations are a telling case since Moscow has referred to them as a "model" for its dealings with nationalist regimes. Soviet trade with India is far greater than that of any other Third World country, and it has received more attention than any other since Mikhail Gorbachev's ascension. Yet it has continued to refuse basing rights for the Soviet navy, rejected Gorbachev's proposed Asian security conference, and generally shown itself to be independent in its political and economic dealings with other countries.[7]

Every Third World country and group of countries has, of course, always been vastly outclassed by the Soviet Union militarily. Yet the single test case does not suggest that the invasion route will prove successful. After nine years of war the USSR failed to attain any more control over Afghanistan than it had prior to 1979. American arms supplies to the Mujahadeen did make an undeniably important contribution to the outcome. Still, at a minimum, U.S. opposition was offset by the exceptional advantage of being able to conduct a war just across the Soviet border. And this is an advantage that can hardly ever be replicated elsewhere. What does characterize Afghanistan and much of the Third World is one or another kind of terrain that markedly detracts from the Soviet military efforts. And where the Soviets could establish military control, it does not follow that they would be able to acquire more than a few countries whose governance would then require a substantial military presence, and which would involve the distinct possibility of festering insurgencies.

The Soviet presence was greatly extended with the provision of all sorts of military assistance to all sorts of states and "national liberation" movements. Their greatest successes occurred in the 1970s with the shipment of an enormous number of low-cost, attractively financed, reliable, quickly obtainable weapons to some fifty states. By 1979 the USSR replaced the United States as the supplier of choice and the leading arms supplier to the Third World. At its 1980 high point Moscow delivered $8.1 billion in arms and signed agreements for another $14.6 billion. In addition, Eastern bloc military personnel were dispatched to serve as advisers, technicians, combat troops, and palace guards to ward off coup-minded opponents. Between 1970 and 1980 their numbers grew from ten thousand to eighteen thousand. Besides a remarkable extension of the Soviet presence, these efforts were more or less instrumental in producing notable successes in Vietnam, Angola, Mozambique, South Yemen, Somalia, Ethiopia, and Nicaragua. Toward the end of the 1980s the Soviet Union was providing three times as much military aid as the United States, training twice as many military officers and technicians, deploying thirty times as many military advisers, and supplying more arms in all but one category.[8]

There is no doubting that the USSR has been able to make numerous gains in the Third World, some of them important, by way of providing military aid. On the other hand, this is the only means by which it has been able to do so. Gains that have been made in other ways are few in number, sporadic successes attributable to a concatenation of unusual circumstances.

Whatever the ways that extensions of the Soviet presence have come about, they have not had anything like a multiplier effect. They have not made for additional gains, even proving to be somewhat counterproductive in this regard. Contrary to a crucial justification for quasi-global containment, states are not given to bandwagoning with the currently successful rival. They do try to balance against a threatening "winner." Kenneth N. Waltz has highlighted the seeming paradox in which "winning leads to losing" in international politics. "No country wants to be dependent upon another. If a country becomes dependent because of weakness, its neighbors will resist suffering a similar fate. We have been misled by a vision of falling dominoes. . . . States try to balance each other off; they do not climb on the bandwagon of a winner."[9] Stephen M. Walt has fully developed the underlying dynamics of this generalization and put it to some diverse and demanding tests in the Middle East. He found that balancing against a threat—by heightening resolve, forming alliances, and upgrading defenses—is far more common than bandwagoning. Although small states are less given to balancing against a major power, weakness may be offset by the latter's unpalatable ideology, past aggressive actions, and by the constraints of distance and topography.[10]

If Third World states have even a mild tendency to bandwagon with the Soviet Union it should certainly have shown up during the 1970s. During these years the Soviets achieved strategic parity, acquired force-projection forces and a blue-water navy, made considerable territorial gains, intervened effectively in "distant" Angola, and announced a decisive shift to socialism in the overall correlation of forces. The United States suffered a major defeat in Vietnam, diluted its containment efforts, experienced the oil shock, and publicly lamented its decline. Yet the Soviets suffered rejections and losses in Egypt, the Sudan, Somalia, Uganda, Equatorial Guinea, Guinea-Bissau, Chile, *and* pre-1979 Afghanistan. Of these, only Egypt, and Chile at the margins, are attributable to American efforts. According to one calculation, the total number of countries in which Moscow enjoyed substantial influence or control did not increase at all between 1970 and 1980.[11] Moreover, some countries balanced against the threat despite and because of our retrenchment. The ASEAN countries did so in response to the U.S. withdrawal and Hanoi's invasion of Cambodia. The Nixon administration's reduction of U.S. forces in South Korea led it to compensate with a 300 percent increase in defense outlays between 1976 and 1980; the Carter administration's proposed troop withdrawal prompted another 200 percent rise over the next four years.[12]

A final observation about the resilience of Third World states is about as significant as the previous ones taken together. The latter refer to extensions of the Soviet presence, the former has to do with its translation into influence-control. Whatever success the Soviets have had in expanding their presence, it bears primarily upon American security to the degree that their allies and clients can be managed and put to good use.

Moscow has never been able to turn its presence, connections, and assistance into widespread control, leverage, or palpable influence. At any one time it has only enjoyed considerable leverage over a handful of Marxist and "fraternal" states in the Third World. Their number was "greatest" between the late 1970s and the late 1980s, when Mongolia, Cuba, Vietnam, and probably Ethiopia, South Yemen, Cambodia, and Laos were under Moscow's sway. Yet even in South Yemen with its "vanguard" socialist party and Moscow's extensive penetration, it was unable to prevent a civil war between two Marxist factions. As for limited influence, it is difficult to discern more than an occasional instance in which the Soviets prevailed on a major external or internal issue—voting at the United Nations and restraint in condemning the invasion of Afghanistan not being major ones. Not only have the Soviets invariably departed with alacrity when asked to do so, but their continued presence has also usually been conditional, depending upon convergent strategies for the realization of common objectives. "When a Third World leader perceives the USSR as being overbearing or unsupportive, the question 'what have you done for me recently?' is more relevant to him than 'what did you do for me in the past?'. . . . The status of the Soviet Union typically has not been that of imperial overlord but of a guest worker."[13]

Soviet clients have asserted their autonomy, even when exceptionally dependent on their patron's support. Despite the Angolan regime's need for some fifty thousand Cuban troops and Soviet largesse to assure its survival, it refused base rights for the Soviet navy, signed a nonaggression accord with South Africa that was opposed by Moscow and mediated by Washington, declined to mesh its economy with the East, and maintained extensive ties with the West. During the nearly twenty years in which Egypt depended upon Moscow as its largest source of economic aid and only important source of military equipment, it imprisoned local communists, carried out the union with Syria, quarreled with Iraq, rejected the Rogers Peace Plan, and began the War of Attrition and the 1973 War, all contrary to Soviet advice and pressure.[14] By 1976 Iraq had received more than $1 billion in Soviet aid and more military equipment than any other Middle Eastern client, yet Moscow's influence "had been very limited," Iraq giving "relatively little in the way of political obedience in return."[15]

Future extensions of the Soviet presence and the heightening of Soviet influence-control look to be bleaker than in the past. There are no promising improvements in expansionist means or the conditions that make for their effectiveness, while some developments will probably make it more difficult not just to extend, but to maintain Moscow's position. Socialism as an ideology will probably be further denuded of its energizing and guiding impact. Modernization programs will require a sharper focusing of trade relations with the industrialized countries. Economic needs that have already constrained military and economic assistance will become more pressing, at least in the short run. And with the ebbing of the Cold War, the American trade embargoes and military support for anti-Marxist insurgents that have made some clients highly dependent upon Moscow are likely to fade away.

Turning to Western Europe, to claim that it has most probably been resilient enough to insulate the United States is to take issue with this long-standing, central unquestioned premise; in the absence of the Atlantic alliance Europe is incapable of warding off Finlandization or of deterring and defending against a Warsaw Pact invasion. To make the case admittedly involves some hypotheticals since the United States has been invariably involved as the alliance leader; to rely upon inferences from what has been to what probably would have been under different conditions makes for a relatively weak argument. However, the attempted demonstration of the reverse claim—that a Western Europe on its own would have proved insufficiently resilient to ward off pressures, threats, and attacks—runs up against the very same problem. The fact that the USSR has not extended its influence and control into Western Europe is only germane if it can somehow be shown that it would have done so in the hypothetical absence of the American presence.

Paradoxically, assessing Western Europe's will to negate Soviet blandishments, pressures, and threats by extrapolating from the one country that has been Finlandized is barely relevant. As a small country, situated on the Soviet border, formerly part of the Russian empire, and a German co-belligerent it is hardly surprising that it acceded to Moscow's demands. Except for its size, no other country in Western Europe shares any of these features with Finland, while the two other small states that were subjected to Soviet demands reacted very differently. Yugoslavia maintained its independence in the face of a six-year "little cold war" between Moscow and Belgrade. Soviet efforts to dissuade Norway from joining NATO not only failed, but they also helped move it into the alliance. Were it not for the availability of American commitments, Norway might have reacted differently, but this cannot be said about what was then a virulently anti-American Yugoslavia.

If the resilience of Western Europe were ever such that it would have shifted eastward except for the American connection, there should have been some movement toward Finlandization, especially when there was some special cause for concern. In the 1960s American worries were prompted by Charles de Gaulle's vision of a Europe poised and mediating between the superpowers, and by Willy Brandt's Ostpolitik which could have helped overcome the East-West divide. Neither development was followed by any steps toward Finlandization. Yet more telling is their absence when American anxieties were at their high point during the late 1970s. The communist parties of Spain, Portugal, and Greece had made substantial strides toward power. Yet the spectre of Eurocommunism turned out to be a minor, short-lived surge, and its demise could hardly be attributed to U.S. policy.

It is one thing to acknowledge America's part in managing the Atlantic alliance, even in keeping it together. Yet it would seem that the characteristics of Western Europe itself would have been sufficient to obviate Finlandization. During the late 1980s its GNP was bigger than our own, twice that of Japan's, and twice as large as the Soviet Union's, West Germany's alone constituting 40 percent of the Soviet GNP. With a population of 320 million, Western Europe's is one and a half times bigger than that of the USSR. "Totaling" up its population, industrial output, and technological resources at any point after 1960 makes for a somewhat greater military potential than that of the USSR and Eastern Europe together. Groupings of this absolute and relative size, economic might, and military potential are not at all given to acceding to other states. There are also the individual state's characteristics to consider: their autonomous histories, national pride and traditions, commitments to liberal democracy, political unity, and stable institutions. Under just about any circumstances such states are almost sure to have the necessary will to maintain their full independence, to expend their resources to whatever extent is thought necessary. As for the question of political-military solidarity, the European Community is easily the most impressive instance of interstate institution-building in the postwar period. The coordination of a plethora of recalcitrant domestic interests suggest as much success in organizing a defense against a common external threat.

And just how were the Soviets to have their way in the past? Western Europe has been more open and friendly toward the USSR than has the United States, but at times it has been anything but implacably opposed to Soviet threats and demands. Nor has it had any illusions about the Soviets or shown any disposition to rely upon Soviet good will rather than their own military forces for their security. As for inducements, West German hopes for reunification could not be taken much beyond cosmetics due to the Soviet fear of German power, while proposals for mutual military reductions ran squarely up against the Europeans' insistence upon conventional parity. As for Soviet leverage, dependency relations ran almost exclusively in the wrong direction, with capital, credits, trade, and technology moving from West to East. What kind of palpable pressures could then have been exerted over Western Europe, according to what sort of plausible scenario, bringing which additional pressures to bear after the first proved inadequate?

There is an answer to this question, one that has long been viewed as an alternative route to Finlandization. Assistance to Greece and Turkey in 1947 was intended to close off the Middle East to the spread of communism and Soviet control, thereby obviating the use of the oil weapon to detach Western Europe from the United States. The most recent concerns have involved Moscow's gaining control over Iran (and its oil fields) via a cross-border invasion, intervention in a civil war, or the installation of a pro-Soviet government. Military pressures could then be focused upon Saudi Arabia and the other Gulf states until they adhere to Moscow's demands. After gaining physical access to or political control over Middle Eastern oil supplies, the Soviets could threaten an embargo unless Western Europe (and Japan) shifts eastward, or sell the oil and create a dependency relationship.[16]

Such a scenario hinges on each of three conditions. Contrary to what was just said about the Third World as a whole, the Middle Eastern states turn out to be insufficiently resilient to guard against extensions of Soviet influence and control. Contrary to some powerful incentives, Western Europe does very little to diversify its suppliers and to become more energy self-sufficient when prompted by America's disengagement—over and above the promptings that led to a reduction in Gulf oil imports from 60 to 35 percent of total imports between 1980 and 1985.[17] Contrary to conventional market behavior, Europe is unable to obtain additional oil from Third World suppliers despite its willingness to pay premium prices, their need of funds, and a possible excess of world oil supplies.

Since approximately 1960 Western Europe has most probably been capable of deterring and defending against a Warsaw Pact invasion —about as well without its American ally as with it. It was just seen to have the will to ward off the Soviet Union. What needs to be shown here is that a Europe on its own would have maintained military forces whose size and special advantages would fully compensate for the withdrawal of the American military and its nuclear umbrella. As already noted, around 1986 is the most appropriate reference point for such a discussion.

In monetary terms the United States spent about $135 billion annually on the defense of Europe, this being the cost of U.S. forces stationed on the continent and oriented toward it in the event of a conventional war. In terms of personnel, 320,000 served across the Atlantic, and 130,000 were to be sent across in the event of a war. Of the ready forces on the continent, the United States supplied 10 percent of the ground forces, 15 percent of the air forces, and 25 percent of the tanks. Roughly twenty times more American than British and French nuclear weapons were targeted on Central Europe and the USSR.[18]

A look at NATO Europe's military potential and the political feasibility of its mobilization suggests that it would probably have compensated for these sizeable, patently expensive American forces. Its total military expenditures as a percentage of GNP totaled a little more than half of America's, 3.8 percent versus 6.8 percent. Raising the former to the level of the latter would generate an additional $68 billion, which is equal to half the $135 billion American expenditure devoted to Europe. That this comes within the range of political feasibility is suggested by a comparison of U.S. military expenditures of $1,077 per person with NATO Europe's per capita outlay of $263. To double the latter would add $136 billion to Europe's defense spending.[19] Doing so would fully match the U.S. contribution and still leave Europe's per capita outlay at only half of ours. There is, moreover, the Europeans' response to the one time—during and in the wake of the war in Vietnam—that the United States cut back substantially on its material support for NATO. They steadily increased their own expenditures, their share of total NATO spending almost doubling from 23 to 42 percent between 1969 and 1979.[20]

Having raised the financial issue in terms of a full, $135 billion replacement of the American contribution, it turns out that this would not have been necessary. David P. Calleo goes so far as to characterize such a spending requirement as "preposterous," and not for any debatable military reasons. "America's ratio of expenditure to forces is notoriously inferior to Western Europe's—a result that reflects not only America's vast inefficiencies in procurement, management, and weapons acquisition, but also its inherent comparative disadvantage in deploying large conventional forces overseas."[21]

With NATO Europe already providing 3.3 million military personnel compensating for America's would have required a relatively small increase of 10 percent. In gauging its feasibility the most important number is the proportion of the population serving in the armed forces: .96 percent for the United States, 1.0 percent for NATO Europe, and 1.1 percent for Belgium, the NATO country with the highest ratio.[22] Substituting for the full American force of 450,000 would have required an additional one soldier per 1,000 of population. This would have brought Europe's ratio up to 1.1, the same as Belgium's.

A Western Europe on its own would have had three singular military benefits. With a Pact invasion almost certainly taking the form of a blitzkrieg which could easily decide the war's outcome within a week or two, an all-European force would have enjoyed the inestimable advantage of proximity to the battlefield. In contrast, the 130,000 U.S. troops to be transported across the Atlantic—almost one-third of the total U.S. force and all of NATO's "operational resources"—could all arrive only within three months after their mobilization. Nor is it certain that they would escape Soviet submarine attacks and be able to disembark at intact harbors. Given the difficulties in fully compensating for a U.S. withdrawal, West Germany could well have overcome its strong distaste for building defenses near the inter-German border. Antitank ditches, antitank positions, prechambered bridges, and other preparations would have served as exceptionally cheap and effective defenses. A belt of obstacles along the entire inter-German border would have cost less than a billion dollars. Relying upon standard military data, William W. Kaufmann estimates that "such barriers would decrease the relative effectiveness of a given offensive force by as much as 40 percent." These barriers would have allowed seventeen divisions to halt a concentrated attack by as many as thirty Pact divisions.[23]

Compared to the thousands of American nuclear weapons targeted upon Central Europe and the USSR, Britain and France only had hundreds of nuclear-tipped cruise missiles and submarine-launched ballistic missiles. However, an American withdrawal would almost certainly have prompted an expansion, probably complemented by a West German nuclear force. And many times more important than numbers is the credibility of a nuclear deterrent, most certainly so even when a small force cannot be prevented from destroying every large- and medium-sized Soviet city three times over. Britain, France, and West Germany's credibility for carrying out the suicidal threat would have been much greater than ours. Extended deterrence cannot be highly credible when it involves trading Boston for Bonn. Basic deterrence is far more likely to be inherently credible. What Robert W. Tucker has said about America's missiles also applies to a Europe without America. "So long as it is clear that they will be employed only in the direct defense of the homeland, they confer a physical security that is virtually complete, and that the loss of allies cannot alter."[24]

This, the best reasonable case to be made on behalf of Western Europe's resilience,[25] does, of course, feature more than one or two uncertainties. Judgments on this score have differed sharply and there is thus reason to consider the judgment of the Europeans themselves. In fact, the point is applicable to just about all U.S. allies.

America's allies have regularly viewed their own resilience with discernibly greater confidence than has the United States. They have also treated the possibilities of communist expansionism with significantly less anxiety. And there is good reason to accord the allies' judgments special weight. They are geographically closer, politically more exposed, and militarily at greater direct risk. In almost every disagreement about the likelihood of a successful attack by the Warsaw Pact our NATO allies have regarded it with greater equanimity. Our fear of a China with one-quarter of the world's population was strikingly evident throughout the 1950s and the 1960s. Yet this fear was not as great in South Korea, Japan, Southeast Asia, and possibly Pakistan. During the Vietnam War the nearby SEATO countries were less anxious about the threat to their own security than was the United States. And most recently, Marxist Nicaragua and the radical insurgency in El Salvador have caused much greater nervousness in the United States than among the bordering and nearby countries in Central and South America.

But what if the United States is not (seen to be) all that well insulated by other states? The other territorial component of strategic immunity becomes crucial to the extent and at the "point" that they might prove to be insufficiently resilient. The United States is invulnerable insofar as successful extensions of Russian influence-control do not impair either its military capacities—the deterrent-defensive capacities for protecting the core—or its economic well-being.

Militarily, America is invulnerable insofar as Soviet expansionist successes do not offer an advantageous geostrategic position from which to carry out an attack; the military balance is not significantly altered by the forces or potential military resources of the additional Soviet allies and clients; and the latter do not control resources that are needed by the United States for building weapons and fueling them in wartime.

At one time or another, most Third World states have been invested with substantial to critical geostrategic importance as "bridges," "island chains," "barriers," and "flanks." Over and above the Soviets having leapfrogged over them, Robert H. Johnson has pointed out that these concepts often lack meaning and discriminateness. "(I)t has been said that the Persian Gulf region has great importance as a 'bridge' between Europe and all of Asia. The Persian Gulf is unquestionably important, but how is it a bridge and for what purposes and under what circumstances? Why the Persian Gulf rather than Egypt, Suez, and the Red Sea? Moreover, since the globe is a piece with every area ultimately connected to every other, it does not take a great deal of ingenuity to develop a geostrategic rationale for the importance of almost any country."[26]

Some countries are geostrategically important for the defense of America's numerous allies. But if the security perimeter were tightly drawn, that would leave only the Caribbean and Central American countries as possibly advantageous positions from which to threaten the core. As our "backyard," "frontyard," and "southern flank," no Soviet bases within the area is said to constitute the "irreducible minimum security interest." Yet the launching of missiles from nearby locations offers few if any overall benefits, there are no plausible ways in which the Soviets could coerce or attack North America given U.S. conventional superiority, and naval bases would only serve to increase the on-station time of Soviet submarines.[27] Most policymakers view the naval station at Guantanamo primarily as an irritant to the Cuban government; the Panama Canal's military importance is related to the resupply of U.S. forces fighting overseas rather than to the movement of warships.[28]

Nor would Soviet territorial gains significantly threaten the country's sea lines of communication. In part the loss of naval bases can be compensated for by the lengthy patrol capabilities of nuclear-powered ships, if not the leasing of others on a commercial basis. Except for naval bases in the Indian Ocean, the loss of nearly all others would only entail a few extra days to return to American island bases and home ports for repairs and supplies about every two months. Localized Soviet threats to the sea lanes can most probably be deterred and defended against by a superior navy configured for just that role. According to one assessment, what German submarine warfare never came close to achieving in World War II—the severing of the Atlantic—is a more remote possibility for the Soviet Union.[29]

Regarding the military power of third states, the United States continues to enjoy an enormously wide margin of actual and potential superiority over any state other than the USSR—a margin greater than that of any major power relative to those of lesser rank since the seventeenth-century beginnings of the modern state system. The adverse security consequences were indiscernible when fully one-quarter of the world population was "lost" to the Soviets. And when China changed sides again, this time along with a small nuclear capability, America's security was not notably enhanced. Ranking third in the world in military expenditures, China's are less than 20 percent of America's. Its GNP, the largest of any country in the southern hemisphere, is 6 percent of America's. Indeed, the U.S. GNP is fully twice that of the entire Third World, and fifteen times larger than that of Brazil with the largest GNP.[30] For the Soviets to acquire more than the equivalent of American economic resources would entail not the Finlandization, but the exercise of control over the next four wealthiest countries—Japan, Germany, France, and Italy. And even then the United States could not be "spent into the ground" given relatively inexpensive nuclear weapons and the less than onerous requirements for the conventional defense of the core.

Economically, and with respect to imports of military related resources, a state is patently invulnerable if it is autarkic or minimally dependent on others. But as with America, a state may be invulnerable despite such dependencies. The United States is significantly dependent upon imports and exports. More than one-seventh of our GNP derives from trade. The oil imports that are critical to all parts of the economy have increased since 1977 so that they again make up half of total consumption. Non-fuel minerals are essential to civilian and defense industries, with import levels of twenty standing above 50 percent of current consumption.

Yet the United States is still close to being fully invulnerable economically. It has numerous, diverse, reasonably reliable trading partners, the loss of some thus being neutralized by the availability of others. Third states are far more dependent economically upon the United States than vice versa, thereby sharply mitigating if not obviating their leverage. Domestic substitutes for imported materials are available and stockpiles are adequate for emergencies.[31]

More than 60 percent of U.S. trade is conducted with the industrial democracies. With the value of these imports and exports approaching 10 percent of the nation's GNP, a cutoff would obviously have a pronounced economic impact, at least over the short term.[32] This is, however, just about the only economic vulnerability. Canada and Mexico, the first and fourth most important trading partners, lie within the core. They generate one-quarter of U.S. imports and exports. The vast majority of Third World trading partners, including the petroleum producers, is decidedly more dependent upon the United States than vice versa. Only 15 percent of total U.S. trade is conducted with the Third World in its entirety, and at the same time we have so much of what it very much wants or needs: export markets, investment capital, advanced technology, food, and sophisticated weaponry.[33] America's influential positions within the World Bank, the International Monetary Fund, and other multilateral development banks provide considerable leverage. Except for the Arab oil embargo of 1973 and Albania, which has not traded with anyone, not a single country has ever refused to do economic business with the United States. Neither our severing of diplomatic relations nor military support for domestic opponents has prompted any state to break off economic relations.

Then there are the risks of a cut-off or a sharp, politically motivated price increase of crude oil. These risks are decidedly on the low side despite again importing half its oil, with domestic production down by almost one-fifth since 1985 as prices have skidded. For the first- and fourth-ranking suppliers lie within the core. It takes the six largest oil suppliers outside the core to provide half the country's imports. Venezuela, Saudi Arabia, Nigeria, the United Kingdom, Algeria, and Indonesia are found in each oil-producing region outside North America. The number and political diversity of suppliers, as well as their marked dependence on current oil revenues, is such that the Reagan administration experienced few if any constraints in deciding to "reject" Libyan —oil equivalent to one-third of Saudi Arabian imports. The Arab oil-producing states altogether now provide only 15 percent of total imports.[34] Eight years of virtually all-out war between Iran and Iraq did not close the Straits of Hormuz, and had they been closed only 4 percent of imports would have been affected.[35] The Arab and OPEC nations with large oil reserves want to assure the industrialized world of long-term stability in supplies and costs. Their run-up of prices in the late 1970s and early 1980s was admittedly counterproductive. It resulted in plummeting demand for OPEC oil by way of extensive energy conservation measures, a shift to other fuels, economic recession, and an increase in non-OPEC oil production.

As for the nation's own safeguards, there are 600 million barrels of oil currently stored in salt domes along the Gulf Coast. These are equivalent to two and a half months of total imports, and realistically more like nine months, since there is no foreseeable risk of a simultaneous cut-off on the part of all the suppliers. The Strategic Petroleum Reserve's holdings amount to more than three years of imports from all the Arab oil states. They are thus not in a position to contemplate, no less to carry out an embargo, and were it somehow to materialize, the reserves would cushion the economic impact. In addition, there are the policy options for discouraging oil consumption and encouraging domestic and international exploration, options financed by the gradual imposition of federal taxes on oil imports or gasoline consumption. Looking further into the future, there is the development—that is, reducing the cost—of synfuels, geothermal, biomass, solar, and acceptably safe nuclear energy. Public policies for their promotions should prove economically beneficial in any case given the expected depletion of known oil reserves and the sizable export markets for the new technologies.

Of the twenty industrial and strategic minerals whose import levels are above 50 percent of consumption, Canada is the primary supplier of eight, the second-ranking supplier of another, and Mexico is among the chief sources of four. For all but three of the twenty, the major suppliers include Canada, Mexico, France, Britain, Spain, Norway, Austria, and Japan.[36] The Joint Chiefs of Staff have identified seven of the twenty as especially critical: dependency is greater than 75 percent on countries which could "deny us our supplies" in the foreseeable future.[37] Yet Canada is a leading supplier of three, and France, Australia, and Brazil are among the chief sources of another three.[38]

Our greatest vulnerability is to cut-offs of cobalt and chromium.[39] But even here there are sharply mitigating circumstances. On the one hand, 95 percent of cobalt is imported, the biggest suppliers are Zaire and Zambia, and the Soviet Union and Cuba are the next largest producers. On the other hand, Canada is the third-ranking supplier and the fifth biggest producer, the nickel supplied chiefly by Canada can serve as a substitute in superalloys, projects are underway to develop nickel and ceramic substitutes for cobalt's other applications, and stockpiles are fully adequate for most critical defense and industrial needs.[40] Seventy-three percent of chromium is imported, the chief suppliers are South Africa, Zimbabwe, Yugoslavia, and Turkey, and the only other large sources of supply are in the Soviet Union and Albania. Yet other minerals can replace chromium in some of its applications, a wide variety of materials can substitute for the stainless steel of which it is a necessary ingredient, and stockpiles are equal to five years of consumption requirements.[41]

In 1979 Congress enacted a requirement for the stockpiling of minerals to meet military and essential civilian needs on the contingency of a three-year conventional war and total trade disruption. The Reagan administration proposed a downward revision of many specific target levels and the sale of some current stocks, explaining that "strategic materials needs will be sharply reduced in a future war by cutbacks in civilian consumption, keeping the sea lanes open to reliable overseas sources, encouraging substitutions, and stimulating more recycling."[42] This assessment is acceptable. But if not, the 1979 stockpile levels could quickly be reached with an expenditure of $7 billion.[43] Looking further ahead, mineral dependencies could be further reduced by policies that encourage the opening of old mines, research on substitutability, and the development of extensive recycling and conservation programs.[44]

In discussing America's strategic immunity it was assumed that the USSR would undertake frequent and strenuous expansionist ventures. It now becomes possible to ask a prior question about the likelihood of such undertakings. On the possibility that ambitiously or defensively motivated expansionist aims became salient once again, might not the presence and efficacy of the immunity-enhancing conditions that were just delineated persuade Moscow not to act upon them? In prompting Moscow's self-deterrence these conditions would provide for an additional "layer" of security, over and above insulating the United States and rendering it invulnerable.

Just about whatever its intentions and capabilities may be or become, the USSR is likely to dissuade itself from undertaking frequent or strenuous expansive actions in the forseeable future. An appreciation of great scope, potency, and robustness of the immunity-enhancing conditions will discourage costly undertakings that hold out little prospect of success or of special advantage with regard to the United States if successful. Our own disengagement would reinforce Moscow's appreciation and acceptance of the limits and limitations imposed upon it by the immunity-enhancing conditions.[45]

Neither kind of perceptual error is likely that would lead Moscow to overestimate its chances of success. Unmotivated cognitive errors— those stemming from inadequate information, simplifying short cuts, and the like—are much diminished since most of the conditions that make for insulation and invulnerability can be readily perceived and assessed. They tend to be manifest, tangible, clear, and reasonably simple. Their appreciation can only be reinforced by recollections of, and learning from, Moscow's expansionist failures and less than consequential successes. The possibility of America fostering any motivated cognitive errors would be nearly eliminated with a shift toward disengagement. With Moscow not being placed in what could be seen as a circumscribed and pressured position via quasi-global containment, it would not be given the psychological incentive to depreciate the scope and potency of the immunity-enhancing conditions. For it is when states believe their interests to be threatened, each decisional option being seen as unpalatable, that they sometimes alleviate the strains by embracing overly optimistic beliefs.[46]

The years from 1976 to 1978 offer telling evidence of Moscow's past and future ability to recognize externally imposed limits and limitations. A combination of circumstances made these years the incontrovertibly least likely ones for it to do so. Ideological blinders were still being worn and hegemonic ambitions were still in place, the USSR had made some remarkable territorial gains and attained its strategic zenith, the United States had suffered major reverses and was experiencing great anxieties about its security and possible decline. These circumstances "should" certainly have engendered a self-congratulatory mood, along with highly optimistic expectations of continuing successes. Yet it was precisely then that party officials, military officers, and scholarly experts began to distinguish between appearances and realities. Their assessments soon became the bases for Yuri Andropov's policies of retrenchment and Gorbachev's "New Thinking."

Soviet officials and analysts recognized the resilience of clients and other Third World states in meeting Soviet attempts to exercise influence and control. They became disillusioned with "progressive" military regimes, "socialist oriented" states, as well as overtly Marxist ones. These were no longer viewed as sufficiently stable or ideologically committed to make the transition to socialism in the foreseeable future, or to serve as a durable basis for the consolidation of Soviet influence. Even the hegemony of Leninist "vanguard parties" was downgraded into a "prerequisite" for the realization of these goals. Along with much skepticism about the effectiveness and affordability of military and economic assistance to current allies, the prospects for gaining others were minimized. The distinct limits of Soviet influence and socialist development were primarily explained by enduring nationalist, ethnic, and religious values and attachments, concomitantly deemphasizing the changeable variables of neocolonial dependencies and imperialist-backed insurgencies against Marxist regimes.[47]

Were Moscow somehow still to overestimate the likelihood of overcoming the immunity-enhancing conditions there is at least one self-deterrent. It would know that America might shift back toward an adversarial strategy if expansionist actions of some magnitude were successful, and almost surely so if they were seen to have security-deflating consequences. The Soviets would presumably "sacrifice" much in the way of territorial ventures not attempted to avoid this unwelcome prospect.

A high-stakes gamble, such as an attack upon a militarily well-endowed third state, cannot be ruled out despite an accurate appraisal of the attendant costs and odds. But since gambles are almost invariably undertaken when the future looks to be far worse than the present, nonengagement sharply minimizes this possibility. The USSR need not choose between a poor wager on the potency of the immunity-enhancing conditions and an erosion of its relative power or exploitation of its domestic difficulties when we are partly to fully disengaged. The bear is not cornered, its possible decline is not purposefully rushed. If overweening ambitions or security fears were present, they are likely to be kept in check by a culturally imposed risk aversiveness. The interpretations of Nathan Leites, Alexander George, Richard Pipes, and Hannes Adomeit are of a piece in showing that the Soviets regularly behave in accordance with several operational rules when contemplating expansive actions, especially those entailing the use of force. Never undertake actions that are not carefully calculated and planned in advance. Do not move forward when doing so has an uncertain payoff or the distinct possibility of a sizeable loss. When outcomes are unclear, only act if the odds are exceptionally favorable. The attainment of immediate gains needs to be offset by the possibility of longer-range costs. Pull back when resistance turns out to be stronger than expected.[48]

On the record, the Soviets have only carried out one "hare-brained" scheme. The missile emplacement in Cuba is explained by Nikita Khrushchev's faulty assessment of an untried, seemingly irresolute president. But his over-optimism may have been politically and psychologically motivated by the need to do something about the recent "exposure" of the American five to one advantage in strategic weapons and plans to quadruple our ICBMs. The Russians apparently contemplated the use of nuclear weapons once—in 1969 against China's emergent missile force—only to desist after signaling this possibility to the United States and receiving a negative response. Not having struck when the Soviet Union could have escaped nearly if not completely unscathed when the risks and damages are many orders of magnitude higher the use of force becomes all the less likely. The USSR has only once used conventional forces beyond the area occupied by the Red Army in 1945. And not only could the invasion of Afghanistan be viewed as falling within its irreducible security perimeter, that quagmire has much impressed the Soviets with the problematics of defeating irregular forces fighting on hospitable Third World terrain.

Moscow is not likely to desist from all expansive actions. Even with a full appreciation of the immunity-enhancing conditions it will put some estimates to the test, there are bound to be some errors in assessing their potency, and there could well be some ragged edges and small holes in the immunity-enhancing umbrella. But this is to say that expansive actions will not be undertaken frequently or strenuously. They will take the form of occasional, low-cost, low-risk probes for minor imperfections in the immunity-enhancing conditions. When most prove unsuccessful or inconsequential, the Soviets will have firsthand reasons not to pursue others of greater magnitude.

This depiction of the Soviet territorial threat as no more than minimal despite (and partly because of) minimally activist policies for warding it off may be summarily highlighted. American security would only be impaired or put at risk if each of the following four conditions obtained. The Soviets harbor markedly to inordinately revisionist ambitions, or any salient insecurities are not allayed by America's distinctly defensive, self-denying national policies. Moscow does not dissuade itself from expansive ventures by the evident scope and potency of the immunity-enhancing conditions. The insulating conditions do not hold as the Soviets successfully carry out a string of expansive ventures, a small number of effortful ones, or both. And finally, these successes prove to be consequential, which is to say that the invulnerability-enhancing conditions prove inadequate. And this summarizes only half of what is to be said on behalf of America's adoption of a *national* security strategy.

Still, it does not necessarily follow that the United States should disengage fully from the geographically focused rivalry. Full disengagement would constitute such a great sea change in world politics that it would invariably prompt unpredictable events, some of which are likely to have adverse significance for the United States. Nor is it certain that American policies would steadfastly conform to the dictates of nonengagement if the Soviets successfully carried out some expansive ventures, even though they do not in fact impair America's security. There is the distinct chance of erratic, overreactive decision-making after having fully disengaged. There is also the possibility of the strategy's failure to ensure U.S. security, with it being exceptionally difficult or too late to revert back to an international strategy. These concerns can be much mitigated if not entirely overcome. We would move toward a strategy of balanced engagement (or moderate internationalism) over a five-to-ten-year period, going on to "test the waters" and become politically and psychologically acclimated to them for a comparable time, and only then beginning the next shift toward nonengagement.

Whether partly or fully implemented, would not a *national* security strategy detract from other national values and interests? Since the 1940s adversarial policies have been justified in terms of our international ideals. Hawkish measures toward the Soviet Union, its clients and Marxist movements have been thought to further self-determination, democracy, human rights, peace and security. Today it is assumed that an amelioration of the great global problems—extending from the heights of the earth's atmosphere to the level of international terrorism —requires America's full engagement.

There are two responses to these and any other considerations regarding the seeming costs of disengagement. Any security strategy should be evaluated by first distinguishing as clearly and consistently as possible between its manifest aims and all others. If national policies are seen to maximize U.S. security, yet to detract from environmental and other kinds of "security," a value trade-off in favor of the latter may well be called for. But this would be done without at all casting doubt upon nonengagement as a political-military security strategy.

The other response denies and might even reverse the concerns of the first. There are good reasons to suppose that a national strategy would engender very few trade-offs, that it would contribute to the realization of extra-security goals, perhaps even more so than any other security strategy. The roughly 50 percent reduction in defense spending made viable by a national strategy would allow for the furtherance of the country's material interests, and possibly help stimulate economic growth and international competitiveness. In the past Washington regularly gave in to Chile on human rights issues and to Japan on trade disputes, because national security considerations (i.e., good alliance relationships) were seen as paramount. Once we are convinced—and others know that we know—that security-centered alliances are unnecessary, then Washington would have a better opportunity to be a more effective international player outside the security arena. Nonengagement should also contribute to Soviet-American cooperation on global issues, most probably in trying to bring nuclear proliferation and international terrorism under control. For it not only goes much further than conciliatory activism in reassuring the Soviets, but also it obviates the conflicting interests and misunderstandings involved in the negotiation, verification, and interpretation of arms control and territorially centered accords.

At a hardly inconsequential minimum, to acknowledge the country's strategic immunity should help shift the burden of proof to the hawkish and dovish proponents of quasi-global engagement from the shoulders of the "isolationists." Before any new involvement, intervention, or commitment is undertaken in Eastern Europe or elsewhere, it should be clearly shown that the United States would otherwise be poorly insulated *and* vulnerable, with long-standing alliances and deterrent threats also coming to be assessed according to this eminently reasonable security criterion.

# CHAPTER 15 ■
## TAKING PEACE SERIOUSLY:
## TWO PROPOSALS
John Mueller

It certainly seems time to begin to take peace seriously.[1] The major countries of the developed world have now remained at peace with each other for the longest continuous stretch of time since the days of the Roman Empire.[2] Moreover, they have now gone more than a quarter of a century without a significant confrontational crisis: Rather than drawing closer to war with each other as characteristically happened during earlier eras of peace, the major countries seem to be drifting further away from it.

While war between East and West is not impossible in the foreseeable future, it seems far from heroic to assume it to be wildly improbable. Because the consequences of even a non-nuclear major war would be horrendous, it is sensible, of course, to be concerned about it even if its likelihood is slight.[3] Nevertheless, when the probabilities get low enough, a relaxation of concern even about calamity begins to become justified. A nuclear war between Britain and France, or between either (or both) and the United States would be catastrophic but, because of its low probability, none of these once-hostile countries spends much time, effort, money, or psychic energy guarding against the danger.

The likelihood of war between East and West may not be that low, but it seems to be getting there. Lord Carrington, former secretary general and chair of the North Atlantic Treaty Organization, observed in 1988, "I don't think there is a threat in the sense that we're going to get an invasion by the Soviet Union, but what I do think is that the military potential is still there and we have to be prudent."[4] Carrington's call for prudence was certainly sensible in 1988 and, even with the remarkable changes in Europe in 1989 and 1990, it remains sensible still.

Nevertheless, these changes suggest two propositions. First, under present circumstances arms reduction is more likely to proceed efficaciously if it is allowed to come about without explicit agreement. Second, the best way to resolve the divided and still-contentious condition of Europe would not be to fragment or eviscerate the two alliances, but rather to combine them. Specifically, therefore, it is proposed that arms talks be abandoned and that the European alliances be confederated. These proposals are based on the assumption that the probability of a serious war between East and West is extremely small and will remain so. That assumption is examined first.

### The Prospects for War

According to the thinking embraced in the Truman Doctrine of 1947, war with the Soviets could emerge either through "direct" or "indirect" aggression by the Soviets.

To counter direct aggression, the United States escalated its defense budget and forged a series of anticommunist military alliances, the most important of which is the North Atlantic Treaty Organization. But direct, major war between East and West does not seem ever to have been in the cards. While Soviet ideology does not necessarily reject war as a method for advancing revolution, it has never seen Armageddon-risking Hitlerian conquest to be remotely in its interest. Moreover, as William Taubman has pointed out, Soviets early learned the "crucial lesson" that world war "can destroy the Russian regime."[5] Lenin once declared "a series of frightful collisions" between the Soviet republic and the capitalist world to be "inevitable." However the Soviets have seen this war as something that would be started by the capitalist world or would emerge "naturally" when capitalism reached its eventual stage of collapse. By 1935 they decided that even that sort of conflict was potentially avoidable because of the solidarity of the international working class and the growing strength of Soviet armed forces.[6] In the postwar era major war remained unattractive. As John Erickson has put it, "the sole contingency which would persuade any Soviet leadership of the 'rationality' of nuclear war in pursuit of policy would be the unassailable, incontrovertible, dire evidence that the United States was about to strike the Soviet Union."[7]

Although they have been unable to see much advantage in major war, the Soviets have been willing opportunistically to apply limited military force to probe weaknesses in their surroundings, expanding into the Baltic area and Eastern Poland before World War II and into much of East Europe after it. Their most ambitious effort along this line—though one handled by a surrogate—was in Korea in 1950. The spectacular failure of that venture seems to have discredited the tactic permanently: there have been no Koreas since Korea.[8]

Major war has always seemed less likely to evolve from direct, Hitler-style military invasion than from "indirect aggression"—the Soviet

Union's devotion to an expansionary, revolutionary ideology—and from Western efforts to oppose this dynamic. The Cold War contest has taken place almost entirely at such militarily subtle levels as diplomatic posturing, limited and distant wars of national liberation, "contradiction"-manipulation, propaganda, subversion, bluster, and, occasionally, crisis. Throughout, both sides have assiduously sought to keep these sometimes-alarming conflicts contained at low, bearable levels.

As Bernard Brodie has observed, even the largest of their crises never really had the ring of war: "From beginning to end the confrontation we call the Cuban missile crisis—the most acute crisis of any we have had since World War II—shows a remarkably different quality from any previous one in history. There is an unprecedented candor, direct personal contact, and at the same time mutual respect between the chief actors. . . . In effect they are asking each other: How do we get out of this with the absolute minimum of damage to each other including each other's prestige?"[9] It is very difficult to have a war when no one has the slightest desire to get into one. Moreover, as Robert Jervis has suggested, "a major cause of past wars was the belief that armed conflict could not be avoided." The fatalistic belief that war was unavoidable, which obsessed decision-makers in 1914 and which, Jervis argues, is "probably a necessary condition for war" today, has never dominated the thinking processes of important postwar decision-makers even at their gloomiest.[10]

Thus, in retrospect it seems clear that Cold War dynamics have never pushed its major participants close to direct war.[11] And now, under Mikhail Gorbachev, the economically enfeebled, crisis-racked, and perhaps disintegrating Soviet Union has clearly dampened its romantic affection for the sort of threatening expansion that has been the chief motor of the Cold War. There seems to be widespread agreement among analysts that the Soviet Union has lost interest in gathering to its bosom more of the dependencies it collected with so much glee in the late 1970s.[12] With the Soviet withdrawal from Afghanistan and now with its approval of imperial collapse in Eastern Europe, it seems clear that the Soviets are willing to abandon some of the costly and valueless dependencies they have collected over the years.[13]

Moreover this mellowing is probably not dependent on the success of Gorbachev's reforms: the imperatives of the domestic situation are so severe that they seem to require a mellowing of foreign policy whether reform works or not. That is, even if the reform process collapses and another Brezhnev or Stalin or Trotsky or Lenin rises to the top, the Soviet Union, unless it loses all grasp on reality, will *still* need to pursue a gentler and more modest role in its relations with the capitalist world.[14]

In the early 1980s when war alarm was comparatively high, Joseph Nye, Graham Allison, and Albert Carnesale found that specialists tended to estimate the chances of nuclear war before the end of the century to be between 1 in 100 and 1 in 10,000. They were also struck at how difficult it was to come up with a plausible scenario for major nuclear war even when it was assumed that deliberate choices would be confounded by accidents.[15] Now the specialists would surely find these already low estimates to be on the high side. It has never been easy to imagine how the Soviet Union could possibly see advantage in launching an attack on the West or in ardently pursuing ideological adventures around the globe that might provoke or lead to significant direct military conflict with the West. In the Gorbachev era, with its almost daily revelations of internal tensions, frustrations, ethnic rivalry, and desperate economic and social failure, war seems all but inconceivable. And this suggests that it may now be safe and appropriate to explore some new approaches.

## Reducing Arms without Negotiation

Hans J. Morgenthau once proclaimed (his favored form of communication) that "men do not fight because they have arms"; rather "they have arms because they deem it necessary to fight."[16] If that is so, it follows that when countries no longer deem it necessary to fight they will get rid of their arms. A country buys arms because its leaders espy a threat or opportunity which, it seems to them, requires them to arm. Thus, the United States and the Soviet Union have seen each other as threatening and have armed themselves accordingly. The British and the French, on the other hand, do not find each other militarily threatening, and therefore they have not spent great sums on arms designed to counter each other.

Under the present condition of relaxed tension, it seems reasonable —even inevitable perhaps—that a certain degree of arms relaxation will take place. Total disarmament would hardly be in the offing, of course. The possible reemergence of a dangerous hostility would have to be guarded against, and just to keep abreast of things and to avoid severely unpleasant surprises, both sides would presumably want to maintain active research and development programs. Moreover, there are peripheral concerns that might require military preparedness. The United States would certainly want to retain some military options in the Middle East, the Persian Gulf, Latin America, and elsewhere, while the Soviet Union faces variously hostile countries along its Asian border and may also feel it needs troops to keep its factionalized domestic empire intact. Furthermore, neither side would be at all pleased if an arms reduction somehow triggered insecurities that led to the emergence of a vengeful, rearmed Germany or Japan. And both sides would no doubt want to keep some arms around to aid in their quest after "influence" around the globe since that is apparently part of what they take their role to be.

It is not clear, however, that these needs call for ships in the hundreds, for thermonuclear weapons in the tens of thousands, or for standing armies in the millions. And neither side is likely to have difficulty envisioning other ways to spend its money. The United States has built up a burdensome deficit, and many are arguing that its overemphasis on arms expenditures has kept it from being able to compete internationally. The pressures on the Soviet budget, massively bloated by defense expenditures, are even more severe.[17]

However, while the weapons that have been built up during the Cold War may seem increasingly burdensome and even parodic, and while there are strong reasons for wanting to reduce the burden and divert the hilarity, the mechanism for doing so may be difficult to engineer. These difficulties will be enhanced if both sides continue to assume that arms reductions must be accomplished through explicit mutual agreement—that an exquisitely nuanced agreement must be worked out for every abandoned nut and bolt.

Arms agreements tend to take forever to consummate: the nonproliferation treaty of 1968, a very mild measure that was clearly in everyone's best interest, was argued for five years.[18] Indeed, the existence of arms control talks often hampers arms reduction. In 1973, for example, a proposal for a unilateral reduction of U.S. troops in West Europe failed in Congress because it was felt that this would undercut upcoming arms control negotiations—which have been unproductively running on ever since.[19] Similarly, opponents of the MX missile and of Ronald Reagan's Strategic Defense Initiative failed in Congress in part because some of those who consider the weapons systems dangerous or valueless nevertheless support them because the weapons seem to be useful as bargaining chips in arms control talks. Whether those arms reductions were wise or not, they failed in considerable measure because arms control talks existed. A message of George Bush's 1988 campaign for the presidency seems to have been that a weapons system, no matter how costly, stupid, or redundant, should never be unilaterally abandoned if it could serve as a bargaining chip in arms control negotiations.[20]

If arms are reduced by agreement, both sides are going to strain to make sure that all dangers and contingencies are covered, and they will naturally try, if at all possible, to come out with the better deal. Reduction is certainly possible under those circumstances, but it is likely to be slow and inflexible. Arms control is essentially a form of centralized regulation, and it carries with it the usual defects of that approach. Participants will volunteer for such regulation only with extreme caution because once under regulation they are often unable to adjust subtly to unanticipated changes. Moreover they are often encouraged, perversely, to follow developments that are unwise. For example, the Strategic Arms Agreement of 1972 limited the number of missiles each side could have, but it allowed them to embroider their missiles with multiple warheads and to improve missile accuracy, thereby encouraging them to develop a potentially dangerous first-strike capability.

There is an alternative: just *do* it. The arms buildup, after all, was not accomplished through written agreements; instead, there was a sort of free market in which each side, keeping a wary eye on the other, sought security by purchasing varying amounts of weapons and troops. As requirements and perspectives changed, so did the force structure of each side.

If arms can be built up that way, they can be reduced in the same manner. It would be a negative arms race, and there are historical precedents such as the one that began more than a hundred years ago between the United States and British Canada.

Americans and Canadians are so accustomed to living peacefully side by side that it is easy to assume this has always been the case.[21] But once there was enormous hostility between the United States and British Canada, and it was registered in wars from 1775 to 1783 and from 1812 to 1814. After the second war the contestants lapsed into a long period of wary coexistence—of cold war, in fact—but they nevertheless managed to agree to one arms control measure. Impelled as much by economic exhaustion as anything else, the United States reduced its fleet of warships on the Great Lakes and proposed that the British do likewise. The British eventually agreed, and the results were formalized in the Rush-Bagot Agreement of 1817 which placed exact limits on the number, size, and armament of warships. But there was no provision actually to destroy warships, and both sides kept some in dockyards, where they could always be put into action should the need arise. Furthermore, there was quite a bit of evasion and technical violation over the next half-century, and both built ships that could easily be converted to military use if necessary. Both sides continued to build forts along the border, and the British created an extensive and expensive canal system in Canada as a military supply line.

This arms race was accompanied by a series of conflicts between the two neighbors. There were border skirmishes in 1837, a crisis in 1839 in disagreement about the boundary between Maine and New Brunswick, continual war apprehension over the Oregon boundary (settled in 1846), substantial tension during the American Civil War, and sporadic raids by Irish-Americans into British Canada. Meanwhile, many Americans were caught up in the romantic notion that it was somehow in their "manifest destiny to overspread the continent allotted by Providence for the free development of our yearly multiplying millions."

By the early 1870s, however, most of the claims and controversies had been settled. Canada was granted independent status in part because British taxpayers were tired of paying to defend their large, distant colony and, with the Americans focusing on settling the West and recovering from their calamitous civil war, it seemed safe to begin to withdraw the British army from Canada.[22] Without formal agreement, disarmament gradually took place between the two countries. Their forts became museums where obsolete cannon still point accusingly but impotently in the direction of the nearby former enemy; they have been allowed—as the bumper sticker would have it—to rust in peace. "Disarmament became a reality," observes a Canadian student of the era, "not by international agreement, but simply because there was no longer any serious international disagreement."[23]

If the Cold War and the ideological contest have now truly been dampened, a similar arms reduction could come about between West and East. The Soviet Union is under especially severe economic pressure to reduce its arms expenditures and in December 1988, Gorbachev dramatically announced that he was going to begin to do so unilaterally. Months before Gorbachev's announcement Lord Carrington warned about what he called "involuntary or structural disarmament" within NATO, where a relaxation of East-West tensions "has made support for defense spending harder to win." This is of concern, he held, because while Gorbachev clearly "has a real interest in reducing military expenditures," he had apparently not done so yet. However, if the Soviet buildup did begin to swing into reverse, Carrington conceded, NATO's tendency toward "structural" disarmament "would not matter."[24] As if on cue, press reports were observing within days of Gorbachev's announcement that there was a "new reluctance to spend for defense" within NATO.[25] In a month, reports were noting that Gorbachev's pronouncements "make it harder for Western governments to justify large sums for military machines. . . . the Soviet bear seems less threatening to Western publics these days, so that they want to do less on the weapons front. . . . Western perceptions [are] that the Soviet threat is receding and that big armies are expensive and inconvenient—perhaps even irrelevant."[26] A few months later, as more proposals and counterproposals were spun out by both sides, the press was calling the process a "race to demobilize."[27] Reports suggest, in fact, that some officials, alarmed at the disarmament impetus, are hoping to use the formal arms control mechanism to slow the process.[28]

In any such reversal of the arms competition both sides are likely to reduce cautiously, particularly at first, in sensible if perhaps overly sensitive concern that a severe arms imbalance could inspire the other to contemplate blackmail. Moreover, yearly reductions need not be large or traumatic: in the last four years of the Reagan administration, defense budget authorizations declined some 1 to 4 percent per year in real dollars, and little pain was registered.[29] Declines like that could soon cumulate to quite significant levels as a negative arms race is set in motion. (If tensions surge again, formal arms agreements will not make much difference one way or the other because both sides will find ways to evade their spirit.)

It might be useful to point out that this approach differs significantly from the GRIT strategy proposed by Charles E. Osgood.[30] He supposes high tension and then proposes a series of explicit unilateral initiatives to reduce arms tensions in a process he calls Graduated Reciprocation in Tension-reduction. His initiatives have stringent requirements which make them very difficult to engineer in practice. For example, Osgood requires that they be diversified, publicly announced, explicitly capable of reciprocation, executed on precise schedule, unambiguous, and susceptible to verification. Although he refers to his approach as an "arms race in reverse," the arms race has never been so rigorous or formal. It has been filled with deception, guesswork, ambiguity, abrupt lurches, whim, panic, and elaborate efforts to evade verification.

The approach advocated here supposes *low* tension. Because, as Morgenthau suggests, the progress of the arms race has been impelled by high tensions, low tensions, combined with economic pressures, should naturally impel a negative arms race. It may not be entirely fair to characterize disarmament as an effort to cure a fever by destroying the thermometer.[31] But the analogy is instructive when it is reversed: when fever subsides, the instrument designed to measure it loses its usefulness and is often soon misplaced.

The arms-reversal process will be as chaotic, halting, ambiguous, self-interested, and reversible as the arms race itself, but arms would gradually be reduced—and this will happen best if arms negotiators keep out of the way. There might be a role for agreements focused purely on arms control measures that cannot be accomplished unilaterally —like improved communications links, mechanisms to detect surprise attack preparations, or improved methods to verify the size of the other's military forces. But arms reduction will proceed expeditiously if each side feels free to reverse any reduction it later comes to regret. Formal disarmament agreements are likely simply to slow and pedantify this process.

## Resolving Europe by Confederating the Alliances

It seems clear that the internal contradictions of the Soviet Union have now caught up with it, leaving it on view in its true colors as a "third world country with rockets," as one Polish intellectual has put it. It follows that the Soviets will experience a substantial decline in status if economic variables are used to measure status as, increasingly, they are.[32] To begin to reverse their economic problems, the Soviets need to embrace such efficient capitalist remedies as bankruptcy, unemployment, and massive inflation in the prices of essentials like food and housing—remedies which, however, are likely to exacerbate problems of class, region, nationality, and ethnicity. It is possible, of course, that the reformers will be able to turn things around after a period of substantial trauma and dislocation. If they can, comparative decline will be more or less temporary and more or less moderate. If they cannot, decline could go on for decades or even centuries, following the well-trammeled path of such pathetic predecessors as the Ottoman Empire and the Manchu dynasty of China. Utter imperial collapse is also a distinct possibility.

In this process, there is always the danger that the Soviets will be tempted to resort to boisterous behavior or to dangerous rocket-rattling in order to remind the rest of the world that they still exist. Accordingly, it may be useful for the West to engage in various stroking measures to make the Soviets feel that they really are quite important no matter what dismal news the economists may bring. Arms control agreements can help in this, and if, as suggested, they are focused on arms *control* measures, they would not hamper genuine arms reduction. Other methods might also be explored, such as working with the Soviets in the United Nations to resolve issues in troubled areas like the Middle East: whether the issues are resolved or not, the Soviets will at least be made to feel important. Space ventures could serve a similar function and, if carried out in a cooperative mood rather than in a competitive one, they will proceed at a leisurely pace and save money for all sides. (With a little luck, we many *never* have to look at pictures of people hopping around on Mars in spacesuits.) And of course we can all stride together shoulder-to-shoulder in the various marches against such consensual evils as global warming, forest fires, whale depletion, and oil slicks.

East-West coordination can be most productively directed toward resolving the general problem of Europe. Here the Soviet Union has a substantial and substantive role to play, not merely an atmospheric one.

The logical eventual outcome of current trends in Europe would be a sort of continent-wide Finlandization or Austrianization as each country is sent off to pursue prosperity (or whatever it takes its destiny to be) in neutralized and minimally armed independence.

There are two major problems with this process however. One concerns Germany. Without the involvement of the United States and the USSR, Germany would be the most formidable country in Central Europe. Given the history of the last century or two, it is too easy to visualize an independent Germany bent on hegemonic domination, militarization, and war.[33] An effective case can be made that this is highly unlikely. For the foreseeable future — say, ten or twenty years — it is most likely that Germany will follow the direction of postwar Japan and quest after prosperity without conquest. Indeed, in the developed world war seems gradually to have moved over the last two or three centuries into a state of obsolescence following the pattern of other once-ubiquitous institutions like dueling and slavery.[34]

With the experience of two world wars behind them, however, it is understandable that many in the Soviet Union (and elsewhere) would have difficulty finding sufficient satisfaction even in an ironclad guarantee that Germany would not rise again for twenty years. They would want an arrangement that would keep Germany permanently under wraps. The postwar alliance system in Europe may have been absurd, inefficient, and unjust, but at least it seemed to guarantee that Germany could be prevented from again perpetrating a major war on its own. Thus, any resolution of the European situation should include a similar perpetual — or at least seemingly perpetual — guarantee.

A second problem with an abandonment of the alliances is that it would leave the Soviet Union (or a postcommunist Russia), even if there were significant arms reductions, as the dominant military entity in the area. Colin Gray warns that "history does not teach that predatory countries abhor a power vacuum. It is as certain as anything in politics can be that the Soviet Union would hasten to exploit the American withdrawal. . . . [and] press for unilateral advantage over the economically well-endowed former security clients of the United States."[35] Others may question whether things are so "certain." It has become difficult to imagine that the Soviets could see benefit and virtue in policies that might risk a substantial war or provoke substantial discontent in Europe. As an important Soviet official observed in 1987 "Previously we reasoned: the worse for the adversary, the better for us. . . . But today this is no longer true. . . . the better things are going in the European world economy, the higher the stability and the better the prospects for our development."[36] But there is, of course, no guarantee that this point of view is both genuine and permanent. Clearly, an attractive plan for a lasting resolution of the European situation should guard against the possibility that Gray might be right.

Two propositions follow from these considerations. First, because it would allow for the potential rise of German revanchism, the withdrawal of the United States and the Soviet Union from participation in the affairs of Central Europe ought not be an element of a resolution of the divisions and discontinuities of Europe; rather, a solution should require that these two guarantors against German military resurgence be tightly bound into the fate of Europe. Second, because it would allow for the potential Soviet or Russian domination of Europe, the withdrawal of the United States from the affairs of the area is additionally undesirable; a solution should keep the American counterweight in place. In short, Europe is too important to be left to the Europeans alone.

An economic blending of West and East could be part of a solution. But mutual economic dependency has been no guarantee against war in the past; it would be wise for there to be political and military dependency as well. This could be accomplished with most direct dispatch by confederating the two alliances in some way. The chances of a war between East and West are probably not much higher than one between Britain and France; if Britain and France can be linked in the same alliance, so can the United States and the USSR.

It is true that the alliances are there to oppose each other militarily and that an essential mission of each is to defend against an attack by the other. But, traditionally mutual defense has not been the only function of alliances. As Paul Schroeder has pointed out in an illuminating study of alliances between 1815 and 1945, "the desire for capability-aggregation against an outside threat has not always played a vital role in the formation of alliances." In fact, *all* alliances were designed in part to restrain or control the actions of the partners in the alliance, and "frequently the desire to exercise such control over an ally's policy was the main reason that one power, or both, entered into the alliance."[37]

The generalization clearly holds for alliances in the post-1945 era as well. Few would deny that the Soviet Union used the Warsaw Pact to help maintain its control over its East European colonies, and a virtue of NATO to members (and nonmembers) is that it affords some measure of control over a possible German yearning for nuclear weapons or for revenge. American alliances with Taiwan and Japan have been designed in part to control the smaller partners even while guaranteeing their safety from invasion.

In addition, Schroeder observes that "although alliances were commonly used to try to isolate and intimidate an opponent, alliances also were frequently employed in order to group and conciliate an opponent, in the interest of managing the system and avoiding overt conflict." That is, it "need not be true, as is often supposed, that powers must have generally harmonious aims and outlooks if they are to be allies." And he speculates that détente between the United States and the USSR could conceivably develop into some sort of alliance that might be used for peaceful purposes.[38]

A major barrier to East-West alliance has been the Soviet devotion to an ideology built on the notion that the Western political and economic system is fundamentally evil and must ultimately be overthrown. While communists have sometimes productively united with Western capitalists to confront a common enemy (most notably during World War II), their belief in the supreme desirability and necessity of anticapitalist revolution has prevented any of these fronts from becoming permanent. As John Lewis Gaddis has put it, "Moscow's commitment to the overthrow of capitalism throughout the world" has been "the chief unsettling element in its relations with the West since the Russian revolution."[39] As has often been noted, it is this component of postwar international politics that has divided the world into two camps and has kept the two alliances rigid and separate, unlike the situation in much of the previous 150 years when alliance patterns were often remarkably flexible and fluid.

If this ideological component of Soviet foreign policy fades away, it follows that alliance patterns could then take on a nineteenth-century flexibility and that East and West could find it possible and advantageous to confederate themselves into some sort of alliance. Something like this has already happened with the Chinese. When they abandoned their commitment to worldwide anticapitalist revolution and revolutionary war in the 1970s, they were quickly embraced by the capitalist world and may now even be in a sort of alliance with the United States. If the Soviet Union contemplated invading China in the 1950s, it would not have had to worry much about the possibility that the United States would come to China's defense; today, it would.[40] And, after the Yugoslavs broke with the Soviet Union in the late 1940s, the United States sent military equipment to Yugoslavia, declaring that the country was "of direct importance to the defense of the North Atlantic area," and that its "ability to defend itself "was important to the security of the United States." For a while, Yugoslavia was close to becoming an informal participant in NATO.[41]

A similar opportunity may now be coming about with respect to the Soviets. As Francis Fukuyama observed in 1987, "the role of ideology in defining Soviet foreign policy objectives . . . has been steadily declining in the postwar period." While the Soviets might continue to seek expansion and "far-flung military and political interests," he felt the rationale for Soviet policy would become less ideological: "The Soviet Union will still worry about its prestige and commitments, but more in the name of protecting its interests as a great power than as the carrier of a messianic, universal ideology."[42] Then, in a major speech in December 1988, Gorbachev specifically called for "de-ideologizing relations among states" and, while referring to the communist revolution in Russia as "a most precious spiritual heritage," proclaimed that "today we face a different world, from which we must seek a different road to the future."[43]

If the Soviet Union has now become merely a normal, old-fashioned great power, it can comfortably be incorporated into classical patterns of diplomacy and alliance. In 1988, in his last press conference as president, Ronald Reagan was asked if the Soviets might once again become allies with the United States as they were during World War II. Reagan responded, essentially, in the affirmative: "If it can be definitely established that they no longer are following the expansionary policy that was instituted in the Communist revolution, that their goal must be a one-world Communist state . . . [then] they might want to join the family of nations and join them with the idea of bringing about or establishing peace."[44] Six months later his successor, George Bush, was urging, without Reagan's tentativeness, that Western policy should move "beyond containment" and seek to "integrate the Soviet Union into the community of nations."

It is important to observe again that this development is not contingent on the progress of Soviet domestic reform. As long as the Soviet Union, like China in the 1970s or Yugoslavia after 1949, continues to neglect its expansionary and revolutionary ideology, it can be embraced by the West. Illiberal, nonexpansionist Portugal, after all, was a founding member of NATO.

Initially, of course, any confederation of the alliances would feel awkward and peculiar. It could begin with political consultations and lead to a rough coordination of military planning. (The Voice of America is far more likely to bring about a collapse of the Soviet regime than is NATO. VOA now has an office in Moscow; why can't NATO?) Already observers are routinely being sent to watch over the other alliance's maneuvers under a 1986 agreement, and the sanctity of each side's bases is being regularly violated by inspectors from the opposite alliance under the terms of the 1987 Intermediate-range Nuclear Forces Treaty—two ideas that would have been unthinkable only a few years ago. Maneuvers might be coordinated and political consultations could lead to agreement about rules of the game in Europe. Eventually, bases or training camps might even be exchanged. The bases would be at once guarantors of cooperation and hostages to it. This might lead in time to elements of joint command. The role of France within NATO might form something of a model: their forces are not integrated under joint command, but they are coordinated with those of NATO. Eventually, bases or training camps might even be exchanged, as France maintains bases in West Germany.[45]

As military plans and forces became intermeshed, and as the combined alliance becomes more of a political institution and less of a military one, strategists might come to have difficulty figuring out where to point their weapons. Perhaps Switzerland could be a handy target, at least for purposes of calibration, and a situation where thousands of nuclear weapons and millions of troops are directed to a country that has avoided all warfare since 1798 might serve to highlight the essential absurdity of the military enterprise and impel a momentum toward judicious, embarrassed, and overdue arms reduction in Europe.

Whatever the procedures of implementation, the goal would be to create a situation in which every country in the area feels it has some control over the military destiny in the area of every other country and, specifically, one in which both the United States and the Soviet Union maintain control over the military potential of Germany. As Schroeder suggests, such alliances of mutual management have been quite common. In this case the pattern might roughly resemble the Concert of Europe, the alliance-of-the-whole that emerged after 1815.

A confederated alliance structure would facilitate further peaceful blending in what used to be the world's most warlike continent. It could eventually help to facilitate a political unity of the continent—or of the developed world. But this end is not necessary, or perhaps even particularly desireable. The goal should not be to stop conflict, but to keep conflict from taking military form: a wide alliance does not mean that perpetual bliss and perfect harmony would automatically break out.[46] Indeed, a merging of the alliances would not even mean that international war would become impossible in the area. The Soviet Union and Hungary managed to get into a war in 1956 even though they were members of the same alliance, and there was a sort of bloodless intra-alliance war in Czechoslovakia in 1968. At present, wars between Greece and Turkey within NATO, between former Soviet colonies in the East, or between ethnic factions in Yugoslavia are far from inconceivable.

But a confederated alliance would probably be able to help keep such conflicts contained, and it could prevent any single member or cluster from possessing undue influence based on military (as opposed to economic, diplomatic, or political) clout. Contentiousness, rivalry, pettiness, hostility, xenophobia, arrogance, and suspicion would continue to flourish in Europe, but some of the continent's major problems would be resolved and the prospects for major war would be further diminished.

# CHAPTER 16 ■
# AVERTING ANARCHY
# IN THE NEW EUROPE
Jack Snyder

For the past four decades, the division of Europe and the repression of political pluralism in its eastern half have coincided with an unprecedented period of peace among the great powers.[1] Now, however, social change in the Soviet bloc and "new thinking" in Soviet foreign policy are undermining the stable Cold War stalemate in Europe. Simultaneously, mass political participation is expanding in communist Europe, the legitimacy of the old institutions of the communist era is collapsing, and international alignments are becoming more fluid.[2]

Some Western observers have seen these developments as all to the good. In this view, as illegitimate communist rule is rolled back and replaced by liberal, market-oriented regimes, the sources of conflict in Europe will be eliminated and peace will break out. But the difficulties facing perestroika in Russia and the potential for nationalist conflicts throughout the erstwhile Soviet bloc raise the possibility of a much grimmer outcome.

The Soviet Union and Eastern Europe are facing the classic problem that Samuel Huntington described in *Political Order in Changing Societies*: a gap between booming political participation and ineffectual political institutions. In Huntington's analysis this gap is typically filled by the pernicious pattern of "praetorian" politics. "In a praetorian system," says Huntington:

> social forces confront each other nakedly; no political institutions, no corps of professional political leaders are recognized or accepted as the legitimate intermediaries to moderate group conflict. Equally important, no agreement exists among the groups as to the legitimate and authoritative methods for resolving conflicts. . . . Each group employs means which reflect its peculiar nature and capabilities. The wealthy bribe; students riot; workers strike; mobs demonstrate; and the military coup.[3]

Other studies of praetorian societies add that nationalist demagogy becomes a common political instrument to advance group interests and to help unstable governments rule.[4]

Praetorian societies like Germany and Japan have accounted for most of this century's international security problems among the Great Powers.[5] In both cases weak democratic institutions were unable to channel the exploding energies of increasing mass political participation in constructive directions. Instead, elite groups interested in militarism, protectionism, and imperialism used nationalist appeals to recruit mass backing for their parochial ends. Consequently, the Western democracies have a powerful incentive to head off the emergence of more states of this type, especially in the Soviet Union but also in Eastern Europe.

Insofar as Huntington's model signals contemporary dangers, one possible solution would be to recruit reformist Eastern regimes into the West's already well-developed supranational political order, especially the European Community.[6] As in the cases of Spain and Greece, this would create incentives for the emergence of liberal rather than praetorian political patterns, as well as a ready-made institutional framework for acting on those incentives.[7]

This chapter presents three views of the demise of the bipolar division of Europe: liberal "end of history" optimism, which envisions a harmonious European order emerging automatically from the rollback of Soviet influence; Hobbesian pessimism, which anticipates a reversion to pre-1945 patterns of multipolar instability and nationalism; and conditionally optimistic neoliberal institutionalism, which prescribes the implantation of cooperative international institutions as an antidote to the consequences of Hobbesian anarchy.[8] While agreeing with some of the diagnosis of Hobbesian pessimism, I question its policy prescriptions of shoring up the Cold War status quo ante, and if that fails, keeping at arms' length from the impending East European maelstrom. As an alternative to these solutions, I will explore the possibility that a strategy of international institution-building might be able to avert "the war of all against all" that the Hobbesian pessimists see looming on the horizon in Central and Eastern Europe.

In addition to evaluating opposing policy prescriptions, I lay out a theoretical scheme that will help focus the questions that policy advocates ought to address. I argue that the changing European political order requires the field of international security studies to enrich its rather limited repertoire of Hobbesian Realist theories with borrowings from the fields of comparative politics and international political economy.

## Liberal End-of-History Optimism

Liberal optimism anticipates that the erosion of the bipolar division of Europe will make the European political order more peaceful. The Cold War division of the continent has been, in this view, an inherently tense, war-prone situation. The imposition of illegitimate regimes in Europe's Eastern half has been a cause of political frustration and latent violent conflict. If these illegitimate communist regimes in Eastern Europe and the USSR are replaced by liberal, market-oriented, democratic regimes, neither internal nor international bloodshed is likely. As the historical record shows, liberal democratic regimes never fight wars against each other.[9] Insofar as the boom in mass political participation and free speech in the Soviet bloc is a harbinger of democracy, it will also bring a more peaceful international order along with it.

Some might think that this outcome is already all but achieved due to the intellectual discrediting of Marxism-Leninism and the impending victory of liberal ideology throughout the developed world.[10] Others might think that this "ending of history" must be helped along by a strategy of fomenting liberal change in the communist bloc. To promote such developments, the West should, in this view, use whatever leverage it has short of military intervention to roll back Soviet influence and to strengthen liberal, democratic, capitalist forces in the East European countries. No attempt should be made, in this view, to mitigate Gorbachev's fear of "exporting capitalism."[11] Economic aid should be targeted on strengthening the private sector. Trade and financial concessions should be conditional on movement toward a multiparty, market model.[12] Arms control should aim at removing Soviet troops from Eastern Europe. Liberal ideological rhetoric should be used to undermine the social support for what is left of communist authority in Eastern Europe and even in the Soviet Baltic republics. Some elements of current American policy, such as targeting economic aid to Poland and Hungary on the private sector and jawboning in favor of market-oriented pluralism, embody this thinking.

In short, the plausibility of liberal end-of-history optimism rests on two assumptions: first, that states that are well-ordered internally make for a good international order;[13] and second, that states naturally become well-ordered when unnatural, illegitimate oppressors are banished. Such sanguine assumptions are challenged, in different ways, by Hobbesian pessimism and by neoliberal institution-building.

## Hobbesian Pessimism

The prevailing Realist theory of international politics holds that the bipolar stalemate between the two superpowers is the most stable possible power configuration, given the realities of an anarchic international system.[14] This brand of Realism anticipates that the waning of Soviet power, the reunification of Germany, and the erosion of the bipolar division of Europe are likely to lead to the breakup of NATO, and the consequent emergence of an unstable, multipolar balance-of-power system. As a result, major war may come again for the same reasons it came in 1914 and 1939, through the uncertain workings of the multipolar balancing process.[15] Likewise, the balance-of-power policies of small East European states, released from the grip of Soviet hegemony, may help catalyze war among the great powers, as they did before World War I.[16]

Not only recent scholarship, but also some high Bush administration officials seem to hold to this theory. Deputy Secretary of State Lawrence Eagleburger has noted:

> We are moving into, or I should say back into—for such has been the nature of international affairs since time immemorial—a world in which power and influence is diffused among a multiplicity of states. [This multipolar world is not] necessarily going to be a safer place than the Cold War era from which we are emerging. . . . For all its risks and uncertainties, the cold war was characterized by a remarkably stable and predictable set of relations among the great powers. A brief look at the history books will tell us that we cannot say as much about the period leading from the birth of the European nation states up through the outbreak of the Second World War.[17]

However, if the anarchic international setting were the only problem, Hobbesian thinking might not necessarily lead to such pessimistic conclusions. After all, modern Realist thinking includes the idea that the perverse consequences of international anarchy can be mitigated by arms control measures that make states more secure by limiting offensive military capabilities. Although this is harder to contrive in multipolar settings, Realists could find solutions if they really believed that international insecurity were the major, sufficient cause of war.[18]

In fact, Hobbesian pessimism stems not only from the consequences of international anarchy, but also from the effects of international military competition on the domestic political order and from the anarchic nature of domestic political competition itself. Unlike liberal optimism,

Hobbesian pessimism sees domestic order not as arising from a harmonious society but as improved by a coercive state organization—a "Leviathan," in Hobbes's term. The state simultaneously struggles to defend itself against other states, to maintain its monopoly of violence against would-be domestic opponents, and to extract resources from its society for both purposes.

To do these things, the state relies above all on powerful military bureaucracies and nationalist myth-making.[19] The central role of these two pillars of the modern state creates a domestic order prone to provoke nationalistic international aggression. It is not only, as Charles Tilly put it, that war makes the state and the state makes war.[20] Beyond this, the state, to carry out these tasks, needs nationalistic myths that make war more likely.[21] Eagleburger, too, worries that multipolar international anarchy will promote nationalism, remarking that "the process of reform in the Soviet bloc and the relaxation of Soviet control over Eastern Europe are bringing long-suppressed ethnic antagonisms and national rivalries to the surface, and putting the German question back on the international agenda."[22]

Some Realists acknowledge that liberal states sometimes find ways to mitigate the inherently nationalistic tendencies of the modern state, for example, by allowing detailed public scrutiny of the state's conduct of foreign affairs and creating a free marketplace of ideas to evaluate policy.[23] Still, this is the exception rather than the rule. The nature of states in their anarchical setting works against it, in the Hobbesian view. The bipolar post-1945 stalemate has created unusual international circumstances, which have mitigated the exigencies of international anarchy for West European societies, allowing the luxury of the welfare state and widespread antiwar ideology. But to the extent that these benign domestic conditions may in part be consequences of the bipolar stalemate, a shift in international structure may undermine them.[24]

Likewise, Hobbesians view as spurious the connection between economic interdependence among the capitalist powers and the postwar peace. The former does not cause the latter; rather, both are caused by the bipolar stalemate, according to the Realist view.[25] Once the power structure changes, the vulnerabilities inherent in economic interdependence are likely to be a cause of conflict, not of harmony. Extending economic interdependence throughout a new "European Common Home" would, from this point of view, only exacerbate international tensions.[26] Interwar Japan, for example, might have lived much more harmoniously with its neighbors if its fate had not been shaped by its economic dependence on them.

In short, Hobbesian pessimism sees political order as deriving not from a harmony of interests but from a hegemony that quashes the disorder inherent in political anarchy. Tight, co-hegemonic leadership in a bipolar division of Europe is the best that can be hoped for in a Hobbesian world.

Based on these theoretical underpinnings, Hobbesian pessimism can only expect the worst as a result of the erosion of the bipolar order. The structural deformities of multipolarity will ensure that small disturbances will reverberate into a major clash, in the Hobbesian view, while the militarism and nationalism fostered by multipolar insecurity are almost certain to cause such disturbances.

Even if nationalist tendencies have been tamed in welfare-state Western Europe, they are more likely to emerge in the East. In the anarchic conditions prevailing in the reforming states of the Soviet bloc, social groups are likely to use nationalist appeals to establish their right to create a new state, or to seize control of an existing state. Once in power, nationalism will prove useful in strengthening the state's control over society.

Such Hobbesian worries are not without foundation. Conflict-causing nationalism is already proving an indispensable tool for seizing and maintaining state power in the increasingly pluralistic Soviet bloc.[27] Recently, in Soviet Azerbaijan, local intellectuals, using their comparative advantage in propaganda to exacerbate ethnic feeling against Armenia, have succeeded in placing themselves at the head of a popular nationalist movement. Exploiting the power this leadership confers on them, they have successfully bargained with Moscow virtually to supplant the Communist party as the governing institution of Azerbaijan. Although Moscow has rejected their plea to be allowed to set up a separate Azerbaijani army, the mass movement they head seems to be creating one de facto.[28]

Several policy prescriptions follow from Hobbesian assumptions: If at all possible, the West should try to maintain the bipolar order intact, avoid policies that weaken the Soviet Union's resource base, and refrain from undercutting what remains of the Soviet position in Eastern Europe.

But if this is not possible, try to isolate the relatively healthy Western half of the European order, where the effects of anarchy have been partially mitigated, and nationalism and militarism controlled, from Europe's increasingly volatile Eastern half. Do not tinker with NATO and the European Community in pursuit of the will-o'-the-wisp of the European Common Home, which will only embroil the West in the insoluble troubles of the East. Do not oversell the prospects for liberal change in the East—or the West's stake in such changes—to Western publics. As a last resort, count on nuclear deterrence to maintain the peace.

Such a strategy of insulation is likely to be difficult to sustain, given the risks and temptations inherent in the emerging multipolar configuration of power. Under Hobbesian assumptions, at any rate, Germany would be expected to watch political developments in the East with a wary eye, to be sensitive to threats that might emerge from the the unsettled conditions there, and to intervene diplomatically, if not militarily, to forestall such threats. Germany might in fact choose to play a less interventionist role in Eastern troubles, but if so, Hobbesian assumptions could not explain it.

A more innovative Hobbesian strategy might be to give up the bipolar stalemate as lost, and switch to a Bismarckian strategy of defensive multipolar alliances.[29] For example, France, Britain, and the United States might guarantee the security of a reunited Germany against attack by Russia, while "reinsuring" Russia against aggression by Germany. Likewise, small East European states would be guaranteed security assistance only if they were the party attacked, not if they were the attacker. The Locarno Treaty's two-way guarantee of Germany's western border might also provide a model for such a strategy.

Such a scheme might be stabilizing, but history and theory point to many pitfalls along that path. Neither Bismarck's defensive alliances nor Locarno lasted very long. In the multipolarity of the interwar period, states were tempted to ride free on the balancing efforts of others, so defensive alliances lost credibility. Conversely, before 1914 alliance commitments that were originally defensive came to be unconditional, because the power of each major ally was considered essential to maintaining the balance. In such circumstances, as in the German blank check to Austria in 1914, allies had to be supported even if they were the aggressors.[30] Moreover, in checkerboard multipolar alliance patterns, it may be difficult to honor alliance commitments, even defensive ones, without the development of offensive military capabilities and strategies to attack an aggressor in the rear.[31] Such capabilities would exacerbate security fears and undermine the pacific aims of a system of defensive alliances. There is little reason to believe that a strategy of defensive alliances would by itself produce stability. Still, this does not exclude the possibility that in a system moderated by other factors, such as benign patterns of domestic politics, defensive alliances might make a beneficial contribution.

Finally, reliance on a multipolar nuclear stand-off to insure stability also seems problematic. First, the Soviet Union's nuclear arsenal will not protect it from the real challenges to its integrity as a state: ethnic separatism and economic colonization of its periphery by more advanced powers. Second, most of the newly emerging power centers, including Germany, will not have nuclear weapons. In light of the nuclear allergy which currently dominates European thinking, decisions to acquire nuclear weapons could take place only *after* a severe worsening of international tension made them seem necessary. In that context, the uneven proliferation of nascent, vulnerable nuclear forces could be a provocation to war, not a deterrent against it.

The enormity of Hobbesian predictions and the weakness of Hobbesian prescriptions virtually demand asking whether other kinds of measures might not be devised to head off such dire developments. If the pressure of international and domestic anarchy is indeed likely to foster a miscarriage of the balance of power and the spread of militaristic nationalism, then it is natural to ask whether steps can be taken to mitigate this anarchic pressure. Neoliberal institution-building takes up this issue.

### Neoliberal Institutionalism

Neoliberal institution-building offers a more constructive perspective on the creation of a stable political order in Europe. This approach assumes that the Hobbesian condition can be mitigated by an institutional structure that provides legitimate and effective channels for reconciling conflicting interests. Whereas liberal optimism sees political order as arising spontaneously from a harmony of interests, and Hobbesian pessimism sees it as imposed by hegemonic power, neoliberal institutionalism sees it as arising from organized procedures for articulating interests and settling conflicts among them.[32]

When institutions are strong, there is order; the effects of anarchy are mitigated. When institutions are weak, there is disorder; politics are marked by the perverse effects of anarchy.[33] Thus, from this perspective, the problem of creating a new European security order to supplant that of the bipolar stalemate is above all a problem of building institutions. Institutionalist theories borrowed form the fields of comparative politics and international political economy may help illuminate the task ahead.

The classic statement of the institutionalist understanding of political order is Samuel Huntington's *Political Order in Changing Societies.* Huntington is concerned with the consequences for political order when intense political demands are advanced by a mobilized society, but governing institutions are too weak to reconcile those competing claims effectively. In particular, he examines the disorder that emerges in a modernizing society when industrialization, urbanization, and expanding literacy lead to an expansion of political demands, which the traditional political institutions of the ancien régime cannot process efficiently and authoritatively.[34]

In such circumstances, politics becomes disordered. Groups and individuals cannot defend their interests by appealing to legitimate governing institutions and orderly procedures for resolving conflicts, because such channels are unavailable. As a result, groups form to defend their parochial interests through self-help, including direct violent action, as in any anarchical environment. Social groups like students and organized labor may take to the streets or use other means of direct, coercive action, like political strikes, to advance their selfish parochial interests. Government institutions, unable to create order and pursue the state's interests on the basis of legitimate authority, also act as self-interested, coercive groups. The military, because the dominant means of violent coercion lie in its hands, tends to play a central role in this pattern of praetorian politics. As Huntington quotes Hobbes, "when nothing else is turned up, clubs are trumps."[35]

In praetorian societies the problem is not the *lack* of organization, but the character of the institutions that are well organized. Various parochial interests—for example, the military and the trade unions —may be well organized. But institutions for aggregating competing interests—for example, elected representative institutions and mass political parties—are weak and ineffective.[36]

Is this theory relevant to political change in the Soviet bloc? At first glance, it might appear not. Huntington applied his theory to some historical European states, but primarily to modernizing states in the Third World. Moreover, he thought that Leninist party states were antidotes to praetorianism, not causes of it.

Huntington wrote in 1968 that the appeal of the Leninist party-states to newly modernizing countries was that it would help close the gap between high levels of political participation and low levels of political institutionalization.[37] From the vantage point of two subsequent decades, however, it seems clear that Leninist organization was merely an expedient papering over of that gap, not a permanent, stable solution. The Leninist variety of "participation" was too perfunctory and manipulated to serve the real function of channeling and integrating social demands. Likewise, Leninist party-state institutions tended to ossify, thus violating Huntington's dictum that successful institutions must not only be strong, but flexible. Even in the Soviet bloc itself, let alone the Third World, such party-states have failed to meet the challenge of creating a legitimate order.[38]

But will the collapse of Leninist orders produce a praetorian pattern of politics, just as the collapse of institutionally weak traditional political orders often did? Obviously, the situations are not identical. The problem of replacing discredited Leninist institutions is not necessarily the same as the problem of creating strong, diversified, modern governing institutions from scratch in the institutional poverty of a traditional society.

On the other hand, many of the elements of Huntington's praetorian pattern seem present in Soviet bloc states today. In a political environment where governmental legitimacy is weak, the military, organized labor, and intellectuals—indeed almost all the same actors that Huntington found in his praetorian societies—could be among the players taking direct action in defense of their threatened interests.[39]

The main potential difference between collapsing Leninist states and rising traditional ones is that enough of the institutional structure from the communist period might remain to allow a quicker reestablishment of political order than a traditional society could manage. But this could be part of the problem, rather than the solution, if the bureaucratic institutions left over from communist rule act as self-regarding interest groups. In that case, the praetorian pattern would only be reinforced.

Huntington sees the praetorian society as only one model of domestic politics. The Hobbesian condition is not universal in domestic politics. Advanced democracies, says Huntington, have developed strong, flexible institutions that allow groups and individuals to articulate and defend their interests through orderly, universally accepted channels. This pattern he calls the *civic polity*.[40] By implication, if the Soviet bloc succeeds in creating democratic institutions of this type, the praetorian pattern can be avoided. In this sense Huntington's theory might be said to agree with the liberal optimists, although it would be more skeptical about the ease of achieving this favorable outcome.

### Three Pluralist Patterns

By supplementing Huntington with some additional theoretical perspectives, three patterns of pluralistic politics—civic democracy, pretorianism, and corporatism—can be used to analyze the future of the former Soviet bloc. Each offers a description of how interests are aggregated in pluralistic politics, their differences based in part on differing assumptions about the institutional context of political action.

In a civic democracy, well-institutionalized electoral competition drives politicians to compete for the favor of the average voter. In this context politicians tend to promise similar, middle-of-the-road policies that appeal to moderate segments of public opinion, not to ideological extremes. Moreover, pandering to narrow interest groups is politically unadvisable if it entails large costs to the broad electorate.[41]

As a result, costly reckless foreign policies usually lose out in electoral competition in a well-institutionalized democracy, at least in the long run. Mature democracies have been reasonably good at retrenching from strategic overextension and other self-defeating aggressive behavior because such policies threaten the interests of prudent average voters.[42] Moreover, well-developed democratic institutions normally foster a relatively open marketplace of ideas, so that average voters have access to the information and analysis that they need to make a rough calculation of their interests.[43] This does not always work smoothly, but in comparative terms mature democracies have been much better than the German and Japanese praetorian states in avoiding strategic disasters.

In the praetorian pattern, competing groups face each other nakedly, their struggle unmitigated by any effective institutional framework. Compact groups with intense preferences—for example, the military or industrialists—are more likely to organize politically than are large groups with diffuse interests, like average voters. As a result, national policy—both foreign and domestic—can be captured by narrow interest groups, who use their disproportionate influence to extract benefits from and pass costs on to unorganized sectors of society, like consumers and taxpayers. Organized sectors may collude in a logroll that simply exploits the unorganized sectors, or they may try to exploit both the unorganized sectors and each other.[44]

When praetorian patterns hold, foreign policy can be dominated by the interests of narrow military, ideological, economic, or colonial lobbies, who may benefit from reckless policies, while passing their costs on to the taxpayers. In a praetorian system mass interests that suffer from such policies will lack adequate means of redress at the polls.[45]

In the third pattern, democratic corporatism, an overarching coalition may encompass the bulk of the organized interest in the whole society. Because the deals brokered within this encompassing umbrella must aggregate a broad spectrum of society's interests, the power of narrower interest groups is held in check.[46] Such corporatist arrangements are especially common in small European states, who use corporatist brokerage to negotiate the domestic terms of adjusting to the rigors of the international market.[47] Democratic corporatist regimes have typically shunned excessive nationalism and pursued benign foreign policies.

### Emerging Patterns of Pluralism
### in the Former Soviet Bloc

Which model—praetorianism, civic democracy, or corporatism—best captures the likely pattern of pluralistic politics in reforming Soviet bloc countries? On the one hand, these societies seem rife with self-seeking interest groups, many of them the detritus of the period of Leninist rule. Workers and managers in uncompetitive heavy industry, the military, and communist party apparatchiks are compact groups, each with a strong incentive for political action in defense of its threatened corporate interests. Nationalist groups and ethnic minorities are also likely candidates for narrowly self-interested behavior, like the Baltic reformers who press their parochial agenda at the expense of the collective interest in the success of perestroika throughout the Soviet Union. Indeed, varied groups are rapidly forming organizations to push their special interests: wildcat strike committees in Soviet heavy industry, trade unions in the Soviet military,[48] the Great Russian *Rossiya* bloc in the Supreme Soviet, and various ethnic "national fronts."[49]

On the other hand, reforming Soviet bloc states are also creating competitive electoral institutions which should help take power away from compact interest groups and give it to the average voter. A well-developed electoral system with well-developed political parties should prevent the emergence of praetorian politics, according to Huntington's logic.

The problem is that the electoral systems emerging in reformist Soviet bloc countries have a truncated quality that is closer to the Wilhelmine German system than to the modern civic polity. The Wilhelmine precedent offers a sobering example of the consequences of a popularly elected legislature which is not directly responsible for policymaking.[50] The Reichstag, elected on the basis of universal manhood suffrage, had authority to raise taxes, approve budgets, and approve the conscription of soldiers, but it had no power to topple government ministers, who were selected by the kaiser. Forming governments in the Wilhelmine Reich meant logrolling among the members of the uneasy coalition of "iron and rye," which included aristocratic Junker landowners, Ruhr heavy industrialists, Prussian bureaucrats, the army, and the navy. But getting government policies funded meant also coopting swing votes in the Reichstag. For example, to win votes for the expansion of the fleet, the chancellor paid off the Center party with concessions to the narrow concerns of the Catholics who were that party's sole constituency. In short, the Wilhelmine pattern of elite-managed, truncated democracy is more likely to yield a praetorian politics of interest-group logrolling than a civic politics dominated by the diffuse, moderate interests of the average voter.[51]

A similar pattern may be unfolding in some of the truncated democracies in the former Soviet bloc. Despite universal suffrage, contested elections, and diverse representation in a national parliament, the average voter exercises only an oblique influence on state policy in systems like Poland's, let alone the Soviet Union's, for two reasons.

First, in the Soviet case, safe seats for party apparatchiks and members of conservative nationalist organizations like the Great Russian writers' union function like "rotten boroughs," skewing the outcome away from average voter preferences for the benefit of privileged organized groups. Although the safe seats are to be eliminated, party manipulation of the local nominating and campaigning process may still produce a group of delegates to the Congress of People's Deputies that is skewed in favor of conservative coalitions. So will party manipulation of the Congress itself, which acts as a further filter in selecting Supreme Soviet legislators.[52]

But the second and more important flaw is that the resulting elected body has limited authority over policy and over the composition of the governing cabinet. In Poland the defense bureaucracy and the unelected president, with significant authority over foreign and security affairs, remain largely outside the realm of legislative control. In the Soviet Union the main holders of executive power in all issue areas are only loosely accountable to the Supreme Soviet, although some proposed ministers have been rejected by that body and a veneer of legislative oversight is being established even in the military field.[53]

It could be argued that Poland is nearing the threshold of responsible party government, with real power holders directly accountable to fully enfranchised voters. In this view, Poland already passed through a praetorian period in the early 1980s, during which a military dictator aligned himself with conservative industrial and governing elites against a trade union aligned with militant intellectuals. Indeed, this is a common pattern in Huntington's praetorian systems.[54] But now the emergence of real electoral institutions may give Solidarity a strong incentive to act like a Western political party, appealing to the average voter's interest in expanding the economic pie, rather than like a parochial trade union, appealing to the narrow instincts of organized labor.[55] At present, Solidarity seems to be leaning toward market-oriented policies, which would further undercut the power of Poland's protected heavy industries, and away from a policy of continued subsidies, which would retain the hothouse environment of the planned economy. Only if the new system works will the military's interest in political intervention to prevent disorder wane. If so, the praetorian pattern may be averted.

In Hungary elements of all three patterns—democratic, praetorian, and corporatist—could be discerned in the events of 1989. Since the spring of 1989, all major constitutional and economic questions have been the subject of detailed bargaining with representatives of the government, the main political parties, and organized labor all sitting down together for roundtable discussions.[56] Hungary appeared to be taking the route of the small corporatist states, like its neighbor Austria.[57]

However, benign corporatist arrangements serving the broad social interest are not the only deals being struck in pluralist Hungary's smoke-filled back rooms. The plan for the early election of a president, concocted through collusion between communists and conservative nationalists and narrowly defeated in November 1989, smacked of a logroll between parochial interest groups. The communists (now called socialists) had hoped that a monopoly on name recognition would insure the victory of their candidate for president, Imre Pozsgay, if the election were held in January 1990 on the basis of direct popular vote. Pozsgay allegedly expected to use the several months before a new legislature would be elected in the spring of 1990 to assert strong presidential control over the state bureaucracy. The socialists were supported in this plan by the Democratic Forum, a nonsocialist party whose members include many conservative nationalists and anti-Semites. It is widely believed that the Forum, some of whose members have long-standing ties to the communist bureaucracy, was offered the premiership as a quid pro quo.[58]

If successful, this scheme would have shifted Hungarian politics toward a praetorian pattern of truncated democracy, not managed by a benign corporatism, but manipulated through a narrow marriage of communist bureaucrats and Hungarian nationalists. The would-be praetorian logroll was defeated, however, through the power of the average voter at the ballot box. The Alliance of Free Democrats, a truly democratic Western-oriented party, demanded a referendum on the plan for a hasty presidential election. Overcoming a Socialist-Forum boycott, the democratic opposition parties generated the necessary minimum turnout needed to delay a presidential vote until the new constitution and legislature are in place.[59] The power of the average voter turned back attempts by narrowly self-interested cartels to collude in skewing Hungarian corporatism in a praetorian direction.

Whether the reforming East European states are over the crucial democratic threshold remains to be seen. The Soviet Union is of course much farther from having a system of real democratic accountability. Praetorian Wilhelmine Germany's truncated democracy may be the model that describes the Soviet future. Western-style democracy or democratic corporatism may have a better chance to prevail in the smaller states of Eastern Europe.

## International Consequences of
## Praetorian Politics

The emergence of praetorian societies in Eastern Europe would have grave implications for international politics. Two such societies, Japan and Germany, have been the most egregious disturbers of the peace in this century. In Eastern Europe in the first half of this century, even small powers with praetorian political systems provoked international conflicts, which embroiled the Great Powers.

Wilhelmine Germany again illustrates why this occurred.[60] Wilhelmine aggressiveness stemmed from two sources. The first was the terms of the intra-elite logroll. Many of the elite groups had vested interests in policies that embroiled Germany with other powers—for example, heavy industry's and the navy's interest in fleet construction, the army's offensive Schlieffen Plan, the Junkers' need for farm tariffs that hurt Russian interests. In the praetorian Wilhelmine society there was neither a strong central authority nor strong accountability to the median voter to constrain these parochial interests and establish strategic priorities. As a result, Germany made too many enemies and, once encircled, tried to break out of that encirclement through aggression.

The second element feeding Wilhelmine aggressiveness was the relationship between the elites and the mass groups suddenly mobilized into German political life in the 1880s and 1890s. This sudden burst of political participation was due in part to the processes of industrialization and urbanization and in part to the strategies of elite groups who sought to recruit mass allies against competing elites. Thus, Junker landowners recruited smallholding agrarian populists, while industrial and naval circles used the middle-class Navy League to create popular pressure for their pet project. Many of these agricultural and middle-class groups had been whipsawed by market forces which had disrupted their traditional economic activities in the late nineteenth century. Because liberal laissez-faire had been discredited by its disruption of traditional, regulated markets, these mass groups were not hard to recruit for the elites' illiberal protectionist and imperialist schemes. Added to this volatile mixture was nationalistic propaganda, which the elites used as part of their "social imperialist" strategy for managing the explosion of popular participation in politics.

A similar pattern can also be observed in the history of Eastern Europe's small powers during the first half of the twentieth century. Myron Weiner has noted what he calls the "Macedonian syndrome," in which the weak, modernizing states of Central and Eastern Europe were often captured by ethnic groups, the military, and intellectuals touting nationalist themes as tools for their parochial purposes.[61] Their irredentist nationalism embroiled these states in conflicts with their neighbors, contributing further to the hyperpatriotic cultural atmosphere and the praetorian character of domestic politics. Squabbles among the praetorian East European states gave rise to the familiar multipolar checkerboard balance-of-power pattern and triggered interventions by outside

Great Powers. In short, nationalistic, praetorian domestic politics both fed and was fed by sharp competition in the anarchical international setting.[62]

Despite Weiner's findings, the broader historical record does not show that praetorian societies necessarily become nationalistic and expansionist. Huntington's instances of praetorianism include many societies that turned their violence strictly inward. Perhaps the East Europeans internationalized their praetorian violence because of the prevalence of ethnic irredenta in their region, a historical pattern which largely persists today.[63] Another difference between Weiner's cases and Huntington's might be the distinctive historical role played by praetorian Germany as a model of belligerence for its smaller East European praetorian neighbors. If so, a well-behaved Federal Republic of Germany might exert a more benign influence on Eastern Europe in the present era.

How likely is it that the Soviet Union will recapitulate the Wilhelmine pattern of domestic and foreign policy, or that Eastern Europe will relive the Macedonian syndrome? Some obvious parallels can be mentioned. The Soviet Union is a state undergoing a huge leap in mass political participation in the context of an authoritarian tradition and a demonstrable delegitimation of its previous governing institutions. "Traditional" elite groups, in this case the conservative sectors of the party and the military, have corporate interests that in the past have inclined them toward a conflictual approach to international politics.[64] Labor, ethnic groups, the military, and intellectuals are forming organized groups. Existing institutions, including the communist government and truncated democratic bodies, are hard-pressed to reconcile competing demands of these groups in ways that serve collective rather than parochial interests. The mass populace, moreover, is being mobilized into political life at the same time that it is being threatened with unparalleled economic disruptions due to the introduction of market reforms. Potential or actual ethnic conflicts in the Soviet periphery and between some East European states may contribute to an international environment where intense nationalism seems the norm and where peace and security cannot be taken for granted.[65]

Gorbachev himself worries that the pluralism unleashed by perestroika has the potential to degenerate into a praetorian chaos. Explaining the need to maintain the leading role of the communist party, he asserts that "in the efforts to renew socialism, the party may not concede the initiative to either populist demagoguery, nationalist or chauvinistic currents or to the spontaneity of group interest."[66]

On the more positive side, Gorbachev may be in a stronger position and is more liberal than analogous reform leaders in Germany or Japan, like Gustav Stresemann and Shidehara Kijuro in the 1920s.[67] The Soviet military, though an active lobbyist for offensive military programs under Brezhnev, does not have anything like the deep-rooted traditions of domestic interventionism and international belligerency that their German and Japanese counterparts had. Soviet intellectuals, notwithstanding ethnic chauvinist elements among the Great Russians and other national groups, are playing a much more positive role than did the infamous "fleet professors" of the Wilhelmine era and the whitewashers of German war guilt in Weimar Germany.[68]

More generally, the passing of Social Darwinism from pan-European culture, due in part to the passing of praetorian regimes, has made nationalist appeals harder to sell, as have the lessons of two world wars.[69] Inside the erstwhile Soviet bloc, nationalism seems virulent primarily among stateless ethnic groups—Armenians, Azerbaijanis, and Balts. Three reforming nationalities who already form the core of nation-states —Russians, Poles, and Hungarians—have not so far tried to exploit excessive nationalism as a solution to the problems of governing increasingly pluralistic societies. The nationalism and anti-Semitism of elements within the Democratic Forum are not yet playing a dominant role in Hungarian politics. However, one such core nationality, Yugoslavia's Serbs, has been asserting its parochial claims at the expense of the Albanians in Kosovo province. Still, among peoples with states, it was two non-reforming states—Romania and pre-reform Bulgaria—who had recently been engaging in draconian measures to destroy the national identities of their ethnic minorities.[70]

In short, the states of the former Soviet bloc, including the USSR, may degenerate into praetorian politics in response to the problems associated with expanding political participation and the retrenchment of Soviet power, or they may not. And if they do slip into that pattern, they may recapitulate the Wilhelmine and "Macedonian" patterns of foreign policy, or they may not. The outcome remains in doubt.

Precisely for that reason, it seems plausible that the nature of the broader international environment, including the policies of the West, will affect the result. Nationalism may be kept under wraps in Hungary, for example, because the public calculates that a show of overt chauvinistic irredentism toward Romania over the Hungarian minority in Transylvania would kill Hungary's incipient opening to the West.[71] It is therefore to the effects of the international setting that I now turn.

## International Causes of
## Praetorian Politics

Whether a society takes the praetorian path is determined largely by its domestic pattern of development. The prime candidates are late, rapid developers with elites who have a strong interest in resisting the diffusion of political power.[72] But the international environment may also play a role, either for good or ill.

Among small states, one would expect the international environment to play a major role in shaping domestic institutions and their expression in foreign policy. Small, vulnerable states must adapt to their international position because they cannot buffer themselves from its influence. As I suggested previously, the especially malign international setting may explain why Weiner's aggressive Macedonian syndrome prevailed in Eastern Europe in the first half of this century, whereas it was less prevalent in praetorian states elsewhere.[73] Likewise, Peter Katzenstein finds that an "authoritarian version" of corporatism was prevalent in small European states in the 1930s, whereas later a "democratic form of corporatism" was "nourished by the strong effect of a liberal United States on the postwar global economy."[74]

The effect of the international setting on large, would-be praetorian states is just as dramatic. In the 1920s, for example, Weimar Germany and Taisho Japan were societies on the cusp of emerging from praetorian patterns. Liberal, democratic, free-trading, nonmilitarist institutions were potentially emerging in these two states in the 1920s. In part, this was facilitated by a fairly benign international environment. The Washington Naval Treaty of 1922 and the Locarno Pact of 1925 institutionalized a security environment that made aggressive behavior seem unnecessary for achieving security. Financial flows from America, in the form of Dawes Plan loans to Germany and Japanese profits from the textile trade, bankrolled liberal, free-trading coalitions, which counted on an expanded electoral franchise to maintain their position against military, protectionist, and conservative elites. When this relatively liberal international order collapsed because of the Depression at the end of the 1920s, however, the liberal regimes in Germany and Japan collapsed along with it.[75]

The lessons of this case may cut both ways. One is cautionary: links between a tentatively liberalizing state and a liberal international order must be strong and permanent or else they may be counterproductive. Forging such ties and then having them broken is probably more disruptive to domestic political order than never forging them at all.

A more optimistic lesson, however, is that even a relatively weak liberal international order can exert positive effects even on hard-case praetorian societies like Germany and Japan by creating incentives for the formation of liberal coalitions. By implication, a much stronger liberal regime, like the one that the advanced capitalist countries have forged today, should be able to exert an even stronger positive effect on easier cases, like most Eastern bloc states.

The next section uses the neoliberal institutionalist theory of international regimes to examine the current policy implications of this insight.

## Creating Political Order Through International Institutions

How might international institution-building contribute to the creation of a stable, democratic order in the former Soviet bloc? In addressing this question, it will be worthwhile to consider theories of international regimes and to look back to the origins of the postwar order.

Neoliberal regime theory, as articulated by such students of international political economy as Stephen Krasner and Robert Keohane, accepts the proposition that cooperation rarely emerges spontaneously in anarchic conditions.[76] To overcome problems of organizing collective action, successful cooperation requires a push from some powerful provider of incentives to cooperate and the creation of institutions that coordinate the participants' expectations and actions. But once in place, a cooperative regime and its institutions tend to create habits and constituencies that make them self-perpetuating.

One version of the institutionalist view places particular stress on the role of institutional structures in channeling interests toward certain outcomes. This is the part of the institutionalist argument that I draw on most heavily. Kenneth Arrow's famous "impossibility theorem" showed that it is impossible to predict a unique outcome of pluralistic policymaking from the preferences of the participants. A variety of different coalitions and policy outcomes is possible; there is no stable equilibrium. Subsequent theorists have shown, however, that the prevailing institutional setting increases the probability of certain outcomes and favors the emergence of some potential coalitions over others.[77]

The canonical example of a successful attempt to use international institution-building to load the dice in favor of liberal outcomes is the post-1945 international economic regime. Initially underwritten by American power and leadership, this regime is now firmly rooted in its participants' domestic and international institutions in ways that go beyond simple power relations among states. In light of the frequent calls for a "new Marshall Plan" for Eastern Europe, it is especially appropriate to remember precisely how the original Marshall Plan worked to forge the liberal postwar order.[78]

The Marshall Plan's effectiveness lay in its political and institutional strategy, not just in its dollar amount. American money was only a small fraction of the total investment in Western Europe in the late 1940s. America did not just buy a liberal international order. Rather, the Marshall Plan worked primarily because it linked its financial aid to the beneficiary countries' acceptance of institutions of transnational economic cooperation. These included not only multilateral institutions like the General Agreement on Tariffs and Trade (GATT), but regional European cooperative efforts like the European Coal and Steel Community (ECSC) and the European Payments Union (EPU). This had a multiplier effect on economic efficiency, while politically it strengthened internationally oriented sectors and coalitions against their insular, protectionist foes. In short, the Marshall Plan worked by creating international institutions to channel domestic interests in a direction favorable to international cooperation and stability.[79]

Proponents of a new Marshall Plan for Eastern Europe should think in similar terms. The former Soviet bloc needs not just economic investment. More important, it needs to develop a workable set of economic and political institutions that will allow that investment to be put to stable, productive use. Western loans and investment in Eastern Europe in the 1970s failed to spark meaningful economic growth and political change because they were not tied to institutional reform. Moreover, just as Marshall aid backed regional European organizations like ECSC and EPU, so too today's efforts might work best through regional European institutions like the European Community.

### Specific Proposals for Building Pan-European Institutions

Like its original, the new Marshall Plan needs a strategy for using international institutions to fill the gap between booming political participation and a weak domestic order threatened by the competing demands of illiberal organized interests. I will evaluate some ideas of this type that have already been advanced by prominent figures in the West, and also attach some specific ideas of my own to this general framework.[80]

The most effective scheme would gradually integrate reforming Soviet bloc states into the European Community. The EC is a strong, well-developed supranational institution with a proven record of successfully assimilating less-developed European states into its economic system, with favorable effects on their political development. West Germany, the nation that Soviet bloc states are most eager to trade with, is a member of the EC. With backing from Washington and a benign attitude from Moscow, the EC would surely have sufficient resources to play the leadership role that is helpful in setting up a strong international regime. There are economic incentives for the EC to play a more active role in the East, as well as ideological and security incentives.[81]

This is *not* a scheme that relies simply on the erroneous notion that economic interdependence breeds peace. The favorable political effect comes not just from interdependence, but from the institutional structures and changes in domestic interests that may or may not accompany high levels of interdependence. In previous eras of extensive foreign trade and loans, multilateral economic institutions were weaker, as were the effects of interdependence on domestic economic structure. Although trade may have been at high levels, the production process of individual firms was rarely internationalized, as it is now. Consequently, the political effects of a liberal order were not deeply rooted in international institutions and domestic interests.[82] Thus, pointing out that high levels of trade preceded World War I is not an argument against a strategy of neoliberal institution-building in the former Soviet bloc.

How would such a strategy work? According to the most commonly discussed ideas, different East European states would be granted different levels of association with the EC and integrated into its institutions at a varying pace. Progress toward market reforms and full-fledged electoral democracy would be the price of admission to greater participation. Access to capital and markets would be the carrot. The institutionalized, legal character of the relationship would make for predictability, irreversibility, and deeply penetrating effects on the domestic order of the state.

The regime should also have a security component. Alliances that the Soviet Union would find threatening, such as between NATO and Poland, should be forsworn.[83] Arms control should be designed to stabilize not only the East-West balance but also East-East balances.

Two principles should be considered in designing military postures. First, states who have potential irredentist ethnic claims should not be militarily stronger than their neighbors. Thus, Hungary is—and should be—militarily weaker than Romania, which deters irredentism over Transylvania. Romania, in turn, is weaker than the Soviet Union, which deters irredentism over the status of Romanian-speaking Soviet Moldavia.[84]

Second, individual states and the two alliances should have force postures that are optimized for defense. Tank-heavy mobile strike forces and deep-strike ground-attack aircraft should be sharply limited, whereas fixed defenses should be encouraged.[85] Whenever possible, states should prepare to defend their allies by moving forces into defensive positions on the allies' own territory, not by preparing to attack the aggressor on the aggressor's home territory.[86] For noncontiguous allies, this might involve airlifting troops into previously prepared defensive positions.

A cooperative, pan-European security regime should also lay out the rights and responsibilities of ethnic and religious minorities. The purpose would be to head off nationalistic conflicts before they get started. Adherence to such a regime would be a precondition for the deepening of a state's participation in East-West economic ties. Social science has developed a number of ideas about how in general to prevent ethnic tension from creating political instability. Applied social scientists should think about how to use these ideas in the construction of a European minorities regime.[87]

One concrete idea would be to create an International Academy for Nationalities Studies, the aim of which would be to get local intellectuals out of their self-created hothouses of nationalistic mythology and co-opt them into the broader Euro-Atlantic intellectual community. Throughout the history of nationalism, a major role has been played by intellectuals and publicists, who create a wave of nationalist myth and then ride it to positions of prestige and influence.[88] The international community should try to create alternative incentives for restless intellectuals and on-the-make journalists. Conferences, lucrative fellowships, and mid-career retraining at the academy should expose them to objective accounts of the history of their region and its relations with others, and to modern theories of conflict management in multiethnic societies. But to participate, intellectuals and their local institutes would have to be accredited by some international body (much as the international psychiatric organization now imposes professional conditions for Soviet participation). Conditions might include international standards of archival openness, availability of books by international authors, accurate labeling of fact and opinion in journalistic writings, and academic promotions based on international scholarly standards.

### A Role for the United States and the USSR

The United States and the Soviet Union must play a role in the European Common Home. For example, the EC solution to the German problem should not be seen as supplanting NATO and the Warsaw Pact. Restructured along the lines of nonoffensive defense, the alliances should be retained, because they help provide a legal basis for the division of Germany. Moreover, their extant institutional structures have already proved useful in negotiating conventional arms control and more generally in managing the transition to a more cooperative system of European security.

Economic arrangements must also include the two superpowers. The strategy of extending Western economic institutions eastward must include the Russian core of the Soviet Union. Otherwise, the enterprise would seem to Moscow like capitalist imperialism and might therefore provoke a backlash. At all costs, the expansion of the EC must not look like a lure to encourage Baltic separatism, while leaving Muscovy to sink into its economic bog.[89] Although the Soviet Union might be included in the European Common Home more loosely than some other East European states, arrangements must be designed to offer Moscow a net benefit in security and economic terms. A moderate dose of easy credits for consumer purchases, joint ventures, reassuring arms control, and the symbolism of an opening to the West might suffice to achieve this effect. President Bush's proposals on GATT and Most Favored Nation status at the Malta summit are steps in the right direction.

The United States would also have to be included in the Euro-Atlantic system. An open door to an American economic presence in Eastern Europe would help prevent the EC move eastward from becoming a thin veil covering an all-German show. American treaty commitments to NATO and the Four Power Berlin regime should be maintained.

## How International Institutions Would Prevent Praetorianism

A system of international institutions would work to prevent the emergence of praetorian regimes in the former Soviet bloc, first, because increased openness to trading on the world market would help break the power of the self-interested cartels that are characteristic of praetorian politics. As conventional wisdom has phrased it, "the tariff is the mother of trusts."[90] The Bismarckian marriage of iron and rye, for example, was consummated expressly to establish tariff protection for both sectors, which would have been severely weakened without it. In contrast, free trading would make it impossible to return to the domestic political alliances that characterized Brezhnev's Russia and Gierek's Poland, comprising obsolete industry, the military, and the orthodox Communist party.

Second, a negotiated security environment would undercut the plausibility of nationalist appeals and threat exaggeration by the military. Since civilian control over the military would be thereby easier, one of the ingredients of praetorian politics—military intervention in domestic politics—would be missing. At the same time, by co-opting intellectuals into pan-European networks, another potential source of virulent nationalism would be lured toward more benign pursuits.

Third, a democratic institutional requirement for EC membership would directly strengthen the moderating voice of the average citizen in Eastern Europe. Recent developments in Hungary already show this process at work. The Hungarians readily admit that one motive for their democratic constitutional reforms is to make them acceptable economic partners for EC countries. Democratic voting, in turn, has helped to stymie a would-be communist-nationalist ruling cartel in that country.

Finally, successful economic integration into the EC would expand the economic pie in Eastern countries, and thus lubricate the process of political transformation, just as the mid-Victorian economic boom, fueled by expanding international trade, facilitated Britain's transition to a full-fledged, two-party, universal-suffrage democracy.

In short, given the importance of heading off the emergence of praetorian states in the former Sovet bloc, the West has an incentive to extend its successful international regimes eastward in order to help fill the gap between rising political participation and weak governing institutions. One plausible scheme would center on an expanded EC as its core, with the United States and the Soviet Union as more loosely associated members of a Euro-Atlantic Common Home.

## Evaluating the Competing Perspectives

The burden of this discussion is to clarify the reasoning behind three competing perspectives on security in the changing European order, and in particular to explore the logic behind the neoliberal institutionalist view. A definitive evaluation of the three views is a task for the cumulative work of many scholars and public commentators.

Nonetheless, a few judgments are in order. First, liberal optimism seems more like ideological self-indulgence or politicians' rhetoric than a serious analytical position. Any worthwhile analysis must recognize that the dismantling of a stable political order entails grave dangers.

Hobbesian pessimism, in contrast, enjoys a firmer theoretical foundation and offers some insightful diagnoses, but suffers from a few significant flaws. It exaggerates the inevitability that international conflict and nationalistic excesses will follow from the erosion of the bipolar division of Europe. Its assumption is untenable—that profound changes in the domestic character of states since the interwar period will be readily reversed as a consequence of changes in the structure of the international system. The past pathologies of German politics, for example, were caused not primarily by Germany's vulnerable position in the multipolar system, but by the social tensions associated with Germany's pattern of late development.[91] Because this particular phase of development was outgrown long ago, the coming period of multipolarity will take place in a more benign domestic context. If this favorable pattern is reinforced by liberal international institutions, there is no reason to expect a revival of the Hobbesian war of all against all in Europe.

Nor does the Hobbesian viewpoint generate any plausible solutions to the problem of European order. The solution that *is* consistent with its theoretical assumptions—maintaining the bipolar Cold War division of Europe—is no longer available. Russia is too weak and irresolute, and East European publics are too restive for the status quo ante to be restored. More plausible would be a unilateral decision by the NATO alliance to insulate itself from the coming crisis in the East, but this fits poorly with the theoretical assumptions of the Hobbesian theory, which posits as unlikely that a state would impose on itself a geopolitical sphere of abstention, and that an alliance would be maintained after the opposing alliance breaks up. In particular, it is hard to imagine West Germany remaining completely indifferent to the fate of reforms in East Germany, under Hobbesian or any other plausible assumptions.

The third Hobbesian solution, Bismarckian defensive alliances, had a weak track record when it was tried before. If it is to do better this time, it will have to be embedded in a political order of more favorable domestic and international institutions. Insuring that all states in the multipolar checkerboard are simultaneously secure will require elaborate arms control arrangements negotiated on the principles of nonoffensive defense in a well-institutionalized setting. Otherwise, the logic of the strategic solution will mount pressures to develop offensive military capabilities to come to the aid of noncontiguous allies.

Neoliberal institutionalism also entails several serious problems. It envisages a cooperative security regime involving all of the world's great powers, which would be an almost unprecedented historical event apart from the short-lived post-Napoleonic Concert of Europe.[92] Moreover, it fails to reckon with the problem of compensating the many powerful social groups who would be losers in any scheme integrating Eastern societies into the Western political order—for example, internationally uncompetitive economic sectors, those who control locally scarce resources,[93] and the institutional remnants from the Soviet period. Integrating these societies into Western market economies is bound to be disruptive, if not outright explosive.

Inclusion of the Soviet Union in the Western order is the sine qua non of the whole scheme, yet it is by far the most difficult to accomplish. Its economy is too big for the EC to digest as it could a Spain, a Greece, or a Hungary. Moreover, the Soviet economy and polity seem more inherently resistant to successful reform than does Hungary's, for example. The nuclear-armed Soviet Union must be included because a praetorian outcome there would do the most damage, but it is the country for which that outcome may be hardest to prevent.[94]

Finally, neoliberal institution-building will do great damage if it is attempted but does not work. It will damage the West by embroiling it deeply in the possibly insoluble problems of the East. A new Marshall Plan may convince Americans that spreading liberalism in Eastern Europe is their manifest destiny, and they may get so absorbed in the task that they refuse to give it up if it turns sour. As the example of the 1920s suggested, international institution-building might also damage the East by engaging it in disruptive but unsustainable economic ties with the West. Shaking up the social order in order to forge such links, and then breaking them if they fail to work, could generate more profound social disorder than would failing to forge them in the first place.

On balance, a middle road between the Hobbesian instinct for insulation and the neoliberal instinct for institutionalized activism is probably best. East Germany, Hungary, and Czechoslovakia should probably be admitted eventually into the Western institutional framework. It is especially important that the EC solution be adopted for the German Democratic Republic. Poland's role in Western institutions should be tailored to fit Soviet sensibilities, which would probably tolerate a high degree of Polish economic integration with the West, but not close military ties.

The Soviet Union should be offered generous security guarantees, a full seat in Europe's diplomatic councils, and beneficial economic relationships with the West. Given the apparent unripeness of the Soviet economy for reform, however, it is highly risky to encourage a leap into the dark in the form of thorough integration of the Soviet economy into Western markets. Judging from current evidence, this would disrupt Soviet society more than it would spur increased productivity, and consequently might provoke praetorian tendencies rather than dampen them.

Analyzing European security can no longer be reduced to positing the vectors of billiard-ball states and counting their tanks. The European order is being remade by social and economic change, no less than by shifts in the international configuration of power. Strategies to maintain international security must, in this new world, comprehend all of these varied facets of social life.

# CONCLUSION ▄▄

## Robert Jervis

Only two things are clear about the future of Soviet-American relations. First, they will be different, not only from the immediate past, but also from any model the past has given us. Second, most predictions in this area are likely to be wrong. Indeed, the greatest uncertainty is whether there will be any "Soviet-American relations" at all. That is, the Soviet Union may dissolve or be the battleground for a series of bloody civil wars. In my analysis—necessarily speculative—I will draw on the thoughts of the contributors to this book, but I do not mean to implicate them in my views. At a time when each day's newspaper brings new surprises, collective judgments are not possible.

Each era appears unique to those living through it, but my guess is that even later generations of scholars will view the 1990s as unique. World politics has rarely been thoroughly re-ordered without a major war. Yet with any luck that is the situation we are facing. In fact, from what the Soviet Union is doing, one could infer that she had just lost a war. And, in a sense, she has. The Soviet Union has lost the economic, social, and political war against itself, its society, and the forces that restrain economic growth. But this is a war without another country or coalition that acts like a winner. We do not have countries ready to move into the power vacuum that has been created or to structure a new set of rules to guide international behavior. Indeed, although the United States remains by far the most powerful country in the world, its mood—and perhaps its economy—does not fit this position.[1]

The fact that we have not just been through a war makes the efforts to build a new world both easier and harder. Neither hopes nor fears are as high as they were in 1815, 1918, or 1945. The sense of unity of purpose and confidence which characterized the winning coalitions in the earlier period is absent. On the other hand, postwar exhaustion is missing.

The future is also unprecedented because while the Soviet Union is economically and politically weak, it remains the only country that could destroy the United States. Other states which are America's economic rivals (as well as its economic partners) are its close allies (and indeed even its friends). While the United States, Western Europe, and Japan were brought together in significant measure because of the perceived Soviet threat, forty years of cooperation have produced structures, attitudes, and values that will last even though the initial conditions of threat have been removed. Even if they do not get nuclear weapons, Japan and Germany will be two of the most powerful nations in the world. Yet their relations with the United States, although of course characterized by significant frictions, are not likely to develop into real hostility.

We could still look to generalizations from the past about whether bipolar or multipolar systems are more prone to conflict, instability, and war. But not only do scholars differ on these judgments, but it probably will be hard to characterize the future international system in these terms. If Western Europe united and maintained a nuclear force, the system would be tripolar (assuming the Soviet Union stays together). But if Europe does not unify, would the system be unipolar, still remain bipolar, or be multipolar? Would the answer be different if Germany and Japan developed nuclear weapons? And if the latter events did occur, would the past histories of multipolar, but non-nuclear, systems give us much guidance about a multipolar nuclear world?[2]

Paradoxically, the powerful influence of history makes the future more difficult to predict. That is, any number of almost accidental events can strongly influence the directions in which world politics will move. For example, a world in which the Baltic republics peacefully secede is likely to develop quite differently from one in which the Soviet Union uses massive force to coerce the republics, and this world in turn would be very different from one in which the republics are not cowed by demonstrations of force but rather forcibly resist. Likewise, any number of events within the Soviet Union, within or between the countries of Eastern Europe, or in American policy could shape Soviet-American relations for years to come. The world is not solely determined by the international structure and other large-scale variables.

Structural models are inappropriate—or at least insufficient—in this case for a second reason: Soviet-American relations will be deeply influenced by domestic developments within each country as well as by international factors. Gorbachev sees clearly that the fate of his foreign policy is closely linked to the success or failure of his efforts to remake the Soviet internal system. (The extent to which the latter depends on the former is subject to more debate.) On the American side as well, foreign policy choices will rest in part on domestic patterns and coalitions that have not yet emerged and on the success or failure of leadership.

## Possible Forms of Cooperation

If the United States and the USSR have fewer conflicting interests and more common and convergent ones, how might they cooperate? Other chapters in this book have focused on conflict and cooperation in specific issue-areas; here I will outline a few possibilities for the general form that cooperation might take. Eventually, the Soviet-American relations might evolve into something resembling the Concert of Europe.[3] In such a regime the states look to their long-run interests, do not take advantage of the other's short-term weaknesses, refrain from pressing others to the limit, and are willing to trade favors "on account," expecting reciprocation sometime in the future rather than only making bargains in which the values must be traded at exactly the same time. More open processes are also involved—greater and more honest communications, less secrecy, and less deception.[4] The participants have a stake in maintaining this kind of relationship and in not permitting a return to a more conflictual one. Furthermore, they know that their partners have the same incentives. The temptation to exploit the other when this is possible—which both sides did during the détente of the 1970s[5]—is therefore resisted. But concerts have only been established after the shock of having had to fight a long and bloody war against a potential hegemon.

Until 1989 the possibility of a concert seemed visionary. While it may not come about, it is now not so easily dismissed. Kinds of cooperation that were unthinkable until recently are now in place. For example, the superpowers are starting to test highly intrusive inspection mechanisms in order to determine whether they could be sufficient for arms control arrangements. Such ideas had long been rejected by the Soviet Union, but can be pursued now that it has lost its crippling obsession with secrecy.[6] Of course a high degree of openness is necessary but not sufficient to produce a concert-like arrangement. An unusually high degree of common interest, a long-run perspective, and even a degree of trust (which in part is engendered by the other factors) is required. It is still too soon to tell whether these conditions will be met.

A less ambitious form of cooperation would be to try to agree on general "rules of the game," as the United States and the USSR did in the Basic Principles Agreement at the May 1972 summit meeting. This is not a hopeful model: the two sides brought very different expectations to the agreement. While the United States considered it relatively unimportant, the Soviets apparently saw it as ratifying their right as an equal superpower to engage in what the United States considered illegitimate adventures in the Third World.[7] The fact that this experience turned out so badly has soured both sides on this approach. Even if it did not suffer under this handicap, the attempt to develop a general formula that would cover a multitude of problems and situations is not promising. In trying to gain some of the advantages of the concert without being able to build on the same degree of common interest, this approach may be particularly difficult. Stylized and artificial restraints are deployed to restrain what is still a quite severe conflict; there is a disproportion between the strength of the animal to be secured and the strength of the cage.

Instead, better relations might be developed through three processes and channels. First, with the disappearance of the perceived need to deny the other any possible advantage anywhere in the globe, many conflicts can be separated from potential superpower rivalries by mutual disengagement, often through the use of multilateral agencies such as the United Nations.[8] For this to happen, both superpowers must be willing to tolerate a wider range of outcomes in Third World disputes than they have been accustomed to, but this seems quite plausible. Such a stance might increase conflict in the Third World; extensive superpower involvement often keeps them under control. It would have been hard to imagine the Iran-Iraq War lasting for eight years if each of these states had been the client of a superpower. It is possible, of course, that the superpowers could actively work together to dampen conflicts in Eastern Europe or the Third World. Although such joint ventures would have the virtue of allowing each superpower to see that the other did not act unilaterally to gain a competitive advantage, they would require very close coordination between the superpowers and would place a great burden on their relationship. Mutual disengagement probably would be easier, even though it might not be better for the rest of the world.

A second cooperative process seems anodyne, but it is neither easy nor trivial. This is to develop much more consultation between the superpowers. They could discuss many more issues at greater depth and with more honesty. The aim would be to develop greater empathy and predictability. Of course, close and extensive contact does not guarantee understanding; as Richard Neustadt has shown, the close and multilayered communication between the United States and Great Britain did not prevent each country from failing to understand how the other would act over Suez in 1956 and Skybolt six years later.[9] Indeed, part of the problem was that each side was confident that it could easily put itself in other's shoes, which in fact it could not. Furthermore, understanding and predictability can be used to make gains at the other's expense. Nevertheless, if the sources of conflict have diminished and the incentives for cooperation have increased, it will benefit each side not only to understand the interests, perspectives, and alternatives of the other, but to have the other side develop such an understanding of the state. Although no formal agreement or mechanisms can ensure this, a modest step would be to require annual summit meetings, semi-annual meetings of foreign and defense ministers, and even more frequent contacts at lower levels. It would not be too much to suggest that each country's ambassador and high embassy officials should have daily meetings with the host government.

Third, both countries could agree to inform the other of any planned actions that would impinge on the other's interests. Surprise is as potent a weapon in competitive diplomacy as it is in military strategy. For the superpowers to renounce this tool would be to ratify the predominance of managing their long-run relations even at the cost of foregoing short-run gains. It would enhance their ability to avoid crises and make it easier for them to avoid some policies which would unnecessarily harm the other. For example, both the United States and the USSR might have been better off had they had to notify each other of their intentions to aid client factions in Angola in 1975 or if the United States had had to tell the Soviet Union that it was planning to equip its missiles with multiple warheads.

Part of the rationale for the "no surprise agreement" is that both sides have come to realize that when each side can react effectively to the other's attempts to make unilateral and competitive gains, both the hope to exploit the other side and the fear of being exploited are often misplaced because one side's defection is likely to be met by a matching response.[10] In the past, American and Soviet leaders have failed to realize that they could not follow a sharply competitive policy or deploy an effective weapon without the other following suit. In many cases, the real as opposed to the perceived choice has been between mutual cooperation or mutual competition. Thus only for a short period did the United States have MIRVs while the Soviet Union did not. Of course, in some cases a short-run advantage leads to even greater gains, but between major powers such instances are rare. That the advantages accorded by surprise often are short-lived should make it easier for the superpowers to give up this tool.[11] But ingrained habits are powerful and can be overturned only by strong efforts. Such efforts are worthwhile because even if surprises rarely produce lasting advantage, they can increase mistrust and produce spirals of unnecessary conflict which make it hard to maintain good relations.

### New Wars in the New World?

The removal of Soviet control over Eastern Europe greatly increases the chance of wars within that region. These would of course be unfortunate for the peoples and states involved, but the more pressing question here concerns the risks of Great Power wars. Many of the causes of wars fall into one of two categories: aggression or spirals of unnecessary conflict. Of course, many wars contain elements of each and even years later historians can argue about which component dominated. Throughout the Cold War the dominant American analysis was that the major —and almost the only—danger was from aggression. The policy prescriptions were fairly obvious in general, if the specifics were contentious: the United States and its allies had to demonstrate the capability and, even more importantly, the resolve to resist Soviet adventures. Although few areas other than Western Europe and Japan were of vital intrinsic interest, if the United States appeared weak and irresolute anywhere in the world, Soviet leaders might infer that core interests could be undermined without a forcible response. It therefore was necessary to resist Soviet, or even Soviet-inspired, adventures throughout the world. But as long as the West displayed consistent firmness and resolve, the danger that aggressive impulses could actually lead to war was relatively slight. Critics argued that both deterrence theory and American foreign policy overlooked the danger that deterrence policies could create rather than contain conflict if they were applied to a state that was motivated more by fear than expansionism. The security dilemma is ever-present in international politics and was, according to many, the basic cause of Soviet-American conflict. In this view, policy prescriptions are also relatively straightforward. Each side has to reassure the other that its intentions are benign and develop means of making itself secure without unduly threatening the other.

It is hard to believe that important American security interests could be significantly menaced by aggression, at least in the next decade. Even if Soviet power makes it America's main adversary, how are we threatened by the USSR? Direct attack on the United States has never been feasible. To expect military pressure on Japan or a move toward the Middle Eastern oil fields seems out of the question. And the scenario that so preoccupied American defense planners for years of a Soviet conventional attack on Western Europe is impossible now that the Warsaw Pact has for all practical purposes dissolved.

But this does not mean that the United States can simply follow the prescriptions of the theory that holds that wars are caused by spirals of threats and mutual insecurity. Although reassurances will have an important role to play in the coming years, not all dangers to the Soviet Union will come from the United States, and the United States cannot entirely neglect the possibility that moves taken to increase Soviet security could have undesired effects.

Furthermore, even if the danger of Soviet aggression against the

United States—and U.S. aggression against the USSR—is extremely low, other countries in the world may be less satisfied with the status quo, and it is out of these disputes that the greatest dangers to Soviet-American relations arise. In Eastern Europe and, to a lesser extent, the Middle East, the risk of interstate warfare is not only significant but also could involve the United States or the USSR. Although we should not be too quick to assume that external forces were necessary to maintain the peace in Europe or to see the Hungarians and Romanians as positively anxious to grab for each other's throats, such wars could occur.

If they arise, they are likely to grow out of several elements which combine aspects of aggression and insecurity. First, and probably a necessary condition for armed violence in Europe, there would have to be a blossoming of intolerant nationalism. Often a concomitant of widespread social upheaval and rapid social change, extreme nationalism leads states to inflate their ambitions, to exaggerate their abilities to cow or conquer others, and to overestimate the degree to which they face external threats. Compounding the problem, nationalism's domestic face looks to the forced assimilation of ethnic minorities. In Eastern Europe, this is a recipe for international conflict.[12] A second element likely to produce conflict is the belief that offensive political tactics and military strategies are much stronger than defensive ones. When this is the case a statesman must seek competitive advantages and positions from which others can be dominated, whether the goal is to change the status quo or to maintain it. The security dilemma will then operate in an extreme fashion; mutual security is not believed to be possible. Third, such a worldview is particularly likely to be held by military officers.[13] It is too early to tell whether such regimes will rule in Eastern Europe. The United States and the USSR should surely do everything in their power to see that they do not. But even with extensive resources and wisdom, they can only influence, and not determine, what will happen.

The other obvious source of conflict in Europe is Germany. One need not believe that evil is inherited to fear that the European country that suffered the greatest net loss of territory after World War II might seek redress. It is easy for those who live in countries who have not suffered such losses to argue that territory now has little value or meaning. Although an outright German attack on her Eastern neighbors is hard to imagine, her attempt to gain great influence over them is not. Furthermore, such efforts could lead to friction, resistance, and heightened nationalism, which in turn could lead Germany to believe that it was more important than ever to establish a greater degree of stabilizing control in the East. Armed conflict can hardly be excluded as a possible outcome of such interactive processes.

It can be argued that such nightmares can be put aside because no European people or statesman would fight because of the knowledge that war simply does not pay. But economic prosperity is not the only goal people seek; ethnic passions, nationalism, inflated hopes for a quick victory, and inflated fears of what the future will bring if the state does not fight should not be underestimated.

I put more faith in the role of nuclear weapons in inhibiting conflict in Europe if great tensions should arise. Even if the United States and the USSR should declare that they would stay out of wars in Eastern and Central Europe, no one could be sure that such wars would not pull in the superpowers. Aggression in Europe is particularly risky in the nuclear era even if neither the attacker nor the victim has nuclear weapons; the Soviet and American nuclear arsenals provide a degree of extended deterrence to the countries of East Central Europe even if no one intends or desires such a consequence. The result is both that potential aggressors face an obstacle that they cannot remove and that potential victims gain a degree of security. Thus nuclear weapons reduce both the danger of war by aggression and war through the operation of the security dilemma. But some danger remains and so the United States and the USSR could decide either to disengage from conflicts in East and Central Europe or to deter their breaking out in the first place. The difficulty is that the costs of each of these strategies is sufficiently high so that statesmen may be tempted to combine them; yet doing so may bring about the worst of all possible worlds. A strategy of disengagement would carry to the extreme the logic that underpinned Gorbachev's policy in the fall of 1989. Even if he did not expect the communist regimes to be swept from power,[14] he seemed to realize that the fate of the USSR was not necessarily entangled with that of Eastern Europe. If Soviet security is compatible with German unification and the establishment of noncommunist regimes along the Soviet borders, why would it be threatened by squabbles within that area?

If the Cold War began in part because it was impossible to have East European regimes that were both pro-Soviet and freely elected, Gorbachev seems willing to end the Cold War on the basis of putting the latter value over the former. The changes in the social structure in Eastern Europe over the past forty-five years and the lessons the inhabitants have learned will make Finlandization a more likely outcome than virulently anti-Soviet governments, and the Soviet willingness to redefine its security interests makes possible a stance of neutrality on disputes among the former satellites. Indeed, the fact that these regimes are no longer communist means that any conflicts among them will no longer carry dangerous implications for what is left of Soviet ideology.

For the United States as well, in principle it would be possible to declare that events in Eastern Europe were of no material interest. But if the fact that these countries are no longer communist removes any ideological incentives for the Soviet Union to be involved, it creates such incentives for the United States. To allow democracies—or at least potential democracies—to fight each other is repugnant to the United States. Furthermore, ideology, history, and geographical proximity mean that wars in Eastern Europe could involve countries of Western Europe, especially Germany, with the obvious dangers for Soviet-American relations.

If the chance of war within Eastern Europe is greatest if both the United States and the USSR declare their willingness to stand aside, might it not be best for both of them—and for the countries in the region—if the USSR maintained some of its duties as a policeman? As long as the Soviet Union did not reimpose communist rule and reestablish forward military bases that could menace the West, why should the United States object to a Soviet sphere of influence? Of course, the Soviets might object—they have just withdrawn from the region and may see no reason to reassume the burdens. Furthermore, while an abstract consideration of international politics might lead to the conclusion that the United States should permit if not encourage such a Soviet role, American values and domestic politics make this solution very difficult. Could a United States which in early 1990 sought to deter Moscow from using force in Lithuania stand by while force was used against the independent countries of Eastern Europe?

To put this another way, there are serious conflicts between American *security* interests and other American interests. It is hard to see how permitting the Soviet Union to intervene in Eastern Europe would menace American security. Indeed, if such a policy could increase the chances of European stability, it would increase American security. I also doubt that the United States and Western Europe would be more secure if the Soviet Union were to break apart. Of course, none of the inheriting states would have as much military power as the USSR has now, but Russia—and perhaps other newly independent states as well —would still have nuclear weapons. Furthermore, if Eastern Europe is filled with traditional rivalries and ethnic conflicts that could breed wars, this is true to an even greater extent of the area that is now encompassed by the Soviet Union. Perhaps the conflicts and wars that would be likely to erupt in the aftermath of the dissolution of the USSR would not directly menace the United States, but it strains the imagination to see how they would make us more secure and it is all too easy to see how they could present us with grave dangers.

The American security interest is not coterminous with American national interest, however. American values begin with security, but they do not end there. We support self-determination and freedom from foreign domination in part because we think they will help make the world more peaceful, but in larger part because we think it right that peoples rule themselves. Likewise, even if keeping the peace in Eastern Europe did not add much to the American security, American diplomats would devote resources to this end because they wish to minimize bloodshed.

Thus the impulses to gain some influence in Eastern Europe and to deny the Soviets the right to intervene with impunity are likely to be strong. To such considerations of American values will be added the calculations of domestic politics. Although changes in American voting patterns have diluted the strength that the East European voting blocs had in the 1940s and 1950s, recent events in Eastern Europe have reawakened many old sentiments.

If not checked, these impulses could even lead the United States to guarantee the newly found freedom of the East European countries. Far from permitting the USSR to police Eastern Europe or deciding that this region provides a buffer zone which protects Western Europe and allows the United States to reduce its security commitments, the United States might apply the principle of extended deterrence to Eastern Europe. Just as the United States said that it would fight—and use nuclear weapons if need be—if the USSR invaded Western Europe, so it might make a similar commitment to Eastern Europe. This would decrease the chance of Soviet action in this area, but only at the cost of increasing the chance of Soviet-American war if such intervention did occur. Furthermore, Moscow probably would see such an American policy as having not only the effect but also the intent of reducing Soviet security.[15]

The American impulse to move well beyond security goals could be a threat to world peace. But will the American domestic political system support a policy of full engagement with the world for less grandiose objectives? It is chastening to remember that this was the question that Roosevelt faced—and could not answer—in 1943 and 1944. Fearing that the American public would prefer isolationism to participating in international politics when the issues were no longer black and white and American vital interests were no longer immediately threatened, he downplayed the likelihood of postwar friction with the Soviet Union. His successor was able to thrust America into extensive involvement with Europe only by moving to the opposite extreme and exaggerating the Soviet threat. It is yet to be seen whether President Bush and his successors can convince the American people to remain deeply involved with Europe—and even to continue stationing troops there—when the threats to American security are relatively slight and when maintaining good relations with the USSR may involve the sacrifice of some ideals and values in Eastern Europe.

Germany will be central to Soviet-American relations as it is central to European geography and politics. Both insecure and powerful, Germany has been the main disturber of the European peace for much of the last century. From the beginning, one function of NATO was to give others (in the West as well as the East) security from West Germany as well as giving that country guarantees. This function is still needed, but is not easy to manage as the publicly accepted rationale disappears. It is hard for any country to be singled out as the only one that needs restraining; harder still when that state has earned a position of leadership by its economic achievements and the singularity is partly rooted in the stigma of having violated the standards of humanity. But it should not be impossible to help the Germans see that maintaining NATO is in their interests. With fewer American troops and less intensive military maneuvers, the burden can be reduced. And the advantages would not be minor. For if Germany is to have good relations with her Eastern neighbors, they will need to be reassured that Germany is not a threat. Of course membership in a multilateral alliance will not provide an ironclad guarantee of German good behavior—nothing will. But it will decrease the chance that even if Germany should develop malign intentions she would be able to act on them. The East Europeans can only allow themselves to develop close economic ties with Germany and to allow that state to be a protector of the rights of German nationals in their countries if they believe that such positions will not be used to their disadvantage. Even a spontaneous and legally binding renunciation of older borders (and it is too late for the former) cannot banish the possibility that the claims will be resurrected.

Similar calculations apply to the states of Western Europe. They are likely to be much more willing to accede to Germany's economic leadership if they see structures and institutions in place that can channel German energies. Primary among these is the European Community, but as the largest and most powerful member, Germany is in a position to influence it as much as it can contain Germany. NATO, being larger and including the United States is less likely to be hijacked by one member, however powerful. Without it, the other European states will view Germany with suspicion and, following natural balancing propensities, will seek to hem Germany in. It is already clear that Britain and France may pull closer together in reaction to German unification. Should NATO dissolve and the United States withdraw from Europe, such a pattern would become more dominant.

Germany may welcome a continued NATO not only because it reduces others' perception of threat from her, but also because it can reduce threats she faces. Or, to put it more precisely, the end of the alliance could increase the threats. Even though the Soviet Union now has little capability to invade Germany and little incentive to menace her, relations could become strained in the future. Without a supporting alliance, Germany could well feel the need to develop nuclear weapons. But, as the security dilemma operates, the result could easily be to increase first Soviet fear and then Soviet and East European pressure on Germany. Of course, the opposite side of this coin is that this fear could lead the East Europeans to suppress their quarrels, thus removing one threat to world peace. But heightened tension between Germany and the rest of Europe would not make a safe or a restful world.

The future of Soviet-American relations then depends in part on the values and choices of many others. War has frequently arisen out of Germany and Eastern Europe. The United States rarely took an interest in these conflicts until they threatened to envelop it. But the future can be different; seeing the potential dangers, we may be able to avoid them. As a result of domestic changes, especially in the Soviet Union, the waning of each side's ideological imperatives, the relative decline of both superpowers, and the lack of direct bilateral conflicts, the greatest source of friction between the United States and the USSR in the last part of the twentieth century is likely to be their conflicting security requirements. Conflicts and wars can occur even if both sides are satisfied with the status quo. Thus it will require effort and skill on the part of the superpowers to ensure that the world that emerges after the Cold War will be a safer and better one. The hope voiced by Carl Becker seemed foolish for four decades, but may now be within reach: "We can only hope, and do what we can to make it come true, that each of these great states will be disposed to regard the balance of power, not as something to be upset on every favorable opportunity for advancing its own selfish interests, but rather as something to be adjusted by mutual agreement, and with constant and considered attention to the maintenance of peace and the promotion of prosperous intercourse among nations."[16]

# ■ NOTES

## Introduction

1  Arnold Wolfer, *Discord and Collaboration* (Baltimore: Johns Hopkins University Press, 1962), pp. 10–19.

2  Ole Holsti, "American Reactions to the USSR: Public Opinion," Chapter 2 in this volume.

3  Robert Shapiro and Benjamin Page, "Foreign Policy and the Rational Public," *Journal of Conflict Resolution* 32 (June 1988): 211–47; Miroslav Nincic, "The United States, the Soviet Union, and the Politics of Opposites," *World Politics* 40 (July 1988): 452–75; and Bruce Russett, "Democracy, Public Opinion, and Nuclear Weapons," in *Behavior, Society, and Nuclear War*, vol. 1, ed. Philip Tetlock et al. (New York: Oxford University Press, 1989), pp. 174–208.

4  Louis Hartz, *The Liberal Tradition in America* (New York: Harcourt, Brace, and World, 1955).

5  For further discussion, see Robert Jervis, "Will the New World Be Better?" chapter 1 in this volume.

6  Quoted in Robert Dallek, "American Reactions to Changes in the USSR," chapter 3 in this volume, p. 14.

7  Colin S. Gray, "Do the Changes Within the Soviet Union Provide a Basis for Eased Soviet-American Relations? A Skeptical View," chapter 4 in this volume.

8  William Zimmerman, "Economic Reform, Democratization, and Soviet Foreign Policy," chapter 5 in this volume.

9  Seweryn Bialer, "Is Socialism Dead?" chapter 6 in this volume.

10  Jack Snyder, "Averting Anarchy in the New Europe," chapter 16 in this volume.

11  John Mueller, "Taking Peace Seriously: Two Proposals," chapter 15 in this volume; also see his *Retreat from Doomsday: The Obsolescence of Major War* (New York: Basic Books, 1989).

12  George H. Quester, "The Soviet Opening to Nonprovocative Defense," chapter 8 in this volume.

13  Donald S. Zagoria, "Soviet Policy in East Asia: The Quest for Constructive Engagement," chapter 10 in this volume.

14  Eric A. Nordlinger, "America's Strategic Immunity: The Basis of a National Security Strategy," chapter 14 in this volume.

15  Glenn E. Schweitzer, "Environmental Protection and Soviet-American Relations," chapter 13 in this volume.

16  Quoted in Alan Cowell, "Soviets Trying to Become Team Player in Moscow," *New York Times*, December 12, 1989.

17  See Harold H. Saunders, "The Soviet-U.S. Relationship and the Third World," chapter 7 in this volume.

18 Alexander J. Motyl, "Rights, Rituals, and Soviet-American Relations," chapter 11 in this volume.

19 Charles Gati, "East and West in Eastern Europe," chapter 9 in this volume.

20 Toby Trister Gati, "The UN Rediscovered: Soviet and American Policy in the United Nations of the 1990s," chapter 12 in this volume.

21 Saunders, "The Soviet-U.S. Relationship and the Third World."

22 For a discussion of the origins of the CSCE, see John Maresca, *To Helsinki: The Conference on Security and Cooperation in Europe, 1973–1975* (Durham: Duke University Press, 1985); a shorter version is Maresca, "Helsinki Accord, 1975," in *U.S.-Soviet Security Cooperation*, ed. Alexander George, Philip Farley, and Alexander Dallin (New York: Oxford University Press, 1988), pp. 106–22. For the argument that biological evolution can proceed only because structures possess redundancies that permit them to serve functions different from those they originally did, see Stephen Jay Gould, "Not Necessarily a Wing," *National History*, October 1985, pp. 12–25.

23 Quoted in Francis Clines, "'Enough' for Glasnost?" *New York Times*, December 26, 1989.

24 Steven Greenhouse, "France Offers Aid to Ceausescu Foes" and Thomas Friedman, "Baker Gives US Approval if Soviets Act on Rumania," both in *New York Times*, December 25, 1989.

## I Will the New World Be Better?

1 In 1954 Paul Nitze declared that "highly satisfactory conditions" for ending the Cold War would be "(a) the unification of Germany on terms satisfactory to the West Germans and to us; (b) the . . . separation from Moscow of the Chinese Communist regime; (c) a continuing system for the control and regulation of armaments involving complete on-the-spot inspection; and (d) the elimination of an effective iron curtain. This would be an extremely ambitious program calling for such overt U.S. superiority as would induce the Russians to permit" these developments to occur. Paul Nitze, "A Project for Further Analysis and Study," *War Gaming: The Persuasion Phase—Final Report* (Maxwell Air Force Base, Ala.: Air War College, 1954), p. 94.

2 George Kennan, "The Sources of Soviet Conduct," *Foreign Affairs* 25 (July 1947): 566–82; also see the discussion in NSC-162/2, U.S. Department of State, *Foreign Relations of the United States, 1952–1954*, vol. 2: *National Security Policy* (Washington, D.C.: U.S. Government Printing Office, 1984), p. 581. In a recent analyses, the importance of external constraints on the USSR are stressed in Eric Nordlinger, "Prospects and Policies for Soviet-American Reconciliation," *Political Science Quarterly* 103 (Summer 1988): 197–223; domestic changes are emphasized in Richard Ullman, "Ending the Cold War," *Foreign Policy* 72 (Fall 1988): 130–51.

3 "A report to the National Security Council by Task Force 'A' of Project Solarium," July 16, 1953, p. 131.

4 Carl Becker, *How Better Will the New World Be?* (New York: Knopf, 1944).

5 For a debate about the role of nuclear weapons in maintaining the superpower peace, see John Mueller, "The Essential Irrelevance of Nuclear Weapons," *International Security* 13 (Fall 1988): 55–79, and Robert Jervis, "The Political Effects of Nuclear Weapons," *International Security* 14 (Fall 1988): 80–90.

6 John Mueller, *Retreat from Doomsday: The Obsolescence of Major War* (New York: Basic Books, 1989).

7 See Alexander George, "Crisis Management: The Interaction of Political and Military Considerations," *Survival* 26 (September–October 1984): 223–34, and "Problems of Crisis Management and Crisis Avoidance in U.S.-Soviet Relations," in *Studies of War and Peace*, ed. Øyvind Østerud (Oslo: Norwegian University Press, 1986), pp. 202–26.

8  See, for example, Bruce Russett, "Democracy, Public Opinion, and Nuclear Weapons," in *Behavior, Society, and Nuclear War*, vol. 1, ed. Philip Tetlock et al. (New York: Oxford University Press, 1990), and Bruce Russett and Donald DeLuca, "'Don't Tread on Me': Public Opinion and Foreign Policy in the Eighties," *Political Science Quarterly* 96 (Fall 1981): 381–400. Elite opinion—at least in the late 1970s—was much more sanguine. See Michael Kanzelberger, "Hawks and Doves," Ph.D. diss., UCLA, 1982.

9  Zbigniew Brzezinski, *Power and Principle* (New York: Farrar, Straus, Girox, 1983), p. 189.

10  For a further discussion, see Robert Jervis, "Strategic Beliefs and Domino Dynamics," *Dominoes and Bandwagons: Superpower Competition and Strategic Beliefs in the Eurasian Rimland*, ed. Robert Jervis and Jack Snyder (New York: Oxford University Press, 1990).

11  Quoted in Arthur Schlesinger, Jr., "The Origins of the Cold War," *Foreign Affairs* 46 (October 1967): 47.

12  Quoted in Bill Keller, "Gorbachev Deputy Criticizes Soviet Policy Trend," *New York Times*, August 7, 1988. For Gorbachev's changing statements on this issue, see his *Perestroika: New Thinking for Our Country and the World* (New York: Harper and Row, 1987), pp. 144–48 and his speech to the United Nations of December 7, 1988, especially p. 7.

13  A more sophisticated version of this belief that holds that liberal democracies do not fight each other has a great deal of truth: see Michael Doyle, "Kant, Liberal Legacies, and Foreign Affairs," parts 1 and 2, *Philosophy and Public Affairs* 12 (Summer and Fall 1983): 205–35, 323–53.

14  Louis Hartz, *The Liberal Tradition in America* (New York: Harcourt, Brace, and World, 1955).

15  Michael Sherry, *Preparing for the Next War: American Plans for Post-War Defense, 1941–45* (New Haven, Conn.: Yale University Press, 1977), pp. 52–53.

16  Quoted in John Lewis Gaddis, *The Long Peace: Inquiries into the History of the Cold War* (New York: Oxford University Press, 1987), pp. 35–36.

17  Gaddis, *The Long Peace*, p. 34; Thomas Patterson, *Meeting the Communist Threat* (New York: Oxford University Press, 1988), ch. 1. Patterson stresses the perceived analogy between Stalin's Russia and Hitler's Germany; Gaddis sees the American propensity as having deeper historical roots.

18  U.S. Department of State, *Foreign Relations of the United States, 1952–1954*, vol. 8: *Eastern Europe; Soviet Union; Eastern Mediterranean* (Washington, D.C.: U.S. Government Printing Office, 1988), p. 956.

19  *New York Times*, January 26, 1984, p. B8.

20  "Moscow's Vigorous Leader," *Time*, September 9, 1985, p. 29.

21  The Soviet realization that Third World countries would not develop along desired lines pre-dated Gorbachev: see Elizabeth Kridl Valkenier, "Revolutionary Change in the Third World: Recent Soviet Assessments," *World Politics* 38 (April 1986): 415–34. Stephen David argues that coups have proven to be an effective and cheap way for the Soviets to spread their influence. Although this may be correct, the technique has not subverted any of the major countries. See Steven David, *Third World Coups d'Etat and International Security* (Baltimore: Johns Hopkins University Press, 1987).

22  Jack Snyder, "The Gorbachev Revolution: A Waning of Soviet Expansionism," *International Security* 12 (Winter 1987–88): 93–131.

23  John Herz, "Idealist Internationalism and the Security Dilemma," *World Politics* 2 (January 1950): 157–80; Herbert Butterfield, *History and Human Relations* (London: Collins, 1951); Robert Jervis, "Cooperation under the Security Dilemma," *World Politics* 30 (January 1978): 167–214.

24  Quoted in Adam Ulam, *Expansion and Coexistence* (New York: Praeger, 1968), p. 5.

25 See, for example, Bernard Brodie et al., *The Absolute Weapon* (New York: Harcourt Brace, 1946); Michael Mandelbaum, *The Nuclear Revolution* (New York: Cambridge University Press, 1981); Robert Jervis, *The Illogic of American Nuclear Strategy* (Ithaca: Cornell University Press, 1984), and *The Meaning of the Nuclear Revolution* (Ithaca: Cornell University Press, 1989); McGeorge Bundy, *Danger and Survival* (New York: Random House, 1988).

26 It is often argued that second-strike capability cannot provide "extended deterrence"—that is, it cannot protect allies. I think this is incorrect: see Jervis, *Illogic of American Nuclear Strategy*, ch. 5, and *Meaning of the Nuclear Revolution*, chs. 1 and 3.

27 This might not be true when power is quite evenly distributed among a fairly large number of states, so that the two leading actors had little more power than others. A possible exception to the generalization is the relatively good relationship between Britain and the United States from the late nineteenth century through World War II, when the former was the world's leading power and the latter the second-ranking one, even if for most of this period America's power was only potential.

28 Gordon Chang, "JFK, China, and the Bomb," *Journal of American History* 74 (March 1988): 1287–310; Henry Kissinger, *White House Years* (Boston: Little, Brown, 1979), pp. 172–73, 193.

29 George Liska, *Russia and the Road to Appeasement* (Baltimore: Johns Hopkins University Press, 1982). This view may be more prevalent in Russia than in the United States.

30 This is not to say that either superpower is losing economic or military strength in an absolute sense—although in some areas this may be the case for the Soviet Union—but that others are growing much more rapidly.

31 Robert Gilpin, *War and Change in World Politics* (New York: Cambridge University Press, 1981); Paul Kennedy, *The Rise and Fall of the Great Powers* (New York: Random House, 1987).

32 Indeed, the international economic system might be more stable if any of the rising states were to have the ability and willingness to do so. As many scholars have stressed, managing an international economic system in which no one power dominates is extremely difficult.

33 Kennedy, *The Rise and Fall of the Great Powers*. For good critical discussions, see Samuel Huntington, "The U.S.—Decline or Renewal?" *Foreign Affairs* 67 (Winter 1988–89): 76–96; Aaron Friedberg, "The Strategic Implications of Relative Economic Decline," *Political Science Quarterly* 104 (Fall 1980): 401–32; and Joseph Nye Jr., *Bound to Lead* (New York: Basic Books, 1990).

34 Thus the Anglo-German entente preceding World War I may have led the Germans to believe that England would remain neutral in a continental war: for the latest and most thorough statement of this argument, see Sean Lynn-Jones, "Detente and Deterrence: Anglo-German Relations, 1911–1914," *International Security* 11 (Fall 1986): 121–40; also see Harold Saunders, "The Soviet-U.S. Relationship and the Third World," chapter 7 in this volume, pp. 109–32.

35 A change in ideology also was necessary before a Soviet leader would come to believe—perhaps incorrectly–that his values and domestic legitimacy would not be menaced by non-communist regimes in Eastern Europe.

36 The general importance of unilateral measures is stressed by Alexander George in *U.S.-Soviet Security Cooperation*, ed., George, Farley, and Dallin pp. 12, 641–54.

37 See Jervis, "Cooperation under the Security Dilemma"; George Quester, *Offense and Defense in the International System* (New York: Wiley, 1977), and "The Soviet Opening to Non-Provocative Defense," chapter 8 in this volume.

38 Thomas Schelling, *Strategy of Conflict* (Cambridge, Mass.: Harvard University Press, 1960), pp. 16–19.

## 2  American Reactions to the USSR: Public Opinion

1   Observations by George F. Kennan and Hans J. Morgenthau suggest how realists typi-
    cally assess public opinion.
       "But I sometimes wonder whether in this respect a democracy is not uncomfort-
    ably similar to one of those prehistoric monsters with a body as long as this room
    and a brain the size of a pin: he lies there in his comfortable primeval mud and pays
    little attention to his environment; he is slow to wrath—in fact, you practically have
    to whack his tail off to make him aware that his interests are being disturbed; but,
    once he grasps this, he lays about him with such blind determination that he not
    only destroys his adversary but largely wrecks his active habitat" (Kennan, 1951:59).
       "The rational requirements of good foreign policy cannot from the outset count
    upon the support of a public opinion whose preferences are emotional rather than
    rational" (Morgenthau, 1978:558).
2   A more definitive test would link public opinion to systematic data on Soviet behav-
    ior, as well as interpretations of it by political leaders, opinion leaders, the media,
    and the like. Such a research design, currently being employed by Page and Shapiro,
    would require more time and resources than are available for this chapter.
3   However, a survey limited to New York City found that 31 percent of the respon-
    dents believed that Stalin's death improved chances for peace, whereas 25 percent
    felt that it reduced them.
4   For a fuller analysis of public opinion on the likelihood of war, see Mueller (1979).
5   For this discussion, only Gallup poll data on the president's overall job rating are
    reported. The question was posed well over one hundred times between 1981 and the
    end of 1989.
6   The thesis that Ronald Reagan won the 1980 election *despite* rather than because of
    his foreign policy views is developed in Schneider (1983).
7   Even before U.S. entry into World War II, a majority of the public supported Russia
    over Germany. In 1938, the margin was 83 percent–17 percent, and after the Nazi
    attack on its erstwhile ally the margin was 72 percent–4 percent. In July 1941,
    Gallup asked whether respondents favored a peace in which Germany keeps "only
    territory won from Russia" and gives up everything else; only 34 percent accepted
    that proposition.

## 3  American Reactions to Changes in the USSR

1   For continuing American suspicions about the Soviets, see Daniel Yankelovich and
    Richard Smoke, "America's New Thinking," *Foreign Affairs* 67 (Fall 1988): 1, 6–7, 10.
2   For American hopefulness about change in the Soviet Union, see Yankelovich and
    Smoke, "America's New Thinking," pp. 2, 5–6, 8, 17.
3   Richard Smoke et al., *The Public, the Soviets, and Nuclear Arms: Four Futures:
    Alternatives for Public Debate and Policy Development* (Providence, R.I.: Brown
    University, 1987), pp. 5–14.
4   Smoke, *Four Futures*, pp. 15–19; John Lewis Gaddis, *Strategies of Containment: A
    Critical Appraisal of Postwar American National Security Policy* (New York: Oxford
    University Press, 1982).
5   For the *Life* quote and other evidence of this wartime perspective, see Robert Dallek,
    *The American Style of Foreign Policy: Cultural Politics and Foreign Affairs* (New
    York: Knopf, 1984), pp. 138–42.
6   Richard M. Nixon, *RN: The Memoirs of Richard Nixon* (New York: Grosset and
    Dunlap, 1978), pp. 609–11, 613–14, 619–20.
7   George Will, "Reagan's Naivete Is Wearing Thin," *Los Angeles Times*, October 10,
    1985, sec. 2. p. 7.
8   *New York Times*, May 29, 1988, sec. 4, p. 17; *Los Angeles Times*, May 31, 1988, p. 1.

9   *New York Times*, August 28, 1988, p. 1.

10  *Los Angeles Times*, August 30, 1988, p. 1.

11  *New York Times*, June 2, 1988, p. 25.

12  Ibid., May 29, 1988, sec. 4, pp. 1, 3, 17.

13  *Los Angeles Times*, May 31, 1988, p. 1; *New York Times*, June 2, 1988, p. 1.

14  Quotes in *Columbia: The Magazine of Columbia University*, June 1988, pp. 22–28.

15  *New York Times*, August 2, 1988, p. 1; August 28, 1988, p. 1 *Los Angeles Times*, September 13, 1988, p. 9. Also see the comment by Brent Scowcroft, George Bush's national security adviser, who at the start of Bush's term declared that the "Cold War is not over," and warned against Soviet efforts to drive a wedge between the United States and Western Europe, *Los Angeles Times*, January 23, 1989, p. 1.

16  Ibid., April 29, 1989, p. 1; *New York Times*, November 15, 1989, p. A25; *Los Angeles Times*, November 16, 1989, p. B7; *New York Times*, December 23, 1989, p. 1.

17  *Los Angeles Times*, June 1, 1988, p. 1; *New York Times*, May 29, 1988, sec. 4, p. 1.

18  See Robert C. McFarlane, "To Soviets, Reagan Made 'Devil's Leverage' Real," *Los Angeles Times*, September 1, 1988, sec. 2, p. 7; August 30, 1988, p. 1; *New York Times*, May 29, 1988, sec. 4, pp. 1, 3, 17.

19  *Los Angeles Times*, June 1, 1988, pp. 1, 12, 13. Yankelovich and Smoke found that only 14 percent of Americans "consider it absolutely essential to [Soviet] good faith [in dealing with the United States] that 'their customs, culture and language are similar to ours,'" "America's New Thinking," p. 16. Yet however rational Americans may be when asked about the necessity of a Soviet conversion to assure good relations, the appeal of the idea is evident in Reagan's actions as well as in other evidence I cite in this essay.

20  *New York Times*, May 29, 1988, sec. 4, p. 3.

21  Ibid., August 2, 1988, p. 5.

22  *Los Angeles Times*, May 31, 1988, sec. 5, p. 1.

23  George Stein, "Soviet Chic," *Los Angeles Times Magazine*, June 5, 1988, pp. 11–14, 36, 38.

24  Stein, "Soviet Chic," p. 38; *Los Angeles Times*, Jan. 24, 1989, pp. 1, 21.

25  Seweryn Bialer, "The Psychology of U.S.-Soviet Relations," Gabriel Silver Memorial Lecture, April 14, 1983, School of International and Public Affairs, Columbia University, New York City.

26  Marshall D. Shulman, "Missing the Boat on Arms Control," *Los Angeles Times*, July 25, 1988, sec. 2. p. 5.

27  George F. Kennan, "The Gorbachev Prospect," *New York Review of Books*, January 21, 1988, p. 7.

28  For further discussion, see Dallek, *The American Style of Foreign Policy.*

29  For an elaboration of this argument about the impact of shifting domestic moods on American foreign policy, see Dallek, *The American Style of Foreign Policy;* for the changes in public feeling, see *Los Angeles Times*, January 13, 1989, p. 31. The Farewell Adress is in the *New York Times*, January 12, 1989, p. A8.

**4   Do the Changes within the Soviet Union Provide a Basis for Eased Soviet-American Relations?**

1   See John Lewis Gaddis, *Russia, the Soviet Union, and the United States: An Interpretive History* (New York: Wiley, 1978), particularly ch. 1, "A Heritage of Harmony: 1781–1867."

2   Emphasis added. The addition of "and the world" tends to pass notice in much Western commentary. Mikhail Gorbachev, *Perestroika: New Thinking for Our Country and the World* (New York: Harper and Row, 1987).

3   See the title essay in John Lewis Gaddis, *The Long Peace: Inquiries into the History*

*of the Cold War* (New York: Oxford University Press, 1987), pp. 215–45; Colin S. Gray, *The Geopolitics of Super Power* (Lexington: University Press of Kentucky, 1988).

4   It was noticeable that neither side in the Crimean War sought to employ nationalist sentiments among each other's subject peoples. See Hugh Seton-Watson, *The Russian Empire, 1801–1917* (Oxford: Clarendon Press, 1967), pp. 330–31.

5   Summarizing George F. Kennan's view in 1947, John Lewis Gaddis has written that "Ideology, then, was not so much a guide to action as a justification for action already decided upon." Gaddis quotes Kennan's January 1947 opinion that "ideology is a product and not a determinant of social and political reality. . . ." *Strategies of Containment: A Critical Appraisal of Postwar American National Security Policy* (New York: Oxford University Press, 1982), p. 34.

6   Halford J. Mackinder, *Democratic Ideals and Reality* (1919, repr. New York: W. W. Norton, 1962); W. H. Parker, *Mackinder: Geography as an Aid to Statecraft* (Oxford: Clarendon Press, 1982); Brian W. Blouet, *Halford Mackinder: A Biography* (College Station: Texas A&M University Press, 1987); Ronald Reagan, *National Security Strategy of the United States* (Washington, D.C.: White House, January 1988), p. 1.

7   Multinational empire, particular in the modern era of nationalism, by its very nature has a structural problem of legitimacy.

8   To date the military typically has insisted that the path to defensive sufficiency should not be taken by the USSR acting in isolation: "Unilateral implementation of defensive sufficiency is practically impossible. Sufficiency is determined by the nature of the military threat. Therefore, the implementation of the principle of sufficiency is a mutual, bilateral process." Colonel General Nikolay Chervov, "On the Military Doctrines of East and West; In the Interest of Strategic Stability," *JPRS*-UMA-88-014, July 18, 1988, p. 3.

9   Gorbachev has written of "a change in the entire pattern of armed forces with a view to imparting an exclusively defensive character to them," *Perestroika*, p. 203.

10  "The new political outlook calls for the recognition of one more simple axiom: security is indivisible. It is either equal security for all or none at all," ibid., p. 142.

11  An outstanding Western study is Ed A. Hewett, *Reforming the Soviet Economy: Equality versus Efficiency* (Washington, D.C.: Brookings Institution 1988).

12  See Richard Pipes, *Russia under the Old Regime* (New York: Scribner's, 1974).

13  For differing perspectives, see Stephen White, *Political Culture and Soviet Politics* (London: Macmillan, 1979); and Robert C. Tucker, *Political Culture and Leadership in Soviet Russia: From Lenin to Gorbachev* (New York: W. W. Norton, 1987). Cultural sensitivity is pervasive in Christopher Donnelly, *Red Banner: The Soviet Military System in Peace and War* (Coulsdon, Surrey: Jane's Information Group, 1988). Indeed, if anything, Donnelly may overstate the thesis of cultural distinctiveness.

14  In discussing the historical fact that Soviet doctrine has changed, it was useful for David Holloway to warn "that one should not take an 'essentialist' view of Soviet policy, seeing it as springing from some innate characteristic of Russian culture or the Soviet system, impervious to phenomena in the real world," "Military Power and Political Purpose in Soviet Policy," *Daedelus* 109 (Fall 1980): 28. A similar warning is portentously conveyed, with this author allegedly as the guilty party, in Joseph S. Nye, Jr., "The Role of Strategic Nuclear Systems in Deterrence," *Washington Quarterly* 11 (Spring 1988): 54. It is important, as Nye and Holloway warn, to beware of an essentialist view which could well blind one to real changes in Soviet thought. But, it is also important to beware of the reverse error of unduly discounting that which is truly cultural in the U.S. or Soviet approach to security. William E. Odom has noted that "the two aspects [of military doctrine, social-political and military-technical] are viewed [in the Soviet Union] as highly interactive, *and are unique* for each state because the political, social, economic, cultural and geographical realities of no two states are precisely the same. While much of military science holds for all states,

military doctrine must be designed for the realities of a single state. A shared U.S. and Soviet military doctrine, therefore, would strike a student of Soviet military thought as either absurd or a misunderstanding of the definition," "Soviet Military Doctrine," *Foreign Affairs* 67 (Winter 1988–89): 117, emphasis added.

15 Tucker frames the question thus: "was Stalin's transformative decade a resumption and culmination of the Bolshevik Revolution or in basic ways a negation of it?" and favors the second option, *Political Culture and Leadership in Soviet Russia*, p. 52.

16 Understandably, if somewhat unrealistically, our European allies have always wanted their superpower guardian to be prepared to subordinate its interests elsewhere in the world to the cause of peace and order in the European region. It may be recalled that in World War II the British government endeavored none too successfully to hold the United States to fairly strict adherence to the agreed grand-strategic principle of Germany First. "The pull of the Pacific" was a fact of American political culture —obviously magnified by the events of the early morning of December 7, 1941—to which London was notably culturally unempathetic.

17 For a useful collection of reflective essays on the subject, see Terry L. Deibel and John Lewis Gaddis, *Containment: Concept and Policy*, 2 vols. (Washington, D.C.: National Defense University Press, 1986).

18 Prominent among the better studies generically supportive of the NATO enterprise is Stanley R. Sloan, *NATO's Future: Toward a New Transatlantic Bargain* (Washington, D.C.: National Defense University Press, 1985). Variably radical views of NATO are well argued in Melvyn Krauss, *How NATO Weakens the West* (New York: Simon and Schuster, 1986); John Palmer, *Europe Without America? The Crisis in Atlantic Relations* (New York: Oxford University Press, 1988); and David P. Calleo, *Beyond American Hegemony: The Future of the Western Alliance* (New York: Basic Books, 1987).

19 Caspar W. Weinberger, *Department of Defense Annual Report, Fiscal Year 1987* (Washington, D.C.: U.S. Government Printing Office, 1986), p. 29.

20 Of the effects of the successive victories of the Greeks at Salamis (480 B.C.) and Plataea (479 B.C.), J. F. C. Fuller observed: "it was loss of prestige which not only checked the expansion, but undermined the foundations of the Persian Empire, and, like most empires before or since, led to its eventual ruin." *The Decisive Battles of the Western World and Their Influence Upon History*, vol. 1 (London: Eyre and Spottiswoode, 1954), p. 51.

21 For reasons definitively outlined in Carl von Clausewitz, *On War*, ed. Michael Howard and Peter Paret (Princeton, N.J.: Princeton University Press, 1976), Books 6–7.

22 Samuel P. Huntington, "Conventional Deterrence and Conventional Retaliation in Europe." *International Security* 8 (Winter 1983–84): 32–56. Huntington has written one of the best early appreciations of U.S. strategy in the 1980s "U.S. Defense Strategy: The Strategic Innovations of the Reagan Years," in *American Defense Annual, 1987–1988*, ed. Joseph Kruzel (Lexington: D. C. Heath, 1987), pp. 23–43. Huntington argues persuasively that before the Reagan years, U.S. and allied planning for the use of general purpose forces were overly defensive, while U.S. central strategic systems were greatly unbalanced in favor of the offense.

23 Colonel General Makhmut Gareev, "Soviet Military Doctrine: Current and Future Developments," *RUSI Journal* 133 (Winter 1988): 8. Gareev also emphasizes an alleged shift in doctrine from war-winning to war prevention. See also Army General D. T. Yazov, "On Soviet Military Doctrine," *RUSI Journal* 134 (Winter 1989): 1–4. Particularly useful Western commentaries on the current ferment in Soviet military doctrine include: C. N. Donnelly, "Gorbachev's Military Doctrine: Implications for Arms Control Negotiations," unpub. paper, October 1988, and *Red Banner*; Odom, "Soviet Military Doctrine"; and Harriet Fast Scott and William F. Scott, *Soviet Military Doctrine: Continuity, Formulation, and Dissemination* (Boulder, Colo.: Westview

Press, 1988). Fairly sympathetic commentaries on Gorbachev's new thinking on the foreign and domestic contexts for changes in military doctrine include: Jack Snyder, "The Gorbachev Revolution: A Waning of Soviet Expansionism?" *International Security* 12 (Winter 1987–88): 93–131; Seweryn Bialer, "'New Thinking' and Soviet Foreign Policy," *Survival* 30 (July–August 1988): 291–309; and David Holloway," Gorbachev's New Thinking," *Foreign Affairs* 68, no. 1 (1988–89): 66–81.

24　George F. Kennan ("Mr. X"), "The Sources of Soviet Conduct," in *Containment: Documents on American Policy and Strategy, 1945–1950* ed. Thomas H. Etzold and John Lewis Gaddis, (New York: Columbia University Press, 1978), p. 89.

25　Gareev argues that "from the political angle Soviet military doctrine has always had a defensive orientation because the Soviet Union has never attacked anybody but has been forced to fight wars only of the kind which were forced upon it, and to do so with the exclusive aim of repelling aggression," "Soviet Military Doctrine," p. 7. Stalin no doubt acted preemptively in 1939 to forestall Polish and Finnish aggression. As recently as 1984 Gareev was asserting as follows: "The experience of the war demonstrated that a combination of the offensive as the main type of military action and the defensive *is an objective pattern of warfare,* and like any pattern, *it operates with the strength of necessity* and it is very dangerous to disregard it." *M. V. Frunze: Military Theorist* (1984, repr. Washington, D.C.: Pergamon-Brassey's, 1988), p. 208, emphasis added.

26　See Marion William Boggs, *Attempts to Define and Limit "Aggressive" Armament in Diplomacy and Strategy,* University of Missouri Studies, vol. 16, no. 1 (Columbia: University of Missouri, 1941); and Jack S. Levy, "The Offensive/Defensive Balance of Military Technology: A Theoretical and Historical Analysis," *International Studies Quarterly* 28 (1984): 219–38.

27　Donnelly, "Gorbachev's Military Doctrine," p. 8.

28　Ibid., p. 7.

29　On the long-standing character of the Soviet interest in "deep operations," see Bruce W. Menning, "The Deep Strike in Russian and Soviet Military History," *Journal of Soviet Military Studies* 1 (April 1988): 9–28. Also see Kerry L. Hines, "Competing Concepts of Deep Operations," *Journal of Soviet Military Studies* 1 (April 1988): 54–80.

30　See Nicolai N. Petro, "Rediscovering Russia," *Orbis* 34 (Winter 1990): 33–49.

31　See Henry S. Rowen and Charles Wolf, Jr., eds., *The Future of the Soviet Empire* (New York: St. Martin's Press, 1987).

32　Robert M. Gates, "Recent Developments in the Soviet Union and Implications for U.S. Security Policy," speech to the American Association for the Advancement of Science, Colloquium on Science, Arms Control and National Security, Washington, D.C., October 14, 1988, p. 8.

33　For example, see Edward Crankshaw, *The Shadow of the Winter Palace: The Drift to Revolution, 1825–1917* (New York: Viking Press, 1976), particularly ch. 10, "Revolution from Above."

## 5　Reform, Democratization, and Soviet Foreign Policy

1　See, for example, Institute for East-West Security Studies, *How Should America Respond to Gorbachev's Challenge* (New York: Institute for East-West Security Studies, 1987); *New York Times,* October 22, October 27, 1987; Alexander Yanov, *The Russian Challenge and the Year 2000* (New York: Basil Blackwell, 1987); several publications by Timothy Colton including "Approaches to the Politics of Systemic Economic Reform in the Soviet Union," *Soviet Economy* 3, no. 2 (1987): 145–70; and Jack Snyder, "International Leverage on Soviet Domestic Change," *World Politics* 42 (October 1989): 1–30, as well as chapter 16 in this volume.

2   For the classic summary of the views of "second image" political theorists, see Kenneth Waltz, *Man, the State, and War* (New York: Columbia University Press, 1959).

3   Ken Jowitt, "Neo-traditionalism . . . ," *Soviet Studies* (July 1983): 275–97, William Zimmerman, "Mobilized Participation and the Nature of the Soviet Dictatorship," in *Politics, Work and Daily Life in the Contemporary Soviet Union*, ed. James Millar (London: Cambridge University Press, 1987); Dvizhenie sotsialisticheskogo obnovleniia [Movement for Socialist Renewal], "K grazhdanam Sovetskogo Soiuza" [To the Citizens of the Soviet Union], *Arkhiv samizdata* 5724, July 7, 1986.

4   Richard Rosecrance, *The Rise of the Trading State* (New York: Basic Books, 1986).

5   Colton, "Approaches to the Politics."

6   Recall that biases are notorious in surveys. I do not believe, however, that this was a problem in this instance. I sat in on a number of pretests on this question, and the respondents frequently responded in words to the effect that "Of course, now I think the Soviet Union was wrong but at that time. . . ."

7   This and other seven-point scales were collapsed to three categories for analysis.

8   I disregarded a fourth proposition that "Stalin's actions were contrary to the ideals of Marx and Lenin." No consistent pattern emerges, presumably because the question is ambiguous. Some, who by their other responses would be regarded as Stalinist, said Stalin's actions were contrary to the ideals of Marx and Lenin, and others did not. Likewise, those who by other responses seem quite clearly non-Stalinist categorized Stalin's actions as contrary to the ideals of Marx and Lenin, whereas others did not.

9   General questions—whether the respondent favors glasnost—suggest the opposite tendency; surely, however, this is a result of older respondents being more disposed to engage in affirming what they take to be policy line.

10  *Vechernaia Moskva*, June 7, 1989, as reported by APN, *Daily Review*, June 20, 1989.

11  "Inter-generational Change and Soviet Foreign Policy," *Soviet Interview Project Working Papers* (Champaign, Ill.: University of Illinois, 1986).

12  I have not repeated those $tau_b$ statistics reported in the tables.

13  In this and all future references to military spending I disregard the handful—never more than nine among as many as 2,365 coded responses—who said "too little" was spent on the military.

14  Harold K. Jacobson, *Networks of Interdependence: International Organizations and the Global Political System* (New York: Knopf, 1979).

## 6   Is Socialism Dead?

1   The ongoing research of Soviet public opinion and attitudes is conducted by the All-Union Center for the Study of Public Opinion (VCJOM) in Moscow. Most of the data comes from the project "The Soviet Man," the results of which began to appear in March 1990 and were reported in "Sovetskij Chelovek-Eskiz Portreta," in *Moskovskiv Novosti*, no. 11, March 18, 1990.

2   Ibid.

## 7   The Soviet-U.S. Relationship and the Third World

1   John D. Steinbruner, director of the Foreign Policy Studies Program at the Brookings Institution, suggested this formulation as we worked on his edited book, *Restructuring American Foreign Policy* (Washington, D.C.: Brookings Institution, 1988).

2   The dimension of levels or maturation of relationship is developed first from Harold H. Saunders, "Regulating Soviet-U.S. Competition in the Arab-Israeli Arena, 1967–86," in *U.S.-Soviet Security Cooperation: Achievements, Failures, Lessons*, ed. Alexander L. George, Philip J. Farley, and Alexander Dallin (New York: Oxford Uni-

versity Press, 1988), ch. 22, particularly pp. 574–80.

3    I first developed these observations on our changing world and the concept of relationship in two papers: "Beyond 'Us and Them'—Building Mature International Relationships," a draft monograph prepared in 1987–88 under a grant from the United States Institute of Peace in collaboration with the Kettering Foundation; and a version of that paper published as a work in progress, "Beyond 'We' and 'They'—Conducting International Relationships," in *Negotiation Journal* 3 (July 1987): 245–77. The observations were refined under a grant from the Carnegie Corporation of New York for "The Arab-Israeli Conflict in a Global Perspective," in Steinbruner, ed., *Restructuring American Foreign Policy*, where they are applied in detail to that conflict. A fuller presentation written with the support of the Ford and MacArthur foundations appears as "An Historic Challenge to Rethink How Nations Relate," in *Psychodynamics of International Relationships*, ed. Vamik D. Volkan, Demetrios Julius, and Joseph V. Montville, vol. 1: *Concepts and Theories* (Lexington, Mass.: Lexington Books, 1990), ch. 1 They will also appear in the new epilogue to my book, *The Other Walls: The Politics of the Arab-Israeli Peace Process* (Princeton, N.J.: Princeton University Press, 1990). Others will follow. In each case, these observations and the concept of relationship are stated in more or less the same form as the necessary starting point for analysis of a particular question.

4    This statement was made during a 1987 meeting of the Dartmouth Conference Task Force on Regional Conflicts, which I co-chaired. The Dartmouth Conference is a dialogue among private Soviet and U.S. citizens that has met regularly since 1960. It is jointly sponsored on the Soviet side by the Institute of U.S.A./Canada Affairs and the Soviet Peace Committee and on the U.S. side by the Kettering Foundation with support from other foundations. To protect confidentiality in the dialogue, it is agreed practice not to attribute statements to speakers by name.

5    Evgeni Primakov, "New Philosophy of Foreign Policy," *Pravda*, July 9, 1987; English translation printed in Foreign Broadcast Information Service, *Daily Report: Soviet Union*, July 14, 1987, pp. CC5–10.

6    Mikhail S. Gorbachev, "Realities and Guarantees for a Secure World," *Pravda*, September 17, 1987; quoted in English translation in Foreign Broadcast Information Service, *Daily Report: Soviet Union*, FBIS-SOV-87-180, September 17, 1987, pp. 23–27.

7    "Abridged version" of a report by Foreign Minister E. A. Shevardnadze on July 25, 1988, at a conference of the Soviet Ministry of Foreign Affairs "on the 19th All-Union CPSU Conference: Foreign Policy and Diplomacy," FBIS-SOV-88-144, September 22, 1988, annex, p. 10.

8    Mikhail Gorbachev, United Nations Address, December 7, 1988, full text, Novosti Press Agency, December 8, 1988, p. 6.

9    Private conversations during the 1988 Dartmouth Conference plenary.

10    Thoughts on regulation of competition here are taken or developed from Saunders, "Regulating Soviet-U.S. Competition in the Arab-Israeli Arena," esp. pp. 574–80.

11    Soviet views cited are from conversations in the Dartmouth Conference Task Force on Regional Conflicts or between U.S. members of that task force and Soviet officials.

12    Gorbachev, United Nations Address, p. 6.

13    I am grateful for the broad support of the Kettering Foundation and for grants from the United States Institute of Peace, the Carnegie Corporation of New York, and the John D. and Catherine T. MacArthur, the Ira D. and Miriam Wallach, and the Ford foundations. I also thank the Brookings Institution for hospitality and support extended to me as a visiting fellow.

**8 The Soviet Opening to Nonprovocative Defense**

1  For an excellent and detailed analysis of these new statements, see Jack Snyder, "Limiting Offensive Conventional Forces: Soviet Proposals and Western Options," *International Security* 12 (Spring 1988): 48–77. See also Leon V. Sigal, "Conventional Arms in Europe: Signs of a Soviet Shift," *Bulletin of the Atomic Scientists* 43 (December 1987): 16–20.

2  For such a cautious interpretation, see R. Jeffrey Smith, "Soviets Debate Basic Military Posture: Kremlin Leadership Seen as Divided on Future Defense Course," *Washington Post*, August 1, 1988, p. 1.

3  The burdens of the Soviet economic situation are laid out in Stanley H. Cohn, "The Economic Burden of Soviet Defense Expenditures," *Studies in Comparative Communism* 20 (Summer 1987): 145–62.

4  The original turn-of-the-century argument is reprinted in Halford J. Mackinder, *Democratic Ideals and Reality* (1919, repr. New York: W. W. Norton, 1962).

5  For an example of an argument assuming Soviet deception, see Jeffrey Record et al., *The INF Treaty: Pro and Con* (Indianapolis: Hudson Institute, 1988), esp. pp. 38–39.

6  Soviet difficulties in holding control over Eastern Europe are outlined in F. Stephen Larrabee, "Eastern Europe: A Generational Change," *Foreign Policy*, no. 70 (Spring 1988): 42–64.

7  For Soviet allegations that various Western weapons systems favor the attack, see Dmitri Yazov, "The Soviet Proposal for European Security," *Bulletin of the Atomic Scientists* 44 (September 1988): 8–11.

8  On some possibilities by which the conventional confrontation would be favorable to NATO instead of to the Warsaw Pact, see Malcolm Chalmers and Lutz Unterseher, "Is There a Tank Gap?," *International Security* 13 (Summer 1988): 5–49.

9  Particularly useful on this subject is Jack Snyder, "The Gorbachev Revolution: A Waning of Soviet Expansionism?," *International Security* 12 (Winter 1987–88): 93–131.

10  For an argument scoffing at the possibility that the Soviets would ever want to conquer Western Europe, see Richard J. Barnet, "Why on Earth Would the Soviets Invade Europe?," *Washington Post*, November 22, 1981, pp. C1–2.

11  For a valuable set of Soviet analyses of some of the issues discussed here, see the 1987 IMEMO Yearbook, Institute for World Economy and International Relations, *Disarmament and Security 1987* (Moscow: Novosti Press Agency Publishing House, 1988).

12  For the occasion when the French communist leader told the National Assembly that French workers would welcome the Red Army as liberators, see *New York Times*, February 23, 1949, p. 1.

13  On the nature and possibilities of such qualitative distinctions between offensive and defense weapons, see Albrecht A. C. von Muller and Andrzej Karkoszka, "An East-West Negotiating Proposal," *Bulletin of the Atomic Scientists* 44 (September 1988): 39–41.

14  The short-lived enthusiasm for "sufficiency" in the Nixon administration is recounted in John G. Stoessinger, *Henry Kissinger: The Anguish of Power* (New York: W. W. Norton, 1976), p. 86.

15  For an interesting discussion of pre-World War II discussions and negotiations on qualitative sorting of the offensive and defensive, see M. W. Boggs, *Attempts to Define and Limit "Aggressive" Armament in Diplomacy and Strategy* (Columbia: University of Missouri Studies, 1941).

16  For some discussion of Gorbachev's *political* needs for conventional arms control, see Robert Blackwill, "Conceptual Problems on Conventional Arms Control," *International Security* 12 (Spring 1988): 28–47.

17  For a Soviet discussion on the possibilities of some unialteral Soviet concessions, see Vitaly Zhurkin, Sergei Karaganov, and Andrey Kortunov, "Reasonable Sufficiency—Or How to Break the Vicious Cycle," *New Times*, 40 (October 1987): 13–15.

## 9   East and West in Europe

This chapter was completed May 1, 1990; sections draw on my book, *The Bloc that Failed: Soviet-East European Relations in Transition* (Bloomington: Indiana University Press, 1990).

1   Zbigniew Brzezinski, "Special Address," *Problems of Communism* 37 (May–August 1988): 67–70.

2   Charles Gati, "Eastern Europe on Its Own," *Foreign Affairs* 68, no. 1 (1988–89): 99–119.

3   See, for example, [Unsigned], "Winning the War without Fighting: Johail Gorbalin's Strategy," *International Currency Review* (London), 20, no. 3 (1990): 5–21.

4   Edward Jay Epstein, *Deception* (New York: Simon and Schuster, 1989), as quoted in "Winning the War," p. 8.

5   For further details and an excellent analysis, see William H. Luers, "Czechoslovakia: Road to Revolution," *Foreign Affairs* 69 (Spring 1990): 77–98.

6   *Washington Post*, March 18, 1987.

7   *New York Times*, December 5, 1989.

8   Luers, "Czechoslovakia," p. 77.

9   Ibid., p. 97.

10   Compare J. P. Vloyantes, *Silk Glove Hegemony: Finnish-Soviet Relations 1944–1974. A Case Study of the Theory of the Soft Sphere of Influence* (Kent, Ohio: Kent State University Press, 1975.) For a view that denies that Finland belongs to a "soft sphere" of Soviet influence, see Roy Allison, *Finland's Relations with the Soviet Union* (New York: St. Martin's Press, 1985).

11   The White House, Office of Press Secretary, "Text of Remarks by the President to the Citizens of Hamtramck, Michigan," April 17, 1989.

12   Michael Mandelbaum, "Ending the Cold War," *Foreign Affairs* 68 (Spring 1989): 21. For another insightful Mandelbaum essay on the subject of Eastern Europe and the legacy of the cold war, see "The United States and Eastern Europe: A Window of Opportunity," in *Central and Eastern Europe: The Opening Curtain?*, ed. William E. Griffith (Boulder, Colo.: Westview Press, 1989), pp. 366–87.

13   For further details and a penetrating assessment, see Zbigniew Brzezinski, "Post-Communist Nationalism," *Foreign Affairs* 68 (Winter 1989–90): 1–25.

14   Creation of a confederation in Eastern and Central Europe is not a pipe dream. There are already preliminary discussions going on in the region about such issues as a "Baltic Union" (Poland, Sweden, Norway, and Finland, as well as Estonia, Latvia, and Lithuania), about a "Danubian Federation: (Italy, Austria, Yugoslavia, Hungary, and Czechoslovakia), about a Polish-Czechoslovak-Hungarian confederation, and about a "neutral belt" from the Baltic to the Adriatic.

## 10   Soviet Policy in East Asia:
## The Quest for Constructive Engagement

1   For a translation of the Vladivostok speech of July 1986, see Foreign Broadcast Information Service, *Daily Report: Soviet Union*, July 29, 1986, pp. R/1-20. The foreign policy portion of the Krasnoyarsk speech appears in "News and Views from the USSR," Soviet Embassy Information Department, Washington, D.C., September 19, 1988, pp. 1–11.

2   For reviews of Gorbachev's initiatives in East Asia, see Donald S. Zagoria, "Soviet Policy in East Asia: A New Beginning?," *Foreign Affairs: America and the World, 1988/89* 68 (1989): 120–38; Rajan Menon, "New Thinking and Northeast Asian Security," *Problems of Communism* 38 (March–June 1989); and "Gorbachev's Asian Policy, a Joint Report of the United Nations Association of the USA and the Asia Pacific Association of Japan" (New York: United Nations Association, March 1989).

3  The major obstacle to a border settlement is the status of Heixiazi, a three-hundred-square-kilometer island at the confluence of the Amur and Ussuri rivers. The island is claimed by the Chinese but controlled by the USSR. Because Heixiazi overlooks Khabarovsk as well as the point at which the Trans-Siberian Railway crosses the Amur River, the Soviets are reluctant to give it up.

4  See the writings of Banning Garrett and Bonnie Glaser, who have conducted a number of substantial interviews with Chinese strategic thinkers in recent years.

5  On China's foreign trade, see in particular the writings of Nicholas Lardy, especially *China's Entry into the World Economy* (New York: Asia Society, 1989).

6  See Zbigniew Brzezinski, "America's New Geostrategy," *Foreign Affairs* (Spring 1988):

7  On Soviet-Japanese relations, see the prolific writings of Peggy Falkenheim, Hiroshi Kimura, and Tsuyoshi Hasegawa.

8  Foreign Broadcast Information Service, *East Asia*, September 8, 1987, pp. 30-32.

9  On the formidable problems of reforming the Soviet economy and improving Soviet foreign trade, see the writings of Ed Hewett.

10  On the problems of developing Siberia, see John P. Hardt, "Soviet Siberia: A Power to Be?," in *Siberia and the Soviet Far East*, ed. Rodger Swearingen (Stanford, Calif.: Hoover Institution Press, 1987).

11  Richard Armitage and Gaston Sigur, "To Play in Asia, Moscow Has to Pay," *New York Times*, October 2, 1988, p. E25.

12  See *Defense of Japan* (Tokyo: Japanese Defense Agency, 1988).

13  My observations on Japanese thinking are based on several conversations with high-ranking Japanese officials and on the talks and papers that some of these officials have delivered to international conferences.

14  As Charles Krauthammer has pointed out, "No country [in East Asia] from South Korea to China to Thailand to Australia—not even Vietnam—fears the deployment of American troops. What they do fear is American withdrawal. Not that they expect immediate Japanese rearmament. But in absence of Pax Americana there would be enough nervousness about ultimate Japanese intentions and capabilities to spark a local arms race and create instability and tension of a kind that has not been seen in Asia for decades." "Universal Dominion: Toward a Unipolar World," *National Interest* (Winter 1989–90): 48.

15  For a sobering but acute analysis of Gorbachev's dilemmas, see John B. Dunlop, "Will the Soviet Union Survive Until the Year 2000?," *National Interest* (Winter 1980–90): 65–75.

## 11  Rights, Rituals, and Soviet-American Relations

1  The notion of a "conceptual essence" is problematic, yet it is probably indispensable to theoretical arguments involving definitional precision. For thoughtful discussions of the issues involved, see *Social Science Concepts*, ed. Giovanni Sartori (Beverly Hills: Sage, 1984).

2  Not surprisingly, some scholars claim that human rights are a distinctly Western notion. See *Human Rights: Cultural and Ideological Perspectives*, ed. Adamantia Pollis and Peter Schwab (New York: Praeger, 1979). To some degree, this objection is irrelevant, as almost all states, Western and non-Western, currently claim to observe human rights.

3  It is legitimate at least to ask whether the concept of human rights can retain its force after being set loose from its religious underpinnings.

4  See *The Politics of Aristotle*, ed. Ernest Barker (London: Oxford University Press, 1958).

5 On the mechanics of the categorical imperative, see Immanuel Kant, *Foundations of the Metaphysics of Morals* (Indianapolis: Bobbs-Merrill, 1959).

6 Any allusions to the incompatibility of the City of God and the City of Man are, of course, intended. See St. Augustine, *City of God* (Garden City, N.Y.: Image Books 1958).

7 On multiple sovereignty, see Charles Tilly, *From Mobilization to Revolution* (New York: Random House, 1978).

8 See *The Human Rights Reader*, ed. Walter Laqueur and Barry Rubin (Philadelphia: Temple University Press, 1979), pp. 195–232, for a sampling of international documents. Some of the most radical sentiments are contained in the International Covenant on Economic, Social and Cultural Rights: "All peoples have the right of self-determination. By virtue of the right they freely determine their political status and freely pursue their economic, social and cultural development"; The State Parties to the present Covenant . . . shall promote the realization of the right of self-determination, and shall respect that right. . . . The State Parties to the present Covenant recognize the right to work, which includes the right of everyone to the opportunity to gain his living by work which he freely chooses or accepts, and will take appropriate steps to safeguard this right" (pp. 209–10).

9 Eurocommunists once claimed to have abandoned this notion, yet it is hard to interpret Marx otherwise, especially in light of *The German Ideology*.

10 Jean-Jacques Rousseau, *The Social Contract* (Harmondsworth, Eng.: Penguin, 1968).

11 Thomas Hobbes, *Leviathan* (Harmondsworth, Eng.: Penguin, 1968).

12 John Locke, *Two Treatises of Government* (New York: Mentor, 1963).

13 For an excellent discussion of these issues, see Vernon Van Dyke, "The Individual, the State, and Ethnic Communities in Political Theory," *World Politics* 29 (April 1977): 343–69.

14 For a discussion of this and related propositions, see Richard Falk, *Human Rights and State Sovereignty* (New York: Holmes and Meier, 1981), 33–62.

15 The notion of state autonomy, although Marxist in inspiration, has substantial heuristic and analytical value. For a non-Marxist interpretation, see Eric Nordlinger, *On the Autonomy of the Democratic State* (Cambridge, Mass.: Harvard University Press, 1981).

16 This proposition seems valid in all but crassly determinist interpretations of history.

17 An excellent collection on civil society is *Civil Society and the State*, ed. John Keane (London: Verso, 1988). Rhoda E. Howard and Jack Donnelly, in attempting to correlate human rights violations with regime types, conclude that only liberal regimes are consonant with international human rights standards, which are liberal in essence, "Human Dignity, Human Rights, and Political Regimes," *American Political Science Review* 80 (September 1986): 801–17. True enough, perhaps, but the argument has the ring of tautology. I have therefore avoided regime inclinations or types as relevant intervening variables in my argument.

18 A perceptive article on this subject is Karl Deutsch, "The Crisis of the State," in *Comparative Politics*, ed. Roy C. Macridis and Bernard E. Brown (Chicago: Dorsey, 1986), pp. 44–55.

19 See Clifford Geertz's remarkable *Negara: The Theatre State in Nineteenth-Century Bali* (Princeton, N.J.: Princeton University Press, 1980).

20 For obvious reasons, as the sins of communism cannot be the sins of capitalism by definition.

21 In this volume see chapter 15 by John Mueller and chapter 1 by Robert Jervis; George F. Kennan, "After the Cold War," *New York Times Magazine*, February 5, 1989.

22 See Eric Nordlinger's provocative chapter in this volume (ch. 14).

23 An analogy with the Catholic church's attempt during the Middle Ages to construct a city of God on earth is, perhaps, appropriate.

## 12 The UN Rediscovered: Soviet and American Policy in the United Nations of the 1990s

My research assistant, Edmund Piasecki, provided invaluable documentation and analysis during the writing of this chapter.

1 The United Nations Association of the United States of America (UNA–USA) and the Soviet UN Association are engaged in a multiyear study on the future of the UN. The two groups have held several high-level meetings on peace and security issues, multilateral arms control, UN reform, global environment issues, and human rights. Additional meetings are planned on economic development, peacekeeping, and other political and disarmament issues. The two groups publish joint statements periodically outlining new areas for cooperative action.

2 The historical review of Soviet UN policy in this chapter draws on Edward C. Luck and Toby Trister Gati, "Gorbachev, the United Nations, and US Policy," *Washington Quarterly* 11 (Autumn 1988):

3 The Congo operation, run by the independent-minded Dag Hammarskjöld until his death in 1961, convinced the Russians that the secretary general could not be entrusted with overall supervision of peacekeeping forces. The death of the Soviet-supported Congolese Prime Minister Patrice Lumumba reinforced their belief that peacekeeping operations were inherently biased toward the West. The Soviet's failure to pay their assessed contributions for the Congo and the UN Emergency Force (UNEF) in the Middle East authorized in 1956 led to such large Soviet arrearages that during the 1964 General Assembly an effort was made to deprive them of their right to vote in the General Assembly, the "Article 19" crisis.

4 In general, Soviet proposals can be divided into four categories: (1) measures to improve UN conflict control capabilities; (2) measures to make better use of the main UN organs; (3) measures to promote economic, humanitarian, and ecological well-being; and (4) measures to make international law more comprehensive. These proposals differ greatly in terms of specificity and practicality. A listing of all of them appears in the Appendix to this chapter.

5 Although the UN Charter contained most of these "new" ideas, the Soviet Union insisted that the pre-nuclear genesis of the charter did not sufficiently take into account the need for a broader definition of security.

6 Even by UN standards, the initial draft was vague and confused, serving as a poor advertisement for "new thinking." (Indeed, at the time it was introduced Soviet delegates had a hard time explaining why it was needed.) After many amendments and despite strong opposition from the United States, it easily passed the 41st General Assembly. One year later, Gorbachev presented his more detailed and positive view of the United Nations. His call for an "exchange of views" at the UN was greeted with great interest, but the attitude toward comprehensive security remained skeptical. Sensing that the Soviet resolution was not just a run-of-the-mill peace initiative but might portend a more substantive approach to the UN, many countries which supported the USSR at the 41st General Assembly abstained during the voting at the 42nd General Assembly. At the 43rd General Assembly, a watered-down version of the resolution on comprehensive security was passed, only after the word *approach* was substituted for *system* and numerous other changes were made. The United States, after countless speeches against the proposal, informally said it would abstain rather than oppose the resolution if the Soviet Union would agree not to include a review of the item on the 1989 General Assembly agenda. No deal.

7 Although the UN diplomatic community expressed concern about the *re*ideologization of the UN as a consequence of the debate on comprehensive security, much of Gorbachev's December 1988 address to the General Assembly was devoted to the reasons why it is in the Soviet interest to *de*ideologize Soviet foreign policy. This part of the speech was perhaps read with greater interest in Moscow than in foreign countries.

8    In a socialist bloc working document of the early 1970s an effort was even made to remove the word *interdependence* from all UN documents. See "General Guidelines for the New International Development Strategy" submitted by the socialist bloc to the UN Second Committee on a New International Development Strategy in which the following statement appeared: "The different concepts which have recently emerged, particularly 'global interdependence' and 'the satisfaction of basic needs,' should be treated with attention and caution in the formulation of the new international development strategy. The interpretation of certain circles of the concept of 'global interdependence,' for instance, is totally unacceptable. In its guise they are trying nothing less than to impose so-called collective responsibility for what happened in the world economy and intensify the exploitation of developing countries. For this reason the term 'interdependence' should be replaced by the term 'interrelationships.'" Cited in Toby Gati, "The Soviet Union and the North-South Dialogue," *Orbis* (Summer 1980): 246. The Soviet approach to the fourth United Nations Development Decade is much simpler: "Bloc approaches run counter to the universal significance of the development problem," according to a statement by Sergei Lavrov, USSR representative to the UN General Assembly Ad Hoc Committee of the Whole for the Preparation of the International Development Strategy for the Fourth United Nations Development Decade, June 1989 (press release no. 111, Soviet Permanent Mission to the United Nations, June 7, 1989, p. 2).

9    In 1988 the Soviet Union contributed $4.2 million to UNDP versus $113 million given by the United States.

10   Eduard Shevardnadze, minister of foreign affairs of the USSR," Address to the 43rd UN General Assembly," (press release no. 159, Soviet Permanent Mission to the United Nations, September 27, 1988, p. 6). The foreign minister's statement seems to reflect some of the points made by Georgy Shakhnazarov in two articles (*Pravda*, January 15, 1988 and *International Affairs* [Moscow], March 1988) in which Shakhnazarov argues that the internationalization of all aspects of human endeavor has created the necessity for a voluntary delegation of national sovereignty to supranational powers in order to create a more governable world. Alexander Bovin, writing in *Pravda* takes issue with the notion of a "world government" inasmuch as no stable balance of interests exists from which such authority can be derived. The decisions of the UN, Bovin continues, will never be implemented by any sovereign state if they contradict its national interest (February 1, 1988).

11   In explaining the about face on Afghanistan, for example, Deputy Foreign Minister Vladimir Petrovsky noted: "[B]earing in mind the fact that our action was condemned by over one hundred members of the United Nations we came to realize eventually that we had set ourselves against the international community, violated rules of conduct and defied man's universal interests. As a result, we have withdrawn our troops from Afghanistan," "Disarmament and Multilateralism," First Committee of the 44th General Assembly of the United Nations, October 26, 1989, p. 6.

12   Soviet receptivity to a strengthening of the World Court followed closely the Reagan administration's refusal to accept the World Court's mandatory jurisdiction in a case involving the mining of Nicaragua's harbors. It is hard to avoid the conclusion that the outcome of this case influenced at least some of Moscow's newfound interest in the World Court.

13   In February 1989 the Soviet Union announced the withdrawal of its reservations regarding compulsory ICJ adjudication of any disputes which may arise from the interpretation or application of six international human rights treaties to which it is already a party. The treaties cover genocide, slavery, women's rights, racial discrimination, and torture.

14   This duality is well expressed in many public opinion polls on the United Nations. A 1989 Roper poll commissioned by UNA-USA shows a large degree of support for the

United Nations, but a sharp decline when people were asked if the UN is doing a good job. In the area of peace and security, Americans were strongly in favor of multilateral over unilateral intervention in regional conflicts (49 percent to 17 percent); of increasing financial support for UN peacekeeping activities (46 percent to 11 percent); and of expanding the UN's role in controlling chemical weapons (49 percent to 33 percent) and even nuclear (46 percent to 33 percent) weapons. Furthermore, 58 percent of those polled thought the United States should abide by World Court decisions even when the decisions went against us (15 percent were opposed), and 56 percent favored giving the UN more power to deal with global environmental problems (27 percent disagreed). Increasing UN funding for environmental protection was supported 58 percent to 6 percent. Despite these high marks for UN accomplishments in specific fields, the UN's overall job performance rating was low. Only 38 percent thought it was doing a "good job"; 29 percent rated its overall performance as "poor"; and 33 percent were undecided. Poll after poll dispute often-repeated claims that Americans are fed up with the UN. In a 1985 Gallup poll 81 percent of the American people want the United States to remain in the United Nations.

15 The deployment of the UN's first international peacekeeping force, UNEF, in 1956 provided a face-saving way out of a major political embarrassment for Britain and France in the Sinai. Both nations had sent troops to protect their interests at the Suez Canal after Egypt nationalized the canal and an Israeli invasion of the Sinai (prompted by Palestinian terrorist attacks) had endangered free trade through the waterway. Irked that neither Britain nor France had bothered to consult their NATO ally and fearing a Soviet use of force in the Middle East, the United States strongly backed a Canadian-sponsored draft in the General Assembly requesting Secretary General Dag Hammarskjöld to draw up a plan to "secure and supervise the cessation of hostilities" through the use of an emergency international force. The Soviet Union had pushed for ever stronger measures to effect the withdrawal of foreign troops, but did not object strongly to the steps proposed. In the end the Eastern bloc abstained in the vote on the Canadian draft.

16 While commentators throughout the 1970s frequently criticized Third World and socialist bloc attacks on U.S. policy at the United Nations, the phrase is perhaps best known as the title of former UN Ambassador Daniel Patrick Moynihan's *A Dangerous Place* (Boston: Little, Brown, 1978), in which he criticized those delegates who followed "an unexamined routine of going along with the Non-Aligned while the Non-Aligned went along with the Russians" (p. 256). Moynihan ascribes the "natural ally" comment to Algeria's UN ambassador at the time, Absulaziz Bouteflika, who made it in his official capacity as president of the General Assembly during Moynihan's eight-month tenure in 1975 and 1976 (p. 135). President Gerald R. Ford had warned the United Nations about the tyrannical majority in his 1974 address to the 29th General Assembly, and then U.S. Ambassador John A. Scali reiterated it at the end of the session (pp. 33–34). After the adoption of the Zionism Is Racism resolution in 1975, Moynihan warned the assembled delegates that in the United States "people will begin to say, indeed they have already begun to say, that the United Nations is a place where lies are told" (p. 198).

17 Over the years the U.S. assessment had declined from 40 percent to 33 percent to 25 percent, where it still is. The size of the Soviet assessment, including Byelorussia and the Ukraine, has ranged from 7.7 percent to 17.5 percent. In 1989 it was 11.6 percent. In 1988 the United States paid $502 million in voluntary contribution, while the USSR contributed $23 million (4.6 percent of the U.S. total). It is hard to imagine that if the Soviet Union had paid as much as the United States did year after year that it, too, would not have been more vocal in demanding its money's worth from the United Nations.

18 The UN operation in Lebanon (UNIFIL) was the sole peacekeeping operation author-

ized during this period, but it lacked a well-thought-out mandate and eventually lost support from even the United States and Israel, its original backers.

19　The institutionalization of a secret ballot procedure in 1979; the rare censure of an Eastern bloc state, Czechoslovakia, in 1978 for violations of workers' rights; and the ILO's vigorous pursuit of complaints against Poland and the Soviet Union allowed the United States to return to full membership in 1980.

20　This policy did not apply only to the Soviet Union, East European, and Third World states. An effort was also undertaken to monitor the voting records of countries receiving U.S. bilateral aid in order to reduce the gap between the state of bilateral relations (often very good) and the international profile as reflected in anti-U.S. votes at the United Nations. Although this effort was resented by many nations, it served to put countries on notice that what they did at the UN mattered to Washington.

21　Address by President Ronald Reagan before the General Assembly, September 26, 1983, UN Doc. A/38/PV.5.

22　The permanent members of the Security Council had been holding a series of informal meetings since late 1986 to discuss the settlement of regional disputes.

23　John R. Balton, "The Concept of the 'Unitary UN,'" address before the Geneva Group consultative-level meeting, Geneva, June 29, 1989, *Current Policy*, no. 1191, (Washington D.C.: U.S. Department of State, Bureau of Public Affairs, July 1989).

24　As the drug problem illustrates, U.S. attempts to expand UN responsibilities while applying the unitary UN concept may prove impractical. The secretary-general has argued that "normal deployment" of funds (as called for in the unitary approach) will not provide sufficient resources for the proposed expansion and that additional funds from member states will be required. Although Secretary James Baker agreed that contributions should be increased, he gave no indication that the United States intended to do so.

　　Two international drug control treaties, negotiated under the auspices of the United Nations are in force: the Single Convention on Narcotic Drugs (1961) and the Protocol amending it (1972), and the Convention on Psychotropic Substances (1971). The 1988 UN Convention against Illicit Traffic in Narcotic Drugs and Psychotropic Substances, ratified by the United States on February 13, 1990 and four other countries, entered into force with fifteen additional ratifications.

25　During the Carter administration, the United States signed—but has yet to ratify —two other human rights treaties on civil and political rights and on economic, social, and cultural rights. Washington has not even signed three other conventions on racial discrimination, discrimination against women, and apartheid. The majority of the UN membership, including the Soviet Union, has signed and ratified all seven treaties.

26　The president's fiscal year 1991 budget request called for full funding ($695 million) of assessed contributions to fifty-one international organizations (including $507 million for the UN system) and payment of cumulative U.S. arrears of $464 million to be paid at 20 percent per year over five years. The president also requested $247 million to fund assessments for UN peacekeeping activities ($91 million), as well as cumulative peacekeeping arrears ($157 million).

27　This is particularly true on questions concerning Middle East policy, most importantly, on the question of Israeli credentials in the General Assembly and attempts by the PLO to gain admission as a "state" to UN-specialized agencies such as WHO, UNESCO, and FAO.

28　"Joint Statement of Soviet Deputy Foreign Minister Vladimir Petrovsky and United States Assistant Secretary of State John Bolton," (press release no. 202, Soviet Permanent Mission to the United Nations, November 3, 1989; and UN Document A/RES/44/21.

29　The following discussion draws heavily on conversations with Soviet scholars and diplomats during trips to the USSR. Glasnost has not yet advanced sufficiently for me to thank them by name.

30   "International Control?" a discussion with Telmuraz Ramishvili, Soviet member of the UN Sub-Commission on Prevention of Discrimination and Protection of Minorities, *Moscow News*, no. 4, 1989, p. 30.

31   The Soviet Union was not yet ready to vote its new philosophy on this point in 1989. When a vote was taken in the Commission on Human Rights on a Hungarian complaint about the treatment of minorities in Romania, the Soviet delegate absented himself from the hall.

32   Until 1987 the Soviet Union and its allies abstained on resolutions relating to fuller disclosure of military expenditures. The USSR promised to present data on the Soviet military budget to the General Assembly in 1990 using the UN standard reporting system.

33   "What Worries Soviet Diplomats?" Interview with Eduard Shevardnadze, *Moscow News*, no. 1, 1989, p. 9.

34   Several legal scholars have already begun to stress this point: "Another international aspect of a rule-of-law state is open democratic discussion of foreign policy problems and the adoption of decisions regarding them in accordance with a procedure strictly defined by law. . . . If the Supreme Soviet is to play a full-fledged role in the foreign policy sphere, it would also be worthwhile to envisage as an independent function of the Standing Commissions of the Chambers of the USSR Supreme Soviet consideration of matters pertaining to the implementation of the Soviet Union's international treaties ratified by the USSR Supreme Soviet." Yuri Rybakov, Leonid Skotnikov, and Alexander Zmeyevsky, "The Primacy of Law in Politics," *International Affairs* (Moscow), May 1989, p. 65.

35   "Internationalizing the Dialogue and the Negotiating Process," *International Affairs* (Moscow), no. 2, February 1989, p. 138.

36   "What Worries Soviet Diplomats?," p. 8.

37   The latter two are particularly important because they address two of the three conditions outlined in the 1985 Kassebaum-Solomon amendment on withholding of UN dues.

38   A Joint Statement issued by UNA-USA and the Soviet UN Association in April 1989 on "The UN's Role in Enhancing Peace and Security" outlines in some detail the new possibilities for improving the UN's effectiveness. Many of the themes reoccur in the joint U.S.-Soviet resolution described earlier.

### 13   Environmental Protection and Soviet-American Relations

1   A discussion of the four-point agenda is included in George Shultz, "Managing the U.S.-Soviet Relationship," *Current Policy*, no. 1129 (Washington, D.C.: U.S. Department of State, Bureau of Public Affairs, November 1988). A subsequent view is presented in James Baker, "Statement at Senate Confirmation Hearings," *Current Policy*, no. 1146 (Washington, D.C.: U.S. Department of State, Bureau of Public Affairs, January 1989). An overview of cooperation in the environmental field is set forth in "U.S. and Soviets Spur Scientific Collaboration," *Letter*, no. 1, Conservation Foundation, 1988. Illustrative of calls for expanded cooperation is David McClave, *U.S.-Soviet Relations: An Agenda for the Future*, no. 14. *Cooperation to Protect the Environment and Conserve Resources* (Baltimore: Johns Hopkins University, School of Advanced International Studies, 1988).

2   A. Lyutiy, "Responsible Citizens of the Planet: Forum in Moscow," *Pravda*, January 13, 1990, p. 6.

3   For the first time, nationwide data, albeit in large aggregations, on the state of the environment in the USSR were published in *Report of the Condition of the Natural*

*Resources in the USSR in 1988* (Moscow: State Committee for the Protection of Nature and All Union Institute for Scientific and Technical Information, 1989), and in *Protection of the Environment and Rational Use of the Natural Resources in the USSR*, Statistical Handbook (Moscow: State Committee for Statistics of the USSR, 1989).

4   "Terms of Reference; ASUSSR-NAS Interacademy Committee on Global Ecology," National Academy of Sciences, December 1988, pp. 1–2.

5   A sobering view of the impact of continued hot summers on the food supply is set forth in Lester Brown, "Re-examining the World Food Prospect," *State of the World, 1989* (New York W.W. Norton, 1989), p. 58.

6   A revealing discussion of Soviet environmental problems is included in A. V. Yablokov, "State of Nature in the USSR," report to the seminar East European Environmental Challenge, Ecology 89 International Congress, Gothenburg, August 28–31, 1989. Among the many published discussions of Soviet environmental problems are "The Greening of the U.S.S.R.," *Time*, January 2, 1989, pp. 68–69; Valentine A. Koptyug, "From Concern to Effective Policy," *Komunist*, no. 7, May 1988; Keay Davidson, "Poll: Environment No. 1 Soviet Worry," *San Francisco Examiner*, November 22, 1989, p. A-10; Jeff Trimble, "Soviets Get Serious about Environmental Crises," *San Francisco Chronicle*, December 14, 1988, p. 2; Bill Keller, "Developers Turn Aral Sea into a Catastrophe," *New York Times*, December 20, 1988, p. C1; *The Political Economy of Environmental Protection in the Soviet Union* (Washington, D.C.: American Committee on U.S.-Soviet Relations, 1989).

7   Changes in Soviet environmental policies and organizational responsibilities are discussed in Nicholas A. Robinson, "Perestroika and Priroda: Environmental Protection in the USSR," *Pace Environmental Law Review* 5 (Spring 1988): 351–423.

8   Activities under the U.S.-USSR Environmental Protection Agreement are described in Nicholas A. Robinson and Gary R. Waxmonsky, "The U.S.-U.S.S.R. Agreement to Protect the Environment: 15 Years of Cooperation," *Environmental Law* 18 (1988): 403. An update is included in "US-USSR Environmental Agreement Joint Committee 1990 Memorandum," U.S. Environmental Protection Agency, January 12, 1990. Examples of projects of mutual interest are included in Glenn E. Schweitzer and Anna S. Phillips, eds., *Monitoring and Managing Environmental Impact; American and Soviet Perspectives* (Washington, D.C.: National Academy Press, 1986).

9   With regard to the Supreme Soviet, see "USSR Supreme Soviet Resolution on Urgent Measures to Promote the Country's Ecological Recovery," *Pravda*, December 3, 1989, pp. 1–3; for a discussion of environmental groups in the USSR, see "Russia's Greens," *The Economist*, November 4, 1989, p. 23.

10  See, for example, Koptyug, "From Concern to Effective Policy."

11  For an overview of Soviet-American scientific cooperation see Glenn E. Schweitzer, *Techno-Diplomacy: US-Soviet Confrontations in Science and Technology* (New York: Plenum Publishing, 1989), and Glenn E. Schweitzer, "Who Wins in U.S.-Soviet Science Ventures?" *Bulletin of the Atomic Scientists* 44 (October 1988): 28–32. Additional details are presented in U.S. Congress, House Subcommittee on Europe and the Middle East of the Committee on Foreign Affairs, *United States-Soviet Exchanges, 1988: Hearings*, 99th Cong., July 31, 1986.

## 14   America's Strategic Immunity:
### The Basis of a National Security Strategy

1   The case for a strategically immune state's disengagement, in Eric A. Nordlinger, *Masterly Inactivity: A National Security Strategy* (forthcoming), also highlights the singular weakness of all engagement strategies. To tailor and premise an encompassing engagement strategy upon an interpretation of the rival's intentions as aggressive

and/or defensive is exceptionally problematic. Not only are many interpretations usually wide of the mark, but overly adversarial and conciliatory policies also have security-deflating consequences, with mistaken ones then being difficult to recognize and correct for. To adopt an agnostic position that rejects a tailoring of policies to ascribed intentions is not to deny that they need to be squarely addressed. A national strategy does so for the entire spectrum of possibilities. And it is more effective than adversarial policies in deterring and conciliatory ones in reassuring the rival.

"Given" a rival with revisionist aims a national strategy is at least as effective as adversarial measures in guarding against expansive actions beyond the core and unacceptable actions in and around it. Additional hawkish measures cannot improve upon the deterrent threat. On the premise of a Soviet Union motivated by defensive concerns and security anxieties, national policies are maximally effective—markedly more so than their conciliatory counterparts in reassuring the rival that it need not undertake expansive or unacceptable actions to improve upon its security position. And national policies are maximally effective, much more so than any actively hawkish or dovish ones, in negating our involvement in any kind of war—be it "low-intensity," limited, or general, conventional or nuclear, and whether brought on purposefully or inadvertently. In the shorthand language of game theory, a *national* security strategy turns out to be the "dominant" one.

2   Strategic immunity's other dimension refers to the rival's attempts to improve upon quantitative and qualitative military capabilities. Insofar as the Soviets' military efforts fail, the United States is said to be impermeable; insofar as any successes do not impair its security, it is impervious. The United States is said to be immune in both regards in Nordlinger, *Masterly Inactivity*. A narrow security perimeter bears upon military deployments by allowing for about a 50 percent reduction in conventional forces. It also obviates the need for a less credible strategic force designed for extended deterrence. A national military posture is as distinctively defensive as allowed for by the need to deter and defend against challenges in and around the core perimeter, which still allows for U.S. superiority in surface ships and attack submarines to protect sea lines of communication without threatening the Soviet Union.

3   William Zimmerman, *Soviet Perspectives on International Relations, 1956–1967* (Princeton, N.J.: Princeton University Press, 1969), pp. 253–54.

4   Elizabeth Kridl Valkenier, *The Soviet Union and the Third World: An Economic Bind* (New York: Praeger, 1983).

5   Stephen T. Hosner and Thomas Wolfe, *Soviet Policy and Practice Toward Third World Conflicts* (Lexington, Mass.: D. C. Heath, 1983), pp. 11–78 passim; Robert H. Donaldson, "The Second World, the Third World, and the New International Economic Order," in *The Soviet Union in the Third World: Successes and Failures*, ed. Robert H. Donaldson (Boulder, Colo.: Westview Press, 1981), pp. 358–83; Peter Shearman, "Gorbachev and the Third World: An Era of Reform?," *Third World Quarterly* 9 (October 1987): 1089–99.

6   Richard E. Feinberg, *The Intemperate Zone: The Third World Challenge to U.S. Foreign Policy* (New York: W. W. Norton, 1983), pp. 136–38.

7   Francis Fukuyama, "The Tenth Period of Soviet Foreign Policy," paper delivered at the national security conference held by the Center for International Affairs, Harvard University, June 1987, pp. 8, 11–12; Shearman, "Gorbachev and the Third World," pp. 1093–100. Admittedly, it is not certain that India's resilience would have been such in the absence of U.S. involvements in South Asia and the Indian Ocean.

8   Roger F. Pajak, "The Effectiveness of Soviet Arms Aid Diplomacy in the Third World," in *The Soviet Union in the Third World*, ed. Donaldson, pp. 384–408; Mark N. Kramer, "Soviet Arms Transfers to the Third World," *Problems of Communism* 36

(September–October 1987): 52–68; *Discriminate Deterrence*, the Report of the Commission on Integrated Long-Term Strategy (Washington, D.C.: GPO, January 1988), p. 19; *Supporting U.S. Strategy for Third World Conflict* (Washington, D.C.: Department of Defense, June 1988), p. 9.

9   Kenneth N. Waltz, "Another Gap?" in *Containment, Soviet Behavior, and Grand Strategy*, ed. Robert E. Osgood, Policy Paper 16 (Berkeley: Institute of International Studies, 1981).

10   Stephen M. Walt, *The Origins of Alliances* (Ithaca, N.Y.: Cornell University Press, 1987), esp. pp. 29–30, 172–78.

11   Stephen Goose, "Soviet Geopolitical Momentum: Trends of Soviet Influence Around the World from 1945 to 1980," *Defense Monitor*, January 1980; also see Donaldson, ed., *The Soviet Union in the Third World*, p. 302.

12   *The Military Balance 1976–1977* (London: International Institute for Strategic Studies, 1976), p. 57; *The Military Balance 1980–1981* (London: International Institute for Strategic Studies), p. 71; Richard Sneider, *The Political and Social Capabilities of North and South Korea for the Long-Term Military Competition* (Santa Monica: Rand Corporation, 1985), p. 44.

13   Stephen S. Kaplan, *The Diplomacy of Power: Soviet Armed Forces as a Political Instrument* (Washington, D.C.: Brookings Institution, 1981), pp. 661–62. The various studies that find Soviet influence to be distinctly circumscribed are reviewed in Joseph L. Nogee, "The Soviet Union in the Third World: Successes and Failures," in *The Soviet Union in the Third World*, ed. Donaldson, pp. 438–51. For an update, see Rajan Menon, "Soviet Arms Transfers to the Third World," *Journal of International Affairs* 40 (Summer 1986): 59–76; and S. Neil MacFarlane, "The Soviet Union," in *Superpower Competition and Security in the Third World*, ed. Robert S. Litwak and Samuel F. Wells (Cambridge: Ballinger, 1988), pp. 67–71, 74.

14   Walt, *Origins of Alliances*, pp. 225–27, and the studies cited there.

15   Ibid., pp. 229–30, and the studies cited there.

16   The writings that give credence to these developments are found in Robert H. Johnson, "The Persian Gulf in U.S. Strategy: A Skeptical View," *International Security* 13 (Summer 1989): 133, n. 41; 139, n. 56.

17   Ibid., p. 127.

18   Earl C. Ravenal, "Europe without America: The Erosion of NATO," *Foreign Affairs* (Summer 1985). Gene R. La Rocque has come up with a figure of $125 billion in "A New Strategy to Defend America," *Harper's*, July 1988, p. 43. The other figures are calculated from Gordon Adams and Eric Munz, *Fair Shares: Bearing the Burden of the Atlantic Alliance* (Washington, D.C.: Center on Budget and Policy Priorities, March 1988), pp. 50–52.

19   These calculations are based on figures from *World Military Expenditures and Arms Transfers 1987* (Washington, D.C.: Arms Control Disarmament Agency, March 1988), pp. 44, 81.

20   Robert J. Art, "Fixing Atlantic Bridges," *Foreign Policy*, no. 47 (Summer 1982): 70.

21   David P. Calleo, "The American Problem" *Ethics and International Affairs* 3 (1989): 237–38.

22   *World Military Expenditures*, pp. 44, 50, 81.

23   William W. Kaufmann, "Non-Nuclear Deterrence," in *Alliance Security: NATO and the No-First-Use Question*, ed. John Steinbruner and Leon V. Sigal (Washington, D.C.: Brookings Institution, 1987), p. 62.

24   Robert W. Tucker, "Containment and the Search for Alternatives: A Critique," in *Beyond Containment: Alternative American Policies Toward the Soviet Union*, ed. Aron Wildavsky (San Francisco: Institute for Contemporary Studies Press, 1983), p. 81. Tucker has also pointed out that if Soviet strategic forces were superior to America's, our deterrent threat on behalf of the homeland would still enjoy "maximum

credibility." See *The Nuclear Debate: Deterrence and the Lapse of Faith* (New York: Holmes and Meier, 1985), p. 111. The most extensive argument that nuclear superiority does not matter is found in Robert Jervis, *The Illogic of American Nuclear Strategy* (Ithaca N.Y.: Cornell University Press, 1984).

25 After the necessary adaptations, the analysis also applies to Japan—a defensible island country with a population one-half of the Soviet Union's, a larger GNP, stable and cohesive institutions, and a tradition of independence. In addition, there is the China "factor."

26 Robert H. Johnson, "Exaggerating America's Stakes in Third World Conflicts," *International Security* 10 (Winter 1985–86): 34–35.

27 Jerome Slater, "Dominoes in Central America: Will They Fall? Does it Matter?" *International Security* 12 (Fall 1987): 124–25. Also see the studies cited in Lars Schoultz, *National Security and United States Policy Toward Latin America* (Princeton, N.J.: Princeton University Press, 1984).

28 Schoultz, *National Security*, pp. 166, 173, 217–18.

29 Karl Lautenschlager, "The Submarine in Naval Warfare, 1901–2001," *International Security* 11 (Winter 1986–87).

30 These data come from the *Handbook of Economic Statistics, 1989* (Washington, D.C.: Central Intelligence Agency, May 1988), passim; *World Military Expenditures,* p. 54.

31 This conceptualization of economic invulnerability very much overlaps that of others. See, for example, Boleslaw Adam Boczek, "Resource Rivalry in the Third World," in *East-West Rivalry in the Third World: Security Issues and Regional Perspectives,* ed. Robert W. Clawson (Wilmington: Scholarly Resources, 1984), pp. 184–86; Bohdan O. Szuprowicz, *How to Avoid Strategic Minerals Shortages: Dealing with Cartels, Embargoes, and Supply Disruptions* (New York: Wiley, 1981), p. 286.

32 *Direction of Trade Statistics* (Washington, D.C.: International Monetary Fund, 1988), pp. 93, 139.

33 For some illustrative specifics, see Feinberg, *The Intemperate Zone*, pp. 88, 109–10, and L. Harold Bullis and James E. Mielke, *Strategic and Critical Materials* (Boulder, Colo.: Westview Press, 1985). pp. 93, 130.

34 The data upon which these calculations are based are taken from the *Monthly Energy Review* (Washington, D.C.: Energy Information Administration, April 1989), pp. 42–43.

35 During the Iran-Iraq War just over 1 percent of shipping was affected as it passed through the Straits. It increased after the U.S. naval forces began patrolling. Johnson, "The Persian Gulf in U.S. Strategy," p. 146.

36 W. Wendall Fletcher and Kirsten Oldenburg, "How Technology Can Reduce U.S. Import Vulnerability," *Issues in Science and Technology* 2 (Summer 1986): 79, Figure 1. The information in this article is drawn from *Strategic Minerals: Technologies to Reduce U.S. Import Vulnerability* (Washington, D.C.: Office of Technology Assessment, 1985).

37 Cited in Feinberg, *The Intemperate Zone*, p. 117.

38 Fletcher and Oldenburg, "How Technology Can Reduce," p. 79, fig. 1.

39 Barry M. Blechman, *U.S. Security in the Twenty-First Century* (Boulder, Colo.: Westview Press, 1987), p. 49. Cobalt and Chromium are, of course, included among the previously mentioned seven minerals on the Joint Chief's most critical list.

40 Fletcher and Oldenburg, "How Technology Can Reduce," p. 79, Figure 1; Bullis and Mielke, *Strategic and Critical Materials*, pp. 115, 121, 172, 222.

41 Fletcher and Oldenburg, "How Technology Can Reduce," p. 79, fig. 1; Bullis and Mielke, *Strategic and Critical Materials*, p. 119; Feinberg, *The Intemperate Zone*, p. 118. There are also mineral deposits that may be exploited by deep sea bed mining.

42 Simon D. Strauss, "Why the Strategic Stockpile is Essential," *Issues in Science and Technology* (Summer 1986): 89.

43 Bullis and Mielke, *Strategic and Critical Materials*, p. 223.

44 Ibid, pp. 178–229.

45 Nordlinger, *Masterly Inactivity*. Since Earl C. Ravenal is the writer most closely identified with the strategy of disengagement, it should be noted that his case is very different. In contrast to the emphasis on American strengths and nonengagement's *advantages* in Nordlinger, Ravenal emphasizes "the unmanageable diffusion of power," "the dissolution of [American] alliances," "the practical demise of extended deterrence," and America's inadequate resources for quasi-global containment. He has not attempted to demonstrate America's strategic immunity; he is not all that sanguine about its economic aspects. Ravenal's most extensive rationale is found in "The Case for Strategic Disengagement," *Foreign Affairs* 15 (April 1973): 505–12. His other analyses include "Counterforce and Alliance: The Ultimate Connection," *International Security* 6 (Spring 1982):26–43; "Europe without America," *Foreign Affairs* (1985); and "Containment, Non-Intervention, and Strategic Disengagement," in *Containing the Soviet Union*, ed. Terry L. Deibel and John Lewis Gaddis (Oxford: Pergamon, 1987).

46 Richard Ned Lebow, "The Deterrence Deadlock: Is There a Way Out?" in Robert Jervis, Richard Ned Lebow, and Janice Stein, *Psychology and Deterrence* (Baltimore: Johns Hopkins University Press, 1985), pp. 211–17; Irving Janis and Leon Mann, *Decisionmaking* (New York: Free Press, 1977).

47 Mark N. Katz, *The Third World in Soviet Military Thought* (Baltimore: Johns Hopkins University Press, 1982); S. Neil MacFarlane, *Superpower Rivalry and Third World Radicalism: The Idea of National Liberation* (London: Croom Helm, 1985); Elizabeth Kridl Valkenier, "Revolutionary Change in the Third World: Recent Soviet Assessments," *World Politics* (April 1986); Francis Fukuyama, *Moscow's Post-Brezhnev Reassessment of the Third World* (Santa Monica: Rand Corporation, 1986); Jerry F. Hough, *The Struggle for the Third World: Soviet Debates and American Options* (Washington, D.C.: Brookings Institution, 1986).

48 Nathan Leites, *A Study of Bolshevism* (Glencoe, Ill.: Free Press, 1953); Alexander L. George, "The 'Operational Code': A Neglected Approach to the Study of Political Leaders and Decision-Making," *International Studies Quarterly* 13 (June 1969): 190–222; Richard Pipes, "Operational Principles of Soviet Foreign Policy," *Survey* 19 (Spring 1973): 41–61; Hannes Adomeit, *Soviet Risk-Taking and Crisis Behavior* (London: George Allen and Unwin, 1982).

## 15  Taking Peace Seriously: Two Proposals

1 I would like to thank Robert Jervis and Richard Rosecrance for helpful comments. An earlier and somewhat shorter version of this chapter appeared under the title, "A New Concert of Europe," in *Foreign Policy*, no. 77 (Winter 1989–90).

2 Previously, the period between the conclusion of the Franco-Prussian War in 1871 and the outbreak of World War I in 1914 was the longest era of peace among major European countries. That record was broken on November 8, 1988. Both eras of peace were marred by minor wars in Europe: those in the Balkans in the earlier era, the one between Hungary and the USSR in the later one. The earlier era was also marked by a major war outside Europe between Russia and Japan. The longest era of peace among all major countries before the present one was from 1815 to 1854, a record broken on May 15, 1984. While the periods from 1815 to 1854 and 1871 to 1914 were generally free of international war in Europe, there were many civil wars during those periods. See also Paul Schroeder, "Does Murphy's Law Apply to History?" *Wilson Quarterly* 9 (New Year's 1985): 88; and Evan Luard, *War in International Society* (New Haven, Conn.: Yale University Press, 1986), pp. 54–56, 395–99.

3 As Colin Gray cautions, one must "focus more than passing attention upon the

prospects for general nuclear war [because] the low probability of occurrence is more than counterbalanced by the prospective horrors of the hypothetical, if admittedly unlikely, event," Colin S. Gray, "NATO: Time to Call It a Day?" *National Interest*, no. 10 (Winter 1987–88): 26.

4　"MacNeil/Lehrer Newshour," PBS, May 10, 1988.

5　William Taubman, *Stalin's American Policy* (New York: W. W. Norton, 1982), p. 22.

6　See Frederic S. Burlin, "The Communist Doctrine of the Inevitability of War," *American Political Science Review* 57 (June 1963): 337–41.

7　Quoted in Robert Jervis, *The Illogic of American Nuclear Strategy* (Ithaca, N.Y.: Cornell University Press, 1984), p. 166. For similar conclusions by some of the most anti-Soviet writers, see Arkady N. Shevchenko, *Breaking with Moscow* (New York: Knopf, 1984), pp. 285–86; Michael Voslensky *Nomenklatura: The New Soviet Ruling Class* (Garden City, N.Y.: Doubleday, 1984), pp. 320–30; Richard Pipes, *Survival Is Not Enough* (New York: Simon and Schuster, 1984), p. 65. See also Nikita Khrushchev, *Khrushchev Remembers: The Last Testament* (Boston: Little, Brown, 1974), pp. 511, 531, 533. For the argument that stability has been inherent in the postwar condition and is not due to the peculiar effects of nuclear weapons, see John Mueller, "The Essential Irrelevance of Nuclear Weapons: Stability in the Postwar World," *International Security* 13 (Fall 1988): 55–79; for counterargument, see Robert Jervis, "The Political Effects of Nuclear Weapons," pp. 80–90 in the same issue.

8　Soviet military intervention in Afghanistan in 1979 was an effort to prop up a faltering pro-Soviet regime. As such, it was not like Korea, but more like American intervention in Vietnam in 1965 or like Soviet intervention in Hungary in 1956 or Czechoslovakia in 1968. Voslensky notes that Soviet military ventures before and after World War II have consistently been directed only against "weak countries" and only after the Soviets have been careful to cover themselves in advance—often withdrawing when "firm resistance" has been met (*Nomenklatura*, pp. 329–30).

9　Bernard Brodie, *War and Politics* (New York: Macmillan, 1973), p. 426.

10　Robert Jervis, *The Meaning of the Nuclear Revolution* (Ithaca, N.Y.: Cornell University Press, 1989). See also James Joll, *The Origins of the First World War* (New York: Longman, 1984), pp. 167–68, 201–3.

11　For an elaboration of this argument, see John Mueller, *Retreat from Doomsday: The Obsolescence of Major War* (New York: Basic Books, 1989), esp. chs. 5–9.

12　See Seweryn Bialer, *The Soviet Paradox: External Expansion, Internal Decline* (New York: Knopf, 1986), pp. 337, 343; Francis Fukuyama, "Gorbachev and the Third World," *Foreign Affairs* 64 (Spring 1986): 726; Timothy J. Colton, *The Dilemma of Reform in the Soviet Union*, rev. ed. (New York: Council on Foreign Relations, 1986), pp. 192–93; Dimitri K. Simes, "Gorbachev: A New Foreign Policy?" *Foreign Affairs: America and the World 1986* 65 (1986): 489; George W. Breslauer, "All Gorbachev's Men," *National Interest*, no. 12 (Summer 1988): 100; Ilya Prizel, "Latin American: The Long March," *National Interest*, no. 12 (Summer 1988): 111.

13　In 1988, the Kremlin's chief ideologist, Vadim A. Medvedev, rejected the notion that a world struggle is going on between capitalism and communism, Bill Keller, "New Soviet Ideologist Reject Idea of World Struggle Against West," *New York Times*, October 6, 1988, p. A1.

14　See, for example, Michael Wines, "C.I.A. Says a Gorbachev Removal Is the Sole Threat to Soviet Change," *New York Times*, March 2, 1990, p. A8.

15　"Analytic Conclusions," in *Hawks, Doves, and Owls: An Agenda for Avoiding Nuclear War*, ed. Graham T. Allison, Albert Carnesale, and Joseph S. Nye, Jr. (New York: W. W. Norton, 1985), pp. 207–8.

16　Hans J. Morgenthau, *Politics Among Nations: The Struggle for Peace and Power* (New York: Knopf, 1948), p. 327.

17　See, for example, Robert Pear, "Soviet Experts Say Their Economy Is Worse Than U.S.

Has Estimated," *New York Times*, April 24, 1990, p. A14.

18  Moreover, they have often become irrelevant because while one weapons system is being controlled by laborious negotiation, a better one is being invented. And they don't have much of a history of reducing overall defense spending—reductions in one defense area have characteristically been compensated for by increases in another. See Bruce D. Berkowitz, *Calculated Risks* (New York: Simon and Schuster, 1987), esp. ch. 2.

19  See Richard Smoke, *National Security and the Nuclear Dilemma* (New York: Random House, 1987), p. 195.

20  See, for example, his arguments in debate: *Congressional Quarterly*, October 1, 1988, p. 2750.

21  For a valuable overview of these issues, see C. P. Stacey, *The Undefended Border: The Myth and the Reality* (Ottawa: Canadian Historical Association, 1953). See also Stanley L. Falk, "Disarmament on the Great Lakes: Myth or Reality?" *U.S. Naval Institute Proceedings* 87 (December 1961): 69–73.

22  See Richard A. Preston, *The Defense of the Undefended Border* (Montreal: McGill-Queens University Press, 1977), pp. 41–43, 57–59; Reginald G. Stuart, "United States Expansionism and the British North American Provinces, 1783–1871, in *Arms at Rest: Peacemaking and Peacekeeping in American History*, ed. Joan R. Challinor and Robert L. Beisner (Westport, Conn.: Greenwood Press, 1987), p. 119.

23  Stacey, *The Undefended Border*, p. 12. Or as Falk puts it, when "points of dissension disappeared, or could be amicably reconciled, the armaments disappeared with them," "Disarmament on the Great Lakes," p. 73.

24  Lord Carrington, "East-West Relations: A Time of Far-Reaching Change," *NATO Review*, June 1988, pp. 3–5.

25  Amity Shlaes, "Talk Turns to Triple Zero in West Germany," *Wall Street Journal*, December 9, 1988, p. A22.

26  Robert Keatley, "Gorbachev Peace Offensive Jars the West," *Wall Street Journal*, January 20, 1989, p. A18.

27  *Wall Street Journal*, May 31, 1989, p. A1.

28  An especially pungent acknowledgment of this tendency was put forward by John Tower in 1989 in his ill-fated confirmation hearings for secretary of defense in the Bush administration. While he foresaw no early reduction in the Soviet armed threat, Tower observed that if that threat *were* to diminish "we could obviously reduce our dedication of resources to defense. If there were no threat we'd be spending enormously less than we spend now. . . . We'd be maintaining the kind of army we had in 1938 [which was] about half the size of what the Marine Corps is now." Significantly, Tower did not insist that such a remarkable reduction would have to come about through formal agreement, but clearly implied it could transpire naturally, even automatically, if the perceived threat diminished. Confirmation Hearing for John Tower for Secretary of Defense, Senate Armed Services Committee, January 25, 1989.

29  *Wall Street Journal*, January 10, 1989, p. A13.

30  See Charles E. Osgood, *An Alternative to War or Surrender* (Urbana: University of Illinois Press, 1962), esp. ch. 5.

31  The image is proposed, but not adopted, in William E. Rappard, *The Quest for Peace Since the World War* (Cambridge, Mass.: Harvard University Press, 1940), p. 490.

32  Consider in this regard the exuberant boast of Italy in 1987 that its gross domestic product was now greater than Britain's. In countering, the unamused British argued that the Italians were miscalculating the economic statistics and that the British have far more television sets and telephones per capita; but they did not point to, or even slyly imply the relevance of, their military superiority—particularly their nuclear weapons. On this saga, see Philip Revzin, "Italy Boasts It Deserves Britain's Place in Rich Nations Club," *Wall Street Journal*, February 27, 1987, p. 42. When

Americans were asked, "Which do you feel is more important in determining a country's influence in the world today—economic power or military power?" economic power was selected by 62 percent, military power by 22 percent, *Wall Street Journal,* May 16, 1988, p. 7. For a more general discussion of this phenomenon, see Mueller, *Retreat from Doomsday,* ch. 10.

33  As Gray notes, "Very few events plausibly might provoke a deliberate Soviet lunge into West Germany, but a whole range of scenarios can be composed for such an eventuality should Bonn announce an intention to acquire truly national nuclear forces," "NATO," p. 18.

34  For an elaboration of this argument, see Mueller, *Retreat from Doomsday.* See also Richard Rosecrance, *The Rise of the Trading State: Commerce and Conquest in the Modern World* (New York: Basic Books, 1986). Gray observes that "war has become unacceptable and unthinkable for the complex, densely populated, and enormously vulnerable societies of Western Europe," "NATO," p. 19. Something similar can probably be said for most of the peoples of Eastern Europe as well.

35  Ibid., p. 25.

36  Quoted, Jack Snyder, "The Gorbachev Revolution: A Waning of Soviet Expanionism?" *International Security* 12 (Winter 1987–88): 115.

37  Paul W. Schroeder, "Alliances, 1815–1945: Weapons of Power and Tools of Management" in *Historical Dimensions of National Security Problems,* ed. Klaus Knorr (Lawrence: University Press of Kansas, 1976), p. 230.

38  Schroeder, "Alliances," pp. 231, 256–57.

39  John Lewis Gaddis, "Was the Truman Doctrine a Real Turning Point?" *Foreign Affairs* 52 (January 1974): 388.

40  In 1980 there were official discussions between the two about the possible transfer of American defense technology to China and about "limited strategic cooperation on matters of common concern," although these never reached fruition, Jonathan D. Pollack, "China and the Global Strategic Balance," in *China's Foreign Relations in the 1980s,* ed. Harry Harding (New Haven, Conn.: Yale University Press, 1984), p. 159; on the potential for alliance, see also Strobe Talbott, "The Strategic Dimension of the Sino-American Relationship," in *The China Factor,* ed. Richard H. Solomon (Englewood Cliffs, N.J.: Prentice-Hall, 1981), pp. 81–113. Also of interest in this regard is the debate that took place in the mid-1970s when it seemed possible that the government of Portugal might be taken over by communists. The option of keeping a communist Portugal within the anticommunist NATO alliance was seriously considered. See Gerald Ford, *A Time to Heal* (New York: Harper and Row, 1979), p. 285.

41  John C. Campbell, *Tito's Separate Road: America and Yugoslavia in World Politics* (New York: Harper and Row, 1967), pp. 24–27.

42  Francis Fukuyama, "Patterns of Soviet Third World Policy," *Problems of Communism* 36 (September–October 1987): 12–13. Alexander Dallin has also observed "an unadvertised shrinking of communist ideological pretensions. . . . At the same time, the structuring of the foreign-policy and international-security agenda in the Kremlin has moved from the party bureaucrats and ideologists into the hands of more pragmatic and more expert professionals," "Soviet Approaches to Superpower Security Relations" in *U.S.-Soviet Security Cooperation,* ed. Alexander L. George, Philip J. Farley, and Alexander Dallin (New York: Oxford University Press, 1988), p. 605.

43  *New York Times,* December 8, 1988, p. A16; December 9, 1988, p. A18.

44  *New York Times,* December 9, 1988, p. A18.

45  For a discussion, see Michael M. Harrison, *The Reluctant Ally: France and Atlantic Security* (Baltimore: Johns Hopkins University Press, 1981), ch. 5.

46  As Schroeder points out, NATO "has been riddled with rivalries and conflicts over intra-alliance control and management, not only between France and the USA, but

also between France and Germany, Britain and France, and other members," "Alliances," p. 257.

## 16   Averting Anarchy in the New Europe

Jeff Frieden, Gregory Gause, Joseph Grieco, Ted Hopf, Samuel Huntington, Robert Jervis, Robert Keohane, John Mearsheimer, Helen Milner, Alexander Motyl, David Spiro, Stephen Walt, Stephen Van Evera and several participants at seminars at Columbia and Harvard universities either provided helpful comments on this chapter or discussed the ideas leading to it. Gary Sick urged me to write them down.

1   The best treatment is John Lewis Gaddis, "The Long Peace: Elements of Stability in the Postwar International System," *International Security* 10 (Spring 1986): 99–142, reprinted in Gaddis, *The Long Peace* (New York: Oxford University Press, 1987), ch. 8.

2   For background on recent East European developments, see William E. Griffith, ed., *Central and Eastern Europe: The Opening Curtain?* (Boulder, Colo.: Westview Press, 1989). See also Mark Kramer, "Soviet Policy toward Eastern Europe in the Gorbachev Era," *International Security* 14 (Winter 1989–90): 25–67.

3   Samuel P. Huntington, *Political Order in Changing Societies* (New Haven, Conn.: Yale University Press, 1968), p. 196. Philip Roeder, "Modernization and Participation in the Leninist Developmental Strategy," *American Political Science Review* 83 (September 1989): 859–84, also invokes Huntington in analyzing current Soviet developments.

4   Myron Weiner, "The Macedonian Syndrome: An Historical Model of International Relations and Political Development," *World Politics* 23 (July 1971): 665–83, examines praetorian-type states from this aspect. *Political Order*, Huntington discusses nationalism as a response to foreign domination (pp. 304–5).

5   The Nazi period was not praetorian in my use of the term because central state authority dominated parochial interests, but the foreign policy ideology that spurred Hitler's expansionism was an outgrowth of earlier praetorian periods. It developed from ideas that flourished in the political competition among imperialist, militarist, and protectionist groups in the Wilhelmine era. See Woodruff Smith, *The Ideological Origins of Nazi Imperialism* (New York: Oxford University Press, 1986). More generally, arguments about the international aggressiveness of praetorian regimes dominated by imperialist elite coalitions are developed in Jack Snyder, *Myths of Empire: Domestic Politics and Strategic Ideology* (Ithaca, N.Y.: Cornell University Press, 1991).

6   Arguing for this policy, although not linking it to Huntington's analysis, is Robert D. Hormats, "Redefining Europe and the Atlantic Link," *Foreign Affairs* 68 (Fall 1989): 71–91. Anne-Marie Burley, "The Once and Future German Question," *Foreign Affairs* 68 (Winter 1989–90): 65–83, esp. 66, 70–73, notes that this sort of conception is the conventional wisdom in mainstream West German political circles, and has been for most of the 1980s.

7   On the lure of EC membership as a factor promoting the democratic political outcome in Spain, see Edward Malefakis, "Spain and Its Francoist Heritage," in *From Dictatorship to Democracy*, ed. John H. Herz (Westport, Conn.: Greenwood, 1982), pp. 217–19; and Mary Barker Cascallar, "International Influences in the Transition to Democracy in Spain," unpub. ms., Columbia University, spring 1988.

8   These three viewpoints do not precisely reflect the views of any particular author. Rather, in sketching each view, I have adapted the arguments of several theorists and commentators on current events, to present a logically coherent view of their underlying principles.

9   On this point, see Michael Doyle, "Liberalism and World Politics," *American Politi-*

*cal Science Review* 80 (December 1986): 1151–69, and "Kant, Liberal Legacies, and Foreign Affairs," parts 1 and 2, *Philosophy and Public Affairs* 12 (Summer and Fall 1983): 205–35, 323–53. Also relevant is John Mueller, *Retreat from Doomsday? The Obsolescence of Major War* (New York: Basic Books, 1989), and Jack S. Levy, "Domestic Politics and War," *Journal of Interdisciplinary History* 43 (Spring 1988): 653–73.

10　Francis Fukuyama, "The End of History?" *National Interest*, 16 (Summer 1989): 3–18. Fukuyama is neither an unvarnished liberal nor an optimist; he expresses some regret over the universal victory of liberal ideology (p. 18).

11　Gorbachev, quoted in the *New York Times*, November 15, 1989, p. 1.

12　See Mark Palmer, "U.S. and Western Policy—New Opportunities for Action," in *Central and Eastern Europe*, ed. Griffith, pp. 388–400.

13　For the seminal critique of this kind of "second image" theory of war and peace, see Kenneth Waltz, *Man, the State, and War* (New York: Columbia University Press, 1959).

14　Kenneth Waltz, *Theory of International Politics* (Reading, Mass.: Addison-Wesley, 1979). In the following discussion, I use the word *anarchy* when I mean the lack of a central authority to adjudicate disputes between competitors; I use *disorder* or *chaos* to describe the results of anarchic political conflict. On conceptual confusion in the use of the term *anarchy*, see Helen Milner, "Anarchy and Interdependence," *Review of International Studies* (forthcoming).

15　Thomas Christensen and Jack Snyder, "Chain Gangs and Passed Bucks: Predicting Alliance Patterns in Multipolarity," *International Organization* 44 (Spring 1990), present a discussion of the pathologies of multipolar balancing in these cases that builds on, but revised, Waltz's basic insights.

16　Most of the points in this paragraph were discussed by John Mearsheimer in presentations to meetings in Chicago and Princeton, N.J., in the spring and summer 1989, and in "The Future of Europe," a paper prepared for the Flagstaff Conference at Ditchley Park, England, in February 1990. See also Stephen M. Walt, "The Case for Finite Containment: Analyzing U.S. Grand Strategy," *International Security* 14 (Summer 1989): 5–49, esp. 39–40. Walt and Mearsheimer have been helpful in discussing with me the implications of Realist theory for the changing situation in Europe. Their ideas served as background helping me to write this section. However, they bear no responsibility for the direction in which I have developed these ideas. The label "Hobbesian pessimist" is mine, not theirs. Waltz says that his ideas on anarchy were inspired by Rousseau, not Hobbes. To my knowledge, Waltz has not taken a position on the current European changes.

17　Eagleburger speech at Georgetown University, September 13, 1989, reported in the *New York Times*, September 16, 1989, pp. 1, 6. Subsequent statements by President Bush and Secretary of State Baker appear to have rejected this view, however, and Eagleburger has aligned his own subsequent statements with theirs. Andrew Rosenthal, "U.S. Finds Relief in Stand by Gorbachev on the East," *New York Times*, November 16, 1989, p. 21. See also Samuel Huntington, "No Exit: The Errors of Endism," *National Interest*, no. 17 (Fall 1989): 3–11, for a critique of end-of-history optimism.

18　One difficulty with solving the security dilemma through arms control in multipolarity is that allies arrayed in the typical multipolar checkerboard pattern need offensive capabilities to honor their alliance commitments. One solution would be a truly radical adjustment of force postures in a defensive direction, such that every state could be secure against any combination of contiguous states without the assistance of noncontiguous allies. For a discussion of the general problem, see Stephen Van Evera, "Offense, Defense, and Strategy: When Is Offense Best?" paper presented to the annual meeting of the American Political Science Association, Chicago, 1987.

The seminal theoretical work on the security dilemma is Robert Jervis, "Cooperation under the Security Dilemma," *World Politics* 30 (January 1978): 167–214.

19   Exploring these issues is Stephen Van Evera, "Causes of War," Ph.D. diss., University of California at Berkeley, 1984.

20   Charles Tilly, "Does Modernization Breed Revolution?" in *Revolution: Theoretical, Comparative, and Historical Studies*, ed. Jack Goldstone (New York: Harcourt Brace Jovanovich, 1986), p. 56.

21   For a discussion of the nexus among war, the state, and nationalist myths, see Van Evera, "Causes of War." See also Stephen Walt, "The Foreign Policy of Revolutionary States," paper presented to the annual meeting of the American Political Science Association, Chicago, 1987, who quotes Tilly in this connection.

22   *New York Times*, September 16, 1989, p. 6. See also Kramer, "Soviet Policy toward Eastern Europe in the Gorbachev Era," pp. 51–54.

23   Van Evera, "Causes of War," notes that societies with open policy debates are more able to contain nationalist myth-making by state organizations.

24   Mearsheimer, "The Future of Europe," makes this point.

25   Waltz, *Theory of International Politics*, p. 71. For an argument that there is a connection between interdependence and peaceful foreign policy, see Edward S. Morse, "The Transformation of Foreign Policies: Modernization, Interdependence, and Externalization," *World Politics* 22 (April 1970): 371–92.

26   Stephen Walt discusses the points in this paragraph in "Preserving Peace in Europe: The Case for the Status Quo," a paper presented to a conference on U.S.-Soviet relations sponsored by the International Research and Exchanges Board (IREX) in Princeton, N.J., August 1989.

27   On the problem of nationalism under conditions of Moscow's declining power, see Zbigniew Brzezinski, "Post-Communist Nationalism," *Foreign Affairs* 68 (Winter 1989–90): 1–25, and Seweryn Bialer, ed., *Politics, Society, and Nationality inside Gorbachev's Russia* (Boulder, Colo.: Westview Press, 1989).

28   Bill Keller, "Nationalists in Azerbaijan Win Big Concessions from Party Chief," *New York Times*, October 13, 1989, pp. 1, 6. For background, see Mirza Michaeli and William Reese, "The Popular Front in Azerbaijan and Its Program," Radio Liberty, "Report on the USSR," August 25, 1989, pp. 29–32.

29   Stephen Van Evera mentions this approach in "The Future of Europe," unpublished ms., November 1989. On the distinction between Bismarck's defensive alliances and the offensive ones that supplanted them, see Stephen Van Evera, "The Cult of the Offensive and the Origins of the First World War," *International Security* 9 (Summer 1984): 96–103.

30   Waltz, *Theory of International Politics*, pp. 166–69; Christensen and Snyder, "Chain Gangs and Passed Bucks."

31   Van Evera, "When Is Offense Best?"; and Scott Sagan, "1914 Revisited: Allies, Offense, and Instability," *International Security* 11 (Fall 1986): 151–76.

32   Differentiating between neoliberal institutionalism and classical liberalism is Robert Keohane, *International Institutions and State Power* (Boulder, Colo.: Westview Press, 1989), pp. 10–11.

33   Two influential studies embodying this type of analysis are Stephen Krasner, ed., *International Regimes* (Ithaca, N.Y.: Cornell University Press, 1983), first appearing as a special issue of *International Organization* (Spring 1982), and Robert Keohane, *After Hegemony* (Princeton, N.J.: Princeton University Press, 1984).

34   Huntington, *Political Order*, ch. 1.

35   Quoted in ibid., p. 196; chapter 4 discusses praetorian systems.

36   Ibid., chapter 4, can be read this way.

37   Ibid., pp. 334–43, esp. p. 340.

38   On the failure of Leninist regimes to institutionalize participation successfully, see

Roeder, "Modernization and Participation," pp. 859–72. For additional background, see Seweryn Bialer, "Gorbachev's Program of Change," and other essays in *Gorbachev's Russia and American Foreign Policy*, ed. Seweryn Bialer and Michael Mandelbaum (Boulder, Colo.: Westview Press, 1987).

39  Offering country-by-country analyses of such social forces are Griffith, ed., *Central and Eastern Europe*, chs. 6, 8–13; J. F. Brown, *Eastern Europe and Communist Rule* (Durham, N.C.: Duke University Press, 1988); and the spring 1986 special issue of *International Organization* on "Power, Purpose, and Collective Choice: Economic Strategy in Socialist States," ed. Ellen Comisso and Laura Tyson. The latter addresses in particular the effect of changes in the international economic environment on the economic policies and domestic politics of East European states.

40  For Huntington's discussion of the civic polity and the the contrast with praetorianism, see Huntington, *Political Order*, pp. 78–92.

41  See Anthony Downs, *An Economic Theory of Democracy* (New York: Harper, 1959). Benjamin I. Page, *Choices and Echoes in Presidential Elections* (Chicago: University of Chicago Press, 1978), presents tests of and modifications to Downs's basic argument.

42  Downs himself does not make this deduction from his theory. For theoretical and empirical support for it, see Snyder, *Myths of Empire*. I do not mean to argue that democracies are always pacific or that systems with competitive elections invariably produce moderate, optimal policies. Rather, I argue merely that Downs's reasoning helps to explain why democracies have been good strategic learners who have avoided the extreme forms of self-defeating expansionism characteristic of the praetorian great powers. Paul Kennedy's essays on "The Tradition of Appeasement in British Foreign Policy, 1865–1939," and "Why Did the British Empire Last So Long?," chs. 1 and 8 in Kennedy, *Strategy and Diplomacy, 1870–1945* (London: Allen and Unwin, 1983), might be read with this in view.

43  I thank Stephen Van Evera for discussion of this point.

44  See Mancur Olson, *The Rise and Decline of Nations* (New Haven, Conn.: Yale University Press, 1982), on political systems dominated by selfish interest groups, and *The Logic of Collective Action* (Cambridge, Mass.: Harvard University Press, 1965) for the underlying theory. Olson applies his theory primarily to advanced democracies, not to the undemocratic pluralistic societies that Huntington labels praetorian, but Olson's hypotheses should hold even more strongly in such cases, where diffuse interests lack electoral power to check self-interested compact groups. On bargaining among organized interest groups, see Olson, *Rise and Decline*, p. 37.

45  Olson does not discuss these implications of his argument for foreign policy. I make those deductions and support them with historical evidence in *Myths of Empire*.

46  Olson, *Rise and Decline*, pp. 47–53.

47  Peter Katzenstein, *Small States in World Markets* (Ithaca, N.Y.: Cornell University Press, 1985), p. 24 and passim.

48  "Soviet Army Officers Plan to Create Trade Union," Radio Free Europe/Radio Liberty "Daily Report," October 18, 1989; Bill Keller, "Soviet Military Officers Pressing for Changes and a Trade Union," *New York Times*, October 22, 1989, pp. 1, 16.

49  On the *Rossiya* bloc, see Esther B. Fein, "Soviet Legislature Votes to Abolish Official Seats," *New York Times*, October 25, 1989, p. 13. On the national fronts, see Radio Liberty, "Report on the USSR," August 25, September 15, and October 6, 1989.

50  David Blackbourn, *Populists and Patricians* (London: Allen and Unwin, 1987), pp. 102, 161–62, 190, and esp. 211.

51  See Eckart Kehr, *Economic Interest, Militarism, and Foreign Policy* (Berkeley: University of California Press, 1977), esp. 272–76; and Snyder, *Myths of Empire*, ch. 2.

52  Fein, "Soviet Legislature," p. 13.

53  Jack Snyder and Andrei Kortunov, "French Syndrome on Soviet Soil?" *New Times* (Moscow), no. 44 (1989): 18–20, offer a critical discussion of current Soviet attempts

to institutionalize civilian control of the military. David Holloway, "State, Society, and the Military under Gorbachev," *International Security* 14 (Winter 1989–90): 5–24, stresses the progress that has been made in asserting democratic control over Soviet military policy.

54  Huntington, *Political Order*, p. 214, citing the Chilean case, and ch. 4, passim.

55  For background, see Roman Stefanowski, "Trade Unions and Politics in Poland," Radio Free Europe Reports, "Situation Report," Poland, no. 15, October 12, 1989.

56  Radio Free Europe "Situation Report," Hungary, no. 10, June 23, 1989.

57  Peter Katzenstein, *Corporatism and Change: Austria, Switzerland, and the Politics of Industry* (Ithaca, N.Y.: Cornell University Press, 1984).

58  David K. Shipler, "Letter from Budapest," *New Yorker*, November 20, 1989, pp. 74–101, esp. 90–91, 97; Henry Kamm, "Hungary Opposition Splits," *New York Times*, November 25, 1989, p. 8, and "Hungarians Hold First Free Vote in 42 Years," *New York Times*, November 27, 1989, pp. 1, 11. On the Democratic Forum, see also Radio Free Europe, "Situation Report," Hungary, no. 3, February 24, 1989, pp. 35–36, and no. 5, March 31, 1989, pp. 19–24.

59  Kamm, "Hungarians Hold First Free Vote."

60  The following discussion of German politics is based on Hans-Ulrich Wehler, *The German Empire, 1871–1918* (Leamington Spa/Dover, N.H.: Berg, 1985); Geoff Eley, *Reshaping the German Right* (New Haven, Conn: Yale University Press, 1980); and ideas developed in Snyder, *Myths of Empire*, ch. 2.

61  Weiner, "The Macedonian Syndrome," pp. 665–83. Weiner's cases include almost every East European and Balkan state, before either World War I or II.

62  The best extended treatment of these problems is Joseph Rothschild, *East Central Europe between the Two World Wars* (Seattle: University of Washington Press, 1974).

63  Brzezinski, "Post-Communist Nationalism," p. 3.

64  Jack Snyder, "The Gorbachev Revolution: A Waning of Soviet Expansionism?" *International Security* 12 (Winter 1987–88): 93–131. Celeste Wallander, "Third-World Conflict in Soviet Military Thought: Does the 'New Thinking' Grow Prematurely Grey?" *World Politics* 42 (October 1989): 31–63, presents evidence that the Soviet military has manifested such tendencies even after the emergence of "new thinking" among Soviet civilians.

65  For a theoretically informed analysis of Soviet nationality problems, see Alexander Motyl, *Will the Non-Russians Rebel? State, Ethnicity, and Stability in the USSR* (Ithaca, N.Y.: Cornell University Press, 1987).

66  Mikhail Gorbachev, "The Socialist Idea and Revolutionary Perestroika," *Pravda*, November 26, 1989, as translated in the *New York Times*, November 27, 1989, p. 12.

67  For a comparison of "tentatively liberalizing regimes" in their international contexts, see Jack Snyder, "International Leverage on Soviet Domestic Change," *World Politics* 42 (October 1989): 1–30.

68  Holger Herwig, "Clio Deceived: Patriotic Self-Censorship in Germany after the Great War," *International Security* 12 (Fall 1987): 5–44.

69  Mueller, *Retreat from Doomsday*, "The Essential Irrelevance of Nuclear Weapons," *International Security* 13 (Fall 1988): 55–79, esp. 75–78.

70  For background on these nationalisms, see Griffith, ed., *Central and Eastern Europe: The Opening Curtain?*, chs. 8–14, esp. 11–12 on the Balkans.

71  On the Transylvania issue and the Democratic Forum's relatively guarded attempts to exploit it politically, see Radio Free Europe, "Situation Report," Hungary, no. 3, February 24, 1989, pp. 35–38; no. 5, March 31, 1989, p. 21; no. 12, July 28, 1989, pp. 37–40.

72  Barrington Moore, *Social Origins of Dictatorship and Democracy* (Boston: Beacon, 1966); and Alexander Gerschenkron, *Bread and Democracy in Germany* (1943, repr. Ithaca, N.Y.: Cornell University Press, 1989).

73 For a related argument and evidence about the 1930s, see Deborah Welch Larson, "Bandwagon Images in American Foreign Policy: Myth or Reality?" *Dominoes and Bandwagons: Strategic Beliefs and Superpower Competition in the Eurasian Rimland*, ed., Robert Jervis and Jack Snyder (New York: Oxford University Press, 1990).

74 Katzenstein, *Small States*, p. 38. The corporatisms of the 1930s included both democratic and authoritarian variants, but the latter was more prevalent in the 1930s than it was in the liberal international order after 1945.

75 Snyder, "International Leverage," pp. 6–8; Peter Gourevitch, *Politics in Hard Times* (Ithaca, N.Y.: Cornell University Press, 1986). Of course, Weimar's comparatively restrained foreign policy was also due in part to its military weakness.

76 Krasner, *International Regimes*; Keohane, *After Hegemony*. See also Joseph Grieco, "Anarchy and Cooperation: A Realist Critique of the Newest Liberal Institutionalism," *International Organization* 42 (Summer 1988): 485–508.

77 A good review of this literature is Kenneth Shepsle, "Studying Institutions: Some Lessons from the Rational Choice Approach," *Journal of Theoretical Politics* 1 (April 1989): 131–47. The seminal work is Kenneth Arrow, *Social Choice and Individual Values*, 2d ed. (New Haven, Conn.: Yale University Press, 1963).

78 On the call for a new Marshall Plan, see Flora Lewis, "Watershed for Europe," *New York Times*, November 22, 1989, p. 25.

79 Robert Pollard, *Economic Security and the Origins of the Cold War, 1945–1950* (New York: Columbia University Press, 1985), pp. 158–67, 248–49.

80 In addition to Hormats, "Redefining Europe"; Brzezinski, "Post-Communist Nationalism"; and Burley, "The Once and Future German Question," see various statements by European leaders on the need to manage German reunification and East-West rapprochement within a context of broader European institutions, reported in the *New York Times*: Helmut Kohl, November 29, 1989, pp. 1, 17; Hans-Dietrich Genscher, November 6, 1989, p. 10; Valery Giscard d'Estaing, November, 11, 1989, p. 8; and post-Malta statements by George Bush and West European leaders, December 5, 1989, p. 17.

81 On possible security motives for the EC's 1992 plans, see Wayne Sandholtz and John Zysman, "1992: Recasting the European Bargain," *World Politics* 42 (October 1989): 95–128, esp. 95–96.

82 On the internationalization of firms' operations and interests, see Helen Milner, *Resisting Protectionism* (Princeton, N.J.: Princeton University Press, 1988). On the institutional aspects, see Robert Keohane and Joseph Nye, *Power and Interdependence* (Boston: Little, Brown, 1977).

83 Henry Kissinger, "Untangling Alliances," *Los Angeles Times*, April 16, 1989, part 5, pp. 1, 6, discusses conventional arms control in the context of the broader European political order.

84 For figures on these states' current and potential military power, see International Institute for Strategic Studies (IISS), *The Military Balance, 1989–1990* (London: IISS, 1989).

85 For details, see Jack Snyder, "Limiting Offensive Conventional Forces: Soviet Proposals and Western Options," *International Security* 12 (Spring 1988): 48–77.

86 Van Evera, "When Is Offense Best?" discusses the reasons for this and also the difficulties involved in implementing such a strategy.

87 See Arend Lijphart, *The Politics of Accommodation: Pluralism and Democracy in the Netherlands* (Berkeley: University of California Press, 1968), and other works discussed and cited in Katzenstein, *Small States*, pp. 35, 88, 185, 213–15. Note also the proposals for voluntary ethnic confederations in Brzezinski, "Post-Communist Nationalism."

88 Stephen Van Evera has been the pioneer in reopening the question of the origins and consequences of nationalist myth-making; see "Causes of War." See also Paul Ken-

nedy, "The Decline of Nationalistic History in the West, 1900–1970," *Journal of Contemporary History* 8 (January 1973): 77–100; and Saburo Ienaga, *The Pacific War, 1931–1945* (New York: Pantheon, 1978), ch. 2. On the return of nationalistic history, see Richard J. Evans, *In Hitler's Shadow: West German Historians and the Attempt to Escape from the Nazi Past* (New York: Pantheon, 1989).

89 For a discussion of constructive steps that the West can take with regard to the Baltic states, see Alexander Motyl, "Identity Crisis in the Soviet West," *Bulletin of the Atomic Scientists* 45 (March 1989): 21–24.

90 Ronald Rogowski, *Commerce and Coalitions: How Trade Affects Political Alignments* (Princeton, N.J.: Princeton University Press, 1989); Olson, *Rise and Decline*, ch. 5.

91 See Moore, *Social Origins*; Gerschenkron, *Bread and Democracy*; and Wehler, *German Empire*.

92 On the Concert of Europe security regime, see Robert Jervis, "Security Regimes," *International Organization* 36 (Spring 1982): 357–78, esp. 362–68.

93 Rogowski, *Commerce and Coalitions*, pp. 106–7, 121–22, 175–77, discusses Eastern Europe and the USSR in light of the hypothesis that increasing exposure to trade harms holders of locally scarce factors of production (land, labor, or capital), but benefits holders of the locally abundant factors.

94 According to some critics, EC expansion into Central Europe might strengthen a German-dominated European Community, creating what amounts to a tripolar configuration of power: the United States, the Soviet Union, and the EC. If, as Waltz argues in *Theory of International Politics*, p. 163, tripolar configurations are unstable, this outcome could be dangerous. But the United States and the Soviet Union should be included as major participants in the European regime, which thus would not exist as a separate pole. Moreover, if the institutional scheme worked, the consequences of tripolar anarchy would be muted. In any event, Waltz's deductions about the instability of tripolar configurations are speculative and not logically compelling. By the broader logic of Waltz's own theory, an attack by one pole should lead to an alliance of the other two, to prevent the achievement of systemwide hegemony by the attacker. The attacker, anticipating this, should be dissuaded from aggression. Finally, adding Japan and/or China would make the global configuration multipolar, not tripolar.

## Conclusion

1 The conventional wisdom is that American power is declining. For rebuttals see Samuel Huntington, "The U.S.—Decline or Renewal?" *Foreign Affairs* 67 (Winter 1988–89): 76–96, and Joseph Nye, Jr., *Bound to Lead: The Changing Nature of American Power* (New York: Basic Books, 1990).

2 If we are to believe Kenneth Waltz in *Theory of International Politics* (Reading, Mass.: Addison-Wesley, 1979), multipolar systems are less stable than bipolar. But if we are to believe Waltz in *The Spread of Nuclear Weapons: More May Be Better*, Adelphi Paper no. 171 (London: International Institute of Strategic Studies, 1981), then we would conclude that a multipolar nuclear world would be quite safe.

3 For a concise description, see Richard Elrod, "The Concert of Europe," *World Politics* 28 (January 1976): 159–74; for analyses, see Robert Jervis, "Security Regimes," *International Organization* 36 (Spring 1982): 357–78, and "From Balance to Concert," *World Politics* 38 (October 1985): 58–79.

4 For the connections between cooperative processes and outcomes, see Morton Deutsch, *The Resolution of Conflict* (New Haven, Conn.: Yale University Press, 1973).

5 The best treatment is Raymond Garthoff, *Détente and Confrontation* (Washington, D.C.: Brookings Institution, 1985).

6 Indeed, it is now West European sensitivities to intrusion that set the limit to inspection schemes.

7 See Alexander George, "The Basic Principles Agreement of 1972: Origins and Expectations," in Alexander George et al., *Managing U.S.-Soviet Rivalry* (Boulder, Colo.: Westview Press, 1983), pp. 107–18.

8 For a discussion of the United Nations in this context, see Toby Trister Gati, "The UN Rediscovered: Soviet and American Policy in the United Nations of the 1990s," ch. 12 in this volume.

9 Richard Neustadt, *Alliance Politics* (New York: Columbia University Press, 1970)

10 For the use of this framework in analyzing conflict and cooperation, see the articles in *World Politics*, October 1985. Alexander George, Philip Farley, and Alexander Dallin, *U.S.-Soviet Security Cooperation* (New York: Oxford University Press, 1988), ch. 1, are certainly correct, however, to stress that it does not fit all situations.

11 Indeed, on at least some occasions, the use of surprise may increase the chance that the policy will fail by adding opposition to the tactic employed to opposition to what the state is trying to achieve. Thus in retrospect it appears that the Russians might have succeeded in putting missiles into Cuba in 1962 if they had done so openly rather than with stealth and deception. The United States declared the Soviet move unacceptable largely on the grounds of how it was done. It is hard to see how international support could have been mustered for bringing the world to the brink of war in order to prevent the Russians from doing what international law and custom permitted and what the United States had done in preceding years.

12 Myron Weiner, "The Macedonian Syndrome: An Historical Model of International Relations and Political Development," *World Politics* 23 (July 1971):665–83; Jack Snyder, "Averting Anarchy in the New Europe," ch. 16 in this volume.

13 See Jack Snyder, *The Ideology of the Offensive: Military Decision Making and the Disasters of 1914* (Ithaca, N.Y.: Cornell University Press, 1984); Barry Posen, *The Sources of Military Doctrine: France, Britain and Germany Between the World Wars* (Ithaca, N.Y.: Cornell University Press, 1984); and Stephen Van Evera, "The Causes of War," Ph.D. diss., University of California, Berkeley, 1984.

14 Charles Gati, "East and West in Eastern Europe," ch. 9 in this volume.

15 Under these circumstances, the USSR could base its deterrence in the face of conventional inferiority on the danger of escalation, as was true for NATO in most of the Cold War; see George Quester, "The Soviet Opening to Nonprovocative Defense," ch. 8 in this volume.

16 Carl Becker, *How Better Will the New World Be?* (New York: Knopf, 1944), p. 86.

Academy of Sciences of the USSR, 226
ADB 164, 168, 180
Adomeit, Hannes, 259
Afghanistan, 27, 69, 123, 125, 126, 131, 132, 159, 197, 209, 210, 218, 244; factions and popular movements in, 111–12; Soviet invasion of, 32, 35, 118, 122, 165–66, 199, 200, 241, 259; Soviet withdrawal from, 43, 54, 56, 175, 194, 264
Africa: central, 235; southern, 125, 126
Agreement on Environmental Protection (U.S.-USSR), 232, 234
Albania, 255, 256; and Kosovo, 161
Alexander II, 65
Algeria, 255
Allende, Salvador: U.S. contribution to demise of, 49; USSR and, 244. *See also* Chile
Alliance of the Free Democrats, 289. *See also* Hungary
Allison, Graham, 265
Almond, Gabriel, 24
American Civil Liberties Union (ACLU), 189
Amnesty International, 189, 191
Amur River border dispute, 166
Andropov, Yuri, 258
Angola, 25, 118, 122, 126, 127, 131, 197, 209, 245, 246, 306; Cuban troops in, 247
Antarctica Treaty, 207
Apple, R. W., Jr.: on change in East Europe, 55
Arab-Israeli conflict, 111, 112, 124, 125, 126, 127, 129
Arafat, Yasser, 209
Argentina, 244

Aristotle, 184
Armitage, Richard, 173
Arms control, 30, 31, 34, 36–37, 69, 266, 270, 296; Comprehensive Test Ban, 209; Conference on Disarmament, 206; conventional and chemical weapons agreements, 177; Conventional Armed Forces in Europe (CFE), 71, 182; Graduated Reciprocation in Tension (GRIT), 269; inspection mechanisms, 304; Intermediate-range Nuclear Forces (INF) Treaty, 31, 39, 40, 42, 49, 54, 56, 59, 67, 70–71, 74, 136, 145, 175, 194, 274; Kennedy Test-Ban Treaty, 32, 59; Limited Test Ban Treaty, 207; Non-Proliferation Treaty (NPT), 207, 209, 266; nuclear disarmament, 133, 136; nuclear freeze, 29, 31, 39; SALT, 10; SALT II, 30–31, 44, 122; Strategic Arms Reduction Talks (START), 31, 39, 40, 70–71, 74, 177
Arrow, Kenneth: on "impossibility theorem," 294
ASEAN. *See* Association of Southeast Asian Nations
Asia, Southeast, 209, 252. *See also* ASEAN
Asian Development Bank (ADB), 164, 168, 180
Association of Southeast Asian Nations (ASEAN), 164, 165, 171, 180; Bali Treaty, 180
Augustine, Saint, 184
Australia, 164, 171, 256
Austria, 28, 256, 288

Baker, James, 127, 130, 212
Balance of power: maintenance of, 62; in Eurasia, 63
Bali: theater-state (*Negara*), 190

Bali Treaty, 180. *See also* ASEAN
Balkanization of Eastern Europe, 161
Basic Principles Agreement, 125, 126, 304
Becker, Carl, 8, 313
Berlin, 8; "deadline crisis," 32
Bialer, Seweryn: on "quick fix" attitude, 58
Bilak, Vasil, 152
Bogomolov, Oleg T.: on Hungary, 152
Bolton, John, 211
Brandt, Willy, 248
Brazil, 100, 242, 243, 244, 256; GNP, 254
Brezhnev, Leonid, 51, 123, 178, 264, 298
Brezhnev Doctrine, 149, 154
Britain, 73, 100, 252, 256, 262, 305; and Jordan, 124
Brodie, Bernard, 264
Brunei, 171
Brzezinski, Zbigniew, 10, 55, 148
Bulgaria, 159, 292; claims on Macedonia, 160
Bush, George, 23, 33, 43, 44, 159, 198, 226, 266, 274, 311; approach to arms negotiations, 59; policy on China, 178; proposal on GATT and Most Favored Nation status, 298
Byrd Amendment, 208

Calleo, David P., 251
Cambodia, 174, 175, 176, 180, 211, 218, 246; invasion by Vietnam, 165–66, 199; withdrawal of Vietnamese troops, 165. *See also* Kampuchea
Camp David Accords, 209
Cam Ranh Bay, 173, 174
Canada, 255, 256; war with the U.S., 267–68
Carlucci, Frank, 54, 57
Carnesale, Albert, 265
Carrington, Lord, 262, 268
Carter, Jimmy, 129, 187, 189, 208; on Afghanistan, 241; and Camp David accords, 209; and human rights, 121
Castro, Fidel, 49
Catherine the Great, 65
Ceauşescu, Nicolae, 148–49
Central America, 26, 125. *See also* individual countries
Cheney, Richard: predicts that reforms will fail, 55
Chile, 246, 261; Allende, 244
China: and Imperial Russia, 135
China, People's Republic of, 15, 96, 98,

164, 167, 172, 174, 175, 176, 177, 181, 242, 252, 274; Amur River border dispute, 166; GNP, 254; Manchu dynasty, 270; Tiananmen Square, 178; trading partners, 168
CMEA, 158, 159
Collective security, 50, 176
Colton, Timothy, 79
Common security, 111
Communist Party of the Soviet Union (CPSU); demotion of, 69; disillusionment of members, 98; loss of vanguard role, 62
Comprehensive Test Ban, 209
Concert of Europe, 275, 300, 304
Conference on Disarmament, 206
Conference on Security and Cooperation in Europe (CSCE), 6
Congress of People's Deputies (USSR), 288
Conventional Armed Forces in Europe (CFE), 71, 182
Converse, Philip E., 24
Council for Mutual Economic Assistance (CMEA or Comecon), 158, 159
Crisis stability, 141
Cuba, 8, 99, 235, 246, 256; Guantanamo, 253; Leninism in, 98; missile crisis, 15, 32, 124, 259, 264
Czechoslovakia: 140, 152, 275, 301; Czech-Slovak conflict, 161; Soviet invasion of, 28; withdrawal of Soviet troops, 159

Dallek, Robert: on "unthinking communism," 25
Dawes Plan, 293
Defensive defense, 133, 141, 179–80
Defensive sufficiency, 74, 142. *See also* Sufficiency
De Gaulle, Charles, 248
Democratic Forum (Hungary), 289, 292
Deng Xiaoping, 179; summit with Gorbachev, 164
Détente, 13, 27, 28, 29, 30, 35, 42, 44, 118–19, 121, 304; decline of, 17; détente II, 40, 43; impact on NATO, 71
Deterrence, 18, 59, 307
Dienstbier, Jiří, 153
Dobrynin, Anatoly: and Kissinger, 130
Dominican Republic: U.S. Marines in, 49
Donnelly, Christopher, 71
Dubček, Alexander, 152, 153, 154

Eagleburger, Lawrence, 279, 280
East-Central Europe. *See* Europe, Eastern
Economic and Social Council (ESOSOC), 206
EEC, 171, 176
Egypt: 246, 247, 253; Aswan Dam, Soviet funding of, 124; Aswan Dam and Helwan steel complex, 243; and Israel, 126; and Soviet Union, 126
Eisenhower, Dwight D., 7, 15; Eisenhower-Dulles campaign, 49
El Salvador, 25, 99, 252
Entente, Anglo-French, 15
Epstein, Edward J., 151
Equatorial Guinea, 246
Erickson, John, 263
Essential equivalence, 142. *See also* Parity
Ethiopia, 99, 122, 126, 245, 246; Leninism in, 98
Europe, Central, 271. *See also* Europe, Eastern
Europe, Eastern, 13, 14, 16, 44, 49, 127, 261, 264, 276, 303, 305, 306, 308, 309, 310, 311; American interest in, 59; political change in, 55, 67, 69, 98, 100; Soviet influence in, 55, 72
Europe, Western, 69, 133, 135–36, 147, 298–99, 250, 303, 307, 310, 311. *See also individual countries*
European Coal and Steel Community (ECSC), 259
European Community (EC), 295–97, 300
European Economic Community (EEC), 171, 176
European Payments Union (EPU), 295

Falkenrath, Richard A., Jr., 218
FAO, 204, 207
Federal Bureau of Investigation (FBI), 50
Finlandization, 147, 156–57, 158, 159, 247, 248, 249, 254, 309
Food and Agriculture Organization (FAO), 204; World Food Program, 207
Ford, Gerald, 209
Forrestal, James, 12
France, 73, 100, 252, 254, 256, 262, 274, 282
Fukuyama, Francis, 273

Gaddis, John L., 12, 50, 273
Gandhi, Rajiv, 177
Gates, Robert M.: on economic reform, 73
GATT. *See* General Agreement on Tariffs and Trade

General Agreement on Tariffs and Trade (GATT), 198, 204, 295, 298
General Assembly (UN), 120
Geneva accords, 201
George, Alexander, 259
Gerasimov, Gennadi, 152
Germany, 8, 11–12, 28, 73, 159, 242, 254, 266, 271, 272, 277, 291, 297, 299, 303, 310, 312; Junkers, 290; militarism, 138; neutralization of, 67; reunification of, 159, 279, 282; and Stresemann, 292; Weimar, 293; Wilhelmine, 287, 289
Germany, West, 248–49, 252, 295. *See also* Germany
Gierek, Edward, 298
Graduated Reciprocation in Tension (GRIT), 269
Gray, Colin, 271
Great Britain. *See* Britain
Greece, 249, 275, 277, 300; communist party, 248
Grenada, invasion of, 126
Gromyko, Andrei, 166; and Kissinger, 130; and Middle East peace conference, 129
Group of 77, 217
Guantanamo, 253
Guatemala, U.S. intervention in, 49
Guinea-Bissau, 246

Hajek, Jiří, 153
Hartz, Louis, 2; "bourgeois fraction," 11
Harvard Russian Refugee Project, 81
Havel, Václav, 154
Hegenbart, Rudolf, 153
Helsinki agreements, 13, 205, 214; Conference on European Security, 174
Hiss, Alger, court case, 49
Honecker, Erich, 148–49
House Armed Services Committee: report on Soviet military goals, 55
Hungary, 96, 140, 151–52, 275, 278, 288–89, 296, 299, 300, 301; tension with Romania, 160, 292; withdrawal of Soviet troops, 159
Hun Sen, 180
Huntington, Samuel P.: "conventional retaliation," 69, 291; *Political Order in Changing Societies*, 276–77, 283–85
Husák, Gustáv, 152

IAEA, 201, 207, 209
Ideology, 63, 119, 263, 264, 273–74;

Leninism, 98, 158; Marxism, 100, 119; Marxism-Leninism, 11, 34, 35, 66, 99, 121, 278
IMF, 198, 204, 208, 255
India, 167; and Imperial Russia, 135; and Pakistan, 111
Indochina, 167, 180, 235
Indonesia, 171, 244, 255
INF. *See* Arms control
Institute of Sociological Research (USSR Academy of Sciences) survey, 78–96
Intermediate-range Nuclear Forces (INF) Treaty. *See* Arms Control
International Atomic Energy Agency (IAEA): 207, 209; and Chernobyl, 201
International Civil Aviation Organization (ICAO), 201
International Council of Scientific Unions, 234
International Fund for Agricultural Development (IFAD), 204
International Labor Organization (ILO), U.S. withdrawal from, 209
International Monetary Fund (IMF), 198, 204, 208, 255
Iran: Khomeini revolution in, 112; U.S. intervention in, 49; WWII confrontation over, 28
Iran-Contra scandal, 33
Iraq, 247; war with Iran, 210, 255, 305
Israel, 130; and Arab states, 111, 124, 128; criticism of, 208; and Palestinians, 112; U.S. interest in, 117–18
Italy, 100, 254

Jacobson, Harold K.: on "networks of independence," 96–97
Jakeš, Miloš, 148–49, 153
Jamaica, 244
Japan, 8, 11, 15, 100, 164, 173, 175, 176, 181, 242, 248, 252, 254, 256, 261, 266, 271, 272, 277, 289, 291, 294, 303, 307; and Imperial Russia, 135; interwar, 280; Shidehara Kijuro, 292; Taisho, 293; territorial dispute with USSR, 165, 168; trade with China, 168
Jiang, Zemin, 179
Johnson, Robert H., 253
Jordan, U.S. aid to, 124

Kampuchea (Cambodia), 125, 126
Kassof, Allen, 58
Katzenstein, Peter, 293

Kaufmann, William W., 251
Keller, Bill: on Americanization of Soviet Union, 52
Kennan, George, 50, 59–60; containment hypothesis, 70; Project Solarium, 7; "X" article, 76
Kennedy, Paul: on "imperial overstretch," 16
Kennedy Test-Ban treaty, 32, 59
Keohane, Robert, 294
Khmer Rouge, 180
Khrushchev, Nikita, 167, 243, 259; reforms, 74
Kijuro, Shidehara, 292
Kim Il-sung, 170
Kirkpatrick, Jeane, 210
Kissinger, Henry, 44, 50, 232; and Arab-Israeli peace process, 119, 127, 129; and Dobrynin, 130; and Gromyko, 130
Korea, 167, 170, 174, 175, 176, 179, 263
Korea, North, 172, 174
Korea, South, 164, 243, 252; reduction of U.S. forces in, 246
Korean Air Lines (KAL) flight 007, 32, 200, 201, 232
Kosovo, 161, 292. *See also* Albania; Yugoslavia
Kosygin, Alexei, 74
Kozyrev, Andrei, 203
Krasner, Stephen, 294
Krenz, Egon, 150

Laos, 246
Latin America, 162, 265. *See also* Central America
Lebanon, U.S. marines in, 125
Legvold, Robert, 44, 54
Lenin, 11, 54, 61, 263, 264; change from above, 65; and NEP, 53
Leninism, 98, 158
Levada, Iurii, 102
Lewis, Anthony: on changes in Soviet society, 51–52
Lewis, Flora, 53, 56; on Gorbachev, 52
Ligachev, Yegor, 11
Limited Test Ban Treaty, 207
Lippmann, Walter, 23
Lippmann-Almond thesis, 24, 25, 26, 34

McCarthy, Joseph, 49
Mackinder, Halford J., 63, 135
Malta summit meeting, 33
Mao Tse-tung, 43

Marx, Karl, 100
Marxism, 100, 119
Marxism-Leninism, 11, 34, 35, 66, 99, 121, 278
Martlock, Jack, 54
Mexico, 100
Military parity, 30, 31
Mondale, Walter, 43
Mozambique, 99
Mutual security, 14, 17, 18

Namibia, 131; SWAPO, 132
National Security Council (U.S.), 116
National War College, 24
New Economic Plan (NEP), 53
Nicaragua, 25, 127, 131; Contras, 49; Sandinistas, 99, 127
Nixon, Richard, 44, 50–51; visit to China, 43
Non-intervention, 126
Non-Proliferation Treaty (NPT), 207, 209, 266
Nonprovocative defense, 133
North Atlantic Treaty Organization (NATO), 5, 25, 26, 66, 67, 134, 137; and reunified Germany, 68
Nuclear disarmament, 133, 136
Nuclear freeze, 29, 31, 39

Ottoman empire, 73

Pakistan, 111
Palestine Liberation Organization (PLO), 127
Palestinians, 112
*Pamyat'* (Memory), 72
Panama, U.S. troops to, 126
Parity, military, 30, 31
Parks, Michael: on Gorbachev's reform, 52
Patterson, Thomas, 12
Peaceful coexistence, 54, 61, 120
People's Commissariat for Internal Affairs (NKVD), 50
Persian Gulf, 10, 132
Peter the Great, 65
Phillips, Howard, 40
Piasecki, Edmund, 218
Pipes, Richard: on Bush, 43
Podhoretz, Norman, 40
Populism, rise of, 111
Portugal, 73
Primakov, Evgenii, 119

Progressive Party (U.S.), 50
Project Solarium, 7

Quadripartite Agreements, 13

Rapacki Plan, 136
Real socialism. *See* Ideology
Reasonable sufficiency, 64, 70
Red Scare, 49
Revel, Jean-François, 24
Roosevelt, Franklin, 50
Rosecrance, Richard, 77, 96
Rosenberg spy trial, 49
Rosenthal, A. M.: on Bush, 43

Safire, William, 52–53; on Bush, 43
SALT, 10
SALT II, 30–31, 44, 122
Samuelson, Robert J., 55
Sandinistas, 99, 127. *See also* Nicaragua
Scandinavia, and Imperial Russia, 135
"Scientific socialism," 100. *See also* Ideology
Security dilemma, 14, 18, 64
Shevardnadze, Eduard, 11, 120; and Baker, 130
Shipler, David K., 57; on Reagan, 56
Shulman, Marshall D.: on American opinion, 59
Shultz, George, 53, 127
Socialism. *See* Ideology
South Africa, 132
Southwest African People's Organization (SWAPO), 132. *See also* Namibia
Soviet Interview Project (SIP), 78–96
Spain, 73
Stalin, Joseph, 28, 67, 72; and change from above, 65
Stalinism, 53
Star Wars. *See* Strategic Defense Initiative
Stein, George: on Soviet Chic, 58
Strategic Arms Limitation Talks (SALT), 10, 30–31, 44, 122
Strategic Arms Reduction Talks (START), 31, 39, 40, 70–71, 74, 177
Strategic Defense Initiative (SDI), 44, 56; Soviet opposition to, 67
Suez Canal: and War of Attrition, 125
Sufficiency, 133
Sulzburger, Arthur Hays, 12
Sweden, 73
Syria, 124, 126

Tamas, Gaspar, 100–101
Test-Ban treaties. *See* Arms control
Third World, 16, 36; competition in, 13; nuclear weapons in, 42; Soviet and Chinese influence in, 35
Truman, Harry S., 50
Turkey, and Imperial Russia, 135

United Nations (UN), 5, 125; General Assembly, 120

Vance, Cyrus, 129
Vandenberg, Arthur, 23

Vietnam: escalation of troops, 49; popular movements, 112

Wallace, Henry, 50
War of Attrition, 125
Warsaw Pact, 134, 136, 137
Wick, Charles Z., 57
Will, George, 40, 51; on Bush, 43
Wilsonian politics, 11, 12, 13, 25, 50
Wolfers, Arnold, 1

Yalta Conference, 28
Yarsike, Deborah, 84
Yugoslavia, 96

About the Authors

Seweryn Bialer is Belfer Professor of Social Sciences and International Relations and Director of the Research Institute on International Change at Columbia University. Among his books are *The Soviet Paradox, Stalin's Successors,* and *Politics, Society, and Nationality Inside Gorbachev's Russia.*

Robert Jervis is Adlai E. Stevenson Professor of International Relations and member of the Institute of War and Peace Studies at Columbia University. His most recent book, *The Meaning of the Nuclear Revolution,* won the Grawemeyer Award for the best contribution to ideas promoting improved relations between nations.

---

Library of Congress Cataloging-in-Publication Data
Soviet-American relations after the cold war / edited by Robert Jervis and Seweryn Bialer.
Includes bibliographical references and index.
ISBN 0-8223-1080-5 (cloth). — ISBN 0-8223-1098-8 (pbk.)
1. United States—Foreign relations—Soviet Union. 2. Soviet Union—Foreign relations—United States. 3. United States—Foreign relations—1989–   4. Soviet Union—Foreign relations—1985–   I. Jervis, Robert, 1940–   . II. Bialer, Seweryn.
E183.8.S65S5763   1990
327.47073—dc20   90-42413 CIP